WHERE TO WATCH
BIRDS IN
BRITAIN AND
EUROPE

*This book is dedicated to the memory of my father, Edwin,
and my mother, Winifred, from an eternally grateful son.*

HAMLYN BIRDWATCHING GUIDES

WHERE TO WATCH BIRDS IN BRITAIN AND EUROPE

JOHN GOODERS

HAMLYN

CONTENTS

Published in 1994 by Hamlyn Limited,
an imprint of Reed Consumer Books Ltd
Michelin House, 81 Fulham Road,
London SW3 6RB and Auckland, Melbourne,
Singapore and Toronto

Copyright © John Gooders 1994

Artwork by John Davis and Dan Powell
Maps drawn by John Gilkes

ISBN 0 600 58007 5

A CIP catalogue record for this book is available
from the British Library

Printed in Hong Kong

INTRODUCTION

Where to Watch Birds in Europe was first published in 1970 and has, with a few brief gaps, been in print ever since. Common sense would have it updated on an annual basis, but publishing just does not work that way. Suffice it that the present edition is the fifth major revision, expansion and re-write of a book that has proved immensely popular over the years. In these days of mass twitches, large circulation magazines, huge membership societies and clubs and whole industries devoted to optics, travel and specialist publishing, it is difficult to understand the disapproval and sometimes outright condemnation by the ornithological establishment that greeted my first *Where to Watch* books. 'We don't want too many birdwatchers'; 'Some things are best kept secret'; 'This is private land and birdwatchers (except me) are not allowed'; 'Birdwatchers will disturb the birds and contribute nothing to the science of ornithology'. These and similar such statements were prevalent at the time, though I suppose those who made them were, even then, only a tiny minority of backwoodsmen who condemned anyone who stepped even a little out of line.

How things have changed! Now everyone seems to be writing a *Where to Watch... somewhere or the other* and I find myself annoyed that they borrow my title without so much as a by-your-leave. Have I too become a backwoodsman over the years? I trust not. In 1970 I believed, as I believe now, that the conservation movement will only succeed if it speaks with a single voice for masses of people. If guide books such as *WWB* and *WWBE*, as they have become known, help to swell the numbers then I am content. The aim of this book remains the same as that of its predecessors – to put birders in touch with birds in the most simple and efficient manner possible.

To this end *WWBE* is composed of a selection of the very best bird spots in Europe. There are famous places like Doñana in Spain, the Camargue in France and the Hortobágy in Hungary. But there are also many more obscure places like the island of Rügen in the former East Germany where 25,000 Cranes appear in autumn. Like Matsalu Bay in Estonia where 40,000 Whooper Swans stop-over in spring. Or like the superb Peñafalcon in Extremadura, where vultures and eagles are so common that birders seek to extend their trip lists by concentrating on Crested Tit and Black Redstart among the woods.

As in earlier editions I have sought to extend – some might say 'stretch' – the boundaries of Europe to include more and more of the Western Palearctic. In the east the reunification of Germany has opened up superb wetlands and shorelines to ordinary visitors who no longer find themselves confined either to the dreadful Interhotel chain, or to prescribed, non-sensitive places. Similarly, one can visit Poland, Hungary, Bulgaria and the Czech Republic and Slovakia without fear of accidentally causing an international crisis by aiming a telescope at the People's Pickle Factory, or whatever. There is, inevitably, a temptation to include the new republics of Russia, Belorussia and the Ukraine, but the former Soviet Union still has a few problems to solve before birding crews are made really welcome. Meanwhile, I have included the Baltic republics of Latvia and Estonia for the first time. Israel and Turkey were first included in *WWBE* in 1986 and it would be nice to extend coverage throughout the eastern Mediterranean. Yet somehow the 'Birds of Beirut' do not quite have the appeal they should. Similarly, there do not seem to be many birders working their way through Armenia or Syria. So I have settled for Jordan and Egypt as reasonable extensions to the European birding domain. I have also included The Gambia for the first time – not because it is in any sense a part of Europe, but because of the number of Euro-birders who now visit this West African state. I know it is illogical, but the travel business makes it as easy to visit The Gambia as almost anywhere else in this book. Who knows, the next edition may include Timbuktoo!

At the other end of 'Europe' I now include the Canary Islands for the first time. Here there are seabirds that make twitchers twitch, pigeons that have a similar effect and vagrants that may eventually turn these islands into the Scilly Isles of the twenty-first century. To the south it would have been a real pleasure to work my way along the North African coast eastwards from Morocco, but once again the unwelcoming states of Algeria and Libya barred my way. Right at the heart of Europe, I had reluctantly to omit the emerging and warring states of the former Yugoslavia. This is particularly sad for, having spent five years leading tours to this wonderful part of the Balkans, I could have produced some really mouthwatering accounts of several outstanding bird haunts. So Kopacki Rit, Carska Bara, Obedska Bara and Deliblato Sands will have to wait for the next edition while we in turn wait, hope and pray for the survival of all the White-tailed Eagles, Red-footed Falcons, Great White Egrets and Glossy Ibises that may still find peace enough to survive in this disaster zone.

Inevitably, the years between this and the previous edition of *WWBE* have seen considerable changes in our knowledge of European birds. Only as recently as 1986 was I able to remark on the existence of Dupont's Larks in Spain. Even then they were known only from the steppes around Lerida. Now they can be found around Almeria and in large numbers north of Madrid and elsewhere. Anyone who knows these birds will realise that they are hardly likely to have flown to these far- flung regions of Spain.

Travelling birders have played an invaluable part in improving our knowledge of bird distribution in many parts of the Continent. It is to be hoped that they will continue to do so. How often has one discovered a new place by chatting to other birders or by reading their reports, only to remember that one has passed by the area several times without realizing its value? Thus I drove through Trujillo in Extremadura several times without realizing that magnificent Monfragüe lay only 50 km north and superb La Serena a similar distance south. In fact, I have to admit that I did not realize that these were the Spanish Steppes and that I was surrounded by Great Bustards. So, while this book is no more than a record of where others have watched birds, it at least forms a basis by which the enterprising birder can recognize that he is exploring off the beaten track.

Inevitably, accounts of the different areas included in this book vary considerably. Some are more general, while others are laced with precise 'stake-outs' for particularly sought-after species. Where a bird is highly localized, as with the Finnish Red-flanked Bluetail for example, a general account is of little value and precise (or as precise as possible) directions are given to put the birder in touch with the bird. Similarly, where a bird returns to exactly the same nest year after year, it may be possible to provide details of an exact watchpoint. Such species are usually large and obvious and very often birds of prey. Here I face the perennial dilemma that has bugged me since 1970 – publish details of a raptor's nest and when it is robbed it is your fault. With a few exceptions I have erred on the side of caution. I could, for example, precisely locate several nests of Spanish Imperial Eagle, of Bonelli's Eagle, of Black Stork, Black-shouldered Kite, White-tailed Eagle, Red-footed Falcon and so on. Mostly I have intentionally avoided doing so. In compensation I have detailed viewpoints that, with a little patience, will produce these birds without the remotest chance of anyone actually disturbing them.

And, on the subject of disturbance, I have nowhere recommended anyone to call-up birds by the use of tapes. This is a very thorny subject because with so many secretive or thinly spread species, tapes are so effective in producing views of the birds. Travelling and showing people birds (as I do) puts considerable pressure on a tour leader and, I admit, that in some areas for some species I do resort to calls to attract the birds within binocular range of my fellow travellers. I think that the practice is justified if, but only if, the individual bird is going to be disturbed on just one occasion. Thus I have specific spots where I can call up Marmora's Warbler, Rüppell's Warbler, Corsican Nuthatch, Krüper's Nuthatch, Scops Owl and others. I am also quite sure that these are 'my spots', known to no one else and that the birds are going to be disturbed once, for a few minutes and then be left in peace. The result is a very happy group of travellers and a soon forgotten piece of territorial defence to a few individuals of relatively widespread and mostly common birds. This seems to me quite different from visiting a known stake-out and playing tapes to attract a bird that may spend a large part of its life chasing off phantom opponents. I would, therefore, request great caution in 'taping' any bird specifically located by directions found in *WWBE*.

The subject of English bird names has always caused controversy, though never more so than at present. The work of Sibley and Monroe and the proposed changes that follow has turned the established order on its head. The changes to English names proposed, withdrawn, and proposed again by the British Ornithologists' Union (BOU), and the modifications proposed and adopted by *British Birds* magazine, have left many ornithologists and most birders in a state of utter bewilderment. As an instinctive supporter of a more rational approach to the vernacular names of birds (I was once put to task by a nameless reviewer in *Birds* magazine for daring to use names that are now 'official') I find the change for change's sake somewhat frustrating. Thus, this edition of *WWBE* uses the names most generally used by birders and birdwatchers in the field, rather than those used in ornithological journals. I apologize for this further example of backwoodsmanship but I have a strange feeling that most of my readers will appreciate birds being called by names that they know and which have been used for many, many years. I may well think again before *WWBE VI* is published about the turn of the century.

John Gooders

ACKNOWLEDGEMENTS

I am often asked whether the *WWB* books are the result of a personal investigation, or based on the work of others. The answer, of course, lies somewhere between these two extremes. I remember in the mid-1960s spending several weekends hunched over maps in the back of a friend's car while he drove through Wales and the Midlands from one reservoir to the next to check access details to these (mostly) highly productive waters. My other companions wanted to see birds. I wanted only to check viewpoints. It was a frustrating experience, but we did once manage twelve waters in a single winter's day and see some birds as well. Europe, of course, could not be attacked in the same way, so friends and correspondents have been prevailed upon to provide details for areas that I have been unable to visit personally. As ever I am eternally grateful for their help, which varies from a full and complete write-up in *WWBE* style, to a few scribbled notes that pick out a particular hot spot. Sadly, I am unable to acknowledge the help of everyone, because I do not know who they are.

If, for example, I am birding at a well-known Euro-site, there is every chance of meeting other birders from a variety of countries. Conversation immediately centres on what has been seen and what missed, followed by intensive map consultation and a free interchange of information. Over the years the stake-outs of others have been checked and discarded, or checked and added to my own itineraries. Most of what I have gleaned can be found in these pages, but I cannot say who supplied what because, in most cases, we never exchanged names and addresses.

I have also been fortunate in having access to the 'trip reports' of many car-fulls of birders who have taken the trouble to write up the results of their holiday bird tours. Some of these are beautifully produced and illustrated volumes. Some aim less high. All have been invaluable in helping to cover many of the more obscure areas and put me in touch with the birds. Many of these reports have been sent to me directly by the participants and, if you find this edition of *WWBE* useful, I would be pleased to have a copy of your report on your trip. I have also benefited from the work of the Foreign Birdwatching Reports and Information Service organized by Steve Whitehouse. Over the years he has built up a formidable library of bird-trip reports covering most of the world. It now consists of over 370 items from a total of 120 countries all of which are listed in his Catalogue. For your copy send £1 to: Steve Whitehouse, FBRIS, 5 Stanway Close, Blackpole, Worcester WR4 9XL (Tel. 0905 454541). Though you may be inspired to travel by *WWBE* and find the guide invaluable in the field, it is still a good idea to spend a little on the most up-to-date gen available by contacting Steve before setting out on an expensive bird trip. I even find that many of my clients on Birding Holidays brandish the appropriate FBRIS report to check that I am not missing anything! Oh ye of little faith! To Steve I am, as always, particularly grateful.

Correspondents and friends all over Europe have rallied round once again to check over my accounts of areas in their own countries and

Black Woodpecker

ensure that they are up to date and as accurate as possible. Nevertheless, if there are mistakes (and there must be in a book of this nature which is out of date before it is published) they are mine.

If I were to list everyone who has, over the years and through its various editions, contributed or helped with information on *WWBE*, this section would grow to quite unreasonable proportions. So if I have missed your name please forgive me. Particular help with this new edition has been received from:

John Adams, N.W. Addey, Marten Ajne, Paul Atkinson, Sherif Baha El Din, Janis Baumanis, Pat Bonham, Brian Clasper, Jacqueline Crozier, Peter Dunn, Gonçalo Elias, Philip Etherington, John Fairfax-Ross, Annika Forsten, Graham and Carla Goodall, Gerard Gorman, Marco Gustin, George Handrinos, Chris Hatch, Ian Hillery, Jóhann Óli Hilmarsson, Andy Howes, Ed Kemble, Aivar Leito, C. and E.M. Marsh, Sean McMinn, Robin Morden, Mark and Carol Newlon, Tapaui Numminen, Lee O'Dwyer, William Oliver, Howard Papworth, Maxine Pastore, Gunnlaugur Petursson, Brian Rasmussen, Hadoram Shirihai, Richard Smith, Soren Sorensen, Karel Štăstný, Tadeusz Stawarczyk, Colin Titcombe, Tommy Tyrberg, Magnus Ullman, Tony Williams.

I should also like to thank all those correspondents who contributed to earlier editions and laid the foundations on which this guide has been built. Finally, my thanks to Marion Waran who has turned my scribble into readable English via the magic word processor. What I would do without her does not bear thinking about, and how we managed on typewriters I cannot remember. Thanks also to Cathy Lowne for her understanding and care in production, to Sylvia Sullivan for such sympathetic editing, and to my wife, Robbie, who let me off a thousand things that urgently needed attention so that I could meet the deadlines of my publisher, Jo Hemmings formerly of Hamlyn.

AUSTRIA

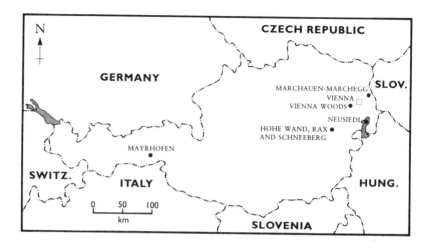

Hohe Wand, Rax and Schneeberg

These three mountain areas lie south-west of Vienna and offer the opportunity for really good, high-class birding at no great distance from either the city itself or the Neusiedl area.

The Hohe Wand (literally 'High Wall') is a vertical, rock outcrop about 12 km long by 3 km wide. It is well covered with forest and is a noted beauty spot that attracts many visitors in summer, particularly at weekends. The woods hold a good variety of birds, including Black Woodpecker, Capercaillie, Hazelhen, Nutcracker, Crested Tit, Ring Ouzel and Buzzard. As elusive as ever is the Wallcreeper, but it is definitely here.

Similar birds can also be seen in the Rax and Schneeberg Mountains that lie a little farther south-west on either side of the village of Hirschwang. Rax is reached by cable car, Schneeberg by rack-and-pinion railway from Puchberg. The high tops of both produce Golden Eagle, Alpine Chough, Raven and Ptarmigan, with Citril Finch on the way down. The secret is to walk down at least one stop/station, and the general opinion is that the railway up Schneeberg is the better bet.

SUMMER Golden Eagle, Buzzard, Capercaillie, Hazelhen, Nutcracker, Three-toed Woodpecker, Black Woodpecker, Wallcreeper, Alpine Accentor, Ring Ouzel, Crested Tit, Water Pipit, Alpine Chough, Hoopoe, Red-backed Shrike, Snow Finch, Citril Finch.

ACCESS Access is by road from Stolloff along the eastern side. Climb the zigzag road to the plateau. Turn left and keep right on the road that crosses to the western escarpment. There is a car park near the 'Naturpark'. Tracks lead northwards through good woodpecker territory to a raised viewing platform. For Rax and Schneeberg see above.

ROUTE Both areas are easily found from Vienna or the Neusiedl area.

MARCHAUEN–MARCHEGG

This WWF reserve lies in the far east of Austria, right against the Czech border. At this point the River March regularly floods its banks, inundating the surrounding meadows and forests and creating what is a more typically eastern European marsh landscape. The special species here are Black Stork and River Warbler, but there are plenty of raptors, including both kites, Honey Buzzard, and Saker. There are seven species of woodpecker and an equal number of owls, including Ural Owl. Warblers include Grasshopper, Savi's and River, providing a good opportunity to sort out the songs of the three species, and there are Thrush Nightingale, Penduline Tit, Little Bittern and sometimes Black-tailed Godwit.

SUMMER Black and White Storks, Night and Purple Herons, Spoonbill, Little Bittern, Red and Black Kites, Lesser Spotted Eagle, Buzzard, Honey Buzzard, Saker, Hobby, Grey-headed, Green, Great Spotted and Middle Spotted Woodpeckers, Ural and Tengmalm's Owls, Pied and Collared Flycatchers, Thrush Nightingale, Grasshopper, Savi's and River Warblers, Short-toed Treecreeper, Golden Oriole, Penduline Tit, Hawfinch.

ACCESS The village of Marchegg lies north of the Danube on Route 49. From the south continue through the village and, at the far end, take a track to the right to the reserve car park. A major floodbank runs northward from here. Walk along this for 3 km and then return via paths through meadows and, later, woods. The best views of Black Stork are in the north, over the meadow area. Walking south from the car park for a few hundred metres provides an excellent viewpoint for soaring birds of prey. Thereafter there is no access along the bank. Take mosquito repellent.

ROUTE Little more than an hour's drive from Vienna or the Neusiedl area, but worthy of a thorough exploration.

MAYRHOFEN

This is a small resort in the Tirol about 70 km south-east of Innsbruck. The surrounding hills are covered with conifers and, where these reach their highest point, there are grassy meadows. The valley floor is grassland, with smaller areas of cultivation. Two cable cars give access up to about 2440 m – the Penkenbahn and the Ahornbahn – with good zigzag paths down through the various habitats. The former has better birding.

Citril Finch, at the tree line, may be quite numerous, and the woods have Three-toed Woodpecker, Nutcracker, Bonelli's Warbler and Crossbill. The valley floor has Dipper and Grey Wagtail, while more widespread species include Goshawk and Alpine Swift.

For higher-altitude species the summer ski resort of Hintertux, with Snow Finch and Alpine Accentor, lies to the south-west.

SUMMER Honey Buzzard, Goshawk, Buzzard, Alpine Swift, Great Spotted and Three-toed Woodpeckers, Water Pipit, Grey Wagtail, Red-backed Shrike, Nutcracker, Alpine Accentor, Dipper, Bonelli's and Wood Warblers, Firecrest, Ring Ouzel, Fieldfare, Crested Tit, Serin, Crossbill, Citril and Snow Finches.

ACCESS The cable cars are easily reached from the village, with relatively easy walks down. Hintertux lies to the south-west.
ROUTE Leave Innsbruck, with its international airport, and take the motorway eastwards before turning south to Mayrhofen.

NEUSIEDL

Lake Neusiedl is Europe's fourth largest lake, extending over 30 km in length and 8 km in width, yet nowhere is it much deeper than 2 m. Occasionally the whole lake dries up, but because it is fed by underground springs this is a fortunately rare event. This shallowness is responsible for its remarkable appeal. Huge reedbeds line almost every shore and, though they are initially annoying and frustrating to the birder seeking open water, they have had the effect of seriously reducing tourist development and thus maintaining the bird population.

Neusiedl is the only example of a steppe lake in western Europe, and offers a landscape more typical of the Hungarian plains than of our image of Austria as an alpine country. Indeed, to the east the plains of the Seewinkel and particularly those of the Hansag extend straight across the Hungarian border and still offer chances of birds such as Great Bustard, Goshawk and Lesser Spotted Eagle, more typical of that country.

For its many visitors, Neusiedl ranks alongside the Camargue, the Coto Doñana and the Danube delta as the greatest bird spot in Europe. Its birds are plentiful, varied and, in some cases, most certainly rare. Great White Egret has its major western stronghold here, while Spoonbills are as numerous as anywhere else in Europe. Seven species of woodpecker can be found, including Black and Syrian. There are Black-necked Grebe, Little Bittern, and decidedly eastern birds such as River and Barred Warblers and Red-breasted and Collared Flycatchers. There are even Eagle, Pygmy and

Great Bustard

Tengmalm's Owls here, though you will need extreme good fortune or local expertise to find them. Altogether, nearly 300 species have been recorded.

The Neusiedl area is not one that can be rushed through in a few days. Several tour operators find enough to occupy their groups for a fortnight, and many visitors return year after year.

SUMMER Black-necked Grebe, Bittern, Little Bittern, Squacco Heron, Great White Egret, Little Egret, Purple Heron, White Stork, Black Stork, Spoonbill, Greylag Goose, Garganey, Ferruginous Duck, Honey Buzzard, Red Kite, Black Kite, Goshawk, Lesser Spotted Eagle, Short-toed Eagle, Hen Harrier, Montagu's Harrier, Marsh Harrier, Saker, Peregrine, Hobby, Red-footed Falcon, Great Bustard, Black-tailed Godwit, Black Tern, Roller, Hoopoe, Grey-headed Woodpecker, Black Woodpecker, Syrian Woodpecker, Tawny Pipit, Woodchat Shrike, Lesser Grey Shrike, Great Grey Shrike, Savi's Warbler, River Warbler, Moustached Warbler, Marsh Warbler, Great Reed Warbler, Icterine Warbler, Barred Warbler, Bonelli's Warbler, Red-breasted Flycatcher, Collared Flycatcher, Bluethroat, Bearded Tit, Penduline Tit, Ortolan Bunting, Serin, Golden Oriole.

ACCESS Save at the village of Podersdorf on the eastern shore, the whole lake is protected by a dense growth of reeds and access is, therefore, concentrated at several strategic points. At the village of Neusiedl-am-See, where most birders tend to stay, a causeway leads to the See Bad where there is a marina and restaurant, but birding is probably best along the road itself. The local railway runs south of the village along the shore of the lake and is handy both for getting about and for offering one of the best bird-walks in the area. Eastward towards Weiden leads to areas of poplars where Penduline Tits nest, but there are plenty of warblers as well. Thereafter, head for the lake at the next level crossing by turning right, and then continue eastward on a cycle path.

Along the western shore there is access at Oggau, where a track leads past barracks towards the shore, and on the reserve of Gade-Lacke, where there are good heronries. Here there are some hides on stilts that are for hunting purposes, but they can be useful for watching over the reed tops for Ferruginous Duck, Bittern and the ever-present Marsh Harrier.

Just to the north, near Schützen, is the Tiergarten, with Black and other woodpeckers, Golden Oriole and definitely no access: much can be seen from the road. Rust, to the south, is famous for its White Storks and for another walk through the reeds along a causeway to the See Bad. Here Little Bittern may oblige, as well as warblers.

To the east of Neusiedl lies the lakeland of Seewinkel. Each lake varies in its attractions and is, in any case, best found with the aid of a map. The most important lakes are listed, with their specialities.

Zicksee has Black-necked Grebe and Bittern. It should not be confused with Zick Lacke near Illmitz. To the south is Hulden Lacke, not visible from the road, but worth the effort of finding, being good for passage waders and herons. The small woodland between Illmitz and Neusiedler See has Barred and Bonelli's Warblers, woodpeckers and Penduline Tit, and is excellent for passage flycatchers and chats. The Unterstinkersee (and Oberstinkersee) is the best water for passage waders, with all the usual west European species present in excellent numbers. There are also Black and White-winged Black Terns, occasional Caspian, and this is an excellent spot for Great White Egret. The walk between the two lakes is certainly worthwhile.

East of Apetlon is the Lange Lacke, a WWF reserve with Great White Egret, Spoonbill, Garganey, Avocet and more passage waders and terns. Farther south near Pamhagen the border runs along the Einser Canal, with Barred and River Warblers, Black-tailed Godwit, Montagu's Harrier and drifting Spotted and Lesser Spotted Eagles, Goshawk, Honey Buzzard and Black Stork; many of the soaring birds are actually in Hungary, over the Kapuvarer Erlen Wald. The plains east of here and south of Tadten still hold small populations of Great Bustard, and there is a special reserve for this species about two-thirds of the way from Tadten to the Hungarian border.

ROUTE Vienna airport has worldwide flights and is even on the right side of the city.

VIENNA WOODS

The famed Vienna woods are adjacent to the city and are noted as the haunt of relatively scarce birds such as the woodpeckers and Red-breasted Flycatcher. Areas such as the Lainzer Tiergarten to the south-west of Vienna have attracted birders for many years. More convenient perhaps are the Schonnbrunn Palace Gardens, which are actually well within the city itself. Here Great Spotted and Middle Spotted and Green and Grey-headed Woodpeckers may all be seen in a remarkably confined area. Other species here include Short-toed Treecreeper, Golden Oriole and Serin.

SUMMER Great Spotted Woodpecker, Middle Spotted Woodpecker, Green Woodpecker, Grey-headed Woodpecker, Red-breasted Flycatcher, Wood Warbler, Short-toed Treecreeper, Golden Oriole, Serin.

ACCESS The Schonnbrunn Palace is most easily found by using the A23 motorway to Altmansdorf, from where the Palace is only 3–4 km due north. Pass through the Palace archway and walk across a flat area between high hedges to the pond. Then take the wooded track half-left and watch for the birds.

ROUTE Vienna. Probably worth doing on a flying visit to Vienna or on the way to Neusiedl.

BELGIUM

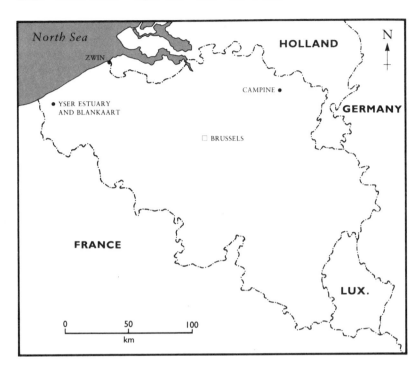

CAMPINE

The Campine is an infertile stretch of Belgium lying north of Antwerp, from the Schelde estuary to Maastricht. Here are numerous heaths, plantations, forests, lakes, marshes and ponds, all of which sounds splendid. It is, however, so vast that concentration at particular points is essential.

In the west, the reserve at Kalmthout Heath has pinewoods with Black Woodpecker, Black Grouse and Long-eared Owl. To the east, the area around Herentals, Geel and Kasterlee has several small reserves, and excellent woodland with heath and marshes. Black Woodpecker, Teal, Curlew and Bluethroat breed. Farther east is Genk, with a reserve at the nearby Stiemerbeck valley. The lakes and marshes here are favoured by Hobby, with Nightjar on the heaths, and Black Woodpecker, Goshawk, Honey Buzzard and Long-eared Owl in the woods. Much of the area is a military zone, but much can be seen at open areas and from roads.

SUMMER Bittern, Hobby, Goshawk, Honey Buzzard, Water Rail, Curlew, Long-eared Owl, Nightjar, Black Woodpecker, Crested Tit, Bluethroat.
ACCESS Though the above areas are widely scattered reserves, they can be visited by roads and tracks. The forests in particular are superb, and the high population of raptors should present no difficulties.
ROUTE Off the E9 from Antwerp.

YSER ESTUARY AND BLANKAART

The Yser is not a large river and its main interest lies in its position on what is otherwise an inhospitable coastline for birds. The small estuary downstream from Nieuwpoort has many passage waders, as well as breeding Avocet and Kentish Plover. Part of the area, including the Yser channel, the Lombardzijde creek and some other creeks and dunes, is a reserve. In autumn, Little Stint, Curlew Sandpiper, Wood and Green Sandpipers and Spotted Redshank and Greenshank may build up to substantial numbers.

Farther south, the right bank of the Yser near Woumen is a fine area of reed-marsh, including the reserve of Blankaart. This is heavily overgrown with reeds and surrounded by water meadows. Despite its abundance in Holland, the Black-tailed Godwit is a scarce bird in Belgium and this is one of its few regular breeding areas with up to 60 pairs. The reedbeds hold Bittern, Little Bittern and Marsh Harrier, and Garganey, Ruff and Short-eared Owl also breed. Passage brings hordes of waders, and in winter there are thousands of Bean and Pink-footed Geese and regular Bewick's Swan.

SUMMER Bittern, Little Bittern, Marsh Harrier, Garganey, Kentish Plover, Little Ringed Plover, Black-tailed Godwit, Ruff, Avocet, Great Reed Warbler.
PASSAGE Hen Harrier, Merlin, Golden Plover, Greenshank, Spotted Redshank, Wood Sandpiper, Green Sandpiper, Little Stint, Ruff, Little Gull.
ACCESS Both reserves can be visited by permit, but a great deal can be seen from roads and tracks at both areas.
ROUTE South-westward on the coastal road from Ostend to the Yser estuary, thence inland to Blankaart near Woumen.

ZWIN

The Zwin reserve lies on the coast, tight against the Dutch border, and extends across the frontier. It is probably Belgium's most famous bird reserve and is the former mouth of the River Zwin through which medieval ships sailed to Bruges. The marshes here do not compare with those of the Rhine delta, but they do hold Marsh Harrier, Avocet, Black-tailed Godwit and Kentish Plover. There are colonies of gulls (including regular Mediterranean) and terns, and Icterine Warbler is a regular breeder. During passage there is a good population of waders, and geese frequent the inland fields during the winter with Bean and White-fronts reaching four figures. Smew, Hen Harrier and Merlin may be quite numerous at this season.

This is a reserve 'for all the family' and the wildfowl collection and tea-room atmosphere may put off some birders. For those whose families insist on seeing Bruges, the Zwin offers an ideal escape.

SUMMER Shelduck, Kentish Plover, Black-tailed Godwit, Avocet, Mediterranean Gull, Common Tern, Icterine Warbler.
PASSAGE Waders.
ACCESS Follow the minor road that skirts the old airfield and the reserve signs. Entrance fee.
ROUTE Northward from Bruges on Route 67, then left to Knokke.

BRITAIN

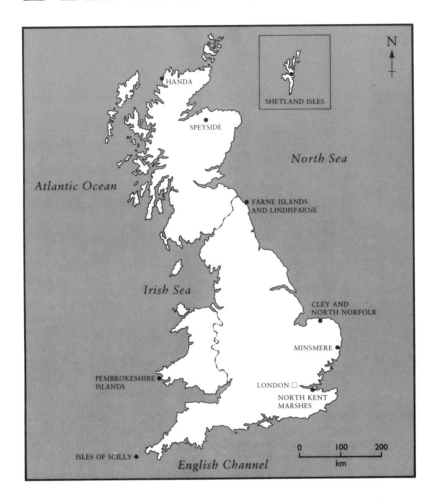

Cley and North Norfolk

A string of bird reserves now extends westwards from Cley along the North Norfolk coast, offering some of the best birding to be had in Britain. It is a cliché to call this 'the ornithologists' Mecca', but the area always has been a major attraction to British birders. Not a day passes without birders scouring the marshes, fields, woods and saltings, and during the peak spring and autumn periods there often seem to be more watchers than birds.

Cley is a reedbed and lagoon reserve with plentiful hides, a good reserve centre and an excellent variety of species. Here one can see all the regular waders that pass through Britain, plus a few scarce species that breed at hardly any other location. Wildfowl are abundant in winter and the sea produces one of the best passages of birds to be found along the East Coast.

Blakeney Point is a splendid ternery and an excellent place to see grounded migrants. Being awkward to reach (long slog along the beach or by boat), it is less worked than it merits. Blakeney Harbour is a good estuary, with wildfowl and the more regular waders. The adjacent fields have begun to become the retreat of birds in need of peace and quiet away from birders.

Holkham is known primarily for its ability to produce rarities, especially warblers in autumn. These haunt the pines or rough scrub behind the beach, but the foreshore has geese and waders, as does Wells Harbour. Parrot Crossbills bred here in the early 1980s and are worth looking for.

Scolt Head is a low, sandy island reached only by boat. It is home to a substantial ternery and is best visited, after contacting the warden, in early summer. Next, to the west, is Titchwell, where the RSPB has created a superb lagoon and reedbed reserve of completely free and unhindered access. Bittern, Marsh Harrier and Bearded Tit breed, and the passage of waders vies in quality with that of Cley. Black Tern and Little Gull have become passage specialities. There are plentiful large hides and a good reserve centre and shop.

Just 'round the corner' and into The Wash is another RSPB reserve at Snettisham. Here the old gravel workings with islands lie just inland of one of Britain's top estuaries, and the number of waders that fly past, or in to roost, is simply staggering. Mostly these are the more common species, but all manner of things do occur here.

SUMMER Bittern, Marsh Harrier, Water Rail, Ruff, Black-tailed Godwit, Common Tern, Sandwich Tern, Bearded Tit, Savi's Warbler.
PASSAGE Manx Shearwater, Gannet, Brent Goose, Hen Harrier, Wood, Green and Curlew Sandpipers, Little Stint, Temminck's Stint, Whimbrel, Spotted Redshank, Greenshank, Arctic Skua, Little Gull, Short-eared Owl, Bluethroat, Barred Warbler, Snow Bunting, Lapland Bunting.
ACCESS The whole of this coast is easily reached northwards from Norwich. Many visitors start at **Cley** and work their way eastwards, choosing their sites according to season. Along the way one is bound to meet other birders and exchange information. Cley permits can be obtained from the reserve centre at the eastern end of the village, but many just walk the loop from the Coastguards along the beach to the East Bank and then back through the village. **Blakeney Point** can be visited by boat from Morston – well advertised in this small village. The walk along the beach from Cley Coastguards is somewhat tedious. The Harbour is adjacent to Blakeney Quay. Take the wall directly north, alongside the quay car park. **Holkham** lies directly north of Wells Harbour and has a large car park at the eastern end of the pines. The sites are of free access. The pines can also be approached via Holkham Gap, opposite the entrance to Holkham Hall. Scolt Head is really only for the terns; boats can be arranged in Overy Staithe or Brancaster Staithe. Access is free, but the terneries are protected by fences. **Titchwell reserve** lies just west of the village to the north of the coast road. There is a car park, and access to hides is free at all times. **Snettisham** reserve is approached by driving to the beach car park and continuing southwards on foot to the reserve with useful hides overlooking the lagoon.
ROUTE Roads radiate northwards from Norwich.

Farne Islands and Lindisfarne

The Farnes consist of some 30 small islands lying off England's north-east coast between Tynemouth and the Scottish border. Most of them belong to the National Trust and are of straightforward public access, though The Brownsman is closed during the breeding season. Seabirds are the main attraction and include auks, Kittiwake and Fulmar on the cliffs, Puffin and Eider inland, and four British terns on the low-lying areas. In particular this is a famous stronghold of Sandwich and the now rare Roseate Tern, though Eiders vie for popularity with the closeness of their sitting and immense numbers. There is a variety of waders and other species on passage.

Immediately west of the Farnes is Lindisfarne. Most of this area is intertidal and rich in birds, particularly during passage periods and in winter. To the birdwatcher the names of the various areas conjure up pictures of different exciting species. Fenham Flats, Skate Road, Ross Links, Holy Island Lough, Budle Bay – all are outstanding for birds. Wildfowl include a wintering flock of some 2000 of the light-bellied race of Brent Goose, up to 3400 Greylag Geese and a herd of up to 350 Whooper Swans. Skate Road is the favourite haunt of sea-duck, divers and three species of grebe. The number of waders in Lindisfarne runs into tens of thousands every winter. Even the summer visitor to the Farnes should not miss Lindisfarne.

SUMMER Fulmar, Eider, Oystercatcher, Ringed Plover, Kittiwake, Common Tern, Arctic Tern, Sandwich Tern, Roseate Tern, Guillemot, Razorbill, Puffin.
AUTUMN AND WINTER Divers, Slavonian and Red-necked Grebes, Brent, Pink-footed and Greylag Geese, Whooper and Bewick's Swans, Eider, Scoter, Whimbrel, Wood Sandpiper, Spotted Redshank, and Sanderling.
ACCESS The Farnes are reached by motor boat from Seahouses village and there is a landing charge. The best island is the Inner Farne. The **Lindisfarne reserve** is of free public access, though the surrounding

Razorbills, Guillemots, Kittiwakes and Fulmar.

farmland is private. The most important access points are: Fenham near Mill Burn, north of Fenham le-Moor at Lowmoor Point; the road east of Beal and the causeway (beware: covered at high tide) across to Holy Island; north of Elwick to Whitelee Letch; east of Ross a footpath leads across Ross Links to Ross Back Sands and Skate Road; north-east of Budle north-west of Budle at Heather Cottages; on Holy Island, the road leading north to the Links; east of Holy Island to Sheldrake Pool.
ROUTE The A1 passes within 2 km of the area north of Newcastle.

HANDA

Handa is a small island off the north-west coast of Scotland about 5 km north of Scourie. It is everyone's idea of what a seabird colony should be, with 100,000 breeding birds creating an amazing spectacle of non-stop movement and noise. Most of the species one could expect are here, and the Rock Doves are the genuine article.

SUMMER Red-throated Diver, Fulmar, Shag, Kittiwake, Guillemot, Razorbill, Puffin, Black Guillemot, Arctic Skua, Great Skua, Rock Dove.
ACCESS Day trips can be arranged easily from Scourie Harbour, but not on Sundays.
ROUTE Leave the A894 at Tarbet. The nearest airport is at Inverness.

ISLES OF SCILLY

These islands in the south-western approaches have, over a period of thirty years, replaced Fair Isle (Shetland) as the prime producer of rare birds. Though the islands have a good collection of breeding seabirds, the main time for birding is October. Throughout that month there are upwards of 2000 birders combing every nook and cranny of the five inhabited islands, as well as several that have no permanent residents. Their goal is the hyper-rare, the birds that make twitchers twitch, the 'new to Britain', 'new to Europe', 'new to the Palearctic'.

As the 'Scilly Season' has developed, so too has the infrastructure to cater for the hordes. At first the locals were disturbed by the damage to crops, but today the well-ordered birders are welcomed as a new tourist boom. A considerable array of functions, entertainments and meeting places is organized and a network of communications is designed entirely for birders. It may not be to everyone's taste, but the 'Scilly Season' is a quite remarkable gathering of skilful and enthusiastic people.

Birds vary from the commonplace to the rare. The interest is mostly in small lost passerines from North America, but Siberian birds are often present and there is generally a scattering of interesting waders. Anything can turn up here, and one has the feeling that very little is missed.

AUTUMN Vagrants.
ACCESS The main island is St Mary's and the majority of birders make their base there, near the Harbour for quick inter-island transportation. Accommodation may be in short supply and should be booked in advance.
ROUTE Regular sailings and helicopter service from Penzance to St Mary's. Penzance has excellent rail connections with London.

MINSMERE

Minsmere is one of the best places to go birdwatching in Britain, and if the number of species seen is the test of a good day then Minsmere is tops. It is an RSPB reserve on the Suffolk coast. A cross-section of habitats from the sea westwards comprises the dune beach (outside the reserve), with interesting areas of *Suaeda* bushes; a sand-covered protective sea-wall; 'the Scrape', reedbeds and open pools; flat farmland; deciduous woodland; and open heather heath. The Scrape is the area of coastal pools, improved and extended to provide feeding grounds for waders on passage, and contains a series of islands, numbered to facilitate reference, for breeding birds. This direct interference with the process of nature has attracted Common Terns, and enabled the Avocet to breed successfully. Waders here are as good as in any other east coast area and a few rarities turn up every year. Farther inland the reedbeds have Marsh Harrier, which can be seen all year round. Bearded Tits also breed, and Spotted Crakes have done so on occasion, though they are far from regular even as visitors. The farmland and woodland hold most of the birds one would expect to find in such areas of southern England, and the heath has Nightjar.

Minsmere is just one, albeit the best, of a series of coastal marshes in Suffolk that make an excellent birdwatching holiday.

SUMMER Shoveler, Garganey, Spotted Crake, Marsh Harrier, Avocet, Sandwich Tern, Common Tern, Little Tern, Nightjar, Bearded Tit.
PASSAGE Spoonbill, Spotted Redshank, Little Stint, Curlew Sandpiper, Black Tern.
ACCESS Though Minsmere can be seen from two free public hides, entrance to the reserve is strictly by permit. Permits are available on various days of the week, varying from season to season. At present the reserve is closed only on Tuesdays. Parties should write in advance.
ROUTE Leave the A12 eastwards just north of Yoxford, signposted Westleton. There, take the Dunwich road and turn right after 3 km, signposted Minsmere. Continue along a rough track, park at the end and walk along the coast to the reserve entrance. Permit holders can drive to the reserve centre direct from Westleton.

NORTH KENT MARSHES

The visitor to London, with only a day or two to spare, need look no farther than the marshes that line the Thames estuary in North Kent. Here, among the power stations and refineries, is some of the best birding in Britain. The Thames itself has exposed mud-banks at low tide that are the haunt of waders, ducks and geese. Behind the protective sea-wall are huge areas of rough grazing broken by dykes, fleets and flooding, providing roosting and additional feeding areas for these birds and a home for many others. If time is really short, concentrate on either Cliffe or Sheppey; if time allows, the area between the two is worth full exploration.

Cliffe boasts a series of pits that have been excavated to provide material for the local cement industry. Mostly the water is deep, therefore providing a home for grebes and duck, with divers in winter. During passage periods, however, they also attract waders and terns and regularly boast a good rarity each season. From Cliffe Pools it is possible to walk the sea-wall eastwards, passing the marshes at Cooling to Egypt and St Mary's Bays, before cutting back inland to the RSPB reserve with its large heronry at Northward Hill. At Allhallows there is access to Yantlet Creek, a noted wader haunt, while farther east lies the huge and rich Medway estuary.

Sheppey is a place on its own, separated from the mainland by the Swale channel, but connected by the Kingsferry Bridge. Here lies the RSPB reserve of Elmley. Often regarded as a winter birding area, Elmley is excellent at all seasons. It has good breeding birds, fine wader passage and a splendid collection of winter raptors.

SUMMER Pintail, Wigeon, Greylag Goose, Marsh Harrier, Black-tailed Godwit, Redshank, Avocet, Common Tern.

PASSAGE Marsh and Montagu's Harriers, Curlew Sandpiper, Little and Temminck's Stints, Spotted Redshank, Greenshank, Green and Wood Sandpipers, Black-tailed Godwit, Ruff and Grey Plover.

WINTER Red-throated Diver, Bewick's Swan, White-fronted and Brent Geese, Wigeon, Shoveler, Hen and Marsh Harriers, Rough-legged Buzzard, Merlin, Peregrine, Short-eared Owl, Knot, Grey Plover, Bar-tailed Godwit.

ACCESS From **Cliffe** village turn left on a track out to the pools. Beyond the coastguard cottages the sea-wall leads eastward to the Cooling Marshes. Northward Hill can be reached at the far end of this walk, at the south-eastern corner of St Mary's Bay. Alternatively, take minor roads from Cliffe to High Halstow, park at the village hall, and walk down Northwood Avenue to the reserve footpath. Continue to Decoy Farm and Swigshole to the Thames. Yantlet Creek is reached by walking eastwards along the sea-wall from Allhallows. The huge **Medway** complex can be worked from its northern shores near Stoke Lagoon, just by the A228 where it crosses to the Isle of Grain. Alternatively, take the A249 toward Shellness and turn left just before the Kingsferry Bridge, signposted Lower Halstow. Turn westwards off this (with the aid of the OS map) and stop where a track leads to Chetney Cottages. Follow this and fork left to the sea-wall. For **Elmley**, continue on the A249 over Kingsferry Bridge and turn right on the first farm track after 2 km. Follow signs to the RSPB reserve.

ROUTE Take the M2 from London, using the M25 ring road if starting in the west. Heathrow to Sheppey takes about two hours by road.

PEMBROKESHIRE ISLANDS

Pembrokeshire with its cliffs and islands is one of the most accessible and important of British seabird areas. Though Continental birdwatchers can go to the Channel Islands and the Sept Îles reserve on the Channel coast of France to see Gannets, in no way do those sites compare with the thousands of pairs at Grassholm. What is more, the teeming colonies of auks, Kittiwakes and Fulmars of Skokholm, Skomer and the many mainland headlands are on a different scale from that of the Channel sites.

Though holding the gannetry, Grassholm is the smallest, least accessible and, Gannets apart, the least attractive of the islands. Skomer is only 2 km from the mainland and is the largest, the most easily accessible and the best island for birds. Its 60-m cliffs hold large numbers of common auks, Kittiwake, Fulmar and Chough, while inland there are vast puffinries and

Manx Shearwater and Storm Petrel colonies. Short-eared Owl and Buzzard can be seen in summer.

Skokholm lies 5 km west of the mainland and the same distance south of Skomer. Though breeding birds include Storm Petrel, Manx Shearwater, Guillemot and Razorbill, the emphasis on the island is on migration. Movements of chats, warblers and flycatchers are frequently very heavy, and in the latter part of the autumn movement of finches and thrushes is dramatic. Rarities of all shapes and sizes turn up with regularity.

SUMMER Storm Petrel, Manx Shearwater, Gannet, Buzzard, Puffin, Guillemot, Razorbill, Chough, Short-eared Owl.
PASSAGE Seabirds, chats, warblers, flycatchers, finches, thrushes.
ACCESS For **Grassholm**, landing arrangements must be made with the West Wales Trust for Nature Conservation (WWTNC), 7 Market Street, Haverfordwest, SA61 1NF. Such landings are extremely infrequent. A nature trail is laid out for visitors to **Skomer** and the island is open daily in the summer, boats leaving under normal conditions at 10.30 a.m. from Martins Haven; there is a landing fee, though members of the WWTNC land free and may stay on the island in the hostel. Access to **Skokholm** is via the WWTNC. For transport arrangements and enquiries, write to The Warden, Dale Fort Field Centre, Haverfordwest.

SHETLAND ISLES

The Shetlands lie 6 degrees south of the Arctic Circle, and stretch 120 km from north to south and about half that distance from east to west. Only nineteen of the hundred or so islands are inhabited. In such a vast and difficult landscape visiting ornithologists have inevitably to be choosy, as spending a full holiday on just a single island can be very rewarding. Nevertheless, the traveller, having come perhaps 1000 km to see northern birds, can be forgiven if he tries to cram everything in. This account, therefore, concentrates on those areas generally considered most worthwhile.

Shetland is a grim and rugged land with thick peat bogs underlain by hard igneous rock. The vegetation is mainly rough grass, supporting sheep, though Fetlar is called 'the green isle' because of its comparative fertility. This northern island group is one of the most accessible areas for seabirds in Europe, and also has several other northern species which usually involve visiting far higher latitudes. The seabirds are fantastic. Huge cliffs towering out of the sea are splattered with birds. Vast numbers of auks, Kittiwakes and Fulmars line the ledges, and there are two easily-seen colonies of Gannets. Manx Shearwater and Storm Petrel breed out of sight, though the former is often seen on the sea on early-season evenings. Of the northern species Great and Arctic Skuas are both numerous, and the former (called Bonxie locally) can be seen more conveniently here than anywhere else in the northern hemisphere. Red-throated Diver, Dunlin and two scarce birds – Whimbrel and Red-necked Phalarope – frequent open land and inland lochs. Among wildfowl found in the same areas are Red-breasted Merganser, Wigeon and Scoter and the occasional pair of Whooper Swans. The visitor who examines every gull in Lerwick Harbour may be rewarded by a summering but non-breeding Glaucous or Iceland Gull. A pair of Snowy Owls bred in 1967–75, but only females have been seen since.

SUMMER Red-throated Diver, Gannet, Fulmar, Manx Shearwater, Storm Petrel, Eider, Scoter, Red-breasted Merganser, Dunlin, Snipe, Common Sandpiper, Golden Plover, Whimbrel, Red-necked Phalarope, Arctic and Common Terns, Arctic and Great Skuas, Kittiwake, Guillemot, Razorbill, Puffin, Black Guillemot, Wren, Twite, Hooded Crow.
ACCESS Almost anywhere in Shetland is good for birds and a holiday could be had on any of the inhabited islands. Unst, in the extreme north of the group, is 20 km by 8 km. The southern half is well cultivated and as green as nearby Fetlar. The cliff scenery is among the best in Britain, and Hermaness in the north of the island is the culmination of many a bird-watcher's dream. Cliff-nesting seabirds fill the air and offshore lie the stacks around Muckle Flugga with their large gannetry. The clifftops are honey-combed with the burrows of Puffins, while the moors inland are the strong-hold of Great and Arctic Skuas. The Hermaness reserve was established in 1955; there are no restrictions on access. The nearby Loch of Cliff is a favourite freshwater bathing place for many of the seabirds. Baltasound, the main village, is served by a regular boat from Lerwick, and the ferries between Mainland and Yell and between Yell and Unst provide an over-land route. Fetlar is the smallest of the main islands. Although its cliffs are not so impressive as many in Shetland, the usual auks, gulls and Fulmars manage to breed. Apart from waders, Fetlar also boasts both skuas and from 1967 to 1975 held breeding Snowy Owls. Mainland is not to be over-looked by birdwatchers arriving hot-foot for the other famous Shetland islands. It has most of the specialities and with better services and facili-ties can provide a more varied holiday than any other island, and it is, of course, the best centre for seeing all the others by day trips. Gannets can be seen fishing in Lerwick Harbour and there are numerous cliffs with sea-birds. Both species of scoter (only one breeding) regularly occur in Weisdale Voe, and Whiteness Voe is also worth a good look. Ronas Hill lies on the north-western side of Mainland and extends along 20 km of coast, in-cluding cliffs up to 230 m with seabirds and skuas. There is a wide choice of accommodation, including a wealth of guest houses. Noss lies 5 km east of Lerwick and its cliffs, although they drop a mere 180 m, seem as high as the famous 430-m Conachair of St Kilda. Over 5200 pairs of Gannets breed and the cliffs are covered with auks, Kittiwakes and Fulmars. On the top are Puffins and Great and Arctic Skuas. There are many tourist trips around Noss by boat from Lerwick, which provide an ideal way of seeing the seabird cliffs. Fair Isle lies mid-way between Orkney and Shetland and because of its isolation, geographical position and small size is world famous as a bird observatory. Though Fair Isle is mainly a migration study station, it does have interesting breeding species such as Great and Arctic Skuas, auks including Black Guillemot, Storm Petrel, Fulmar and the Fair Isle subspecies of the Wren. Vagrants, however, are the Observatory's life blood and turn up weekly, if not daily, during the autumn. Loganair operate a twice-weekly service and an Observatory charter once a week. Full-board accommodation is available. Details from The Warden, Fair Isle Bird Observatory, Lerwick, Shetland, Scotland.
ROUTE Daily air services between Sumburgh and Kirkwall (Orkney) and Aberdeen, and also from Wick. There are connections with other parts of Britain, and twice-weekly sailings from Aberdeen to Lerwick via Kirkwall, and Loganair operate an inter-island service.

Black Grouse

SPEYSIDE

Continental birders visiting Britain expect two distinct types of birding: they expect the best seabird colonies in Europe, plus the chance to see several northern birds otherwise rather awkward. For the latter they are well advised to follow the path beaten by successive generations of British birders to the Spey valley. Here, around Aviemore, they find a land of moors and mountains, forests and lakes not much different from that of Scandinavia. Here they can seek Golden Eagle, Peregrine, Hen Harrier, Ptarmigan, Dotterel and the otherwise localized northern grouse. Here too there are Scottish Crossbills, now recognized as a distinct species from their Continental (and English) counterparts. There are the more widespread Crested Tit and Osprey, and some very scarce waders, but above all there is some of the most beautiful countryside in the whole of Britain.

Once this landscape was the haunt of fishermen, stalkers and a few birdwatchers. Today, Speyside is a tourist resort in both winter and summer. The charm of Aviemore has disappeared, but the area is more accessible.

SUMMER Red-breasted Merganser, Capercaillie, Black and Red Grouse, Water Rail, Hen Harrier, Golden Eagle, Goshawk, Sparrowhawk, Merlin, Peregrine, Dotterel, Golden Plover, Wood Sandpiper, Crested Tit, Scottish Crossbill, Snow Bunting.

ACCESS The Caledonian forest remnants at **Rothiemurchus**, **Glenmore** and **Abernethy** have been surrounded by modern plantations but maintain their unique fauna. Everyone should visit **Loch an Eilean** and **Loch Morlich** and spend time walking the forest tracks. **Loch Garten** is the home of Osprey and is well signposted from the A9 and elsewhere. For higher-altitude birds, drive past Loch Morlich to the Cairngorm ski-lift terminal and take the easy way to the tops; weatherproof clothing, map and compass are essential, even in brilliant sunny summer weather. To the south, the RSPB reserve at **Loch Insh** is more than a winter home of wildfowl.

ROUTE The A9 runs right through the Spey valley. There are also regular trains from London that stop at Aviemore.

BULGARIA

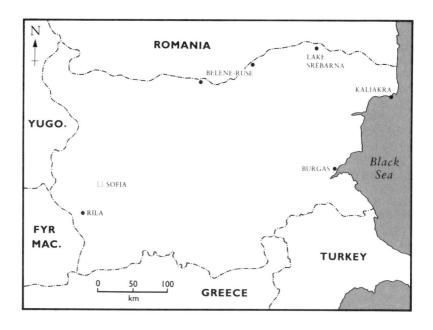

BELENE-RUSE

The Bulgaria–Romania border runs along the middle of the main channel of the River Danube. Sadly, for most of its length, the lakes, marshes and backwaters that have resulted from the river changing its course together with its low-lying seasonal floods, lie to the north in Romania (see Cǎlǎraşi-Giurgiu Floodland). Across the river from Giurgiu lies the town of Ruse and upstream from here are the best marshes in Bulgaria. Here many of the typical birds of the Danube floodlands can be found, especially on the islands of Belene and Vardim, and along the course of the major tributary the Rusenski Lom. Here breeding waterbirds include Pygmy Cormorant, Night and Squacco Herons, Glossy Ibis, a few pairs of Spoonbills and a pair of White-tailed Eagles at each site. At Belene, in particular, some of these species breed in internationally important numbers. Along the Rusenski Lom the riverine forests also hold Black Stork, Lesser Spotted Eagle, Saker, Eagle Owl and Imperial Eagle is often seen and may well breed. The limestone cliffs here also hold Egyptian Vulture and Lesser Kestrel.

SUMMER Pygmy Cormorant, Cormorant, White and Black Storks, Night, Purple and Squacco Herons, Little Egret, Spoonbill, Glossy Ibis, Ruddy Shelduck, Saker, Lesser Kestrel, Long-legged Buzzard, Lesser Spotted, Golden, White-tailed and Imperial Eagles, Whiskered Tern, Eagle Owl, Roller.
ACCESS The two Danube islands are nature reserves but much can be seen along the river banks and, from a good viewpoint, soaring over the

forest. Local boatmen can be hired in Belene and Vardim to ferry you to the islands, but permission from local wardens should be sought in advance. Boating around the islands should present no problems. The Rusenski Lom can be viewed from Route 125 (175) south of Ruse at several points.

ROUTE Ruse has a domestic airport, though anyone exploring the Bulgarian coast northwards could take in Lake Srebârna and this area.

BURGAS

This area has been famous ever since it appeared in the first edition of this book. Such fame rests on two factors: three excellent lakes nearby that attract some of the best waterbirds to be found in the country; and the arrest and interviewing of many birders as to why they were 'spying' on a local factory that seems to produce nothing more strategic than pickles. With the changes that swept through eastern Europe in the late 1980s the second is hopefully a thing of the past and Lakes Burgas, Mandra and Atanassovo can be enjoyed without fear of the local police.

Over the years the nature of each lake has been drastically changed by development, resulting in the loss of much habitat and many breeding birds. Despite Mandra's conversion to a freshwater reservoir, Atanassovo's development as saltpans and Burgas' oil pollution, together they still hold really good birds. Atanassovo is now recognized as a Ramsar site and one of the best birding sites in the country. Breeding species include Little Bittern, Ferruginous Duck, a huge Avocet colony, Collared Pratincole, Gull-billed Tern (only Bulgarian site), together with (probably) Ruddy Shelduck. Migrants are often abundant and White Pelican (15,000), Black Stork (2900), White Stork (135,000), Honey Buzzard (3700) and Lesser Spotted Eagle (5700) have been counted in autumn (figures are averages per year).

Lake Burgas remains a freshwater lake with an outflow to the sea. It has some extensive reedbeds and, therefore holds somewhat different species to Atanassovo. Night and Purple Herons, Little Egret and Glossy Ibis are additional breeders found here. Strangely enough Lake Mandra has actually been improved by its conversion to a reservoir with a remnant brackish lagoon acting as an overflow. Pygmy Cormorant, Squacco Heron, Glossy Ibis and Spoonbill all breed, with sometimes also Great White Egret. Winter birds here are also good, while passage waders are excellent at Atanassovo.

SUMMER White Stork, Little and Great White Egrets, Night, Purple and Squacco Herons, Little Bittern, Spoonbill, Glossy Ibis, Ferruginous Duck, Ruddy Shelduck, Marsh Harrier, Spotted and Little Crakes, Black-winged Stilt, Collared Pratincole, Gull-billed, Common, Little and Black Terns, Syrian Woodpecker, Tawny Pipit, Short-toed Lark, Olive-tree Warbler, Spanish Sparrow, Black-headed Bunting.

AUTUMN White and Dalmatian Pelicans, White and Black Storks, Spoonbill, Glossy Ibis, Honey Buzzard, Short-toed and Lesser Spotted Eagles, Crane, Avocet, Kentish Plover, Ruff, Little Stint, Mediterranean and Slender-billed Gulls, Gull-billed Tern.

ACCESS Burgas is the ideal centre and Route 11, to the north, gives access to the saltpans at Atanassovo. Although getting good views can be frustrating, access to the northern and best part is straightforward. The main road runs along the western shore with adjacent reedbeds holding Bearded

Tit. Avocet and terns can be found on the old saltpans in the south. The road then crosses the north end of the lake, with excellent saltpans beyond on the left. A farm track to the left runs northwards along the eastern side of the saltpans. Sophia University have a migration watchpoint at the end of this track. The road west to Ezerovo provides access to Lake Burgas. Route 31 crosses Lake Mandra near the sea with an excellent reedbed to the east.
ROUTE Although Burgas has an airport, most birders take in the area during exploration of Greece or Turkey.

KALIAKRA

Cape Kaliakra lies on the Black Sea coast of Bulgaria 43 km south of the Ukraine border. Once a no-go area, it can now be visited by outsiders, though it may not be ready for the influx of European listers/birders who should follow its becoming known in the west. It is the most outstanding migrant concentration point along the western shores of the Black Sea with most soaring migrants that fly the Bosporus passing through. It is also a concentration point for smaller birds and a decent seawatching site. Add some interesting breeding birds and some fine winter visitors and it can be seen that Kaliakra may be destined for greatness, at least in ornitho-circles.

Migration, however, will be the first draw on western birders with Black Stork, Honey Buzzard, Black Kite, three harriers, Levant Sparrowhawk, Lesser Spotted and Short-toed Eagles all passing through in numbers. White Pelican can also be numerous (perhaps as many as 10,000) and there are also good numbers of Pygmy Cormorant. Breeding species include Shag, Eagle Owl and Pied Wheatear, while falls of smaller migrants include Red-breasted Flycatcher, Tawny Pipit, Lesser Grey and Red-backed Shrikes.

Lakes Shabla and Durankulak lie to the north, behind the coast, and are variably fresh to saline in nature. Breeding birds here include Ruddy Shelduck at Shabla; and Bittern, Little Bittern, Marsh Harrier and Pratincole at Durankulak. Both lakes are very important in winter with Shabla boasting a population of 7600 Red-breasted Geese (max 17,000) together with 36,000 Whitefronts. Durankulak has similar numbers of Whitefronts, but only 400 Red-breasted. Other wintering species include Pygmy Cormorant, Great White Egret and Smew. Both of these lakes are good for passage waders including Broad-billed Sandpiper as well as small birds such as Calandra and Short-toed Larks, Spanish Sparrow and last, but by no means least, Paddyfield Warbler, which breeds here and virtually nowhere else in Europe outside the former Soviet Union. This high-value bird can be found among the sedges rather than the tall stands of reeds at Durankulak.

With migrant raptors, concentrations of migrant passerines, breeding waterbirds and Paddyfield, Kaliakra and its neighbouring wetlands could become one of the standard ingredients of a Greek or Turkish bird trip.

SUMMER Shag, Bittern, Little Bittern, Greylag Goose, Ruddy Shelduck, Ferruginous Duck, Egyptian Vulture, Marsh Harrier, Stone-curlew, Collared Pratincole, Eagle Owl, Alpine Swift, Short-toed Lark, Pallid Swift, Roller, Bee-eater, Lesser Grey Shrike, Pied Wheatear, Olivaceous Warbler, Paddyfield Warbler, Black-headed Bunting.
PASSAGE Pygmy Cormorant, Black and White Storks, White Pelican, Honey Buzzard, Black Kite, Buzzard and Long-legged Buzzard, Marsh,

Glossy Ibis

Montagu's, Hen and Pallid Harriers, Sparrowhawk, Levant Sparrowhawk, Lesser Spotted and Short-toed Eagles, Marsh and Broad-billed Sandpipers, Lesser Grey and Red-backed Shrikes, Tawny Pipit, Red-breasted Flycatcher. **ACCESS** From Kavarna there is road access to the cliffs at Cape Kaliakra for seabirds and migrants – visible and grounded – and Pied Wheatear. There is a car park and useful café near the point. The two lakes lie northwards on Route 131 then Route 31. Both can be explored on minor roads. **ROUTE** Varna to the south has an airport that is used by package holiday charters and is only a short drive away from Kavarna.

RILA

The highest posint of Bulgaria lies in the south-west, some 105 km south of Sofia. Here too is the famous Rila Monastery, with murals covering every inch of wall space inside and frescoes proliferating outside. This well-trodden tourist route makes a perfect base for birders intent on high-altitude and forest birds. Most of the real gems can be found here, but as always they are somewhat scarce and need searching for. Wallcreeper and Hazelhen fall into the category – they do not give themselves up lightly.

Woodpeckers, including Black and Grey-headed, can be found among the conifers on the slopes above the monastery, while higher still there are Golden Eagle, Alpine Chough, Rock Nuthatch and even Shore Lark and Alpine Accentor. The last two do require some hiking through the forests to more open countryside above. Around the monastery itself the deciduous woods hold Sombre and Willow Tits, Treecreeper, Siskin and Hawfinch, while Nutcracker, Rock Partridge, Rock Bunting and raptors may be seen virtually anywhere.

A good spot for high-altitude species is above Borovec on the eastern side of the massif, where ski resorts and their paraphernalia make access considerably easier. Here Alpine Accentor, Shore Lark, Crag Martin, Wallcreeper, Rock Thrush and Water Pipit may oblige.

SUMMER Golden, Short-toed and Booted Eagles, Capercaillie, Hazelhen, Goshawk, Buzzard, Honey Buzzard, Peregrine, Alpine Chough, Nutcracker, Scops Owl, Alpine Accentor, Alpine Swift, Crag Martin, Red-rumped Swallow, Wallcreeper, Rock Partridge, Shore Lark, Water Pipit, Black and Grey-headed Woodpeckers, Rock Thrush, Firecrest, Sombre, Willow and Crested Tits, Rock and Cirl Buntings, Siskin, Crossbill, Hawfinch.

ACCESS Leave Sofia southwards on Route 2 and turn left (east) on Route 164 at Kočerinovo. Rila has a tourist hotel and camp site and there are plentiful walks through the forests and above. For the Borovec area leave Sofia in the same direction on Route 2, but turn left at Stanke Dimitrov to Samokov, then right to Govedarci and the ski resorts beyond. At Maljovica there are several ski hotels, a camp site and two ski lifts to the south. Facing the ski lifts a path leads up on the right to penetrate an apparently wooded valley running westwards between two high cliff faces. An hour's walk leads to a prominent stone building that may have Wallcreeper in the early morning. The cliff faces on the north side also have this species at the same time of day. One observer reports three different birds at this site.

ROUTE Sofia has an international airport.

SREBÂRNA LAKE

Lake Srebârna is the Bulgarian equivalent of the lower Danube marshes in Romania to the north, and visiting birdwatchers are just as likely to be turned away from what is still a sensitive border zone. Nevertheless, this is a first-rate wetland and one of the most important wetlands in the country for breeding marsh birds.

The lake lies west of Silistra in the north-east of the country and was declared a reserve in 1948. At that time it was separated from the Danube by a dam, but was reconnected in 1978. Open water is surrounded by reeds and thickets holding Purple, Squacco and Night Herons, Great White and Little Egrets, Little Bittern, Glossy Ibis, Spoonbill and White-tailed Eagle. There are also Marsh Harrier, Ferruginous Duck, Black and Whiskered Terns, Penduline Tit, Barred and Icterine Warblers and a good cross-section of the species that one could expect in south-eastern Europe. It is also the only breeding site in the country of Dalmatian Pelican with up to 200 pairs. Altogether, Srebârna and the surrounding land offer an excellent opportunity for first-rate birding in what is still a little-known area.

SUMMER Red-necked and Great Crested Grebes, Pygmy Cormorant, Dalmatian Pelican, Purple Heron, Great White and Little Egrets, Squacco and Night Herons, Little Bittern, Glossy Ibis, Spoonbill, Greylag Goose, Garganey, Red-crested Pochard, Ferruginous Duck, White-tailed Eagle, Marsh Harrier, Little and Spotted Crakes, Black, White-winged Black and Whiskered Terns, Penduline Tit, Roller, Golden Oriole, Hoopoe, Icterine, Savi's, Great Reed, Marsh and Barred Warbler.

ACCESS Though the area is a reserve, much can be seen without disturbing the sanctuary. By contacting the warden and seeking permission to visit, however, one may avoid any complications with the local police.

ROUTE Drive westward on Route 23 from Silistra. The area makes a fine day out for those using a package holiday based on the coast at Zlatni pjasāci (Golden Sands) north of Varna.

CYPRUS

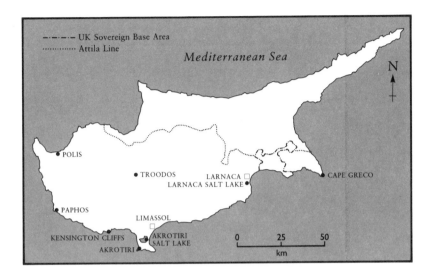

Cyprus, at some 225 km from east to west and nearly 100 km north to south, is the third largest island in the Mediterranean. It is also the most easterly island and, lying south of Turkey, is on the major route between eastern Europe and the Middle East. Though it has several good-value breeding birds, among them the Cyprus Warbler and Cyprus Pied Wheatear as well as Black Francolin and Dead Sea Sparrow, the main attraction is undoubtedly the migrants that pour through in spring and autumn. These include an interesting passage of birds of prey in the east, and hosts of warblers, chats and flycatchers that form the basic diet of very large colonies of Eleonora's Falcons.

Waders have a distinctly eastern bias and regularly include Greater Sand Plover along with Terek, Broad-billed and Marsh Sandpipers. There are often really substantial flocks of Little Stint in autumn. Gulls include Slender-billed and Audouin's, and White-winged Black is more abundant than Black Tern. Among the smaller birds, Cretzschmar's and Black-headed Buntings breed and Ortolans are regular. Masked Shrikes breed and three other species of shrike pass through, only Great Grey being absent. Collared Flycatchers are regular in spring and Semi-collared are probably overlooked among them. Most of the Mediterranean warblers breed and Olivaceous are widespread and common.

Cyprus has endured a somewhat tumultuous history, and even today there is conflict between the Turkish-speaking people of the north and the Greek-speaking population of the south. Partitioning means that visitors must still choose which half to visit. Birders have little choice: the best bird spots are in the south and the Greek part is, in any case, best served by flights and hotels. Unfortunately, British military bases occupy some of the very best birding areas and access is either restricted or requires discretion. It is best not to carry a camera when birding around these areas and, wherever signs prohibiting photography are displayed, it is wise not to use binoculars. The major birding areas, from east to west, are listed.

Cape Greco, where grounded migrants are often abundant, is itself out of bounds owing to the presence of a booster station for Radio Monaco. The surroundings, however, are still good and the invariably dry Lake Paralimni holds a good variety of open-country species.

The salt lake south of Larnaca holds Flamingo, as well as many waders and gulls, plentiful egrets and many open-country birds. To the west of the lake at the Tekke Mosque is an area of reeds and woodland that holds migrants. Spiro's Beach Restaurant is south of the main airport runway and adjacent to various pools that often hold good waders, as well as Flamingo. Further south still, Cape Kiti is often a good seawatch spot.

Probably the most famous birding area on the island is the peninsula of Akrotiri, south of Limassol. Here a large salt lake is a major haunt of Flamingo, waders and herons, while there are plentiful small birds in the varied surroundings of woodland, scrub, orchards, gravel pits, shoreline and cliffs. This is the best area for Greater Sand Plover and Broad-billed Sandpiper, as well as an outstanding one for small migrants. Cape Gata and the southern part of the peninsula lies within RAF Akrotiri and is generally out of bounds. It is, however, still possible to drive around the salt lake, picking up species such as Dead Sea Sparrow, Penduline Tit and Moustached Warbler. It is also possible to view Kensington Cliffs, where Eleonora's Falcon and Griffon Vulture breed. The mouth of the Paramali River to the west is excellent for small migrants and waders and is a noted haunt of Black Francolin, while farther west still is Cape Aspro, where there are the largest colonies of Eleonora's Falcon.

Paphos is another excellent bird area, as well as a fine place for a holiday. It is a small, historical, attractive area, which has good birding sites nearby – ideal for family holidays. To the east, the Dhiarizos River has good reedbeds and a combination of scrub and pools that holds Black Francolin and many warblers. The western part of Cyprus is best for the endemic warbler. To the north, the Troödos Mountains hold Pallid Swift, Crag Martin and Griffon, while there is just a chance of Imperial Eagle.

SPRING Little Bittern, Night and Squacco and Purple Herons, Little Egret, White Stork, Glossy Ibis, Flamingo, Honey Buzzard, Black Kite, Griffon Vulture, Pallid Harrier, Bonelli's Eagle, Imperial Eagle, Lesser Kestrel, Red-footed Falcon, Peregrine, Black Francolin, Spotted and Little Crakes, Crane, Demoiselle Crane, Black-winged Stilt, Collared Pratincole, Greater Sand and Spur-winged Plovers, Little and Temminck's Stints, Broad-billed and Marsh Sandpipers, Slender-billed and Audouin's Gulls, White-winged Black Tern, Black-bellied Sandgrouse, Great Spotted Cuckoo, Scops Owl, Bee-eater, Roller, Calandra and Short-toed Larks, Red-rumped Swallow, Tawny Pipit, Thrush Nightingale, Isabelline and, Cyprus Pied Wheatears, Moustached, Olivaceous, Cyprus, Rüppell's and Bonelli's Warblers, Collared and Semi-collared Flycatchers, Golden Oriole, Lesser Grey and Masked Shrikes, Dead Sea Sparrow, Ortolan, Cretzschmar's and Black-headed Buntings.
AUTUMN Osprey, Pallid Harrier, Red-footed and Eleonora's Falcons, Cyprus Pied Wheatear, Red-backed Shrike.
ACCESS Cape Greco is easily reached to the entrance of Radio Monaco's booster station. Finsch's Wheatear is a winter speciality along this road.

Cyprus Pied Wheatear

Excellent seawatching and grounded migrants. **Lake Paralimni** lies north of Greco. The surrounding fields are worth exploring for migrants, even when the lake is dry. **Larnaca Salt Lake** lies south of Larnaca on the main road. Work your way around the runway to the lake. Watch for Tekke Mosque on the right and later for the Meneou Kiti Beach road. Left off this leads to Spiro's Beach and pool and views of the main lake. For **Akrotiri** leave Limassol west and turn left signposted 'Ladies Mile Beach'. Continue to Zakaki Marshes and then take the track parallel to the beach, with side tracks leading to the eastern shore of the salt lake. Tracks lead west around the southern shore; there is a gate that leads to Bishop's Pool, and eventually to the main Akrotiri base road. Turn right and explore the western shoreline. Before an area of woodland turn left to the reeds and pools of Phasouri, or right to those at the salt lake. At this north-western corner there are Dead Sea Sparrows, but they are highly elusive. For **Kensington Cliffs** take a left at the top of a hill soon after passing a sign for the military base about 20 km west of Limassol. There is a bus-stop lay-by immediately preceding the turning, but even frequent visitors sometimes miss it. The road leads to a chapel and a path continues to the dangerous cliff tops. Griffons can be seen on nests to the right. For **Dhiarizos River** stop on the road to Paphos at Kouklia and explore up- and downstream for Black Francolin and Stone-curlew, the latter often in quite sizeable flocks. In **Paphos** drive to Paphos Lighthouse and explore on foot over the short grassland area that leads south and west to the sea. This area is often alive with migrants in spring and is regularly frequented by visiting birders from whom up-to-date local news can be obtained. **Smyies Ridge and the Baths of Aphrodite** lie north of Paphos, beyond Polis, and consist of hillside olive groves of no apparent distinction. They are, however, strategically situated to receive hordes of small migrants and warblers, flycatchers and chats often abound. Smyies Ridge can be driven over tracks and the Baths are a favoured tourist outing. **ROUTE** The international airport is at Larnaca, but there are frequent charter flights to Paphos.

THE CZECH REPUBLIC

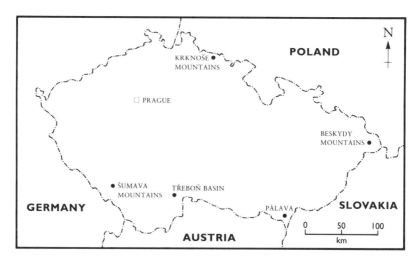

BESKYDY MOUNTAINS

The Beskydy Mountains lie on the borders of Poland and Slovakia within the Carpathians. Though not so spectacular as the neighbouring Tatras, Beskydy has important populations of several sought-after species and is generally easier to work. There are outstanding numbers of Black Stork (20 pairs) and Hazelhen (200 pairs), together with Eagle, Ural, Pygmy and Tengmalm's Owls, good numbers of woodpeckers including up to 150 pairs of both White-backed and Three-toed Woodpeckers, and really great numbers of both Red-breasted and Collared Flycatchers.

SUMMER Black Stork, Honey Buzzard, Hazelhen, Capercaillie, Corncrake, Eagle Owl, Ural, Pygmy and Tengmalm's Owls, Nightjar, Grey-headed, Black, White-backed and Three-toed Woodpeckers, Ring Ouzel, Barred Warbler, Redstart, Red-breasted and Collared Flycatchers, Firecrest.
ACCESS The area can be driven on roads and tracks, or walked. Information from Besdyky Protected Landscape Area, Nădražni 36, 75661 Roznov p. Radh. (Tel. 42 651 55592).
ROUTE Leave Prague eastwards on the N11 to Hradec Králové. Take the N35 through Olomouc and continue on the N35 to Ruznov p. Radh.

KRKNOŠE MOUNTAINS

This area lies close to the Polish border and is a national park with seven State Nature Reserves. The hills are covered with extensive coniferous forests suffering from aerial pollution. The situation is not improved by the 8–10,000,000 tourists. Despite this, the Krknoše form an excellent (and important) area for birds with their forests, marshes, peat bogs and open 'tundra' habitats. Among the attractions are Black Stork (5–7 pairs), Lesser Spotted Eagle, Merlin, Peregrine, Black Grouse, Capercaillie, Dotterel which was regular but now down to a single pair, Alpine Accentor with ten isolated pairs at its most northerly European outpost, Greenish Warbler and the entire Czech population of Red-spotted Bluethroat. Fortunately, no less than 60 per cent (ten pairs) of Red-spotted Bluethroat breed at Pančavská and Labská louka peatbogs in the Prameny Lube State Nature Reserve. The forests boasts excellent populations of owls and woodpeckers, probably including a highly elusive pair of White-backed Woodpeckers.

SUMMER Black Stork, Honey Buzzard, Hen Harrier, Lesser Spotted Eagle, Merlin, Peregrine, Black Grouse, Capercaillie, Corncrake, Dotterel, Eagle, Pygmy and Tengmalm's Owls, Green, Black, Middle Spotted and White-backed Woodpeckers, Woodlark, Alpine Accentor, Bluethroat, Red-breasted Flycatcher, Ring Ouzel, Red-backed Shrike, Greenish Warbler, Scarlet Rosefinch.
ACCESS There is no need for permits to enter the National Park, but the Prameny Nature Reserve should be contacted via Krknoše National Park, 54301 Vrchlabí-Zámek (Tel. 42 438 21011).
ROUTE Leave Prague north-eastwards on the N10 to Jablonec and turn right 10 km later to Vrchlabí which is the best base.

PĂLAVA

Close to the Austrian border two rivers join to form the March (see Marchegg in Austria). These rivers, the Morava and Dyje, meet at Soutok, near Lednice, among a maze of marshes, channels, islands and back-waters to form one of the most important Czech wetlands. At first sight it would seem that this is another of those huge Central European wetlands that are so rich in birds, but so difficult to work. Fortunately much of the area lies in a Protected Landscape Area and there are several workable wetlands such as the five Lednice ponds and the three Pohořelické ryb-niky ponds as well as the grounds of Lednice Chateau, with its seven species of woodpeckers, and the Nové Mlýny Reservoir. Much of the appeal of the area lies in the limestone outcrops, which dominate the otherwise rolling landscape, and in the extensive areas of riverine forest.

The confluence marshes at Soutok are the centrepiece of the area with Black Stork, Saker, Honey Buzzard, both kites, Marsh Harrier, and a single pair of White-tailed Eagles. There are Red-crested Pochard, Little Bittern, Purple Heron, Spoonbill and Mediterranean Gull. Woodlands, including the chateau, have good numbers of Grey-headed, Black, Syrian and Middle Spotted Woodpeckers as well as Barred Warbler and Collared Flycatcher.

In winter and on passage there are vast hordes of Bean and White-fronted Geese, a few Great White Egrets, up to 25 White-tailed Eagles, and Wallcreeper in the town and nearby quarries.

SUMMER White and Black Storks, Grey, Night and Purple Herons, Bittern and Little Bittern, Spoonbill, Greylag Goose, Red-crested Pochard, Honey Buzzard, Red and Black Kites, White-tailed Eagle, Marsh Harrier,

Saker, Mediterranean Gull, Common Tern, Grey-headed, Black, Syrian and Middle Spotted Woodpeckers, Bluethroat, Barred and Savi's Warblers, Collared Flycatcher, Red-backed Shrike, Hoopoe and Bearded Tit.
WINTER White-tailed Eagle, Great White Egret, Bean and White-fronted Geese.
ACCESS No permits are required, but it might be both courteous and informative to contact Pălava Protected landscape, Námestí 32, 69201 Mikulov (Tel. 42 625 2585). Explore the various areas i.e., Lednice ponds, Lednice Chateau, Pohořelické ponds, Nove Mlýny reservoir and especially Soutok with the aid of a good map.
ROUTE Brno is the nearest large town, but the crossing from Austria at Drasenhofen-Mikulov offers a speedy route from Vienna (for cheap flights avoid the skiing and music seasons) and for crews working Neusiedl.

ŠUMAVA MOUNTAINS

These mountains extend 120 km along the Germany-Austria border and 40 km into the Czech Republic. Over half the area is conifer forests, there are extensive peat bogs, often covered with dwarf trees, and damp meadows line the lowland valleys. The whole area forms a rich and important landscape, much of which is incorporated in a National Park and Protected Landscape Area. Itis attractions include Black Grouse (200 pairs), Capercaillie (60 pairs) and Hazelhen (are you ready for this? – 'hundreds of pairs'). Additionally, there are Eagle (10 pairs), Pygmy (250 pairs), Tengmalm's Owls (200 pairs), plus woodpeckers that include Black, Grey-headed, Three-toed (hundreds of pairs) and the most sought-after of all, White-backed Woodpecker (10–20 pairs). Add in a few pairs of Black Stork, Lesser Spotted Eagle, Hen Harrier, Peregrine, and a good population of Honey Buzzard, and the attraction of this superb area of hills becomes instantly obvious. Ural Owl has been regular here since it was reintroduced to the adjacent national park in Bavaria in the 1970s.

SUMMER Black Stork, Honey Buzzard, Lesser Spotted Eagle, Hen Harrier, Peregrine, Hazelhen, Black Grouse, Capercaillie, Corncrake, Eagle, Pygmy, Tengmalm's and Ural Owls, Grey-headed, Black, White-backed and Three-toed Woodpeckers, Woodlark, Bluethroat, Ring Ouzel, Red-breasted Flycatcher, Red-backed Shrike, Scarlet Rosefinch.
ACCESS There are numerous roads and tracks that facilitate exploration. However, it is good advice to get the best out of the area by seeking a permit (and advice) from the Šumava National Park centre at 38501 Vimperk-zămek (Tel. 42 339 21355).
ROUTE Take the road (N4) southwards from Prague through Přibram and Strakonice to Vimperk.

TŘEBOŇ BASIN

The landscape of Třeboňsko consists of innumerable peat bogs covered with forests of pine and spruce, plus groves of old oaks. It is generally regarded as one of the most valuable ecosystems. Additionally, there are some 180 fish-ponds, some of which date from the eighteenth century, which are used for rearing carp in this land-locked country. The ponds

White-backed Woodpecker

hold waterbirds including Bittern, Black Stork (5-10 pairs), White-tailed Eagle (4 pairs), Honey Buzzard (20 pairs), Marsh Harrier (70 pairs), and Hen and Montagu's Harriers, Black Tern and Spotted and Little Crakes. The forests are also rich in species – Hazelhen, Black Grouse and Capercaillie all breed, though they are elusive. Eagle (5 pairs), Tengmalm's (50 pairs), and Pygmy (50 pairs) Owls are present as are Black, Grey-headed and Middle Spotted Woodpeckers. At several areas Collared Flycatcher is regarded as common, while there are also Red-breasted Flycatcher, Bluethroat, Penduline Tit, plus Savi's and Barred Warblers.

Passage brings a variety of wildfowl and waders, including Greylag and Bean Geese and Red-crested Pochard. Particularly in autumn, a pond drained to harvest the fish may attract hundreds of varied waders, and many herons including Great White Egret and Spoonbill. In winter the area is a regular haunt of numbers of White-tailed Eagle.

SUMMER Cormorant, Bittern, Night, Grey and Purple Herons, Black and White-Storks, Greylag Goose, Honey Buzzard, Red and Black Kites, White-tailed Eagle, Marsh, Montagu's and Hen Harriers, Spotted and Little Crakes, Black-tailed Godwit, Common and Black Terns, Eagle, Pygmy and Tengmalm's Owsl, Nightjar, Black, Grey-headed and Middle Spotted Woodpeckers, Woodlark, Bluethroat, Red-breasted and Collared Flycatchers, Red-backed Shrike, Barred and Savi's Warblers, Penduline Tit.
PASSAGE Greylag Goose, Bean Goose, Red-crested Pochard, waders.
WINTER Geese, White-tailed Eagle, Hen Harrier.
ACCESS Much of the area lies within the Třeboňsko Protected Land-scape Area – a Ramsar site. A seemingly formidable area to work, visitors could do no better than to head for the Velky Tisy fish-ponds, north of Třeboň. Here the Czech Ornithological Society have a cottage that may be let to visitors. Contact Dr J. Hora, National Museum, Vǎclavskě nǎmesti, Prague. The reserve headquarters can be contacted (Tel. 42 333 3097).
ROUTE Southwards from Prague with its international airport to Veselí n. Luž and Třeboň.

DENMARK

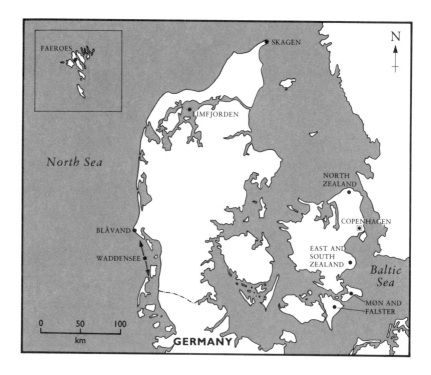

BLÅVAND

The Waddensee ends north of Esbjerg at the promontory of Blåvandshuk. This sandy area has a lighthouse and a bird observatory (with accommodation for a few people) and is one of the best areas in Denmark for migration. Waders and wildfowl pass in huge numbers and after westerly winds there can be good movements of divers, grebes, Gannet, skuas and sometimes shearwaters, storm petrels and Sabine's Gull. The promontory is excellent for movement of finches, thrushes and pipits, and often there are rarities of international status among migrants, as well as semi-rarities such as Tawny Pipit, Stonechat, Barred Warbler and Lapland Bunting.

Inland, but extending to the south, lies the tidal inlet of Ho Bugt, a haunt of a good variety of waders including several hundred Avocets in autumn. These birds breed on the islands of Fanø and Rømø to the south, as well as the peninsula of Skallingen that separates Ho Bugt from the sea.

At Ringkøbing Fjord, about 40 km north of Blåvand, lies Tipperne, water meadows and salt-marshes surrounded by a vast area of shallow water with a few islands. Breeders include Bittern, a large colony of Avocets, Black-tailed Godwit, Ruff, Sandwich Tern and a host of ducks and gulls. Tipperne is a protected reserve, good during autumn passage, when most west European waders and wildfowl occur, often in large numbers. The similar Vaerneengene area, which is open to the public, is worth a visit.

Between Oksbøl and Nørre Nebel, lies Filsø, which is a small lake where thousands of geese (especially Pink-feet) roost.

SUMMER Marsh Harrier, Bittern, Avocet, Black-tailed Godwit, Ruff, Curlew, Sandwich Tern.

AUTUMN Divers, grebes, Gannet, Whooper and Bewick's Swans, Pink-footed, Greylag and Brent Geese, ducks, Peregrine, Merlin, waders, skuas, gulls, terns, auks, pipits, thrushes, finches.

ACCESS Blåvandshuk lies west off Route 12 north of Esbjerg. A road leads to the lighthouse and the best spot to see migration is the extreme western tip. **Tipperne** is open on Sundays April–August from 5– 10 a.m. and September–March from 10 a.m.–12 noon. Leave Blåvand to Oksbøl and then through Norre Nebel to Nymindegab. Just east turn right to Tipperne. Skallingen is reached via a small road from Ho, east of Blåvand.

ROUTE Reached from Esbjerg, which has regular ferries from Britain.

COPENHAGEN

An outstanding area for birds, by virtue of its geographical position. The city has a number of public parks, several of which have large lakes and are known for their numbers of wildfowl, gulls and other waterbirds. Utterslev Mose has a wealth of birds in summer including three species of grebe, Greylag Goose, Pochard, Thrush Nightingale and sometimes Bearded and Penduline Tits, all in a park surrounded by heavily built-up areas.

The major bird areas lie in the south of Copenhagen on Amager. Sjaellandsbroen overlooks the largest area of open water in the harbour at the southern end, and holds large numbers of birds, including Smew, in hard winters. In mild winters these birds stay on lakes at Ishøj Strand just south of Copenhagen (Smew up to 100 and Scaup up to 600). When the lakes freeze over, the birds move to Kalveboderne, and can be seen from Valbyparken and Sjaellandsbroen. Just north of Sjaellandsbroen at Amager Faelled is a small lake, Grønjordssøen, which holds Red-necked, Black-necked and Little Grebes and numbers of passerines, including Thrush Nightingale and Penduline Tit. South-east of Sjallandsbroen is a huge partly open area, Vestamager, which has raptors in winter, including Hen Harrier, Rough-legged Buzzard and sometimes White-tailed Eagle. Vestamager is the major Danish site for Grasshopper Warbler, with more than 100 singing in spring. South of here is Kongelunden, a mixed wood with thick undergrowth. A lot of the passerines one would expect in Denmark are present, including Thrush Nightingale, Icterine Warbler and sometimes Golden Oriole. West and south of the forest is an area of salt marshes that regularly holds good numbers of waders on spring and autumn passage.

During autumn passage, birds of prey can be seen over the city. The best time is late August–late October, and Buzzard, Honey Buzzard and Sparrowhawk are sometimes very numerous. The best migration watch-points in the area are Kongelunden, Utterslev Mose and Ishøj Strand.

SUMMER Great Crested, Red-necked and Black-necked Grebes, Greylag Goose, Pochard, Avocet, Arctic, Common and Little Terns, Thrush Nightingale, Grasshopper, Marsh and Icterine Warblers, Bearded and Penduline Tits.

AUTUMN Wildfowl, raptors, waders, passerines.
WINTER Duck, Smew, Hen Harrier, Rough-legged Buzzard.
ACCESS All the areas mentioned are served by public transport. Uterslev
Mose: a public park in the north-east of the city. Sjaellandsbroen: part of
Copenhagen harbour. Kongelunden: a wooded area in south Amager.
ROUTE Copenhagen has a wealth of accommodation.

EAST AND SOUTH ZEALAND

A few kilometres north of Køge lies Ølsemagle Strand, with a small sand
bank, shallow lagoons, reedbeds and muddy areas, and a sandy beach.
This is one of the best for shorebirds in the east of Denmark. From late
July–mid-October there are regularly several thousand waders and good
numbers of wildfowl. A good day at the end of July or early August
should produce 25 species of shorebird, including, with luck, rarer
species, such as Broad-billed Sandpiper and Red-necked Phalarope.
Many gulls and terns are present in autumn, sometimes including
Caspian Tern. A strong east wind may produce migrating wildfowl and
gulls, terns and skuas. Migration is best during periods of rainy/cloudy
weather with an east wind, but there are always many species to be seen.

For raptors continue through Køge to Stevns Klint, a steep cliff at the
easternmost point of the Stevns peninsula. This is the best site for migrating raptors, in autumn, in Denmark. The birds arrive from Falsterbo,
Sweden, 25 km to the north-east. It is best from the end of August to
mid-October. Depending on the weather, numbers vary from none to a
few thousands per day. The average number is about 20,000 per autumn
Buzzard, Honey Buzzard, and Sparrowhawk are dominant, but there are
also good numbers of Red Kite (400–500), Marsh Harrier (400–500) and
Rough-legged Buzzard (max. 1000). On good days one can see 10–15
species of raptor and sometimes rarities such as Black Kite, White-tailed
and other eagles.

Another autumn watchpoint is Stigsnaes at the south-western point of
Zealand. The numbers of raptors is not so high as Stevns Klint, but there
are dramatic movements of wildfowl, pigeons, larks, pipits, finches and
other passerines. 4 km east of Stigsnaes is Borreby Mose, which consists
of several small lakes and meadow areas. It is easily viewed from the road
to Stigsnaes and there are always lots of wildfowl and shorebirds here.

AUTUMN Brent and Barnacle Geese, ducks, Honey Buzzard, Red Kite,
harriers, Sparrowhawk, Buzzard, Rough-legged Buzzard, Osprey, fal-
cons, Curlew Sandpiper, Temminck's and Little Stints, Knot, Sanderling,
Spotted Redshank, Bar-tailed Godwit, Whimbrel, Little Gull, Sandwich,
Common, Arctic and Black Terns, Snow Bunting.
PASSAGE Wildfowl, pigeons, larks, pipits, finches and other passerines.
ACCESS Ølsemagle Strand About 4 km north of Køge there is a causeway (Revlen) to the sand bank. Stevns Klint Take road 261 from Køge to
Store Heddinge. Continue to Hojerup and park by the church. This is the
southern part of the cliff. Stigsnaes From Skaelskør head towards the oil
refinery. Park at the small forest of Stigsnaes, just north of which is the
watchpoint 'Ørnehoved'.
ROUTE Southwards from Copenhagen.

FAEROES

Eighteen inhabited islands lying half-way between Shetland and Iceland. The weather is never wonderful even during the best time for a visit (June) though it is better than reputed. The seabird colonies are among Europe's finest. There is a gannetry on Mykines, and colonies of Guillemot, Puffin, Kittiwake and Fulmar on most islands, particularly on Streymoy, Nólsoy, Mykines, Eysturoy, Kallsoy, Vidoy, Fugloy, Sandoy and Skúvoy. There are Great and Arctic Skuas on Streymoy, Mykines, Svinoy, Sandoy and Skúvoy; also Leach's Petrel on Mykines and Manx Shearwater and Storm Petrel on Mykines, Skúvoy, and Nólsoy which has the largest Storm Petrel colony in the world. Eider, Whimbrel, Golden Plover, Snipe, Faeroe Starling and Faeroe Wren breed all over the place, while one or two lakes hold Red-necked Phalarope and Red-throated Diver. There is also a chance of Purple Sandpiper and Snow Bunting high up on the fjells.

SUMMER Red-throated Diver, Gannet, Manx Shearwater, Fulmar, Leach's and Storm Petrels, Greylag Goose, Wigeon, Pintail, Scaup, Scoter, Red-breasted Merganser, Eider, Purple Sandpiper, Whimbrel, Golden Plover, Oystercatcher, Snipe, Red-necked Phalarope, Great and Arctic Skuas, Kittiwake, Great Black-backed Gull, Arctic Tern, Guillemot, Black Guillemot, Razorbill, Puffin, Rock Dove, Rock Pipit, Redwing, Wren.

ACCESS There is a good public transport system with buses, boats and helicopters. Car rental, taxis and boat charters are also available. There is accommodation in most areas, though it may be primitive on the smaller islands. Large hotels are confined to the capital, Tórshavn. Alcohol is not on sale. **Streymoy** The main island. The town plantation holds breeding Red-wing and the cliffs north of Westmanna have good seabird colonies. The fjell beyond Saksun in the north of the island has a Great Skua colony. Information, charters, tours, and accommodation in houses on this and other Faeroes can be arranged through The Faeroe Tourist Board, Kunningarstovan, Vaglid, FR-100 Tórshavn. (Tel. 15877: Fax. 14883) **Mykines** The most famous bird island, with the only gannetry. There are colonies of cliff-breeding seabirds, Storm and Leach's Petrels, Manx Shearwater and Arctic Skua. Boats run from Vágar, which also has the airport. **Eysturoy** The lake of Toftavatn near the southern tip holds Red-throated Diver. The lake is easily reached by boat from Tórshavn. **Kallsoy, Vidoy, Fugloy and Svínoy** Part of the north-eastern group of islands with large seabird colonies at their northern ends. Access is by boat from Tórshavn to Klaksvik. **Sandoy** South of Streymoy and one of the best islands for birds. The lakes, especially those around Sand (Sandsvatn and Gróthusvatn), hold Red-throated Diver, wildfowl and waders, including Red-necked Phalarope. Seabirds breed on the cliffs in the west, and Arctic and Great Skuas nest on the hills. There are regular boats from Tórshavn to Skopun, and buses to Sand. Accommodation is possible in private homes. **Skúvoy** A small island south of Sandoy with magnificent seabird cliffs. Manx Shearwater and Storm Petrel breed on the grassy slopes, and Great and Arctic Skuas among the hills. Boats go from Sandoy and accommodation is possible in houses. The seabird cliff of Hovdin at the north-west is easily seen from land, but one can charter a boat from Sand. **Nólsoy** This island has the world's largest colony of Storm Petrels along

the coast south-east of the village. An overnight stop is necessary to experience the colony, but there are several boats a day from Tórshavn.
ROUTE Daily flights from Copenhagen and weekly ones from Glasgow and Reykjavík. Boats in summer from Denmark and Norway.

LIMFJORDEN

The Limfjord all but separates the 'cap' of Denmark from the rest of Jutland. It is a huge shallow inlet, rich in birds. One can narrow down the search to the outstanding area along the northern shore between Thisted and the Aggersund Bridge. This excellent area is worth thorough exploration and a holiday here can be splendidly rewarding. Indeed, one need look no farther than the areas of Vestlige Vejler and Østlige Vejler, two splendid marshland reserves that hold most of Denmark's specialities.

Vejlerne is an area of wet grazing meadows with wet marshes, lagoons and Denmark's largest area of reedbed. Østlige Vejler was created when a sea-wall across one of the bays of the Limfjord failed in the nineteenth century. The marsh has the largest colony of Black Tern in Denmark, with Red-necked and Black-necked Grebes, White Stork (Vesløs village), Marsh Harrier, Spotted Crake and sometimes Savi's Warbler. The area holds the largest breeding population in Denmark of Bittern, Black-tailed Godwit, Black Tern and Bearded Tit. At Hanstholm to the north-west, seabirds and wildfowl are the main attractions. In Hanstholm Vildtreservat a few pairs of Cranes breed, but access is difficult and Crane-watchers would do better in Sweden. Vigsø Heath has breeding Wood Sandpipers. Bulbjerg, which is the only 'real' bird cliff in Denmark, has 400–500 pairs of Kittiwake, and a few Fulmars stay here in summer. Just east of Bulbjerg, lies Vester Torup Klitplantage, a plantation of conifers that holds Nightjar and Crested Tit.

Agger Tange lies beyond Thisted. It affords good views of Avocet, Godwit and Ruff and is excellent for passage waders and wildfowl.

SUMMER Red-necked and Black-necked Grebes, Bittern, White Stork, Greylag Goose, Garganey, Shoveler, Marsh Harrier, Spotted Crake, Black-tailed Godwit, Wood Sandpiper, Ruff, Dunlin, Curlew, Avocet, Black Tern, Nightjar, Grasshopper and Savi's Warblers, Crested and Bearded Tits.
AUTUMN Whooper and Bewick's Swans, Bean and Pink-footed Geese, ducks, shorebirds, Merlin, Peregrine.
ACCESS Østlige Vejler can be viewed from the dam at Bygholm east of Øslos where there is parking. Vestlige Vejler can be seen from minor roads around Arup, south of Østerlid. Hanstholm is 20 km north-west of Østerlid. Migration is best seen from the point east of the harbour or from Bulbjerg, which can be reached via minor roads north of Lund Fjord.
ROUTE From the south, the area is reached by Route 11 and the Oddesund Bridge in the west and by Route 26 and Aggersund Bridge in the east.

MØN AND FALSTER

The small island of Møn is a favoured bird area, especially in spring, when birders from the whole of Denmark visit. As a result of its position in the south-east of the country, there are a number of species rare elsewhere in Denmark, including Barred Warbler, which breeds among hawthorn.

Møn is a major migration point and rarities such as Black Stork, Lesser Spotted Eagle, Hoopoe and Bee-eater, as well as semi-rarities like Red-footed Falcon, Turtle Dove and Bluethroat are regularly found. Østmøn and the wetland areas of Nyord/Ulvshale are the best bet.

At Busemarke Mose in Østmøn is a small lake surrounded by reedbeds. There is a bird tower west of the lake by a small plantation of conifers. In spring many wetland species including Marsh Warbler, Thrush Nightingale and sometimes Spotted Crake, Savi's Warbler and Bearded Tit can be found. Just east of Mandemarke is an area of bushy hills (*Høvblege*) which holds grounded passerines, among them frequently a few rarities. Breeding species include Red-backed Shrike and Icterine Warbler.

The wooded areas of Busene and Busene Have are good for Scarlet Rosefinch and Golden Oriole. The east of the island has steep limestone cliffs 143 m high. Along the cliff there is a rather large deciduous wood, which in spring holds Greenish Warbler, Red-breasted Flycatcher and Golden Oriole. Walk the path along the cliff between Liselund Park and Jydelejet.

Nyord, north-west of Møn, is a sanctuary with a tower beside the road. The island is flat, with meadows and small ponds and in passage periods has many wildfowl and shorebirds. Breeding species include Greylag Goose, Garganey, Shoveler, Pintail, Avocet, Black-tailed Godwit and Ruff.

Ulvshale Nordstrand, the northern beach of the Ulvshale peninsula, is good for shorebirds in autumn. Gedser lies at the southernmost point of Falster, another favoured migration watchpoint. In autumn seabirds, raptors and passerines pass in huge numbers. With a strong east wind in the last half of September and October, movements of seabirds regularly involve thousands of Brent and Barnacle Geese and tens of thousands of duck, mainly Pintail, Wigeon, Scaup, Long-tailed Duck and Eider. Many divers, gulls, terns and skuas can also be seen. If the wind is north-west or northerly good numbers of raptors leave Denmark from here. The most common species are Honey Buzzard, Sparrowhawk, Common and Rough-legged Buzzards. The migration of passerines is sometimes huge, with tens of thousands of finches. About 10 km north of Gedser lies Bøtø Nor, which is a small bay, now isolated from the sea, surrounded by meadows. There is a bird tower, and the area is easily worked. Good numbers of wildfowl and shorebirds stop over and the area also attracts raptors.

SPRING/PASSAGE Honey Buzzard, Red Kite, Marsh Harrier, Osprey, Hobby, Crane, Wryneck, Marsh, Icterine, Barred and Greenish Warblers, Red-backed Shrike, Ring Ouzel, Red-breasted Flycatcher, Thrush Nightingale, Bearded Tit, Golden Oriole, Scarlet Rosefinch, Ortolan Bunting.
AUTUMN Divers, Brent and Barnacle Geese, ducks, Red Kite, harriers, Sparrowhawk, Buzzard, Honey and Rough-legged Buzzards, Osprey, falcons, waders, Little Gull, Black Tern, Arctic and Pomarine Skuas, passerines.
ACCESS Østmøn Take Route 287 from Stege through Borre to Magleby and from here south to Mandemarke. Hovblege hills lie just east of Mandemarke, just west of which lies Busemarke from where you should head west to Råbymagle; east is a small road leading south to the bird tower at Busemarke Mose. From Mandemarke head east to Busene and from there south to the wooded area of Busene Have. There is a small road through the forest along the cliff from Busene to Liselund Park.
Nyord/Ulvshale Take the road north along Stege harbour and follow

signs to, respectively, Nyord and Ulvshale. **Gedser/Bøtø Nor** Gedser is reached via the motorway E47/E55 to Falster. Pass through Nykøbing southwards to Gedser, and from there continue 3 km south-east to the spit of Gedser. The watchpoint lies 100 m north of the spit beside a military radar installation. Bøto Nør is reached via the village of Bøtø; from where you should head south following signs to the bird tower.
ROUTE A two-hour drive on motorways E47/E55 from Copenhagen.

NORTH ZEALAND

North Zealand has beech woods, with a scattering of oak and lime, plantations of conifers and some marshes. The best known are Gribskov to the north of Hillerød – the largest forest in Denmark, and Dyrehaven, a Royal deer park with areas of rough pasture north of Copenhagen. Icterine Warbler, Thrush Nightingale and Red-backed Shrike are typical birds in these forests. Black Woodpecker is the star species. It breeds in Gribskov, and in Tisvilde Hegn and Jaegerspris Nordskov, both to the north-west.

A few Green Sandpipers breed, as do Common and Honey Buzzards, but raptors are best on spring passage. Gilbjerg Hoved is the best, particularly in March–May and when there is a south or south-east wind. The northernmost point of Zealand is popular with locals, who gather at a cliff-top watchpoint 2 km west of Gilleleje. Pigeon, thrush and finch movements can be dramatic, with several, sometimes tens of thousands, per day. A lot of raptors pass here, up to several hundreds per day when the wind is right. Common Buzzard and Sparrowhawk dominate, but harriers, Honey and Rough-legged Buzzards, Osprey and falcons occur in good numbers. In west or north winds migration passes south of Gilleleje, and can be seen from Gribskov and from Hellebaek, 5 km west of Helsingør. Hellebaek is popular with raptor enthusiasts and there is an average of over 9000 raptors in spring and of over 14,000 in autumn. Species are the same as at Gilleleje.

Barred Warbler

SUMMER Honey Buzzard, Buzzard, Green Sandpiper, Black Woodpecker, Nightjar, Woodlark, Red-backed Shrike, Icterine Warbler, Thrush
Nightingale, Hawfinch, Crossbill.
SPRING Raptors, pigeons, thrushes, larks, pipits, finches.
ACCESS Gilbjerg Hoved Take road 237 from Helsingør or 227 from
Hillerød to Gilleleje. 2 km west of the town, park on the right before some
pines. Walk north to a mound with a large stone at a point overlooking the
sea. **Gribskov** Leave Hillerød north toward Gilleleje. Black Woodpecker
breeds. Free Access. **Dyrehaven** Take road 152 towards Helsingør, just out-
side Copenhagen, the forest is accessible at the town of Tarbaek. **Tisvilde
Hegn** Pines along the coast south-west of Tisvildeleje (via Helsinge). Nightjar, Black Woodpecker and Woodlark breed. **Jaegerspris Nordskov** Via
Frederiksund. West over the bridge across Roskilde Fjord, turn right to
Jaegerspris. The woods lie to the east (right) of the road and hold Green
Sandpiper, Honey Buzzard and Black Woodpecker. **Hellebaek** The watchpoint in spring is Hellebaek Avlsgård between the villages of Hellebaek
and Nygård. In autumn the watchpoints are different spots on the beach
between Ålsgarde and Helsingør, but mainly Hellebaek and Julebaek beach.
ROUTE This area is easily worked from Copenhagen, though those intent
on migration-watching may be able to get a chalet near Gilbjerg Hoved.

SKAGEN

Skagen, at the northern tip of Jutland, is primarily a migration watchpoint.
The best time is from mid-April to the beginning of June: movements are
most dramatic during periods of east winds, when birders from across
Scandinavia gather here. Huge flocks of finches, thrushes and pipits pass
along the coast before setting off across the sea towards Norway and
Sweden. Birds of prey, mainly Sparrowhawk, Honey, Rough-legged and
Common Buzzards, but also Marsh and Hen Harriers, Osprey and falcons are to be seen in good numbers. As at other such places, there are
favoured spots for different times of the day and different types of birds.
In the morning at Nordstrande, on the north coast just east of the lighthouse you can see divers, ducks, gulls, terns and passerines. Another
favoured spot in the morning is Grenen, the tip of the peninsula. There are
invariably numbers of grounded passerines among the bushes here and
among the bushes and trees north of the road before it enters the town.
    In the late morning many birders move to Flagbakken Hill, just west of
the town of Skagen on the road south of the railway. Local birders use a few
other hills in this area depending on the wind. In conifer plantations south
of Flagbakken Hill are Nightjar, Woodlark, Tawny Pipit and Crested Tit.
Rarities occur annually and include Great Northern and White-billed
Divers, Black Stork, Black and Red Kites, White-tailed and Golden
Eagles, Montagu's Harrier, Red-footed Falcon, Turtle Dove, Bee-eater,
Golden Oriole, Red-breasted Flycatcher and Bluethroat. Both Glaucous and
Iceland Gulls can be found in the harbour almost throughout the year.

SPRING Red-throated and Black-throated Divers, Honey Buzzard, Marsh
and Hen Harriers, Sparrowhawk, Buzzard, Rough-legged Buzzard, Osprey,
Hobby, Merlin, Arctic Skua, Nightjar, Crested Lark, Tawny Pipit, Ring
Ouzel, Crested Tit, Scarlet Rosefinch, Lapland and Ortolan Buntings.

ACCESS Take the E45 from Ålborg to Frederikshavn and from here Route 40 to Skagen. Grenen Camping, a camping site just north-east of Skagen, is a meeting place for birders. There is a youth hostel west of the town.
ROUTE Frederikshavn and Aalberg are the nearest large towns.

WADDENSEE

The Waddensee, the most important intertidal zone in Europe, extends from Holland to south-west Jutland. One of the best places in the Danish part to watch birds is the causeway to Rømø. In autumn there are huge numbers of Avocet with over 7000 in a single flock. The island itself has dunes, with ponds and meadowland with Red-necked Grebe, Bittern, Marsh and Montagu's Harriers, Kentish Plover, Black-tailed Godwit, Ruff, Avocet and sometimes Gull-billed Tern.

North of Rømø lies Fanø, which holds much the same birds, including the now, in Denmark, very rare Kentish Plover. Fanø, however, is better known as a migration watchpoint for pipits, thrushes and finches, which on 'good' days pass in tens of thousands. Sparrowhawk and falcons also occur in fair numbers. The best place to watch is at Sønderho at the southernmost point of the island and the best time is September–October.

Saltvandssøen at Højer, one of the best wetlands in Denmark, is open only a few days a year. It was established in the early 1980s as compensation for wetland destroyed when a new dyke was built. A sea lake was created between the two dykes and is now important for wildfowl and shorebirds. Denmark's largest Avocet breeding colony is here, as well as Kentish Plover. Thousands of wildfowl and shorebirds stop over on passage. The marshland east of the salt lake, Tøndermarsken, formerly held much of the Danish population of Garganey, Montagu's Harrier, Black tailed Godwit and Black Tern together with other scarce Danish species. White Stork (at Rudbøl), Bittern, Ruff, Marsh Harrier and Short-eared Owl all once bred. During the later 1980s Tøndermarsken lost much of its value, but the area has been preserved and many of these birds can still be seen.

Ballum Enge is one of the most important sites for geese in Denmark during mild winters and early spring. Thousands of geese roost and at sunrise they fly east to feed on the marshland south-east of Højer.

SUMMER Red-necked Grebe, White Stork, Bittern, Garganey, Marsh and Montagu's Harriers, Kentish Plover, Black-tailed Godwit, Ruff, Avocet, Sandwich, Gull-billed and Black Terns, Grasshopper and Savi's Warblers.
AUTUMN Brent and Pink-footed Geese, ducks, Merlin, waders, Shore Lark, pipits, thrushes, finches, Lapland Bunting.
WINTER/EARLY SPRING Whooper and Bewick's Swans, Barnacle, Brent, Greylag, White-fronted, Bean and Pink-footed Geese, ducks, waders.
ACCESS Rømø Take the causeway west of Skaerbaek and park at Havenby. Walk along the dyke to the southernmost point of the island (1.5 km). Look over the small lake of Lakolk and at Juvre Sand at the northern part of Rømø. Fanø By ferry from Esbjerg. Ballum Enge Head south of Højer to Højer Sluse (sluice) for sunrise during February-March.
Saltsoen The southern part of the salt lake can be seen from Germany.
Tøndermarsken Watch from minor roads between Højer and Rudbøl.
ROUTE Regular ferries between Esbjerg and Britain and road links.

EGYPT

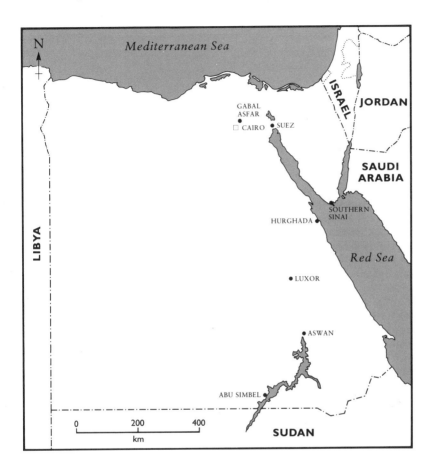

ABU SIMBEL

Abu Simbel lies on the western shore of Lake Nasser and is as famous as the pyramids, the Sphinx and the Valley of the Kings. It is an essential ingredient of any tour of Egypt. Avid, head-down, ornitho-philistines do not despair . . . it is excellent for birds, for migration and has some fine specialities. It is not a place to be rushed, for even the great temple has birds and a *feluca* trip around the surrounding lake could produce Skimmer, Kittlitz's Plover, Egyptian Goose, Senegal Thick-knee and Pink-backed Pelican...not a bad list for the Western Palearctic. Migrant raptors and storks can be seen virtually anywhere and a hotel balcony is probably as good a vantage point as any. To the north of Abu Simbel, just beyond the airport, an agricultural area is good for migrants, while the adjacent lake bay to the south has many waterbirds sometimes including Yellow-billed Stork. This is also the vantage point to scan 'Skimmer Islands'.

SUMMER Pink-backed Pelican, Yellow-billed Stork, Egyptian Goose, Egyptian Vulture, Lanner, Senegal Thick-knee, African Skimmer, Spotted Sandgrouse, African Collared Dove, African Rock Martin, Blue-cheeked Bee-eater, Brown-necked Raven.

PASSAGE White Stork, Spoonbill, Black Kite, Short-toed Eagle, Pallid Harrier, Black-winged Stilt, Kittlitz's Plover, Greenshank, Gull-billed, Little and White-winged Black Terns, Turtle Dove, Roller, Short-toed Lark, Tawny Pipit, Isabelline, Black-eared and White-crowned Black Wheatears, Rock Thrush, Golden Oriole, Woodchat and Masked Shrikes, Spanish Sparrow.

ACCESS Leave Abu Simbel Temple or village and take the road to the airport. North of the airport and beyond it a track beside the boundary fence leads some 3 km or 4 km to the shores of Lake Nasser though it gradually disappears along the way. At the end there are views to the north over 'Skimmer Islands', over a deep bay for Pink-backed Pelican and beyond to the agricultural area. The bushes around the Temple are good for migrants and any hotel balcony is good for visible migration of storks and raptors. Boat-trips can be easily arranged in Abu Simbel village, but get a 'captain' who understands your language and insist on birding.

ROUTE Aswan has an airport. It is possible to do Abu Simbel in a day from here, but much better to stay one or two days at a local hotel. The road from Aswan is good for the first 50 km, but boring for the next 250 km.

ASWAN

Aswan is as far as one can go up the River Nile by plane. After that it is a long and dusty road south to Abu Simbel and Sudan, but above Aswan the Nile has been dammed to create Lake Nasser and its character is quite different. The river and lake hold many resident and migrant birds and, as elsewhere in Egypt, the grounds of hotels offer excellent cover for both. The Nile Valley Sunbird, for example, is typically found drinking at garden sprinklers and with Palearctic warblers among the flowering shrubs. Hotel balconies also offer good opportunities for watching visible migration of raptors. Stake-outs are comparatively few, but a Barbary Falcon has sat on the temple on Elephant Island for years. Similarly, driving south towards Abu Simbel is the area for Lappet-faced Vulture. Watch for it all the way over the first 50 km. After about 50 km a waterhole has produced Saker, Lanner, Barbary Falcon, Egyptian Vulture, Montagu's Harrier and Spotted Sandgrouse, but any waterhole might do the same.

SUMMER White Stork, Purple Heron, Black-shouldered Kite, Egyptian, Griffon and Lappet-faced Vultures, Montagu's Harrier, Lanner, Saker, Barbary Falcon, Spotted Sandgrouse, Lesser Pied Kingfisher, Little Green Bee-eater, Hoopoe, Crag Martin, White-crowned Black Wheatear, Nile Valley Sunbird, Masked Shrike, Clamorous Warbler.

ACCESS Aswan is a tourist centre with plentiful hotels, excursions, boat-trips, etc. Elephant Island can be seen without a boat-trip. The road south to Abu Simbel is clearly marked and should be explored thoroughly, at least for the first 50 km. To do this properly involves either a return to Aswan, or an overnight stay at Abu Simbel. A day-trip will mean missed species.

ROUTE Cairo–Aswan by air.

GABEL ASFAR

Cairo is a huge urban sprawl that is inevitably the starting point for any Egyptian birding trip. The pyramids are in the desert a few kilometres to the west at Giza and it is relatively straightforward to combine a visit to these amazing structures with nearby birding. Try to be first at the pyramids in the morning before the masses arrive, and first away to spend the latter part of the day at Gabel Asfar. This area is a desert reclamation project utilizing the rich waters of the Cairo sewage system. Birders used to the old-fashioned sewage farms of northern Europe will feel at home here. Specialities here include Senegal Coucal, Senegal Thick-knee, White-breasted Kingfisher, Little Green Bee-eater, Avadavat and, particularly, Painted Snipe. After dark the area is a noted haunt of Egyptian Nightjar.

Gabel Asfar lies near the airport off the Cairo–Ismailia road and is very awkward to find. Its ornithological importance was discovered by Egypt's top birder Sherif Baha el Din, to whom I am most grateful.

SUMMER Night and Purple Herons, Glossy Ibis, Short-toed Eagle, Water Rail, Senegal Thick-knee, Painted Snipe, Little Owl, Little Green Bee-eater, White-breasted Kingfisher, Egyptian Nightjar, Senegal Coucal, Fan-tailed Warbler, Avadavat.
PASSAGE Glossy Ibis, Ruff, Snipe, Spotted Redshank, Green and Wood Sandpipers.
ACCESS Start at Cairo Airport and locate the Cairo–Ismailia road. Head toward Ismailia for 2.5 km and watch for a sign on the right to 'El Khanka-Bilbies'. Pass it, make a U-turn at the next gap, turn right at the police station onto 'El Khanka-Bilbies' road and continue for 5.5 km and take a left signposted 'Abu Zabel-El Khanka'. Continue past military bases and,

Painted Snipe

51

at a major fork, go left. Continue through an industrial development to a white police station on the right. Carry on until the canal and walk right along the bank. Return to the police station and take a right following the road to the canal and walk left. Cross the canal back at the road and continue to a pond on the right. There are many other good areas here. **ROUTE** Cairo Airport.

HURGHADA

Hurghada is the primary birding area along the Red Sea coast of Egypt. It also happens to be a popular and expanding tourist resort, with plenty of hotels and other useful infrastructure including boat-trips to the offshore islands with their interesting seabirds. It should be no problem to see Sooty and White-eyed Gulls here and, at least until mid-October there are also White-cheeked Tern and Sooty Falcon. The latter, the desert equivalent of Eleonora's Falcon with a breeding season geared to the autumn migration of small birds, can regularly be seen in the late afternoon hunting over the town or shoreline. A Swedish crew heartily recommend the pier at the Arabia Hotel where falcon-watching can be enjoyed while drinking beer. Passage, in both spring and autumn, can be excellent and the gardens of the various hotels the best places to search. Offshore passage can be good with Crested and Lesser Crested Terns, both of which can be found on the islands, plus Bridled Tern, which only arrives in June to breed. Brown Booby, Osprey, Green Heron, and a variety of waders that includes Greater Sand Plover, can all be seen. Small migrants include Masked and Lesser Grey Shrikes, Golden Oriole, Thrush Nightingale and Wryneck. A drive south to Bir Beida, some 10 km west of Quseir, is worthwhile for the concentration of Crowned Sandgrouse that come to drink soon after dawn.

SUMMER Brown Booby, Osprey, Sooty Falcon, Green Heron, Greater Sand Plover, Crowned Sandgrouse, Sooty and White-eyed Gulls, White-cheeked, Crested, Lesser Crested, Caspian and Bridled Terns, Kingfisher.
PASSAGE White Pelican, Western Reef Heron, Black and White Storks, Spoonbill, Honey Buzzard, Black Kite, Oystercatcher, Black-winged Stilt, Collared Pratincole, Kentish, Greater Sand and Grey Plovers, Little Stint, Curlew Sandpiper, Spotted Redshank, Turnstone, Red-necked Phalarope, Pomarine, Arctic and Long-tailed Skuas, Slender-billed Gull, Common and Little Terns, Roller, Hoopoe, Wryneck, Thrush Nightingale, Golden Oriole, Lesser Grey and Masked Shrikes.
ACCESS Hurghada lies on the Red Sea and is reached on the road south from Suez. There are several hotels with good gardens for grounded migrants and virtually any vantage point will produce migration at the right time. The offshore islands are mostly too distant to see properly, but there are regular tourist boat-trips to Gifton Kabir, the largest island, which produce birding opportunities. The smaller, inner island of Abu Mingar can be visited by boat, ensure you land (wet-footed) on the eastern shore and explore to the north. **Note:** oil may ruin your shoes – take a disposable pair. **Bir Beida** to the south for sandgrouse should not be missed, arrive at dawn and wait 30 minutes to an hour for massed concentrations. **ROUTE** Cairo–Suez–Hurghada–Luxor is the regular birding route, though one could avoid Suez by flying Cairo–Luxor.

Cream-coloured Courser

LUXOR

Luxor is the Nile resort that boasts the most impressive of all Egyptian remains – at least I think so. Here, and at Karnak down the road are the most magnificent temples and across the river (on the eastern bank) is the Valley of the Kings – dry, arid, crowded and, when empty, devoid of life. No one should miss these sites, but there are birds too. The grounds of Crocodile Island attract Nile Valley Sunbird, while any rocky area will produce Trumpeter Finch, Blue Rock Thrush and White-crowned Black Wheatear. Waders along the river banks include White-tailed Plover, while Pale Crag Martin can be found at several of the east bank monuments.

SUMMER Green and Purple Herons, Little Egret, Little Bittern, Purple Gallinule, Black-shouldered Kite, Spur-winged and White-tailed Plovers, Whiskered Tern, Little Green Bee-eater, Roller, Hoopoe, White-crowned Black Wheatear, Blue Rock Thrush, Nile Valley Sunbird, Trumpeter Finch.
ACCESS The main hotel area lies on the west bank of the Nile with the temples to the south. A walk through the agricultural land between the two will produce many birds. There are frequent ferries across the river with connecting buses to the Valley of the Kings, the Valley of the Queens, the Colossi of Memnon and Dier el Bahri. Exploring the ruins beneath the cliffs here is not on every tourist's itinerary, so it is possible to get to grips with some crag and desert species. As always, an eye to the sky is recommended. Visit the Crocodile Island hotel as if you owned it for the sunbird.
ROUTE Luxor has internal flights from Cairo and Aswan.

SOUTHERN SINAI

A little knowledge of eastern Mediterranean migration and a glance at a map will pinpoint southern Sinai as a likely place to produce migrants in numbers, particularly in autumn, but Sinai has more to offer, including seabirds found in the western Palearctic only in the Red Sea, and several elusive desert species such as Blackstart, Desert and Hooded Wheatear, Namarqua Dove, Lichtenstein's Sandgrouse, Tristram's Grackle, Sand Partridge and Scrub Warbler. There are also good roads and modern hotels to facilitate exploration. This is a little worked area that would repay those prepared to explore new ground for unexpected species.

SUMMER Sand Partridge, White-eyed and Slender-billed Gulls, Bridled Tern, Namarqua Dove, Tristram's Grackle, Desert Lark, Palestine Sunbird, Little Green Bee-eater, Blackstart, Hooded, Mourning, Desert and White-crowned Black Wheatears, Sinai Rosefinch.
AUTUMN White Pelican, Honey Buzzard, Red-footed Falcon, Crane, Roller, Bee-eater, Wryneck, Red-backed Shrike, Olivaceous Warbler.
ACCESS Explore along the Gulf of Suez, particularly inland at Wadi'l Raha, including the Monastery of St Catherine. Accommodation here is surrounded by desert and rocky crags for Sand Partridge and Scrub Warbler. Nuweiba, on the Gulf of Aqaba, has Blackstart and Namarqua Dove. Near the tip of Sinai a hotel at Sharm el Sheikh has Lichenstein's Sandgrouse and Desert Wheatear. At the tip lies the promontory of Ras Mohammed, a protected area, but one that should produce outstanding migrants.
ROUTE Cairo to Suez then along the coast of the Gulf of Suez to St Catherine's: 450 km and a long day's drive.

SUEZ

Suez lies at the head of the Gulf of Suez and at the southern entrance to the Suez Canal. Most visitors write it off as a 'dump' and there is little point in exploring it. However, just outside the town and a short distance southwards along the Gulf of Suez is the major watchpoint for migrant birds of prey. Concentrations of these birds are particularly impressive in autumn, but visitors intent on getting to grips with the Red Sea specials and the birds of the southern deserts should not ignore the possibilities of spring. Steppe and Spotted Eagles are both regular as well as more usual eagles and other raptors, including Pallid Harrier and Eleonora's Falcon. The migration of small birds can also be good and there are always a few resident desert birds to provide interest during flat migration periods.

PASSAGE White Stork, Short-toed, Steppe, Lesser Spotted, Spotted Eagle, Imperial and Booted Eagles, Buzzard, Long-legged and Honey Buzzards, Montagu's, Marsh and Pallid Harriers, Eleonora's Falcon.
ACCESS The base for raptor-watching is the road southwards along the western shore of the Gulf of Suez. A short distance out of town the Ain Suchna Hotel will be found on the left-hand side of the road. A little farther south a café on the right nestles beneath the ridge of a substantial hill. This forms an excellent raptor watchpoint with suitable refreshments instantly available. Sometimes, depending on weather conditions, birds pass farther to the north. In such circumstances head back toward Suez and turn left past an army camp. Stop after 1.5 km for a good watchpoint. A further 1.5 km along this road a turning right leads through Wadi Hagul, good for desert birds including Mourning Wheatear.
ROUTE 134 km east of Cairo. The Ain Suchna Hotel was closed in May.

ESTONIA

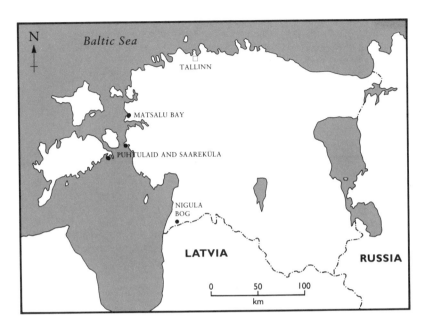

MATSALU BAY

Matsalu Bay is a shallow inlet, actually the delta of the Kasari River, on the west coast of Estonia, much of which is included in the State Nature Reserve of the same name. At the head of the bay there are large areas of water meadow that are regularly flooded, together with extensive reedbeds. Beyond the bay there are numerous islands and islets, while inland there are meadows and substantial areas of woodland. No fewer than 270 species have been recorded here, of which 170 have bred. Breeding birds include Bittern, Greylag Goose, Marsh Harrier, Spotted and Little Crakes, Great Reed and Savi's Warblers. Barnacle Goose has bred since 1981 and there is the only colony of Caspian Tern along the Baltic states coastline. The flooded meadows hold Garganey, Dunlin, Ruff and outstandingly, a few Great Snipe. Both River Warbler and Scarlet Rosefinch nest in the meadows, while the adjacent woodlands hold Wood Warbler and Thrush Nightingale.

All of this, however, pales into insignificance when compared with the huge migration that sweeps through the area each spring and autumn. In spring no less than 5000–12,000 Whooper Swans stop over with a maximum of 40,000 individuals. Bewick's Swan is scarce in comparison with annual totals of a mere 5000. Barnacle (12,000), White-fronted (2000–3000) and Bean Geese (several thousand) are all present, but are outnumbered by more than a million diving duck, predominantly Scoter and Long-tailed Duck, as well as by several hundred thousand Ruff. In autumn the species are slightly different, though all of the swans and geese are present in large numbers. There are, however, regular flocks of 5000–6000 Cranes here, with a maximum of 17,000. That this superb site has been largely hidden from the eyes of western birders for so long is a great tragedy. No doubt the situation will soon be rectified.

SUMMER White Stork, Bittern, Greylag and Barnacle Geese, Pochard, Eider, Goosander, White-tailed Eagle, Marsh Harrier, Water Rail, Spotted and Little Crakes, Corncrake, Common Gull, Caspian, Common, Arctic and Black Terns, Oystercatcher, Turnstone, Dunlin, Ruff, Great Snipe, Great Reed, Savi's, Grasshopper and Wood Warblers, Thrush Nightingale, Scarlet Rosefinch.
PASSAGE Whooper and Bewick's Swans, Greylag, Bean, White-fronted and Barnacle Geese, Eider, Scoter, Long-tailed Duck, Smew, White-tailed Eagle, Crane.
ACCESS The bay can be viewed from several vantage points along both the north and south shorelines and from the surrounding roads and tracks. Start at Penijõe near Lihula on the south-east shore, where the Nature Reserve Office can not only offer you a permit, but also advise you about particular vantage points and tracks.
ROUTE Take the A207 from Tallinn towards Virtsu and stop after 110 km (about two hours) at the bay.

NIGULA BOG

Nigula Bog lies in south-western Estonia between the Bay of Riga and the Latvian border. This treeless waste forms the nucleus of the State Nature Reserve of the same name and is surrounded by mixed forests. The large Lake Nigula lies near the eastern boundary and is the main point of access. Although the bog itself is important, with breeding Wood Sandpiper, Golden Plover, Whimbrel, Great Grey Shrike and Crane, the surrounding forests hold the best birds of the area. Some of these, such as Golden and Lesser Spotted Eagles and Black Stork, are best watched for over the open bog area. Others, such as Capercaillie, Black and Three-toed Woodpeckers, Eagle and Ural Owls must be sought within the forest itself. Here too are Nutcracker, Icterine Warbler and the only place in this book where White-backed Woodpecker is 'relatively abundant'.

SUMMER Black-throated Diver, Black Stork, Golden and Lesser Spotted Eagles, Crane, Golden Plover, Curlew, Whimbrel, Wood Sandpiper, Common Gull, Black, Three-toed, Great Spotted and White-backed Woodpeckers, Eagle and Ural Owls, Nutcracker, Whinchat, Yellow Wagtail, Tree Pipit, Great Grey Shrike, Wood and Icterine Warblers, Pied Flycatcher, Crossbill.
ACCESS Take the Tali to Nurme road and stop just past Vanajärve Station. From a pavilion a track leads westwards to Nigula Lake, skirts the northern side and continues through marsh and forest to the centre of the reserve. Contact the nature reserve office (Tel. 92470) from whom you may obtain permission to spend the night at Vanajärve Station.
ROUTE Head southwards from Tallinn to Pärnu on the M12. This is 150 km and takes about two hours. Continue to Häädemeeste and on to Tali and Vanajärve, another 50 km.

PUHTULAID AND SAAREKÜLA

These two areas are separated by some 20 km of the Baltic Sea, but are treated jointly because they produce similar birds and form the two outer arms of a migrational funnel that concentrates birds in quite staggering numbers.

Puhtulaid lies on the western mainland coast of Estonia about 3 km south of Virtsu. Until the nineteenth century it was an island, but is now connected to the mainland via a causeway. The peninsula is mainly covered with deciduous forest together with smaller areas of pine and fir. From the southern tip visible migration, especially in spring, can be dramatic, with several hundred thousand Scoter, Velvet Scoter and Long-tailed Duck offshore. Additionally there are thousands of Barnacle and Brent Geese plus similarly impressive numbers of Black-throated Divers. The Puhtu area has a good selection of breeding species including Goosander, Eider, Icterine and Great Reed Warblers, and Thrush Nightingale and Scarlet Rosefinch.

Saareküla lies at the south-eastern corner of the island of Saaremaa and is the centre of a bay with many offshore islands. To the east the peninsula of Kübassaare, with its lighthouse, is covered with beautiful deciduous woods. In spring 10,000 Barnacle Geese stop-over here between mid-April and mid-May and, since 1983, several have stayed on to breed. Divers and other wetland birds, as well as many passerines can also be found in both spring and autumn. Breeding birds include Greylag, Turnstone, Dunlin, Black-tailed Godwit and Little Tern, as well as Thrush Nightingale and Scarlet Rosefinch.

SPRING Black-throated Diver, Barnacle Goose, Scoter, Velvet Scoter, Long-tailed Duck, White-tailed Eagle.
SUMMER Barnacle and Greylag Geese, Goosander, Eider, Turnstone, Dunlin, Black-tailed Godwit, Little Gull, Little Tern, Wryneck, Sedge, Great Reed and Icterine Warblers, Thrush Nightingale, Scarlet Rosefinch.
ACCESS Take the A207 from Tallinn to Virtsu. **Puhtulaid** is 3 km south. It is possible to find accommodation at the Virtsu hostel or, with advance warning, at Puhtu Bird Station (Tel. 75565) who are worth contacting anyway. **Saareküla** is more awkward of access, though the route starts at Virtsu. Take the car ferry from Virtsu to Kuivastu on the isle of Muhu. From there one can drive to the isle of Saaremaa, and on to Saareküla via Orissaare. Allow four hours from Tallinn. Accommodation may be available in Saareküla in private homes, or use the hotel at Orissaara.
ROUTE As above.

FINLAND

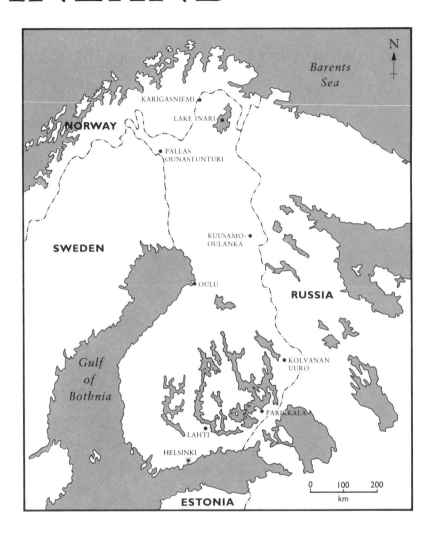

HELSINKI

Despite being the capital and the largest city in the country, Helsinki is one of the best areas for birds in Finland. There are many scarce eastern species to be found, a wide variety of habitats and an efficient 'grapevine' that is only too pleased to help visitors find the specialities of the area. It offers considerably more than a chance for the hard-pressed businessman to fill in an hour or two between appointments. Right in the middle of the city is Vanhankaupunginselka Bay. At Sannalahti is an extensive reedbed with Marsh and Great Reed Warblers, possible Bittern and Little Gull. Grönträsk is a reed-fringed lake of more manageable proportions in the north-western suburbs where Red-necked and Slavonian Grebes breed and Caspian Terns are regular. Laajalahti is a large bay in the western suburbs with the area of Otaniemi on its western shore. This is another Caspian Tern spot, but there may also be a few interesting landbirds here.

SUMMER Red-necked and Slavonian Grebes, Water Rail, Caspian and Arctic Terns, Marsh, Sedge and Great Reed Warblers.
ACCESS A good map of Helsinki shows all of these sites.
ROUTE Helsinki.

KARIGASNIEMI

To the north of Inari the road divides, offering two routes into Norway. Most birders take the eastern route to the Varanger Fjord, but some use the westerly one toward the Porsanger Fjord. Both provide excellent birding along the way, with a marsh some 10 km north of Utsjoki regularly attracting stops on the way to Varanger. On the westerly route Karigasniemi serves the same purpose. Actually there is nothing much here but a few huts, a couple of hotels, a youth hostel and a camp site, but it is an excellent base for the surrounding countryside.

This is mainly open tundra, with dwarf birch in the valleys and many marshes. Some 11–13 km from Karigasniemi and to the east is a marsh with a reputation for breeding waders. Broad-billed Sandpiper, Spotted Redshank, Temminck's Stint and possibly Bar-tailed Godwit usually breed, and Golden Plover, Whimbrel and Rough-legged Buzzard are to be seen. The river valleys hold Waxwing and Arctic Warbler (try the Tenojoki River towards Utsjoki), while the peak of Ailigas to the north has real tundra species such as Shore Lark, Lapland Bunting and possibly Gyrfalcon.

This is splendid country, with fine birding in every direction. Do, however, treat it with the respect that any remote wilderness deserves; compass, map, emergency rations and lots of warm and waterproof clothing even in mid-summer. Also take mosquito repellent.

SUMMER Whooper Swan, Long-tailed Duck, Gyrfalcon, Rough-legged Buzzard, Wood Sandpiper, Spotted Redshank, Ruff, Whimbrel, Broad-billed Sandpiper, Temminck's Stint, Dotterel, Red-necked Phalarope, Long-tailed Skua, Ptarmigan, Shore Lark, Great Grey Shrike, Waxwing, Siberian Tit, Red-throated Pipit, Bluethroat, Arctic Warbler, Pine Grosbeak, Lapland and Snow Buntings.
ACCESS Use Karigasniemi as a base or extended stop-over and explore the road on foot. A smaller road leads north along the Tenojoki River.
ROUTE Buses do run along the road, but most birders arrive by car from the south or from Norway.

KOLVANAN UURO

This small but deeply wooded valley lies just north of Joensuu in east central Finland. The woodlands are mixed and well developed and the stream that has formed the 'canyon' opens out at one point to form a small lake sufficient to harbour a pair of Black-throated Divers. The woods are, however, the main attraction and a likely spot for Greenish Warbler.

Red-flanked Bluetail

Walking conditions are fair and there is little chance of getting lost in the narrow valley though several visitors have found the area much larger than anticipated and required more time than they had allowed. Without exception they have remarked on the birding potential of the valley.

SUMMER Black-throated Diver, Hazelhen, Capercaillie, Thrush Nightingale, Greenish Warbler, Siskin, Red-breasted Flycatcher.
ACCESS Take Route 18 north from Joensuu. Shortly after passing the village of Uuro look for a minor road on the right signposted Kolvanan Uuro. Follow signs through a series of minor roads and eventually stop to look down into the valley. A little beyond here there is a road on the left with parking space and the start of a trail marked in blue. Follow this past a large lake and where the trail crosses the stream continue along the far bank for 3 km or 4 km where steep wooded slopes on the right hold Greenish Warbler and Red-breasted Flycatcher. This streamside trail crosses back to the eastern side just above a smaller lake, by which time the sought-after birds have already been passed. This is a good spot for Hazelhen.
ROUTE Joensuu is on the nearest main road and the area is generally taken as a stop-over between Blyth's Reed Warbler/Spotted Eagle and the Oulu area on the Gulf of Bothnia.

KUUSAMO-OULANKA

Oulanka National Park lies just south of the Arctic Circle near the Russian border and is a superb area of mountains, forests, lakes and streams. There are excellent meadows, deep ravines and some spectacular waterfalls and rapids. The whole area is served by a network of trails and paths making access relatively straightforward to some really excellent birds. Widespread species include Brambling, Siberian Tit, Siberian Jay, Tengmalm's Owl, Wood Sandpiper and Golden Eagle. The outstanding bird is, however, the Red-flanked Bluetail. To the south the lakes around Kuusamo are the place for both Little and Rustic Buntings. Sadly, mosquitoes outnumber them by several billion to one. Try to choose a cold and windy day if choice permits – the mosquitoes will annoy you less.

SUMMER Black-throated Diver, Crane, Golden Eagle, Wood Sandpiper, Temminck's Stint, Whimbrel, Greenshank, Eagle, Tengmalm's and Hawk

Owls, Three-toed Woodpecker, Siberian and Crested Tits, Red-flanked Bluetail, Siberian Jay, Crossbill, Parrot Crossbill, Brambling, Rustic and Little Buntings.

ACCESS Kuusamo lies just east of Route 5. At the junction with Route 20 turn right through the town to the museum (on the right) and beyond. Boggy birch woods on the left are the haunt of Little and Rustic Bunting. To the north 25 km on Route 5 lies the Ruka ski centre. Turn right off the main road and park in front of the hotel. A trail starts on a set of wooden steps to the right of the hotel. At the top of the steps the trail heads left. It crosses roads and ski paths, but is signposted Karhunkirrus and follows a highly scenic ridge called Valtavarra. Red-flanked Bluetail has been seen here. An alternative route to the other end of the trail can be found by continuing north past Ruka on Route 5 to a road on the right signposted Jyrkankoski, Route 8694. Stop after 4.5 km where the trail along Valtavarra crosses the road and walk south. This same elusive little bird may also be found by continuing north to just beyond Käyla where the Oulankajoki River flows under a bridge. Take the trail downstream along the Ristikallio Gorge. By returning to Käyla and turning left (east) the Oulanka Park HQ at Kintaköngas with camping ground, camp shop with good maps, and a trail along the Oulankajoki can be reached.

ROUTE There are hotels in Kuusamo and most visitors drive here after working the Oulu area.

LAHTI

Lahti is a large town a little north of Helsinki and is an easy-to-get-to place for a taste of Finnish birding. North of the town the twin lakes of Kutajarvi and Vesijarvi are among the top-ranked of Finland's wetlands. They hold good numbers of breeding and migrating ducks and waders, as well as typical forest birds in the surrounding woodland. A little farther north is the Vesijako Natural Park with its old forest and several interesting lakes. Here all the usual Scandinavian woodland birds can be seen, along with reasonably regular Osprey, Pygmy and Ural Owls and Red-breasted Flycatcher. The last three are, however, always elusive species.

SUMMER Osprey, Pygmy and Ural Owls, Pied and Red-breasted Flycatchers, Goldcrest, Siskin.

ACCESS Leave Lahti northwards on Route 58 and turn left at Arrakoski; bear left and the park is on the left after 3 km. The twin lakes extend north from the city; try Route 58 on the way towards the Park of Vaasky.

ROUTE Directly north from Helsinki past the airport.

LAKE INARI

Lake Inari lies 260 km north of the Arctic Circle and measures more or less 70 km by 30 km. It is huge, remote, but well worth the effort both in getting there and in exploring its surrounding marshes and forests. The numerous bays, inlets and islands hold important populations of breeding duck, including Smew and Goldeneye. The woods, which in places come right down to the lakeshores, hold many typically Arctic species, including Siberian Jay, Siberian Tit, Pine Grosbeak and the elusive Arctic

Warbler. More open areas have a tundra-type fauna, including Lapland and Snow Buntings as well as Long-tailed Skua.

Throughout this part of Lapland there are strategically sited mountain huts offering basic accommodation to walkers. Those near the roads may be used as a handy base for investigation, though the more adventurous visitor may walk from hut to hut in their exploration. Accommodation and information maps on the hut system can be obtained via the Inari Tourist Hotel which overlooks the rapids of the River Juutuanjoki. This may well be the worst area for mosquitoes in Finland: 'Jungle Formula' (now available in the UK) is the only answer.

SUMMER Whooper Swan, Velvet Scoter, Goldeneye, Red-breasted Merganser, Smew, Goosander, Hen Harrier, Rough-legged Buzzard, Merlin, Willow Grouse, Capercaillie, Crane, Broad-billed Sandpiper, Spotted Redshank, Greenshank, Long-tailed Skua, Hawk Owl, Great Grey Shrike, Siberian Jay, Siberian Tit, Pine Grosbeak, Rustic, Lapland, Little and Snow Buntings.

ACCESS Most birders stay around Inari or at the wooden huts to the north-west. Exploration by road gives access to a number of interesting areas, but some have found the open rocky areas around the huts as good as anywhere. The route eastward toward Akujarvi has a small road to Veskoniemi on the left after 4 km; this leads to the lake. Continue to Akujarvi and keep left to Virtaniemi. Explore here and around Nellimo.

ROUTE Ivalo has an airstrip with connections to Helsinki, but many will arrive via the larger town of Rovaniemi to the south.

OULU

Once a fur and fish trading station, Oulu is now the most important town in northern Finland. It is heavily industrial, has a very busy oil port and is an essential stop-over on any birding trip to Finland. The main attractions are two scarce breeding birds otherwise really difficult outside Russia: Terek Sandpiper and Yellow-breasted Bunting. Even here they are no doddle, and there is the atmosphere of a twitch as one waits for them to put in an appearance. There are, however, many other species to be found in the area, among them Crane, scarce owls, Scarlet Rosefinch and Arctic waders including Red-necked Phalarope and Jack Snipe.

To the south at the marshes of Liminganlahti there is a fine collection of species to be seen, including Red-necked Phalarope, Ruff and Marsh Harrier. There is a WWF visitor centre here together with a watch tower. Near the tower is one of the best places to see Yellow-breasted Bunting. The Sandpiper is usually seen at the Water Purification Works north of Oulu or at the oil harbour – a good map of the city is essential.

SUMMER Crane, Garganey, Red-breasted Merganser, Marsh and Hen Harriers, Rough-legged Buzzard, Spotted Crake, Temminck's Stint, Ruff, Spotted Redshank, Greenshank, Black-tailed Godwit, Terek Sandpiper, Turnstone, Red-necked Phalarope, Caspian Tern, Hawk Owl, Scarlet Rosefinch, Siskin, Yellow-breasted Bunting.

ACCESS Liminganlahti is accessible at several points. Leave Oulu south on the E4/4 towards the airport. Turn right still towards the airport on

Route 815. At a major junction continue towards airport, but watch for a sign on the left to Kylanpuoli. After a few kilometres take a left signed Letto and continue to a bridge over a canal. Just before this a track leads to a bird tower. Continue south to a second bridge, cross and continue for 1 km where a track on the right crosses meadows for the only Black-tailed Godwit breeding in Finland. The road continues to Liminka. Turn right on Route 813 to the WWF centre signed Liminganlahti Opastuskeskus. Watch for Buntings around the bird tower. Terek Sandpiper may be found by taking the E4 around Oulu northwards to the Route 20 intersection. Leave here and head westwards to a T-junction. Turn left and right into Valatie. At a fork, take a right along Koskelantie and turn left into **Suolamänngatie** to the water purification works. Ask for permission at gate to enter (closed Sundays when locals park and walk in). Return towards Oulu and find a way of turning around at the major fork (where you took a right for the water works) so that you can take a left to the oil harbour. Cross a bridge and continue along Hietasaarenti until a gate bars the road. Request permission to enter. Take the track along the embankment on the right. Terek feeds along the shoreline at both places, but the water level must be low enough to expose mud. There are many other good birds hereabouts that a rushed twitch might easily miss.
ROUTE Fly Helsinki–Oulu and work the south of Oulu first.

PALLAS-OUNASTUNTURI

This huge National Park is in north-western Finland, a short distance from Sweden and Norway, and is centred on a mountain ridge of the same name. It lies just south of the coniferous-forest limit, but a little altitude takes one into basically tundra country, with all of the species one would expect farther north. It is, in fact, the combination of landforms that makes the whole area so fine for birds. The park is best penetrated from the south, but the delightful Lapp village of Enontekiö, to the north, is by a lake well away from the 'main road'. This area is typical taiga, with lakes, bogs, marshes and open land holding Crane, Whooper Swan, Smew and many waders. The forests have Siberian Jay, as well as the elusive Great Grey Owl, Golden Eagle and perhaps even Arctic Warbler.

The park can be explored via Mafkmaja, where the Pallastunturi Tourist Hotel is a fine base. The trail north is well marked, with well-spaced huts offering accommodation along the 60-km walk to Enontekiö, but even a walk of a few kilometres should produce Bluethroat, Dotterel, Snow Bunting, Golden Plover and perhaps Ptarmigan. A full walk may produce Snowy Owl, Long-tailed Skua, Lapland and Snow Buntings and perhaps Bar-tailed Godwit. Gyrfalcon breeds among the gorges around the River Könkämä west of Enontekiö and may be seen flying above the valley.

SUMMER Scaup, Long-tailed Duck, Velvet Scoter, Whooper Swan, Gyrfalcon, Crane, Ptarmigan, Rough-legged Buzzard, Greenshank, Spotted Redshank, Red-necked Phalarope, Dotterel, Long-tailed Skua, Snowy Owl, Great Grey Owl, Hawk Owl, Siberian Jay, Shore Lark, Ring Ouzel, Bluethroat, Arctic Warbler, Twite, Lapland and Snow Buntings.
ACCESS Leave Route 79 at Sarkijarvi south of Muonio on Routes 957 and 9571 for the park. The hotel can offer help with maps and advice on a

mountain trek, or you could take the road to Enontekiö from Palojoensuu farther north and explore from there. There is a tourist hotel, but do not rely on unbooked accommodation. A road follows the Könkämä River to Lake Kilpisjärvi for Gyrfalcon. High above this the hill lakes hold many tundra specialities. When leaving the Park HQ and hotel area go left on Route 957 through some excellent forest. An open boggy area about a third of the way to the main road has produced some good scrub birds. ROUTE Most visitors to this part of the world use a car to cover Inari, Varanger Fjord, North Cape and then the present area.

PARIKKALA AND THE RUSSIAN BORDER

In the last edition of WWBE Parikkala was celebrated as the place to see Blyth's Reed Warbler in Europe. The continued westwards expansion of this species has done little to harm the reputation of this fine area of marsh. What has happened, however, is that the growing band of Finnish birders has opened up more of this Russian borderland and passed the information westwards so that foreign birders now have some really good stake-outs in what was already a fine area for birds. The arm of Lake Simpele known as Siikalahti Marsh is a fully protected nature reserve just a short distance east of Parikkala. There is a WWF visitor centre, a boardwalk and an observation tower that facilitates views of Bittern, Osprey, Marsh Harrier and River and Marsh Warblers. A sightings-log and advice on exact locations of Blyth's can be obtained at the Centre, as these birds inhabit the willows at the marsh edge rather than the stands of pure reed – but remember that Marsh and River Warblers are not pure reed-birds either and there may be Booted Warbler here too to add to the confusion.

North of Parikkala Lake Sääperinjärvi near Vartsila is a major site for Yellow-breasted Bunting as well as many other birds at Parikkala. To the south, at Lake Vakevanjärvi, north of Hujakkala, a series of confusing tracks leads to a small hill overlooking the Russian border. This is the only Finnish site for Spotted Eagle, though the birds actually nest in Russia.

SUMMER Black-throated Diver, Red-necked and Slavonian Grebes, Bittern, Whooper Swan, Pintail, Garganey, Osprey, Marsh Harrier, Spotted Eagle, Spotted Crake, Water Rail, River, Blyth's Reed, Marsh and Booted Warblers, Thrush Nightingale, Scarlet Rosefinch, Yellow-breasted Bunting. ACCESS Siikalahti Marsh is signposted from the E3 which runs east of Parikkala. The WWF centre lies just south of the road. Camping is possible here. For Varsila head north on the E3 to Tolosenmäki. Turn right, then left through lovely country with the aid of map GT6. Route 500 runs through the village and just before reaching the lake on the right, turn right and park where an embankment runs off to the left. Walk this to the observation tower. Yellow-breasted Bunting is in the fields before the lake shore. For Lake Vakevanjärvi take Route 387 from the N3 for 15 km to Hujakkala. By now you have already passed the lake, but this is unimportant if the Eagle is required. Continue past the village for 3 km. Turn right and drive another 3 km to a parking spot on the right opposite a small quarry. Walk to the top of Sampolankallio, a hill with excellent views over the Russian forests. There is a birding log in a box. ROUTE Leave Helsinki eastwards through Kouvala to the areas.

FRANCE

BRITAIN

BELGIUM GERMANY

English Channel SOMME
ESTUARY

LUX.

N

FORÊT D'ARGONNE

SEPT ÎLES

☐ PARIS

● LAC DU DER
CHANTECOQ

FONTAINBLEAU ●

● SOLOGNE

● BORGNEUF

Bay of Biscay

● LA BRENNE

SWITZ.

BAIE D'AIGUILLON

ÎLE D'OLÉRON AND
MARENNES MARSHES

● DOMBES

CORSICA

ITALY

CAMARGUE

Mediterranean Sea

GAVARNIE

0   50   100
km

SPAIN

BAIE D'AIGUILLON

The Biscay coast of France is broken by some of the most splendid and important wetlands in western Europe. Among the most significant is the Baie d'Aiguillon, north of La Rochelle. This huge intertidal inlet is so shallow that it almost empties at low tide, offering vast feeding grounds for waders. There is little or no development along the shoreline save for an ever-increasing shellfish industry. The marshes that back the estuary are intersected by dykes, with some wet and reedy areas that hold a good collection of birds. Little Bittern, Night and Purple Herons, Little Egret, Black Kite, Short-toed Eagle, Montagu's Harrier, Corncrake, Black-winged Stilt and Bluethroat breed and harriers hunt throughout the year. It is during passage and, especially, winter that Aiguillon is at its best. Autumn brings almost 250,000 waders, half of which stay through the winter. Knot, Dunlin, Grey Plover, Avocet and especially Black-tailed Godwit are here in their thousands. This is also an important wintering ground for Spotted Redshank and several duck species. In spring, flocks of Black-tailed

Godwit are among the most important in Europe, with up to 50,000 present at a time. Other passage migrants include good numbers of Greylag Goose, Spoonbill, Whimbrel (20,000) and Avocet (6000).

SUMMER Little Bittern, Night and Purple Herons, Little Egret, Garganey, Honey Buzzard, Black Kite, Short-toed Eagle, Marsh and Montagu's Harriers, Little Crake, Corncrake, Black-winged Stilt, Bluethroat, Melodious Warbler.

WINTER Greylag and Brent Geese, Wigeon, Pintail, Shoveler, Marsh and Hen Harriers, Merlin, Peregrine, Avocet, Knot, Black-tailed and Bar-tailed Godwits, Spotted Redshank, Short-eared Owl.

PASSAGE Spoonbill, Whimbrel, Ruff, Black-tailed Godwit, Little Stint, Curlew Sandpiper, Greenshank.

ACCESS With Michelin map 71, the area is explored on minor roads. Mostly these give views over reclaimed fields, but in the north the D60 runs south from St Michel-en-l'Herm to the shore. Beside the drainage ditches behind the sea-wall there is White-spotted Bluethroat, with Little Egret and Montagu's Harrier nearby. The D60 is connected to the D46A via La Dive and south along the Digue de l'Aiguillon. The Point d'Arcay, south of La Faute-l'Aiguillon is the major high-tide roost for the area. A little east of St Michel-en-l'Herme a road leads south from le Vignaud. Follow the Route des Prises to its end, park and walk right to the lock-gate. Turn left to the Digue des Wagons overlooking the mud-flats.

ROUTE La Rochelle lies immediately to the south and is worth avoiding.

BOURGNEUF

This huge bay lies on the west coast of France immediately south of the mouth of the Loire. It is partially enclosed by the Île de Noirmoutier, which is joined to the mainland by a causeway and which has developed into a seaside resort over the past 20 years. Huge intertidal flats make this one of France's primary wetlands, but they are backed by the saltpans around Bouin and the fresh marshes of Machecoul. Farther inland, towards the Loire, lie the great impenetrable marshes of the Lac de Grand Lieu.

The area is a haunt of waders, and reclamation, notably between Port des Champes and Port du Bec, west of Bouin, has done nothing to reduce their numbers. The variety of species is particularly impressive during passage, but several species, including Stilt and Avocet, breed. Wildfowl are good in winter – there are good numbers of Brent Goose. In autumn the seawatching from the far point of Noirmoutier can be excellent with a south-west wind. South of the causeway, the huge dune beach towards St-Jean-de-Monts has extensive pine forest with Bonelli's Warbler, Wood-lark, Hoopoe and Tawny Pipit. The marshes and pools surrounding the bay have excellent breeding birds and should not be ignored. Both bitterns, numerous Marsh and Montagu's and Hen Harriers breed, along with Stilt, Avocet, Black-tailed Godwit and several hundred pairs of Bluethroat.

SUMMER Bittern, Little Bittern, Little Egret, Shoveler, Montagu's, Marsh and Hen Harriers, Black Kite, Quail, Black-winged Stilt, Avocet, Kentish Plover, Black-tailed Godwit, Curlew, Short-toed Lark, Woodlark, Tawny Pipit, Hoopoe, Pied Flycatcher, Bluethroat, Bonelli's Warbler.

PASSAGE Kentish Plover, Spotted Redshank, Greenshank, Avocet.

WINTER Brent Goose, Wigeon, Grey Plover, Curlew.
ACCESS The town of Bouin is probably the best base and saltpans can be
found in all directions. The polders lie to the west and are approached via
Port des Champes (D21) and Port du Bec (D51). The area on either side of
the causeway that leads to the Île de Noirmoutier is a fine vantage point
on a rising tide, but do not get stranded. About 1 km before the causeway a
road leads north to Trente-Salops. Continue towards the sea through
excellent grazing marshes then along the sea-wall to the north. The Lac de
Grand Lieu has many species including Night Heron, Little Egret, Spoonbill and Water Rail but is impossible to work without a boat. Passay is as
near open water as one can get, but several birders have explored the surrounds on local roads and seen a few species. Black Kite is regular.
   The woods and dunes to the south can be explored from La Barre-de-
Monts or Notre-Dame-de-Monts via the D38.
ROUTE From Nantes take the D751 westward, turning left to
Bourgneuf on the D758 and continuing on this road to Bouin.

CAMARGUE

The Camargue remains as popular as ever: it has a wealth of species second only to Spain's Coto Doñana and yet is decidedly closer to northern
Europe. The Camargue proper lies between the two arms of the Rhône,
south of Arles, yet it is unthinkable not to include in any account of the
area the Petite Camargue to the west, the stony wastes of La Crau to the
east, Les Baux to the north-east and the Pont du Gard to the north. Such
a huge area takes time to explore thoroughly, and most birders will take
at least a week to seek out all the species that are regularly found here.
   The Camargue is changing. There are more tourists than ever and, while
most stay near the coast, the cabanes of the 'cowboys' are now mostly
holiday cottages or bijou second homes. The roads are better, there are
many hotels and, of course, more birdwatchers. The heart of the
Camargue, however, remains the Réserve Naturelle on the Étang de
Vaccarès and is still protected as the major French wetland for birds.
   The beach has breeding Kentish Plover and the dunes have both Tawny
Pipit and Short-toed Lark. The southern lagoons are saline and the salt-
extraction industry has an interest in keeping them so. Here is the Flamingo
breeding area, and Black-winged Stilt and Avocet both benefit. Passage
waders may be both numerous and exciting here in season. Still saline, but
not exploited, lagoons lie to the north and here are the best colonies of
gulls and terns, including Gull-billed Tern and up to 20 pairs of Slender-
billed Gull. The surrounding vegetation and larger islands hold Spectacled
Warbler, Crested Lark, Great Grey Shrike and Bee-eater. Farther north
still, drainage ditches and overgrown reedbeds hold Penduline Tit and Fan-
tailed Warbler and offer opportunities for breeding Black Kites – now
common throughout the Camargue – harriers and Scops Owl. The lagoons
and marshes are full of warblers, herons, egrets, waders, terns and Marsh
Harriers. Woodland should not be ignored, for Melodious Warbler and
Golden Oriole occur here. Among the rice-growing areas are Whiskered
Terns, joined over the lagoons by the other marsh terns on passage.
   To the east, La Crau is the delta of the Durance. Though much reclaimed
for agriculture, there are areas with Little Bustard, Stone-curlew, Great

Greater Flamingoes

Spotted Cuckoo, Lesser Grey Shrike, Black-eared Wheatear, Calandra and Short-toed Larks and Pin-tailed Sandgrouse. The rubbish tip at Entressen may produce Egyptian Vulture, though this species is now scarce.

To the north, Les Baux in the Alpilles is excellent for Alpine Swift, Blue Rock Thrush, Subalpine Warbler and sometimes Egyptian Vulture. It is worth the entrance fee to the Roman ruins to sit on the cliffs and watch the birds. Continuing along the Val d'Enfer offers the chance of Peregrine, Wallcreeper, Alpine Accentor and even Eagle Owl.

West of Avignon is the Pont du Gard, a magnificent Roman aqueduct over a gorge. Alpine Swift, Rock Sparrow and Bonelli's Warbler are regular. The Camargue has a wealth of breeding birds, but is splendid all year.

SUMMER Purple, Squacco and Night Herons, Little and Cattle Egrets, Little Bittern, Bittern, White Stork, Flamingo, Garganey, Red-crested Pochard, Egyptian Vulture, Short-toed, Golden and Bonelli's Eagles, Red and Black Kites, Honey Buzzard, Marsh and Montagu's Harriers, Peregrine, Hobby, Lesser Kestrel, Spotted Crake, Little Bustard, Kentish Plover, Redshank, Avocet, Black-winged Stilt, Stone-curlew, Collared Pratincole, Slender-billed and Mediterranean Gulls, Whiskered, Gull-billed, Sandwich and Little Terns, Pin-tailed Sandgrouse, Great Spotted Cuckoo, Scops and Eagle Owls, Pallid Swift, Alpine Swift, Bee-eater, Roller, Hoopoe, Wryneck, Calandra and Short-toed Larks, Crag Martin, Golden Oriole, Penduline and Bearded Tits, Wallcreeper, Rock Thrush, Blue Rock Thrush, Black-eared Wheatear, Cetti's, Savi's, Moustached, Great Reed, Melodious, Spectacled, Dartford, Sardinian, Subalpine and Fan-tailed Warblers, Tawny Pipit, Great Grey and Lesser Grey Shrikes, Serin, Rock Sparrow.

SPRING AND AUTUMN Osprey, Red-footed Falcon, Dotterel, Whimbrel, Black-tailed Godwit, Green, Wood, Marsh and Curlew Sandpipers, Greenshank, Little and Temminck's Stints, Ruff, Little Gull, Black, White-winged Black and Caspian Terns, Orphean Warbler, Woodchat and Red-backed Shrikes.

ACCESS The heart of the Camargue, the **Étang de Vaccarès**, can be viewed from minor roads and tracks extending along the west, north and eastern shores. The Cartes Touristiques 1:100,000 published by IGN are excellent, but the Michelin series is almost as good and more generally available. The area is reached from Arles via the N570 and the D36. The latter leads to Salin de Giraud, the saltworks town, and gives variable views of the riverine forest along the Grand Rhône, which has several large heronries. Beyond the Salin de Giraud lies a network of tracks that lead to the shore and among the lagoons. The D36B is the most famous of the Camargue roads, giving excellent views of Vaccarès as well as access off to the west to **Étang du Fangassier, Étang de Galabert** and **Étang du Fournelet,** which should all be explored. **The Salin du Midi** here has Flamingo, passage waders, terns and many typical birds. In the north, the lagoons and marshes around Mas d'Agon hold Moustached and Great Reed Warblers, Penduline Tit, Whiskered Tern and Collared Pratincole. For **La Crau** take the N113 and turn right on the N568. Watch for good habitat and explore on foot. Farther east, at the intersection of the N113 and the D5, turn left and take the track on the right through the fields of the Croix de Crau area for Little Bustard and Pin-tailed Sandgrouse – especially in winter. Returning to the D5, head southwards, cross the N113 and after 1 km turn left (east) on a track leading along the northern edge of a disused airfield. This is another area for these two special species. Continuing southwards leads to the Entressen area. To see **Les Baux,** take the N570 northwards from Arles, turn right on the D17 and follow the signs. The road along the Val d'Enfer to the west is strongly recommended; this area, together with the route from the castle to the cathedral in the cliff face, regularly produces Wallcreeper (particularly in winter). Take the D27A to the D5, turn left (north) and watch for the road to the radio station at La Caume. Here are Wallcreeper, Alpine Accentor, Alpine Swift and Eagle Owl, the latter often in the gully north-east of the radio station. For the **Pont du Gard,** take the N570 northwards to Tarascon, cross the river to Beaucaire and continue on the N86L, past the A9, to its junction with the N86 at Remoulins. Pont du Gard is 3 km to the north. **ROUTE** The nearest airport is Marseilles, and those serving the Côte d'Azur are not too distant. You can reach the Camargue from the Channel ports in a day with a bit of hard driving, but it is autoroute all the way. Tourist development means that there are now more hotels than ever.

CORSICA

Corsica, or 'Corse', is one of the most beautiful islands in the Mediterranean with spectacular mountains, rugged coastlines and extensive areas of forest. Fortunately it has also been spared the blight of mass tourism and, outside the main towns, retains a gentle even pastoral atmosphere. The language and money are French, the people and food are Corsican. Though it is a large island it is treated as a single site simply because most visitors will wish to spend a week of exploration, though some crews do blitz around for the Corsican Nuthatch and the (perhaps) endemic Citril Finch. The latter is incredibly widespread and even found at low altitudes and the Nuthatch is far more widespread than is generally acknowledged.

The island has other attractions too and Lammergeier is found in all the main mountain massifs along with Golden and Short-toed Eagles. Other high-altitude species include Alpine Chough, Water Pipit, Alpine Accentor and Wallcreeper. Scrub and hillside birds include abundant Subalpine Warbler as well as both Dartford and Marmora's Warblers. Lowlands are mainly confined to the east coast where a series of lagoons look full of ornitho-potential. Sadly, many have been converted to intensive fish culture and are all but devoid of birds. Exceptions are Étang de Biguglia and Étang de Palo. Little Bittern, Purple Heron, Marsh Harrier, Water Rail and Red-crested Pochard can all be found and the lake at Biguglia is also a pretty sure place for Audouin's Gull. This area is also good for passage migrants and a few waders plus Roller and Red-footed Falcon are regular in spring. At this season the Cap Corse area at Barcaggio, in the extreme north of the island, is the primary migration watchpoint. Here the dunes, the maquis area and a shallow lagoon, shelter a variety of species including scrub warblers such as Marmora's, Subalpine, Dartford and Sardinian. There is a temporary ringing station during April and early May. Other good coastal areas are at Bonifacio in the extreme south, where Cory's Shearwater breeds just offshore and the mainland may produce Blue Rock Thrush, Alpine Swift plus Spanish and Rock Sparrows. Eleonora's Falcon is often a migrant here. Near Calvi, in the north-west, is the reserve of Scandola, where Osprey and Peregrine breed; it is best approached by boat.

SUMMER Cory's and Mediterranean Shearwaters, Shag, Red-crested Pochard, Golden and Short-toed Eagles, Lammergeier, Red Kite, Goshawk, Sparrowhawk, Marsh and Montagu's Harriers, Osprey, Peregrine, Hobby, Water Rail, Dipper, Corsican Nuthatch, Wallcreeper, Alpine and Pallid Swifts, Spotless Starling, Alpine Accentor, Red-backed Shrike, Blue Rock Thrush, Marmora's, Subalpine, Dartford, Sardinian, Reed, Great Reed, Cetti's and Fan-tailed Warblers, Citril Finch, Crossbill, Cirl Bunting, Rock Sparrow.

ACCESS Vizzavona lies on the main road, the N193, across the island between Ajaccio and Bastia. Along this road is a sign to 'La Gare de Vizzavona'. A little way to the south is the Office National des Forêts. Opposite this (on the western side), beside a hut, is a footpath leading over a bridge, around a picnic site, past a 'fire' sign, over another bridge and then zigzagging up into the pines. Follow this path, watching and listening for the Nuthatch. Citril Finch has been seen below the pines. It is easy to make a loop back towards the railway station. The **Aitone Forest** lies near the village of Evisa, some 25 km from Porto due west of Corte. There are numerous tracks through the forest for exploration but no definite stake-outs. Reach the **Asco valley** by leaving Bastia towards Corte, but turning right towards Calvi at Ponte Leccia on the N197. After 25 km turn left on the D47 towards Asco. The gorges are before the village, the woods beyond, both are excellent for Lammergeier. Continue to Haut Asco for Alpine Chough and Alpine Accentor. Also in the Corte area are the Gorges de la Restonica, a noted haunt of Lammergeier, Golden Eagle, Alpine Chough and Alpine Accentor. **Lake Biguglia** lies east of the N198, south of Bastia near the airport. The southern end is generally the most productive though the north-east corner is good for Audouin's. If the lake fails in this respect try Bastia Harbour. To the north of Bastia, the Barcaggio area of Cap Corse is reached by following the road to Ersa and then taking the D253 to Barcaggio. Here take the track to the east of the village crossing the river towards the Tour d'Agnellu. At **Bonifacio**, which is very picturesque, descend the cliffs to a point opposite the island of Grain de Sable. At night you can hear Cory's Shearwaters coming in to their burrows. For the reserve of Scandola, go to Calvi and take a boat-trip to the south. Boats are not allowed to stay more than 24 hours at Scandola. ROUTE Regular daily ferries from Nice and Marseilles to Bastia and Ajaccio and flights to both towns.

DOMBES

The ponds of the Dombes north of Lyons are considerably more than a convenient stop-over on the way to or from the Camargue. Indeed, were they not so close to that famous area they would probably become a major ornitho-tourist site. A glance at a map is sufficient to indicate the possibilities. There are literally a hundred or more areas of water centred on the town of Villars and all neatly enclosed in the Rhône valley between the Alps and the Massif Central. Most of the waters are shallow, with emergent vegetation forming considerable reedbeds in some areas. Though there is still some commercial fishery exploitation, the main change in recent years has been the development of water sports in several areas. The nature reserve south of Villars has been partially developed into an ornithological park – a sort of glorified zoo with Chilean Flamingoes, captive wildfowl, a snack-bar and various dioramas with stuffed birds. The free car park here does, however, facilitate exploration of the two large lakes either side of the A83 where parking is otherwise unavailable.

The most significant birds of the Dombes are the herons, which include good colonies of Purple, Night and Squacco Herons and Little Egret. Red-crested Pochard, Stilt, Whiskered Tern, harriers and Black Kite all breed. The Mediterranean influence is evident in the populations of several birds found in the general area. The surroundings are mostly agricultural but there are woods to the east beyond Chalamont.

SUMMER Black-necked Grebe, Grey, Purple, Night and Squacco Herons, Little Egret, Bittern, Little Bittern, Garganey, Gadwall, Red-crested Pochard, Marsh and Montagu's Harriers, Black Kite, Goshawk, Spotted Crake, Black-winged Stilt, Black-tailed Godwit, Black and Whiskered Terns, Woodchat and Red-backed Shrikes, Hoopoe, Bee-eater, Great Reed, Fan-tailed, Savi's and Melodious Warblers.

ACCESS The N83 cuts through the heart of the Dombes, with Villars at the centre making an ideal base. The huge number of lakes should be explored with the aid of a map, for most can be seen from the network of minor roads. The best lakes are the Étang de Glareins and the Grand Étang de Birieux situated on either side of the N83 south of the town. This is where the free parking at the 'bird centre' comes in handy. The Étangs de St Paul-de-Varax are as good as any and the area of Versailleaux-le-Montellier is partly a reserve.

ROUTE Leave the Autoroute du Soleil at Villefranche.

FONTAINEBLEAU

The Forest of Fontainebleau lies some 60 km south-east of Paris immediately east of the Autoroute du Soleil (A6), and has been used by generations of birders as a stop-over on the way to the Mediterranean. The extensive woods, both coniferous and deciduous, are home to a good range of species, including those Continental woodpeckers that have such an appeal to the British. Grey-headed, Middle Spotted and Black Woodpeckers can all be found here, along with Short-toed Treecreeper, Crested Tit, Goshawk and other typical woodland birds of north-central France.

SUMMER Buzzard, Honey Buzzard, Goshawk, Green, Grey-headed, Middle Spotted, Great Spotted and Black Woodpeckers, Wryneck, Short-toed Treecreeper, Bonelli's Warbler, Crested Tit, Hawfinch.

ACCESS The specialities occur throughout the area, so the spots detailed here are, more than most, those where others have managed to find particular birds over the years. This does, of course, create self-perpetuating 'hot spots'. All of these areas are less than 4–5 km from the centre of Fontainebleau, within the minor 'Route Ronde' around the south of the town marked in white on the best map, Michelin 61. On the D409 stop near the Gorges de Franchard and turn south on the ring road. Stop after a short distance and explore the mixed woods left of the road. Leaving the town on the N152, stop where it passes under the Aqueduc de la Vanne at an open show-jumping arena. Take the track south of this. Similarly, the area just north of where the Aqueduc crosses the N7 is also worth exploring. Just a little south of the Aqueduc on the N7 a small turning forks right (west) – the D63E. After 1 km there is an area of pines near a small ridge; explore on both sides of the road. About half way between the D63E and the N7, along the ring road, there is a cottage on the south side of the road. Stop here and walk south behind the cottage to an open area.
ROUTE The Paris motorway ring gives access to the A6; exit at Ury on the N152 to Fontainebleau.

FORÊT D'ARGONNE

The Argonne is a ridge of densely forested hills east of Reims and a completely rural and charming backwater perfect for a leisurely break. To the south lies a less well-defined area of forests, lakes and ponds, and to the west huge rolling cereal plains. The Argonne is an extraordinary contrast to the monoculture plains and its birds are both more numerous and diverse. It is, above all, known for its birds of prey, and Osprey, Honey Buzzard, Black and Red Kites, Goshawk and Hobby all summer. There are also other species that can be seen closer to home here than elsewhere in Europe. Black Stork, Little Bittern, Great Reed Warbler and Bluethroat all fall into this category. Good woodpeckers, the occasional Little Bustard and Collared Flycatcher (perhaps as rare as any) can all be found.

SUMMER Great Crested Grebe, Teal, Gadwall, Osprey, Buzzard, Honey Buzzard, Marsh, Hen and Montagu's Harriers, Black and Red Kites, Goshawk, Hobby, Little Bittern, Bittern, Black Stork, Stone-curlew, Little Bustard, Crested Lark, Barn Owl, Black, Grey-headed, Great Spotted and Middle Spotted Woodpeckers, Wryneck, Red-backed Shrike, Golden Oriole, Dipper, Kingfisher, Short-toed Treecreeper, Crested Tit, Firecrest, Yellow Wagtail, Bluethroat, Grasshopper, Marsh, Savi's, Great Reed and Bonelli's Warblers, Collared Flycatcher, Cirl Bunting, Hawfinch, Crossbill.
ACCESS Sainte Menehould east of Châlons-sur-Marne is the access point for the Argonne, with the most interesting area lying to the south and east. The ridge east of the Vouziers–Sainte Menehould road is the

Argonne proper, and the minor roads that criss-cross the area offer most of the woodland species including raptors. The many lakes to the south are all worth visiting and many have Marsh Harrier. Étang de Belval is one of the best, but the others should not be ignored. Minor roads leading north from Sommeilles into the Forêt de l'Isle are good for Honey Buzzard, Goshawk and Golden Oriole. Near Châlons on the D1 is Marson, from where a road leads high into the chalk hills for Little Bustard and Crested Lark. Eastwards some 6 km beyond le Fresne, the D1 passes through woodland with Bonelli's Warbler. The whereabouts of the small colony of Collared Flycatchers must remain unpublished for security reasons. The Argonne is an area with an established reputation, but one which will still repay careful exploration. It is worth a week of anyone's time.

ROUTE The A4 passes north of Châlons and then just south of Sainte Menehould. Head south to Givry-en-Argonne – an excellent base.

GAVARNIE

Gavarnie is the primary birding site in the French Pyrenees. The Spanish side has more species and is warmer, but this French spot has most of the specialities and is considerably easier to get to. Though Gavarnie itself is a high mountain village, the lowland approach from Lourdes should not be ignored: Booted Eagle is seldom found at any height and Egyptian Vulture is usually a low-level species. The valley is lined with pine forests as you approach, but these gradually give way to more open areas that become progressively more rocky. The scenery is spectacular.

Outstanding here are Lammergeier (which does breed on the French side), Bonelli's Eagle, both choughs, Alpine Accentor and Wallcreeper, but there are many more birds besides.

SUMMER Lammergeier, Griffon and Egyptian Vultures, Booted and Bonelli's Eagles, Goshawk, Ptarmigan, Chough, Alpine Chough, Wallcreeper, Black and White-backed Woodpeckers, Alpine Swift, Alpine Accentor, Crag Martin, Water Pipit, Blue Rock Thrush, Black-eared Wheatear, Dipper, Red-backed Shrike, Bonelli's Warbler, Firecrest, Citril Finch, Rock Bunting, Crossbill, Snow Finch.

ACCESS The approach road should be explored. On arrival at Gavarnie, there are several areas (all easily found) that should be explored. Just before the village is an intersection. Take the road leading to Port de Gavarnie – the pass to Spain (open only in August and September). This leads to the ski centre, where the road is blocked. Stop and explore along the line of the ski lift for Accentor and Snow Finch. The **Cirque de Gavarnie** is reached by track above the village. This leads through woodland to a disused hotel, behind which there is Citril Finch, with Bonelli's Warbler in the lower woods and Accentor high up in the Cirque. The route to the **Vallée d'Ossoue** lies off the road to the Port de Gavarnie – continue straight on where that road veers off to the left. The sheer rock face here is excellent for raptors and Wallcreeper. The **Pyrenees National Park** lies a short distance to the west and includes the valleys of Ossau, Bitet and Souossoueou. Though largely ignored by birders, it too has a pair of Lammergeier as well as 50 pairs of Griffon Vulture that do not breed in Gavarnie. It also has larger populations of Golden Eagle and Peregrine as well as of Ptarmigan and Black Grouse. Black and White-backed Woodpeckers are also present along with Eagle Owl and Chough. **ROUTE** Easily reached via Lourdes. For those wishing to continue to Spain, the route is a huge circle westwards via Escot and Urdos to Jaca (except in August and September).

ÎLE D'OLÉRON AND MARENNES MARSHES

The Île d'Oléron can be regarded as the centrepiece of an excellent birding area around the town of Rochefort. Main interest centres on the marshes and intertidal areas where there is an intensive oyster industry. The island itself was joined to the mainland in 1960, but the flood of holidaymakers and trippers is accommodated by a fine system of roads and is not daunted by the hefty toll that is charged to reach it. By far the best areas are the oysterbeds and saltpans, which can be found at many places, though the northern tip of the island is good for seawatching and has a regular flock of Mediterranean Gull. There are particularly good marshes to the north of St Georges, east of Arceau and south of Allards. There is also a reserve-cum-bird garden at Les Grissotières, well signposted from the main road, where a bird tower gives views over wild, as well as captive, birds. This is a good place to see Short-toed Eagle, three pairs of which breed on Oléron. Best areas for this bird are north-east and west of Dolus d'Oléron. Purple Heron, Little and occasionally Great White Egret, Marsh and Montagu's Harriers, Stilt and Bluethroat can all be found.

The mainland marshes are equally attractive and would repay a thorough exploration. In particular there are three areas that should not be missed – the Yves Marshes, the LPO reserve at Moëze, and the Marennes Marshes on the D123. The Yves area consists of a sandy bay backed by lagoons and reedbeds that has a fine population of breeding birds including White Stork, Purple Heron (up to 100 pairs), Marsh and Montagu's Harriers (20–30 pairs each), Stilt, Black Tern and Bluethroat. The LPO reserve, which is on the coast between Rochefort and the Île d'Oléron, can be viewed from the road and has much the same variety of species. It is considerably nearer the Marennes Marshes, which many regard as one of the outstanding bird haunts on the Atlantic coast of France. Although the Sendre Marshes south of the D728, the marshes around Hiers and Brouage, and the marshes north of Brouage (including the LPO reserve) have been favoured by visiting birders, there is no doubt that the whole area is worthy of exploration. Some have told of the wonders of marshes east of the D123, for example, where White Stork nests on the electricity pylons.

SUMMER White Stork, Little Egret, Purple Heron, Black Kite, Marsh and Montagu's Harriers, Short-toed Eagle, Black-winged Stilt, Bluethroat, Red-backed Shrike, Golden Oriole, Hoopoe.
PASSAGE Spoonbill, Black-winged Stilt, Black-tailed Godwit, Whimbrel, Whiskered Tern, Aquatic Warbler.
WINTER Brent Goose, Pintail, Avocet, Knot.
ACCESS The coast road north from Rochefort to La Rochelle bypasses Yves and the Anse de Foures. For the LPO reserve at Moëze leave Rochefort south on the D3 to Moëze village. Turn west on the D125e to St Froult then south to Plaisance and on through the marshes with the estuary on

the right. This road returns to the D3. Marennes is the gateway to the Île d'Oléron which has marshes to the east of the main island road at Allards, Arceau and to the north of St Georges. Those north of Arceau are a noted haunt of Bluethroat. The D123 runs north-eastwards from Marennes to St Agnant and the Storks nest along a considerable strait halfway between the two. As if all this were not enough, Little Bustard occurs either side of the D739 to the east of Rochefort. One area lies north of this road immediately west of Moragne; the other to the south of the road east of St Coutant-le-Grand. Both areas can be explored on minor roads.
ROUTE Southwards from the port of La Rochelle.

LA BRENNE

A glance at a map is sufficient to show that the area of La Brenne is a highly attractive one for birding. A huge area of ponds and lakes (about 500) is broken by large forests, smaller woods and areas of agriculture. Compared with the Sologne to the north, 'Chasse Gardé' notices are nowhere near as numerous. Though the major waters are grouped together between Rosnay and Mézièrres, there are so many outlying lakes that a thorough exploration would occupy a good week's birding holiday.

The ponds are shallow, with a good growth of emergent vegetation offering breeding security to many species. This vegetation is mostly reeds and in some areas quite extensive reedbeds have developed. As a result, three species of harrier breed along with Bittern, Little Bittern and a good variety of duck. Crakes include Baillon's, and both Black and Whiskered Terns breed. The surrounding dry land holds a good cross-section of species that one would expect in central lowland France, together with Little Bustard and Stone-curlew.

Winter brings large numbers of other species to La Brenne, with wild-fowl being particularly impressive from November on. Terns and waders appear on passage, and raptors pass through in numbers every autumn.

An up-to-date map is essential and the 1:25,000 of the Institut Géographique National is excellent and available locally. This is particu-larly so as fresh ponds are still being created, and these newly flooded waters are rich in food, attracting many wildfowl and waders.

SUMMER Great Crested Grebe, Black-necked Grebe, Purple Heron, Little Bittern, Bittern, Shoveler, Garganey, Marsh Harrier, Montagu's Harrier, Hen Harrier, Red Kite, Black Kite, Baillon's Crake, Water Rail, Snipe, Curlew, Little Bustard, Stone-curlew, Black Tern, Whiskered Tern, Savi's Warbler, Great Reed Warbler.
PASSAGE Osprey, Honey Buzzard, Black Kite, Common Sandpiper, Greenshank, Common Tern, Black Tern.
ACCESS Most of the ponds and lakes are worth a look, and can be watched from the network of surrounding roads with the aid of a good map. The following are easily seen and number among the more productive waters: Notz; Moury – with large areas of reeds; Couvent – a reedbed; Miclos – with reeds and terns; Beauregard – reeds; Gabrière – one of the larger waters, with duck; Gabrieu – water lilies, with breeding grebes and terns; Hardouine – reed-fringed; La Mer Rouge – huge water, with terns and duck; Montiacre – reedbeds and open water; Blizon – with reeds and

islands; **Le Sault** – with reed-fringed banks and the nearby string of three small lakes. The **Étang du Condreau** has a Black-headed gullery with Whiskered Terns, and the Auberge de la Gabrière, adjacent to the lake of the same name, makes an ideal centre.

ROUTE From Paris, take the A10 to Tours and turn south-eastward on the N143 towards Châteauroux. At Châtillon turn right on to minor roads to La Brenne.

LAC DU DER CHANTECOQ

South of Paris, between Troyes and Saint-Dizier, lies a remote backwater drained by the great rivers of the Seine, the Marne and their tributaries. Much of the area is forested, the agriculture poor and the land devoted mainly to grazing; a sharp contrast to the great rolling arable plains to the north and west. Here two huge reservoirs have been constructed, virtually along the traditional migration route of the European Crane population. Not surprisingly, up to 37,000 birds quickly took advantage of the new opportunities and began to use the northernmost reservoir, Lac du Der, as a safe roost and staging-post on their journey between the southern Baltic and winter quarters in Spain. The area proved so much to their liking that variable numbers have, in recent years, stayed on to winter.

The southern lake, Lac de la Forêt d'Orient, has become one of the most regular spots in France for wintering White-tailed Eagle. Together, and along with the surrounding forests, these two lakes have become one of the classic winter birding spots in Europe. White-tailed Eagles also occur at Lac du Der, and the 'digues' along the south-western corner often boast birders from three or four countries in February. This is an excellent spot for the Eagles, as well as late-afternoon roosting flights of Crane.

There are, of course, other attractions too. Hen Harrier is regular, Buzzard abundant, Bean Goose common and Great Grey Shrike, Middle Spotted Woodpecker and Short-toed Treecreeper regular. Ducks include Smew and Goosander, and there is generally a Peregrine present. Some have tried the lakes in spring and summer, though they do not then produce the excitements of winter. Breeding species include Bittern, Little Bittern, Purple Heron, Honey Buzzard, both kites and Marsh Harrier.

WINTER Red-necked Grebe, Bean and Greylag Geese, Shoveler, Gadwall, Wigeon, Goosander, Red-breasted Merganser, Smew, Hen Harrier, Buzzard, Red Kite, Peregrine, White-tailed Eagle, Crane, Ruff, Great Spotted and Middle Spotted Woodpeckers, Great Grey Shrike, Crested Tit, Hawfinch, Crossbill.

ACCESS Both lakes can be explored quite freely from the surrounding roads, some of which run along the banks in the south and west of Lac du Der. The classic spot is the northern end of the Digue de Nord. The boating port east of Giffaumont Champaubert is a good viewpoint, as is the area reached on the D55 across the bay. Cranes feed to the south-west and are best left undisturbed. The Lac de la Forêt d'Orient is best in the north (a bird hide here) and the east, but can be explored at various points. Most of the surrounding forests can be explored by tracks and on foot.

ROUTE The area is easily reached from Paris or the Channel ports via Reims and Châlons. The best routes are toll motorways.

SEPT ÎLES

These islands lie off the north coast of Brittany, half-way between Rennes and Brest, near Perros-Guirec. They form the best seabird colonies in France and hold Puffin and Gannet at their southernmost breeding sites. Gannet first bred on Rouzic in World War II and is well established, reaching 6100 pairs by 1987. It can now be seen in the area throughout the summer, and many pass through the maze of islands off western Brittany on their way to and from Biscay. A good selection of other seabirds can be seen, though the Peregrine is unfortunately no longer here.

SUMMER Storm Petrel, Fulmar, Manx Shearwater, Gannet, Shag, Kittiwake, Sandwich Tern, Razorbill, Guillemot, Puffin.

ACCESS The Sept Îles form a nature reserve and landing is not allowed on Rouzic, Malaban and Cerf – the most interesting ones. However, local boatmen from Perros-Guirec regularly run 'round-the-islands' tours giving excellent views of most of the species from early June.

ROUTE Leave Rennes westward on the N12 to Guingamp, take the D767 to Lannion and follow signs to Perros-Guirec. Many birds can be seen from Ploumanach to the north.

SOLOGNE

The Sologne is an area of heaths and woodland broken by innumerable pools, ponds and lakes. In many areas mature deciduous woodland hides the various waters from the public highways. This region is one of the primary hunting regions of France and is heavily 'keepered'. Prohibiting notices and barbed-wire fences detract from a superb birding area.

Most of the ponds are shallow with a fringe of reeds which often form extensive reedbeds. There are drainage schemes in process of completion and much valuable habitat has already been lost. Nevertheless, there are still plenty of good birds to be seen, including two eagles, three harriers, both bitterns, Purple and Night Herons, Black Tern, Black-tailed Godwit, Black Kite, Goshawk, Honey Buzzard and several woodpeckers.

In the north there is more heath than woodland, though here there is considerable reclamation for agriculture and invasion by birch scrub. There are also large areas of conifer plantations, some of which are old enough to have attracted their own particular bird fauna.

SUMMER Great Crested and Black-necked Grebes, Purple and Night Herons, Little Bittern, Bittern, Shoveler, Short-toed and Booted Eagles, Marsh, Hen and Montagu's Harriers, Black Kite, Goshawk, Honey Buzzard, Black-winged Stilt, Curlew, Black-tailed Godwit, Black and Whiskered Terns, Great Spotted, Lesser Spotted and Black Woodpeckers, Savi's and Great Reed Warblers.

AUTUMN Crane, Black Kite, Black Tern.

ACCESS This is a selective list. In the central area the following can be seen from the road. Marguiliers (marsh and reeds), Favells, Pontbertas, Menne, Malzone and Panama. The Étang de Beaumont requires permission, but is productive. The Étang de Bièvre can be poorly viewed from the north-east corner. Ask for permission to walk 25 m down a track to get better views. In the north-west the Forêt de Chambord is worth

Night Herons

exploring. It is a hunting reserve, but the many roads and tracks make exploration relatively straightforward. There are several other large areas of woodland nearer the central area, including the Forêt de Braudan.
ROUTE From Orleans take the N20 to Nouan-le-Fuzelier. From Nouan, head westward on the D923 and start exploring.

SOMME ESTUARY

The Somme is ignored by birding visitors to France, which is a pity, for it is a major haunt of waders and wildfowl, with a good reserve on the north shore. The reserve is bordered by an experimental 'Parc Ornithologique du Marquenterre', which caters for casual visitors and birders in much the same way as does the Wildfowl and Wetland Trust in Britain. With the Somme as a background, there are wader pools, open marshes and saltings all to be explored, as well as a bird collection, picnic spot, information centre and so on. It is a bit dude, but definitely worth a stop.

At low tide the Somme reveals extensive flats of mud and sand, and in summer masses of holidaymakers descend on the cockle and whelk beds. During passage periods and in winter, the birds have these foods to themselves and there is an excellent collection of waders. Wildfowl still mostly pass through and high-tide roosting flights can be seen from the reserve.

PASSAGE Red-throated Diver, Brent Goose, Shelduck, Spoonbill, Black-tailed and Bar-tailed Godwits, Whimbrel, Little Stint, Curlew Sandpiper.
WINTER Pintail, Wigeon, Greylag Goose, Dunlin, Bar-tailed Godwit.
SUMMER Bittern, Little Egret, Garganey, Shoveler, Pintail, Greylag Goose, Marsh and Hen Harriers, Spotted Crake, Avocet, Kentish Plover, Fan-tailed Warbler.
ACCESS The north shore is accessible at several places, including the Parc Ornithologique from April–November, north of Le Crotoy. There is an admission charge to the Parc. The dunes north of Le Crotoy are free.
ROUTE Easily reached from the Channel ports.

THE GAMBIA

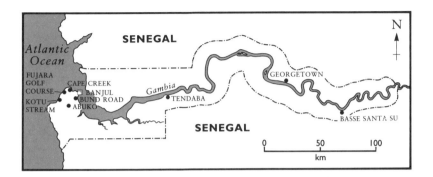

ABUKO

Abuko is the most famous birding site in The Gambia, a testimony to the work of Eddie Brewer who, with the enthusiasm and co-operation of the President, created this reserve. It divides into two halves. The original Reserve contains the last remnant of West African forest near the coast while The Extension is at a more scrub and thicket-like stage of forest development. Every visitor to The Gambia should visit Abuko at least once.

From the entrance a marked trail leads in a few minutes to a lagoon with an adjacent viewing platform. Immediately, there are good birds, including Black-headed and Green Herons, Giant Kingfisher, Hammerkop, Purple Glossy Starling and Grey Plantain-eater. Spur-winged Plover, Purple, Night and Squacco Herons and perhaps Common or Green Sandpipers offer a more familiar diet. Thereafter, the birds of Abuko become tough and elusive. Do not despair! Do not make the mistake of thinking the forest a bird-free zone. Walk the paths at a snail's pace, with extended pauses to wait and see. Many of Abuko's birds are secretive and self-effacing, and any call should be investigated. Though an enormous range of species can be seen, many will be missed. Those that should oblige include Lizard Buzzard, Harrier-hawk, Stone Partridge, Red-billed Wood Dove, Green Crested and Violet Turacos, Pied Kingfisher, Allied Hornbill, Bearded Barbet, Ussher's Spinetail Swift, Grey-headed Bristlebill, Little Greenbul, Wattle-eye, Red-bellied Paradise Flycatcher, West African Thrush, Snowy-headed Robin Chat, Fantee Rough-wing and Pied-winged Swallows and Spectacled and Vitelline Masked Weavers. If, additionally, you get White-spotted Pygmy Rail and Blue-billed Weaver you have done well.

WINTER Grey, Black-headed, Purple, Black, Western Reef, Green, Night and Squacco Herons, Hammerkop, Hooded and Palm-nut Vultures, Lizard Buzzard, Harrier-hawk, Stone Partridge, African Jacana, Spur-winged Plover, Red-billed Wood Dove, Green Crested and Violet Turacos, Yellow-bellied Parrot, Pied and Giant Kingfishers, Swallow-tailed Bee-eater, White-faced Scops Owl, Verreaux's Eagle Owl, Bearded Barbet, Black-throated and Lesser Honeyguides, Fine-spotted and Grey Woodpeckers,

Palm-nut Vulture

Ussher's Spinetail Swift, Grey-headed Bristlebill, Little Greenbul, Black Flycatcher, Wattle-eye, Red-bellied Paradise Flycatcher, West African Thrush, Snowy-headed Robin Chat, Green Hylia, Pied-winged Swallow, Fantee Rough-wing Swallow, Drongo, Purple Glossy Starling, Vitelline Masked, Spectacled and Blue-billed Weavers, Cut-throat, Lavender Waxbill.

ACCESS The entrance to Abuko lies on the south side of the road to Banjul Airport and is well marked and known to all taxi drivers. There is an entrance fee. The first species encountered will probably be vervet or red colobus monkeys, which find this area attractive in winter. Follow the path, slowly, to the pool and viewing platform. Next to the platform is a path to the 'Photographic Hide', worth half an hour waiting for shy species to appear. If tourists appear instead, leave immediately. Continue along this path very slowly. Spend ten minutes at each major bend in the path (every 50–100 m). Eventually arrive at the 'Orphanage' with caged lions, hyenas and wild vultures. Soft drinks available. Continue to the 'Extension'. Peer into the bushes for Pygmy Kingfisher and Stone Partridge and into the air for elusive swallows. If you locate Verreaux's Eagle Owl nest, do not shout to get views of the bird. Return to the 'Orphanage' and take a different path (ask the guards for the 'Exit') and proceed slowly. At a major intersection, ignore signs to 'Exit' and take a right back to the pool.

ROUTE Most birders working The Gambia will be on 'package' holidays or birding tours based at coastal hotels. Abuko is easily reached by taxi or bicycle. Hire cars are expensive, especially for a short trip like this.

BUND ROAD AND CAPE CREEK

The Bund Road is an embankment that extends inland from the docks of Banjul to the main Bakau–Banjul road near the prison. The landward side has a series of marshes with open pools and scrub, and on the seaward side mud-flats give way eastward to vast beds of mangroves. It is an outstanding bird haunt that should not be missed. It is also dangerous and visitors should not venture here alone (see Kotu Stream). There are often policemen at the Banjul end to see that you come to no harm. Ask them to walk with you and reward them with an impressive looking watch or pen. Waders here are excellent and include species such as Dunlin and Knot that are scarce along this coast. Gulls are also good and terns more so with Royal, Lesser Crested and Caspian present. There are regular Pink-backed Pelican and Flamingo and the landward lagoons hold Black and other herons, Great White Egret, Marsh Harrier and occasionally African Marsh Owl. The gulls, terns, waders and pelicans roost on offshore wrecks and it is easy to miss a species or two, but most waders continue feeding on the landward pools and form superb flocks many hundreds strong. Curlew Sandpiper, Ruff, Avocet and Little Stint are usually the most abundant species.

Cape Creek lies next to and towards Banjul from the Hotel Sunwing. It is good for a seawatch and can produce terns, the odd skua and reasonably regular Lanner. From the hotel the Banjul road skirts mud and mangroves to a bridge over Cape Creek set in a saltpan-type landscape. At the bridge take the path seawards beside the creek for views over open sand banks for roosting terns and gulls, and White-fronted Sandplover. This is a hotspot for Slender-billed Gull. Continue to the Bakau–Banjul road. Turn right and stop just beyond where the Serrekunda road forks left at Camaloo Corner. Examine the fields for Plain-backed Pipit and Yellow-throated Longclaw.

WINTER White-breasted and Long-tailed Cormorants, Darter, Pink-backed Pelican, Great White Egret, Purple, Black, Western Reef and Green Herons, Flamingo, Marsh Harrier, Lanner, Ringed Plover, White-fronted Sandplover, Avocet, Black-winged Stilt, Curlew and Wood Sandpipers, Little Stint, Ruff, Turnstone, Redshank, Greenshank, Black-tailed and Bar-tailed Godwits, Whimbrel, Slender-billed, Grey-headed and Black-headed Gulls, Gull-billed, Caspian, Royal and Lesser Crested Terns, Malachite and Pied Kingfishers, Blue-cheeked Bee-eater, Plain-backed Pipit, Yellow-throated Longclaw, Yellow Wagtail, Crombec, Subalpine Warbler, Red-billed Quelea. **ACCESS** Head for Banjul docks and locate Bund Road. The first 200–400 m should provide views over the large landward lagoon. If the mangroves are too tall, return towards Banjul and take the first left, first right, first left, first left beyond the school, leading to the landward side of the lagoon. Return to Bund Road: pause here and there to scan. At the pumping station on the left, stop and check all round. Continue to Bakau–Banjul road, turn left and head for Cape Creek, which is to the right at a major turning. **ROUTE** As Abuko.

GEORGETOWN AND BASSE SANTA SU

Georgetown is 300 km up country from Banjul. A good camp across the river on the north shore, although not luxurious, forms a fine base for exploration of upper Gambia. By leaving the coast soon after breakfast it is possible to reach the camp in time for a late lunch, but do not dawdle on the way. A stop or two may produce Marabou Stork and Bateleur Eagle, but would be more productive if you spent all day birding, though this requires a group of birders, rather than a tourist excursion.

The camp on the river banks provides good birding among the scrub and woodland. Species include Brubru, Sulphur-breasted and Senegal

Puff-back Shrikes, Rufous-crowned Roller, Little and Red-throated Bee-eater, Banded Harrier Eagle, Bruce's Green Pigeon, Didric Cuckoo, White-faced Scops Owl and Pygmy Kingfisher, and the regular herons, storks and egrets and the more widespread birds.

A full-day excursion farther up-river to Basse is *de rigueur* for Egyptian Plover. On entering the town fork left and then turn right alongside the river. The bird should oblige within 10–500 m.

WINTER Yellow-billed and Marabou Storks, Sacred Ibis, Goliath and Green Herons, Spur-winged Goose, Knob-billed Duck, Hammerkop, West Africa Goshawk, African Hobby, Banded Harrier Eagle, Long-crested Hawk and Bateleur Eagles, White-backed Vulture, Lanner, Senegal Thick-knee, Wattled and Egyptian Plovers, Malachite, Pygmy and Striped Kingfishers, Yellow-bellied Parrot, Ring-necked Parakeet, Rufous-crowned and Broad-billed Rollers, Blue-cheeked, Little and Red-throated Bee-eaters, Allied and Abyssinian Ground Hornbills, White-faced Scops Owl, Yellow-fronted Tinkerbird, Fine-spotted Woodpecker, Ussher's Spinetail Swift, Senegal Puff-back Flycatcher, Wattle-eye, Green-backed Eremomela, Red-rumped Swallow, Straight-crested Helmet and Sulphur-breasted Bush Shrikes, African Golden Oriole, Scarlet-breasted Sunbird, Buffalo Weaver.

ACCESS As above. Take a two-night excursion to Georgetown. Explore around the camp after lunch on day one. Take a full-day excursion to Basse for Egyptian Plover on day two. On day three you will be transported down river by boat for the whole morning with lunch on an island. Watch for Red-throated Bee-eater along the way and small birds at lunchtime. Later you transfer back to the coast, reaching the hotels about 8 p.m.

ROUTE From Banjul.

KOTU STREAM AND FUJARA GOLF COURSE

The Kotu Stream's small estuary reaches the sea near the Kombo Beach Hotel which is thus favoured by birders. Together with the golf course (the greens are remarkable), the sewage works and the scrub towards the Casino, this is one of the finest bird areas along the coast and should keep most visitors happy for the first couple of days of their holiday. The estuary is easily worked from the bridge across Kotu Stream near the Kombo Beach. Here a good variety of Palearctic waders makes one feel at home, but there are also Pied and Giant Kingfishers, Senegal Thick-knee, Spur-winged and Wattled Plovers, Grey-headed Gull, Green and Western Reef Herons (beware the last's white phase compared with Little Egret) as well as more widespread birds such as Wire-tailed Swallow and Blue-bellied Roller.

There is a small entrance fee at the sewage works, but it is worth it for close-up views of birds difficult to find elsewhere, including Marsh Sandpiper and White-faced Tree Duck. Painted Snipe are regularly reported, but difficult to find. The Fajara Golf Course lies to the east (north) and offers rough grassland broken by thickets. The chance of being hit by balls is high as the golfers are appalling. Black-headed Plover is virtually assured here as are Piapiac, Gonolek, Beautiful and Splendid Sunbirds, Green Wood-hoopoe, Yellow-billed Shrike and Long-tailed Glossy Starling. Watch for wintering Palearctic warblers in the bushes and Black-headed Bush Shrike.

Between the Kotu Bridge and the sewage works a concrete cycle track leads west (south) to the Casino. This gives access to some excellent scrub broken inland by palm trees. This is an important area for Long-tailed Nightjar at dusk as well as Vieillot's Barbet, Abyssinian and Broad-billed Rollers, Swallow-tailed Bee-eater, the elusive Moho, honeyguides and Yellow-fronted Tinkerbird. Black-shouldered Kite are usually widespread and at Kotu Point the terns may include Royal and Lesser Crested.

WINTER Little Grebe, White-faced Tree Duck, Great White Egret, Green, Western Reef and Purple Herons, Grey Kestrel, Black-shouldered Kite, Black-headed, Wattled and Spur-winged Plovers, Senegal Thick-knee, Avocet, Black-winged Stilt, Wood, Green, Marsh and Curlew Sandpipers, Greenshank, Ruff, Bar-tailed and Black-tailed Godwits, Little Stint, Painted Snipe, Grey-headed Gull, Gull-billed, Caspian, Royal and Lesser Crested Terns, Senegal Coucal, Abyssinian, Broad-billed and Blue-bellied Rollers, Giant and Pied Kingfishers, Green Wood-hoopoe, Long-tailed Nightjar, Yellow-fronted Tinkerbird, Palm Swift, Brown and Blackcap Babblers, Yellow-throated Leaflove, Subalpine and Melodious Warblers, Crombec, Green-backed Eremomela, Grey-backed Cameroptera, Moho, Siffling Cisticola, Red-winged Warbler, Wire-tailed Swallow, Yellow-billed Shrike, Gonolek, Black-headed Bush Shrike, Piapiac, Long-tailed Glossy Starling, Yellow-billed Oxpecker, Beautiful, Splendid and Variable Sunbirds, Village Weaver, Bronze Mannikin, Warbling Silverbill, Lavender Waxbill, Red-cheeked Cordon-bleu, Senegal Firefinch.

ACCESS Most birders stay at either the Kombo Beach or Senegambia Beach Hotels. Hotels nearer Banjul are generally cheaper, noisier and more hassle. The road to the Kombo Beach crosses the Kotu Stream next to the hotel. This bridge is an early morning meeting place for birders, including several local guides – many of whom are called Lamin (not surprisingly as Lamin is usually the name of the first-born son). Though variable, most of them know their birds and will (for a fee negotiated in advance) help you to find several of the more elusive species. White-backed Night Heron and Standard-winged Nightjar are two that fall into this category. The sewage works is on the left towards the main road, surrounded by tall trees. The cycle track to the Casino is half-way between the Bridge and sewage works, and the golf course is a little way beyond Kombo Beach Hotel.

NOTE Hotels in The Gambia are attended by young men attracted by the relative wealth of the guests. They are friendly, helpful and eventually become a painful hassle. They also need pens, sweets, sponsorship and money and are loath to take 'No' for an answer. Birders have been robbed, mugged and stabbed here. *Do not* venture out *alone* anywhere near the city or the coastal strip. If you *have* to bird alone then it might be a good idea to hire a taxi driven by the biggest driver you can find.

ROUTE As Abuko.

TENDABA

To get the best from a week or two in The Gambia it is necessary to make a trip up-river, even if that means leaving an empty hotel room and unconsumed meals. Just getting away from the coast and from salt water makes a difference, species such as Yellow-billed Stork, African Fish

Eagle and Goliath Heron are immediately added to the list. There are three major up-river centres: at Basse Santa Su, Georgetown and Tendaba. The last is the nearest to the coastal hotel area, but Georgetown too can be visited by spending only a single night away from base. Tendaba is, however, well worked and does not involve spending the best part of the day on the roads. It also offers a reasonable standard of accommodation, plus excursions across the river.

The camp lies alongside the Gambia River next to Tendaba village and is backed by rice fields and mangroves to the west, scrubby hills inland, and woods, salt-marsh and fields to the east. The area around the camp has White-necked Stork, Long-crested Hawk Eagle, Abyssinian Ground Hornbill, Blue-breasted Kingfisher, Senegal Puff-back Flycatcher, Puff-back Shrike, Brubru Shrike, Brown-necked Parrot, Lesser Wood-hoopoe, Bruce's Green Pigeon and Black-rumped Waxbill. Searching may produce Black Tit among hillside trees as well as Green-backed Eremomela and Pygmy Sunbird. Crowned Crane, Knob-billed Duck and Mosque Swallow are also to be found. Many of these species are local or even absent from the coastal area, enabling a week-long list of over 250 superb species to be built up.

A cruise across the river and up Tunku Creek is offered to camp residents in order to visit Tunku village. The cruise will provide good creekside birding with Goliath Heron, Sacred Ibis, African Fish Eagle, Osprey, Senegal Thick-knee, Pygmy and Mouse-brown Sunbirds and possible White Pelican. Tunku village lies atop a small hill and you can spend the time here scanning westwards over thin scrub for Swallow-tailed Kite, as well as Carmine Bee-eater. The usual cruise continues to Kisi Bolou, the next creek to the east – ensure that this is on the itinerary before setting out. The creekside trees may hold Pel's Fishing Owl, Darter and Blue-breasted Kingfisher, and Finfoot may also be found. The last may be anywhere along the creek and its side channels, but is easily missed.

WINTER White-necked and Yellow-billed Storks, Pink-backed and White Pelicans, Spur-winged Goose, Knob-billed Duck, Goliath and Green Herons, Great White Egret, Sacred Ibis, Hammerkop, Montagu's Harrier, Osprey, Long-crested Hawk and Brown Harrier Eagles, Swallow-tailed Kite, Finfoot, Senegal Thick-knee, Crowned Crane, Wattled Plover, Collared Pratincole, Caspian and Gull-billed Terns, Pel's Fishing Owl, Malachite Kingfisher, Fine-spotted Woodpecker, Yellow-bellied Parrot, Brown-necked Parrot, Bruce's Green Pigeon, Didric Cuckoo, Swallow-tailed Bee-eater, Lesser Wood-hoopoe, Mosque Swallow, Blue-eared Glossy Starling, Long-crested Helmet, Brubru and Puff-back Shrikes, Black-headed Bush Shrike, Abyssinian Ground Hornbill, Green-backed Eremomela, Yellow White-eye, Grey Tit Flycatcher, Senegal Puff-back Flycatcher, White-crowned Robin Chat, Black Tit, Scarlet-chested, Pygmy and Mouse-brown Sunbirds, Lavender, Black-rumped and Zebra Waxbills, Yellow-fronted Canary.

ACCESS Take a one- or (preferably) two-night excursion from the coastal hotel complex, easily arranged by your tour operator's local rep. There is no point in hiring a car as you will not need it once at Tendaba. Arrange a cross-river excursion at the camp, preferably by yourselves or with other birders. If any difficulties in making arrangements contact West African Tours, PMB 222, Serredunda P.O., The Gambia. (Tel. 95258 or 95532).
ROUTE As above.

GERMANY

BAVARIAN DANUBE

For most of its length the Danube is Europe's most important waterway. Extensive modifications have caused the loss of truly wonderful marshes and flooded forests and the birds that once bred among them. Here and there the river has survived in something like its former state, such as between Regensburg and Vilshofen. The meadows, backwaters, oxbow lakes and marshy woodland here are home to superb populations of good birds, many of which are scarce in this part of Europe. Spotted Crake and Corncrake call noisily during summer nights from the meadows that, by day, hold good numbers of Black-tailed Godwit and Curlew. Reedbeds hold Purple and Night Herons, Marsh Harrier, good numbers of Blue-throat, Great Reed and a few Savi's Warblers. The flooded woods have Black and Middle Spotted Woodpeckers as well as a colony of Collared Flycatcher, while overhead there are both kites and Honey Buzzard.

SUMMER Little Bittern, Night and Purple Herons, White Stork, Garganey, Honey Buzzard, Black and Red Kites, Marsh Harrier, Spotted Crake, Corncrake, Black-tailed Godwit, Curlew, Grey-headed, Black and Middle Spotted Woodpeckers, Bluethroat, Savi's and Great Reed Warblers, Red-backed Shrike, Collared Flycatcher.

ACCESS This is a huge area to explore, but there are several bridges downstream of Regensburg that give access to the riverside marshes and woods. The Bayerischer Wald National Park to the north has some excellent woodland birds and should not be missed. These include Hazelhen, Pygmy and Tengmalm's Owls, Black and Three-toed Woodpeckers and Red-breasted Flycatcher. Reports on visits would be much appreciated.

ROUTE Regensburg lies about 120 km north of Munich.

BAVARIAN LAKES

One of the best areas in southern Germany lies between Munich and the Austrian border, towards Salzburg and Passau with lakes of various sizes, not all worth exploring: concentrate on Ismaninger Speichersee, Ammersee, Chiemsee, Eching and Moosburg and, especially, the Innstauseen. If in any doubt at all head for the latter, often referred to as the Inn Lakes.

The lower reaches of the Inn form the border between Germany and Austria, before it joins the Danube at Passau. A series of dams has turned an area of meadows into a major wetland, with islands, deltas and excellent riverine forest. Soon after their creation, River Warbler spread west to colonize the area. Other breeding birds include Purple and Night Herons, Little Bittern, Red-crested Pochard, many other duck, Marsh Harrier, Black-tailed Godwit, Bluethroat, Grey-headed and Black Woodpeckers, Penduline Tit and the occasional Mediterranean Gull. Waders can be abundant on passage, with several thousand Ruff in spring and autumn. Winter sees thousands of wildfowl including Mallard, Teal, Tufted Duck and Pochard.

Chiemsee is a huge and deep lake with extensive reedbeds at the delta of the Tiroler Achen offering breeding sites for Bittern, Red-crested Pochard, Bluethroat, and Savi's and Great Reed Warblers. The surrounding woods hold Grey-headed and Black Woodpeckers. Though used for recreation, it has passage waders and winter wildfowl including Red-crested Pochard.

Eching and Moosburg Reservoir lies near Moosburg in the Isar valley. It is a passage and winter haunt of duck, with large numbers of Goosander, but does hold the largest breeding colony of Common Terns in Bavaria.

Ismaninger is a substantial reservoir with an adjacent area of fish-ponds north-east of Munich. These rich habitats make the area one of the best in Germany for waterbirds, and there is a large colony of Black-necked Grebes associated with an even larger Black-headed Gullery. Good numbers of breeding duck include Red-crested Pochard, as well as Little Bittern, Water Rail and Penduline Tit. There are many waders on passage, and in autumn there are thousands of duck, many of which winter here.

SUMMER Black-necked Grebe, Purple and Night Herons, Bittern, Little Bittern, Pintail, Garganey, Shoveler, Gadwall, Tufted Duck, Pochard, Red-crested Pochard, Marsh Harrier, Black-tailed Godwit, Water Rail, Mediterranean, Black-headed and Common Gulls, Common Tern, Penduline Tit, Grey-headed and Black Woodpeckers, Bluethroat, River, Savi's and, Great Reed Warblers.
WINTER Teal, Shoveler, Wigeon, Pintail, Tufted Duck, Pochard, Ferruginous Duck, Red-crested Pochard, Goldeneye, Goosander.
ACCESS For the Inn Lakes follow the road along the river south of Passau as far as Simbach. Chiemsee is north of the Munich–Salzburg Autobahn. The reservoir at Moosburg lies just off Route 11 north-east of Munich, Ismaninger lies in the same direction on the road to Ismaning. The last is the private property of an electricity company and accessible only to bona fide ornithologists. Membership of one of our national societies should suffice. Write to Deutscher Bund für Vogelschutz, Achalmstrasse 33a, D7014, Kornwestheim, for details of their current Munich branch.
ROUTE Munich has excellent communications by road and air.

DUMMER

Dummer is a shallow lake some 5 km square north-east of Osnabrück. It is one of the best inland bird sites in Germany and a large area is protected as a nature reserve. There is considerable emergent vegetation, amounting to large reedbeds in some parts, which gives away to natural peat fen, open meadows, and interesting woods. Though mainly known for its typical marshland breeding birds including Little Bittern, Bittern, Marsh Harrier and a wealth of duck among the reeds, it is also noted as a migration and wintering haunt of duck. Some 30 different species have been seen at one time or another. The surrounding meadows hold Black-tailed Godwit and Ruff, and Black Tern breed on the floating vegetation debris. The marshes and moors to the north around Diepholzer hold Montagu's Harrier and are a noted haunt of Crane on migration.

SUMMER White Stork, Grey Heron, Bittern, Little Bittern, Teal, Garganey, Gadwall, Pintail, Shoveler, Pochard, Marsh Harrier, Curlew, Black-tailed Godwit, Ruff, Black Tern, Short-eared Owl.
AUTUMN AND WINTER Greylag Goose, duck.
ACCESS Leave Route 51 at Hude which is 45 km north-east of Osnabrück. Though large areas are in fact nature reserve, most of the lake can be worked from public roads. In spite of being comparatively small, explorations of the local woods adds the typical wealth of German woodpeckers and woodland species, and helps form a useful holiday centre.
ROUTE Via Osnabrück

FEDERSEE

The Federsee is a small reed-marsh and lake, lying just west of Biberach near Buchau, but over 100 species have been recorded breeding here. Among these, Black-necked Grebe, Purple Heron, both bitterns, White Stork, Marsh Harrier, Honey Buzzard, Red Kite, Common Tern, Black Woodpecker, Bluethroat and even Black Grouse can be found. On passage there are often good numbers of waders and up to 150 Black Terns. Today, Federsee is a summer resort, with boardwalks, display signs and visitor amenities, but is still worth more than the hour or so that most non-birding visitors spend here. The staff are usually pleased to meet anyone seriously interested in birds, and can be very helpful in guiding one around.

SUMMER Black-necked and Great Crested Grebes, Garganey, Gadwall, White Stork, Bittern, Purple Heron, Little Bittern, Marsh Harrier, Red Kite, Hobby, Honey Buzzard, Spotted and Little Crakes, Water Rail, Curlew, Common Tern, Long-eared Owl, Black Grouse, Willow and Bearded Tits, Black Woodpecker, Bluethroat, Savi's, Reed and Grasshopper Warblers.
ACCESS From Bad Buchau follow signs to Federsee Museum, where there is a free car park. There is a small entrance fee, and boardwalks lead to open water where boats may be hired. It is a bit dude, but the birds are good.
ROUTE Leave the E11 Autobahn at Ulm and take Route 311 to Riedlingen. Turn left outside the town to Buchau.

KIEL BAY

Kiel Bay lies on the Baltic shores of Schleswig-Holstein and is littered with excellent birding sites. There are so many splendid areas that the region is worth a holiday at almost any time of the year. For simplicity's sake this account is divided into two halves – the coastal area and the inland lakes – though in practice birders will doubtless flick from one to the other.

These lakes are the westernmost extension of a glacier-created string of waters that extends across the north of the former East Germany (the Mecklenburg Lakes) and northern Poland (the Masurian Lakes) to beyond the Russian border. There are so many good lakes that it is hard to pick out the real gems and any visitor should search as many different waters as time allows. Those mentioned may prove best, but do not ignore the hundreds of lesser waters. The area is outstanding as the breeding haunt of White-tailed Eagle, several pairs of which breed at scattered localities. Lebrader, Grosser Plöner See and Warder See all have at least one pair, though the fish-ponds at Boek are generally regarded as the best place to see this bird. Additionally, there are good numbers of Bittern, Marsh Harrier, Great Reed and Savi's Warblers and Red-backed Shrike.

One of the best lakes is Lebrader, north of Plön, where Black-necked and Red-necked Grebes breed, with Bittern, Little Bittern, Marsh Harrier and Great Reed Warbler. Grosser Plöner See has Black-necked Grebe, Bittern, Goosander, Goldeneye, Ruff and Thrush Nightingale, and a tiny population of Mediterranean Gull. Like other lakes in this area, these are good for migrants and winter wildfowl with good numbers of Greylag Goose and ducks. Plön is a good centre to explore all of these waters.

The coast of Kiel Bay is one of the best areas in Germany. There are several estuaries, many marshes and outstanding seabird colonies. There is much worth exploring and selection has had to be rigorous. The area at the mouth of the Flensburger Förde north of Gelting is a winter haunt of waders and wildfowl, including good numbers of Barnacle Geese. To the south, sandbars at the mouth of the Schlei (Schleimunde) are intersected by creeks, marshes and meadows, offering a home to over a thousand pairs of terns, as well as Avocets and Red-breasted Mergansers. This area also holds many waders, duck and Brent Geese on passage and in winter. Approach the peninsula to the south via Olpenitz: it is wardened in the breeding season.

Bottsand is a low half-island of sand with adjacent salt-marsh holding breeding Shelduck, Red-breasted Merganser, Kentish Plover, Avocet and Little Tern. It is also a major wader area. Bottsand lies on the eastern shore at the mouth of the Kieler Förde and is reached by taking the Probsteier road towards Barsbeker and continuing past Barsbeker Lake to the coast. Farther to the east is Hohwacht, a good area for migrants, with the nearby Kleiner Binnensee separated from the Baltic by a dune beach. Breeding birds include Goosander, Marsh Harrier, Ruff, Avocet and Dunlin.

It would be a pity to miss the marshes of the island of Fehmarn. In the west there are several waters with Greylag Goose, Red-crested Pochard, Red-necked Grebe, Bittern, Marsh Harrier and Red-breasted Merganser. The island is connected to the mainland by a bridge.

SUMMER (lakes) Black-necked and Red-necked Grebes, Greylag Goose, Mute Swan, Gadwall, Pochard, Goldeneye, Bittern, Little Bittern, White-tailed Eagle, Marsh Harrier, Ruff, Common and Mediterranean Gulls, Common Tern, Thrush Nightingale, Red-backed Shrike, Great Reed and Savi's Warblers. (coast) Red-necked Grebe, Greylag Goose, Red-crested Pochard, Red-breasted Merganser, Bittern, Eider, Marsh Harrier, Kentish Plover, Black-tailed Godwit, Avocet, Arctic, Common, Sandwich, Little and, Black Terns.

PASSAGE (coast) Greylag, Barnacle and Brent Geese, Bewick's and Whooper Swans, Wigeon, Pintail, Scaup, Eider, Long-tailed Duck, Scoter, White-tailed Eagle, Osprey, Honey Buzzard, Spotted Redshank, Greenshank, Knot, Little Stint, Curlew and Broad-billed Sandpipers, Snow Bunting.

ACCESS Routes and access details are indicated above in the main text.

ROUTE From Hamburg north to the sites area.

MAIN BACKWATERS

Schweinfurt lies due east of Frankfurt on a section of the Main that has managed to survive in something like its natural state. Here there are extensive areas of riverine forest as well as backwater oxbow lakes, marshes, ponds and reedbeds. The whole creates an excellent area for birds, which include both bitterns, both kites, Spotted and Little Crakes, Black and Grey-headed Woodpeckers, Bluethroat, Collared Flycatcher and Great Reed Warbler. Winter brings duck and there are passage waders in some variety. For the birding executive stuck in Frankfurt for any length of time this lovely stretch of river offers an alternative to the similar Rhine Backwaters.

SUMMER Bittern, Little Bittern, Honey Buzzard, Black and Red Kites, Marsh Harrier, Corncrake, Spotted and Little Crakes, Grey-headed, Black and Middle Spotted Woodpeckers, Bluethroat, Great Reed Warbler, Collared Flycatcher, Red-backed Shrike, Ortolan Bunting.

ACCESS The best part of the area lies between Schweinfurt and Volkach to the south, together with the area around Dettelbach. Volkach is right on the river and offers easy access.

ROUTE Take the E5 Autobahn from Frankfurt and exit east of Wurzburg right next to Dettelbach.

MECKLENBURG LAKES

Half-way between Berlin and Rostock lies a 500-square-mile lowland containing over 100 shallow lakes with reedbeds and mixed forests. It is centred on Lake Müritz, Germany's second largest lake, and the Müritz National Park – worth a trip in itself, with 14 breeding species of raptor. Waren, at the north end of the lake, is the administrative centre, with a tourist office (in the Neuer Markt), the Müritz-Museum, seven hotels/pensions, a youth hostel and two good camp sites. One can drive, cycle or walk into the Park from Waren and there are numerous forest trails to the lakes, some with tower hides. Sheet 2 of the 1:75,000 Mecklenburgische Seenplatte map (*Wanderkarte*) is essential and is widely available. Bicycles may be hired (*Fahrradverleih*) by the day from Waren, Ecktannen, Schwarzenhof, Speck and Boek. The last two places have information centres.

Nearly 150 species breed, including White-tailed Eagle (up to 15 feed at the Boek fish-ponds), Osprey (nesting on pylons between Federow and Speck), Crane (flocks of 20–40), both kites, three harriers, Lesser Spotted Eagle, Goshawk, Black Stork and Red-crested Pochard. White Stork nests in Kargow, 7 km east of Waren.

Caspian Tern is regular in autumn and over 1000 Crane gather in October, when 30,000–50,000 White-fronted and Bean Geese begin to arrive. Winter sees large flocks of Whooper and Bewick's Swans and Smew on ice-free lakes, with regular Rough-legged Buzzard, Peregrine and Merlin together with Nutcracker and Waxwing in invasion years. The Müritzhof is a renowned viewpoint for raptors and Crane.

Two other good sites are the Krakower Obersee just west of the Rostock autobahn west of Waren, and Nonnenhof at the southern end of the Tollensee south of Neubrandenburg. Farther east is the Galenbecker See. Drive to Galenbeck village 12 km along a minor road east-south-east from Friedland, and take the path to the observation post on the south-western shore.

SUMMER Red-necked Grebe, Bittern, Little Bittern, Black and White Storks, Red-crested Pochard, Honey Buzzard, Black and Red Kites, White-tailed and Lesser Spotted Eagles, Marsh, Hen and Montagu's Harriers, Goshawk, Osprey, Hobby, Spotted Crake, Crane, Green Sandpiper, Black Tern, Black and, Middle Spotted Woodpeckers, Woodlark, Thrush Nightingale, Savi's, River, Marsh, Great Reed and Barred Warblers, Red-breasted Flycatcher, Bearded and Penduline Tits, Golden Oriole, Red-backed and Great Grey Shrikes, Raven, Crossbill, Scarlet Rosefinch.

AUTUMN Raptors, Whooper Swan, Greylag, Bean and, White-fronted Geese, Red-crested Pochard, Crane, waders, Little Gull, Caspian Tern.

WINTER Whooper and Bewick's Swans, Bean and White-fronted Geese, Rough-legged Buzzard, Peregrine, Merlin, Hen Harrier, Short-eared Owl, woodpeckers, Nutcracker and Waxwing (irregular).

ACCESS The best camp sites, all on Lake Müritz, are: Kamerun, off Route 192 south-west of Waren, with excellent woodland birding around the site; Ecktannen near the park entrance south-east of Waren; and Boek, reached by car via Rechlin at the southern end of Müritz. The fish-ponds are alongside the Rechlin–Boek road at Bolter Muhle. The Ecktannen–Speck road gives access on foot to the main lakes, marshes and forests. There is no access for cars between Speck and Boek.

ROUTE The area lies between the Berlin–Rostock autobahn A19 and the Berlin–Neubrandenburg road Route 96. It may be reached from Hamburg via the A24, turning north onto the A19 just before Wittstock. From Hannover either head north to Hamburg, or east for Berlin and follow the outer ring to the A24 and A19. Do not attempt to go cross-country.

OBERAMMERGAU

Oberammergau is an ideal base for the Bavarian Alps lying in the Ammer valley by the first real mountains south of Munich. The valley north-west to Saulgauts and south-east to Ettal lies between 600 and 900 m and the steep sides of the valley are covered with an extensive growth of conifers. Up to 1400 m firs predominate but then gradually give way to pines, which thin out to the tree limit at 1850 m. The valley floor is mainly meadows of varying dampness and apart from a beech wood at Staffelsee there are few deciduous trees and bushes. Birds found in this habitat include Red-backed Shrike, Pied Flycatcher, Golden Oriole (in the birches near the Wahrubuhel), Black Redstart, Wryneck, Serin and Tawny Pipit, the last on dry cattle pastures. The valley-side fir woods hold Crested Tit, Nutcracker, Fieldfare, Crossbill, Siskin and woodpeckers including Grey-headed (most common), Green and Great Spotted. There are also Lesser Spotted, Middle Spotted, Three-toed, White-backed and Black in the area enabling all the western European woodpeckers to be seen in a single valley, or so I am told! The nature reserve at Karwendel boasts 20–30 pairs each of Black, White-backed and Three-toed, three of the most 'wanted' birds in Europe. Of equal value are the breeding Black Grouse, Capercaillie and 20–30 pairs of Hazelhen, together with Eagle, Tengmalm's and Pygmy Owls. Such quality birds are hard to come by, but abundant Bonelli's Warbler, and good populations of Red-breasted Flycatcher and Citril Finch make birding in this area a real pleasure. There are even a few pairs of Wallcreeper.
   Above the tree line Crag Martin, Alpine Accentor and Alpine Chough can be found, while Golden Eagle, Honey Buzzard, and Goshawk breed in good numbers and are frequently seen overhead.

SUMMER Golden Eagle, Goshawk, Honey Buzzard, Buzzard, Peregrine, Long-eared Owl, Black, Great Spotted, Middle Spotted, Lesser Spotted, White-backed, Three-toed, Green and Grey-headed Woodpeckers, Wryneck, Capercaillie, Black and Hazelhen, Ptarmigan, Eagle, Tengmalm's and Pygmy Owls, Alpine Chough, Golden Oriole, Nutcracker, Fieldfare, Alpine Accentor, Crag Martin, Red-backed Shrike, Tawny and Water Pipits, Short-toed Treecreeper, Firecrest, Crested Tit, Bonelli's Warbler, Red-breasted Flycatcher, Siskin, Citril Finch, Crossbill.
ACCESS The region is easily explored from Oberammergau or Garmish-Partenkirchen. The Ammergauer Berge and Karwendel areas include nature reserves. Access to the high tops is facilitated by development of the area as a ski resort and roads lead through the forests for major specialities. The Staffelsee, north of Murnau, is virtually devoid of birds (add Great Crested Grebe to the trip list), but has beech woods on the south side for woodpeckers. Noth Kar-Spitz is good for altitude species, including Citril Finch.
ROUTE Munich Airport is about 100 km from the area via the N11. Plentiful accommodation and camp sites.

ODER VALLEY AT SCHWEDT

The Oder forms the border with Poland for 180 km. Between Oderberg and Gartz a string of canals runs parallel to the river about 2 km into Germany for 35 km. The land between canal and river is a floodplain dissected by innumerable old channels, forming a sinuous polder-like area. Half-way along, Schwedt stands by the canal and affords the only crossing into Poland. Fortunately it also gives easy access on foot to the best nature reserves. These are known locally as polders and hold such specialities as Spotted Crake (5–15 pairs), Corncrake (about 60 calling males), Bluethroat (up to ten pairs) and Penduline Tit (20–30 pairs), plus an amazing warbler list including Savi's (30 pairs), River (60), Grasshopper (50), Aquatic (10–20), Marsh (150–200), Great Reed (10–20) and Barred (15–30).

In winter and spring the floods hold up to 1000 Whooper and 150 Bewick's Swans, 200 Smew, with many thousands of Bean and White-fronted Geese and other wildfowl. Many of these wildfowl are also present in winter together with up to ten White-tailed Eagle and the odd Peregrine.

SUMMER Black-necked Grebe, Black and White Storks, Garganey, Goosander, Black and Red Kites, Quail, Spotted and Little Crakes, Corncrake, Crane, Ruff, Black Tern, Kingfisher, Thrush Nightingale, Black Woodpecker, Bluethroat, Grasshopper, River, Savi's, Aquatic, Marsh, Great Reed and Barred Warblers, Penduline Tit, Scarlet Rosefinch.

WINTER/PASSAGE White Stork, Bewick's and Whooper Swans, Bean and White-fronted Geese, Garganey, Goosander, Smew, White-tailed Eagle, Crane, waders, Black Tern.

ACCESS Cross the Hohensaaten–Friedrichsthaler Wasserstrasse (canal) from Schwedt and park. Walk north-east 4 km to the best polder, or south-west 4 km. Nearby areas may be explored by crossing the canal at Gatow north of Schwedt or at Zutzen to the south; both villages lie just off Route 2. The nearest campsites are around Angermünde. While exploring this superb area, do not miss the nature reserve of Felchowsee. This fine lake lies only a short distance to the south-west and its reedbeds and wooded shores hold both bitterns, Spotted and Little Crakes, up to 70 pairs of Black Tern and the odd pair of Crane. Some 5–10 White-tailed Eagles are present in winter.

ROUTE From Berlin take A11 (E28) to Szczecin (signposted Stettin), turning off on Route 198 for Angermünde. Follow Route 2 to Schwedt.

RHINE BACKWATERS

Between Karlsruhe and Mainz the Rhine formerly meandered over a wide floodplain, creating a multitude of backwaters and oxbows. Many remain as lakes and marshes, some creating islands. The largest and most famous of these wetlands is the Kühkopf, but there are many others, including the Roxheimer Altrhein on the west bank above Worms, Lampertsheimer Altrhein on the eastern bank and Gimbsheim-Eicher Altrhein and Fischsee to the north. Kühkopf lies downstream west of Darmstadt. An island with areas of open water, reedbeds, damp meadows and belts of woodland, it provides opportunities for over a hundred species to breed, with a hundred more recorded as visitors. Breeders include duck, crakes, Little Bittern, kites, Goshawk, Black and Middle Spotted Woodpeckers, Golden Oriole and Bluethroat. The island is connected to the mainland by bridge, making this a really attractive and easily accessible summer birding spot.

The two other wetlands to the south do not support anything like the same variety of species, though Roxheimer has a good population of Little Bittern, Great Crested Grebe and Little Ringed Plover. Lampertsheimer also has Marsh Harrier, Black Kite and three species of woodpecker.

SUMMER Grey Heron, Little Bittern, Garganey, Shoveler, Goshawk, Red and Black Kites, Buzzard, Honey Buzzard, Hobby, Spotted and Little Crakes, Corncrake, Quail, Curlew, Little Ringed Plover, Long-eared and Short-eared Owls, Grey-headed, Middle Spotted and Black Woodpeckers, Great Grey, Woodchat and Red-backed Shrikes, Hoopoe, Golden Oriole, Bluethroat, Icterine Warbler, Firecrest, Serin.
PASSAGE Osprey, Crane, Garganey, Pintail, Pochard, Tufted Duck, Snipe, Green Sandpiper.
ACCESS Kühkopf is reached by bridge from Stockstadt, which is on Route 44 north of Mannheim. Roads facilitate exploration, though the heronry is fenced off. Lampertsheimer is off the same road to the east, only a short distance from Mannheim, while Roxheimer is reached via Route 9 along the western bank of the Rhine.
ROUTE Frankfurt Airport is one of the busiest in Europe, with fine international connections and access to the Autobahn network.

RÜGEN AND THE BALTIC COAST

Sandbars, peninsulas and islands guard huge shallow lagoons (*Boddens*) and tidal inlets along 200 km of the coast of eastern Germany, from Rostock to the Polish border. This area can be difficult to work and main roads crowded in summer, but away from resorts there are great expanses of wild marshland, dunes and rough grazing unlike anywhere else in central Europe. Rügen and Usedom are the largest islands, joined to the mainland by causeways. The west side of Rügen is a good base, with several nature reserves and spectacular autumn concentrations of Crane and geese. In fact a late September–early October trip is worthwhile for these species alone.

A few Caspian Terns breed on inaccessible islands such as Heuwiese. Feeding and migrating birds may be seen around Rügen and the north of Usedom: over 100 were recorded in one September day. Five pairs of White-tailed Eagle breed on Usedom. Kap Arkona at Rügen's north tip has Scarlet Rosefinch in summer and is well placed for migrants. Jasmund National Park north of Sassnitz has breeding Red-breasted Flycatcher and tourists!. Red-backed Shrike, scattered Barred Warbler and almost certainly a few Greenish and Aquatic Warblers breed. There are several colonies of Avocet, Ruff, Merganser and sea terns and a few pairs of Mediterranean Gull.

En route to this area from Lübeck, do not overlook the Conventer See, by the coast just north of Bad Doberan. This long-established reserve has Red-necked Grebe, Savi's, River, Grasshopper and Marsh Warblers, Thrush Nightingale and both Bearded and Penduline Tits.

In autumn and winter this coast has vast numbers of wildfowl and waders, including over 100,000 Whitefronts, 60,000 Greylag and 20,000 Bean Geese. The main attraction is the 25,000 Crane stopping in September and October at traditional sites such as the Udarser Wiek on Rügen.

SUMMER Red-necked Grebe, Bittern, White Stork, Greylag Goose, Garganey, Red-breasted Merganser, Black and Red Kites, White-tailed Eagle, Marsh Harrier, Avocet, Ruff, Mediterranean Gull, Caspian Tern, Thrush Nightingale, Grasshopper, River, Savi's, Marsh, Barred, Aquatic and Greenish Warblers, Red-breasted Flycatcher, Bearded Tit, Penduline Tit, Red-backed Shrike, Scarlet Rosefinch.
PASSAGE Wildfowl, waders, Crane, Caspian Tern.
ACCESS For **Conventer See** take the Warnemünde road north from Bad Doberan; after 4 km turn left to Börgerende. The lake, with a path to a hide and a tower hide, is on the left 3 km down this road just before the coast. A free causeway leads from the port of Stralsund onto **Rügen**. The tourist office in Bergen, in the centre of the island, sells large-scale maps. On the west side, drive via Gingst over a bridge to the peaceful island of Ummanz where a campsite overlooks the Bodden, with the long island of Hiddensee on the horizon. Rügen has many summer campsites and hotels. Ummanz is virtually traffic-free and bounded by marshes and wet meadows; its east side overlooking the Udarser Wiek is excellent for migrant Crane. North of Gingst a frequent car ferry, the *Wittower Fähre*, gives access to Kap Arkona (via Altenkirchen) and east Rügen, enabling a circular route. Usedom is reached by causeways from Wolgast and Anklam, south-east of Stralsund.
ROUTE From Lübeck take the 105 to Wismar, Bad Doberan, Rostock and Stralsund. This can be congested in summer (there are bypasses) but is the only reasonable route from the west.

SCHLUTTSIEL

This wetland and coastal area lies on the Waddensee coast of Jutland, 25 km south of the Danish border, at the northern end of what is a fine birding area. In fact, good bird habitat extends right along this coast from the border to Hamburger Hallig and beyond. At Schluttsiel, a road runs behind the sea-wall and is separated from the lake by an area of damp meadows. There are good reedbeds that attract Bittern and Marsh Harrier, and among the colony of Black-headed Gulls there are regular Mediterranean. Little Gulls also breed and flocks build up in summer to reasonable numbers. The meadows hold Black-tailed Godwit, plus a good variety of passage species. There is a good movement of birds over the beach at high tide.

To the south, the sand banks offshore hold good populations of Common, Arctic and Sandwich Terns and incredible numbers of passage waders. The figure of 1,000,000 birds has been mentioned. To these can be added 250,000 ducks and a few thousand Barnacle Geese, among which Red-breasted Goose is comparatively regular. Though these populations are centred on the offshore islands, much can be seen from the mainland.

SUMMER Bittern, Marsh Harrier, Black-tailed Godwit, Avocet, Mediterranean and Little Gulls, Arctic, Common and Sandwich Terns.
PASSAGE Dunlin, Knot, Redshank, Oystercatcher.
WINTER Bewick's Swan, Barnacle Goose.
ACCESS The whole of this area can be explored by road and, though there are several nature reserves here, there are few restrictions on access.
ROUTE Husum is the nearest big town.

SCHWERIN AND THE ELBETAL

This group of sites straddles the Hamburg–Berlin autobahn. Schwerin, with its impressive castle almost surrounded by the wide Schweriner See, makes a good centre. Not far to the north are the two shallow Dambecker lakes with 80–100 breeding pairs of Black-necked and ten pairs of Red-necked Grebes, 20–30 pairs of Black Terns and a few Ferruginous Duck.

South-east of Schwerin, near the autobahn, the Lewitz fish-ponds have been a nature reserve since 1938. These cover c.700 ha and support 20–25 pairs of Marsh Harriers and Red-necked (18–25 pairs) and Black-necked Grebes (2–6 pairs) breed. Garganey, Red-crested Pochard and Ferruginous Duck breed most years as well as Osprey, Spotted and Little Crakes, a single pair of Crane and up to 35 pairs of Penduline Tit. Lewitz is excellent in winter too, with up to 1000 Bewick's and 150 Whooper Swans, 2000 Whitefronts, 2000 Bean Geese and 500 Goosander among many thousands of other duck. Four or five White-tailed Eagles are regular at this season.

A little nearer Hamburg is a complex of valley lakes and mainly coniferous forests known as the Naturpark Lauenburgische Seen, around the old towns of Mölln and Ratzeburg on the west side of the former border, with the adjoining Naturpark Schaalsee on the east side. This attractive area has breeding White Stork, Black Woodpecker, Honey Buzzard and Goosander, with White-tailed Eagle and Crane passing through.

To the south and south-east the Naturpark Elbetal stretches along the eastern side of the Elbe as far as Havelberg, with over 130 pairs of White Stork (including over 20 occupied nests in Rünstädt) plus Black Stork, kites, Osprey, White-tailed Eagle, Honey Buzzard, Crane and Black-tailed Godwit. The Untere Havel marshes and Gülper See south of Havelberg have large breeding populations of Savi's and Great Reed Warblers, Penduline Tit, several Black Tern colonies, Black-tailed Godwit and a few Corncrake. Up to 7000 Cranes and 50,000 Bean Geese gather here in late autumn.

SUMMER Red-necked and Black-necked Grebes, Bittern, Black and White Storks, Garganey, Red-crested Pochard, Ferruginous Duck, Goldeneye, Goosander, Honey Buzzard, Black and Red Kites, White-tailed Eagle, Marsh Harrier, Osprey, Hobby, Spotted Crake, Corncrake, Crane, Ruff, Black-tailed Godwit, Black Tern, Black Woodpecker, Savi's and Great Reed Warblers, Bearded and, Penduline Tits, Raven, Crossbill.
PASSAGE White Stork, Bean and White-fronted Geese, Black and Red Kites, White-tailed Eagle, Osprey, Crane.
WINTER Bewick's and Whooper Swans, Bean, White-fronted and Barnacle Geese, White-tailed Eagle.
ACCESS Schwerin has a wide choice of accommodation, and campsites around the Schweriner See. For **Dambecker See** head north from the city up Route 106; after 16 km (2 km past Zickhusen) turn left to Wendisch Rambow along a minor road which leads to the village and lake. Walk north beside the southern lake; the track crosses a stream to reach the northern lake. The **Lewitz fish-ponds** are 15 km north-east of Ludwigslust. Several roads lead east to them from the Schwerin–Ludwigslust Route 106 north and south of its junction with the A24. During the breeding season there are some restrictions on access to both Dambecker See and Lewitz. The **Lauenburgische** district can be explored from Ratzeburg or Mölln each

of which has a good campsite. The A24 just south of Mölln gives access to the Schwerin area. The **Elbetal** extends from Boizenburg, south of Mölln, south-eastwards almost as far as Havelberg. The free leaflet *Der Naturpark Elbetal*, from tourist offices, contains an excellent large-scale map. Accommodation is limited but there are camp-sites at Malliss (Dömitz), Lenzen and Wittenberge. The Untere Havel marshes are directly south of Havelberg, across the Havel; turn left and keep on the south side of the river. After 13 km a car ferry back over the Havel leads to Rhinow from which take the minor road to Gülpe for the Gülper See.
ROUTE East from Hamburg, leave the A24 after about 35 km for Mölln and Ratzeburg, after 80 km for Schwerin, or after 100 km for Lewitz (Ludwigslust junction). The Elbetal lies to the south and may all be worked from Route 5, Boizenburg–Ludwigslust–Perleberg–Kyritz; or east from Hannover on the Berlin autobahn and at junction 70 (Magdeburg) take Route 189 northwards all the way to Wittenberge (120 km).

STECHLINSEE

Between the southern boundary of Müritz National Park and Rheinsberg is a scenic maze of irregular lakes and channels with mixed woodland and small farms. Unlike the Müritz lakes, some of these are quite deep, 68 m in the case of the largest, the 424 ha Stechlinsee. This attractive lake is surrounded by mature mixed forest, through which a walking trail makes a complete circuit of about 15 km. The main interest is in the woodland breeding birds which in 1990 included 30–35 pairs each of Red-breasted Flycatcher and Golden Oriole, some ten pairs each of Black and Lesser Spotted Woodpeckers, with a few Middle Spotted as well. There are also Osprey and both kites and a good chance of Goshawk, White-tailed Eagle and Crane here, as well as 20–25 pairs of breeding Goldeneye.

SUMMER Goldeneye, Goshawk, Red and Black Kites, White-tailed Eagle, Osprey, Crane, Green Sandpiper, Black, Middle Spotted and Lesser Spotted Woodpeckers, Savi's and Great Reed Warblers, Red-breasted Flycatcher, Golden Oriole, Raven.
ACCESS Head for Neuglobsow at the eastern corner of the lake, where there is parking, a camp site and a youth hostel. A well-marked track leads right round the lake and can be comfortably walked in a day.
ROUTE Just on the 1:75,000 map mentioned under Mecklenburg Lakes (*see* page 90), and reached from Waren via Neustrelitz and Fürstenberg (80 km). From the latter take the Menz road south-west and after 5 km turn off west to Neuglobsow. From Rheinsberg, head east to Menz (10 km) then north to Neuglobsow (5 km). The area is 70 km north of Berlin.

VESSERTAL AND SCHWARZATAL

Two forest nature reserves in the Thuringer Wald south of Erfurt. The Vessertal (Vesser valley) covers 1834 ha between Schleusingen and Schmiedefeld, while the 600 ha Schwarzatal reserve follows 5 km of the Schwarza valley south-west of Bad Blankenburg. Both hold a few Goshawk, Pygmy and Tengmalm's Owls and Black and Middle Spotted Woodpeckers. You may also see Black Grouse and Capercaillie at Vessertal, with 15 pairs of Red-breasted Flycatcher and ten of Nutcracker. Schwarzatal also has a pair of Eagle Owl and ten of Grey-headed Woodpecker.

SUMMER Honey Buzzard, Red Kite, Goshawk, Hobby, Black Grouse, Capercaillie, Eagle, Pygmy, Long-eared and Tengmalm's Owls, Nightjar, Wryneck, Grey-headed, Black, Middle Spotted and Lesser Spotted Woodpeckers, Woodlark, Dipper, Firecrest, Red-breasted Flycatcher, Nutcracker, Raven, Crossbill.

ACCESS Take the Suhl road Route 247 north from Schleusingen for 2 km, then turn right to Breitenbach. Park at the north end of the village and walk northwards upstream beside the River Vesser. This track follows the river for 6 km as far as the village of Vesser. For Schwarzatal leave Schleusingen by Route 4 for Ilmenau, where take Route 88 to Bad Blankenburg (63 km). In the town centre turn right (south) just before the road crosses the River Schwarza and keep on the west side of the river. The road follows the winding river along both valley sides but there are parallel walking trails, which start on the edge of the town.

ROUTE Thuringer Wald lies south of the Eisenach–Erfurt–Gera autobahn, the A4 (E40). Turn off by Erfurt along Route 4 for Ilmenau and Schleusingen, or by Weimar along Route 85 for Rudolstadt and Bad Blankenburg.

WESER ESTUARY

The north coast of Germany is lined by the Waddensee and broken by several major estuaries, including the Ems, Elbe and Weser. Each is excellent for birds at all seasons, and it is somewhat invidious to pick out one as being best. In fact, there are splendid birding opportunities along the length of this coast and almost anywhere makes a good base for a holiday.

The Weser, downstream from Bremerhaven, is typical, with huge areas of intertidal mud and sand backed by seawalls and lush grazing meadows. Immediately to the west is Jadebusen, a shallow sea bay with sand banks, mud-flats and an intricate network of creeks. These two areas are a superb feeding ground for waders and wildfowl and a noted haunt of wintering geese and Avocet. Offshore, at the mouth of the complex, the island of Mellum is a strictly controlled nature reserve with breeding Shelduck and a huge gullery. It is also a major high-tide roost for many of the winter waders.

In summer the surrounding marshes hold good numbers of Avocet, Black-tailed Godwit and Ruff, while during passage periods waders pass through in both number in variety.

SUMMER Avocet, Black-tailed Godwit, Ruff, Sandwich Tern.
WINTER Greylag, White-fronted and Brent Geese, Wigeon, Pintail, Shelduck, Bar-tailed and Black-tailed Godwits, Knot, Curlew.
PASSAGE Whimbrel, Black-tailed Godwit, Little Stint, Little Gull.
ACCESS The **Jadebusen** can be worked at several points; around Dangast is as good as any. Even near Wilhelmshaven there are excellent marshes, and the ferry to Eckwarderhörne may prove splendid in winter. The area around this peninsula between two great tidal zones is known as **Butjadinger Land** and the coastline here is fine for marsh and shoreline birds. The island of Mellum may be visited only with the warden's guidance.
ROUTE Wilhelmshaven and Bremerhaven make good starting points.

GIBRALTAR

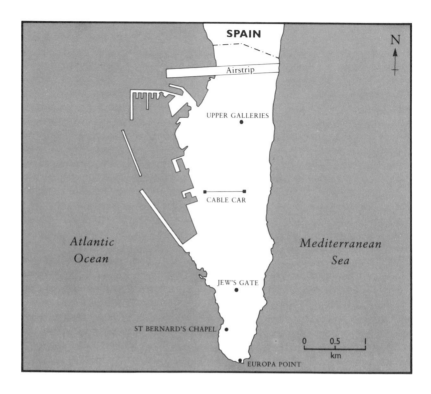

The Rock of Gibraltar stands sentinel at the entrance to the Mediterranean and has been of strategic importance since being described as one of the Pillars of Hercules. Not surprisingly, it has experienced a somewhat turbulent history, but today it is staunchly British, in spite of the fact that Spanish is the national language. Its 'Britishness' is evident everywhere, from tall-helmeted 'Bobbies' to English pubs selling warm English beer. Despite its gross overpopulation, especially of cars, it remains one of the most dramatic birding places in Europe. The 25-km crossing between Europe and Africa is, along with the much narrower Bosporus, the major concentration route of European raptors. Indeed, there are more birds passing overhead during peak seasons than at the more famous site. Most numerous are Black Kite and Honey Buzzard, which often pass over in flocks several hundred strong. Short-toed and Booted Eagles, Goshawk and Sparrowhawk, harriers and, of course, White Stork are also numerous. No fewer than 17 species of raptor regularly pass over Gibraltar. Numbers are largest in autumn, but the birds tend to be higher than in the spring. White Stork is the earliest spring migrant, with Honey Buzzard the latest. Best seasons are late March and late September for the widest variety of species.

WARNING Migration is always best with a westerly wind. If an easterly, the Levanter, is blowing, it is better to cross the border and travel westwards in Spain to the rubbish tip on the right-hand side of the N340 before Tarifa, or to the viewpoint on the left-hand side slightly earlier. In either case, Griffon Vulture will be a bonus.

Best places to watch are Jew's Gate in spring (Peregrines on display almost continuously) and Princess Caroline's Battery and the Upper Galleries in autumn. Other good birds can also be seen, including an excellent passage of seabirds from Europa Point, and Barbary Partridge at St Bernard's Chapel, especially in the evening. Grounded migrants may be sought anywhere on the Rock where there is cover.

Inevitably the visiting raptor-watcher will also wish to see something of adjacent Spain and, indeed, the open border offers easy access to several splendid areas of neighbouring Andalucia. Barbate is described under that country and the Ojen area especially is both close and highly attractive. If a Levanter is blowing, particularly in spring, a trip across the border is essential.

There are several good sites, apart from those mentioned above. Los Barrios has White Stork and Lesser Kestrel and a nearby rubbish tip is a haunt of Black and Red Kites, plus any number of other Strait-crossing raptors. The deserted town of Castellar de la Frontera, now mainly a haunt of peaceful hippies, has Lesser Kestrel and Griffon Vulture. It is also very picturesque and enjoys great views. The Sotogrande Estate to the east is worth a trip for a fine creek with herons, egrets, waders, terns and gulls.

Be quite clear – Gibraltar is superb for raptors in late March and, when a westerly is blowing, there are raptors beating low over the sea in dramatic numbers.

PASSAGE Cory's and Mediterranean Shearwaters, Gannet, White Stork, Short-toed and Booted Eagles, Osprey, Goshawk, Sparrowhawk, Black Kite, Honey Buzzard, Montagu's Harrier, Barbary Partridge, Hoopoe, Sardinian Warbler.

ACCESS Local maps of the Rock are available free at tourist information centres and at most hotels. Taxis are cheap and have a fixed-rate system. Most have radios, so even an occupied cab can be waved down and asked to request another to pick you up from any part of Gibraltar. Car hire is unnecessary, except for trips to Spain. Best excursions are towards Tarifa and to the lovely Castellar de la Frontera. Pass through the frontier to La Linea and take the Algeciras road. At the junction with the N340 turn left, and then after 3 km right towards Jimena. After 10 km fork left and climb to Castellar.

ROUTE Gibraltar has an international airport with an exciting runway extending into the sea.

GREECE

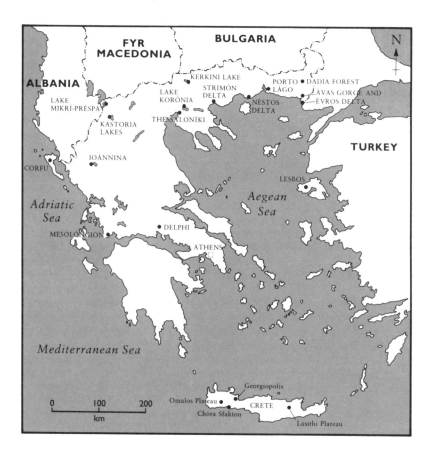

CORFU

Corfu is the 'green' island of Greece, and its trees and meadows present a sharp contrast to the mainland only a few kilometres to the east. It consists of a high rocky area in the wide north and a low-lying narrow region to the south. Though most of the best bird areas lie in the north, at no great distance from the airport, there is one major attraction at the Alikes saltpans that must draw the visitor to the extreme south of the island. The other main birding areas are: Antinioti Lagoon in the north, alongside the coastal road; the northern mountains, rising to over 900 m at Pandokrátor; the plain of Ropa in the 'mid-west'; and Korission Lagoon in the south-west. A cemetery in Corfu town (Kérkira), where gravestones document the British period of control, even boasts a wide variety of carefully protected wild orchids. There are, of course, several other excellent spots, but visitors with time at a premium should certainly include these areas in their itinerary.

Corfu is a splendid migration spot, rather than home to a wealth of exciting birds. Of most interest are Cretzschmar's Bunting, which breeds, and spring migrants such as Collared and Semi-collared Flycatchers, Red-throated Pipit, White-winged Black Tern and Red-footed Falcon, with the chance of Great Snipe, Olive-tree Warbler or Saker Falcon. From April to mid-May birds are always coming and going, and a daily watch at a good area can be rewarding. Do not expect Black-headed Bunting before May.

SUMMER Little Grebe, Pygmy Cormorant, Dalmatian Pelican, Little Bittern, Little Egret, Squacco and Purple Herons, Glossy Ibis, Garganey, Golden and Short-toed Eagles, Buzzard, Marsh and Montagu's Harriers, Hobby, Red-footed Falcon, Quail, Stone-curlew, Little Ringed and Kentish Plovers, Great Snipe, Temminck's Stint, Ruff, Black-tailed Godwit, Curlew Sandpiper, Black-winged Stilt, Collared Pratincole, Mediterranean Gull, Black, White-winged Black and Gull-billed Terns, Scops Owl, Alpine and Pallid Swifts, Roller, Hoopoe, Wryneck, Red-rumped Swallow, Golden Oriole, Red-throated and Tawny Pipits, Red-backed and Woodchat Shrikes, Short-toed Treecreeper, Blue Rock Thrush, Black-eared Wheatear, Cetti's, Moustached, Great Reed, Icterine, Orphean, Subalpine and Sardinian Warblers, Pied, Collared and Semi-collared Flycatchers, Cirl, Cretzschmar's and Black-headed Buntings, Spanish Sparrow.

ACCESS Lake Antinioti lies on the north coast west of Kassiopi and can be viewed from the roadside. Its open waters and reeds are a haunt of Little Bittern among others. **Pandokrátor** is the highest point of Corfu and can be reached by road. Walk the last few kilometres as this is Cretzschmar's habitat. Golden Eagle has been seen near Episkepsia, and the occasional White-tailed Eagle at Antinioti Lagoon. **Plain of Ropa** lies south of Corfu golf course and is best approached by road down the eastern side. The plain is crossed by a track leading to Yiannadhes and a bridge over the river. Walk alongside the river for Great Reed and Moustached Warblers, Red-footed Falcon, harriers, etc. For **Korission Lagoon** take the main road south and stop at the café-garage at Linia before you get to Aghios Georgios Beach. Walk the track to the lake through good small fields with shrikes and wheatears. Continue to the beach and watch for migrants among the juniper. **Alikes Saltpans** are right in the south of Corfu and reached by turning left at a difficult-to-spot road in the town of Lefkímmi. Access is free enough, but avoid weekends and holidays. The pans can be explored on foot and may be disappointing, or staggeringly full of waders, terns, gulls and Osprey. **ROUTE** Corfu has regular flights from most major European cities. As you land, watch for Little Egrets in the lagoons next to the runway. Plentiful accommodation: book early for the old houses on the north-east coast.

CRETE

Crete is some 300 km in length, but only 25 km wide at its narrowest point. It rises steeply to over 2440 m and is essentially a huge mountain chain emerging directly from the sea. Its east-west axis creates a formidable obstacle to birds moving directly north and south and, in poor weather with low cloud, day-flying migrants can be seen to alter course to find their way around, rather than over, the barrier. In some of the high passes, grounded migrants are often abundant during similar conditions.

Most ornithological exploration has occurred in the past 25 years or so and the island's tourist development is only comparatively recent. This has provided a wide and plentiful variety of accommodation, as well as a new major west-to-east road. It has, however, accelerated the process of filling all the rivers and marshes with rubbish and debris. The rivers of Crete mostly run from south to north (the north is more gently sloping and holds most of the human population), but they are inevitably short with only seasonal flows and narrow mouths. The infilling and dumping has only highlighted Crete's lack of substantial wetlands.

Crete enjoys substantial southern influences. The Sirocco often blows warm air over the island and there are wild palm groves in the extreme east at Vai. Huge areas of polythene have sprung up for vegetable-growing and these have reduced the area of lowland available to birds. Unfortunately, the southern influences have had no effect on the bird population – there are no exotic babblers or bulbuls to be found. Also, being so isolated, Crete is not a regular port of call for either migrant raptors or storks. Such soaring birds as do occur are resident.

After a rather depressing picture of disappearing habitat, rapid development and a somewhat impoverished fauna, it is good to be able to report that Crete is a fine place for birds. It has a good population of Lammergeier, is of crucial importance for Eleonora's Falcon, is doing well by its Griffon Vultures and has splendid spring and autumn passage of migrants.

To explore the island fully, use two bases; Aghios Nicholas (east) and Chania (west) are perfect. While Ag. Nick. is fast developing as Crete's most popular resort, Chania remains a fine Venetian city with one of the world's finest waterfronts. Because of the lack of major wetlands, birding can start almost anywhere. The grounds of a good hotel, an olive grove, a scrub area, a rubbish tip – all can, and do, produce birds. Rüppell's Warbler, always an important bird for every visitor, is widespread, though everywhere outnumbered by Sardinian, Migrants too can turn up anywhere, not just on the south coast in spring and the north coast in autumn. Collared, Semi-collared and Pied Flycatchers are regular, Red-throated Pipit may occur in small flocks, there are Whitethroat and Lesser Whitethroat, Black-eared Wheatear and Great Reed Warbler and hosts more.

Crete has other specialities. Lammergeier inhabits the main massifs and is relatively easy around the Lasithi Plateau (east), at the top of the Samaria Gorge (west), and in the Kourtaliotiko and Kotisphos Gorges north of Plakis. Griffons are particularly numerous on the climb up to Lasithi from Ag. Nick. and may easily be seen at the Selinari Gorge on the main road west of Ag. Nick. Eleonora's Falcon arrives in May and can then be seen in flocks several hundred strong in the areas of Sitía and Heráklion. The world's largest colony of these birds, estimated at some 180–230 pairs, lies on the island of Dia north of Heráklion, while the Dionisides Islands off the north-east coast hold some 290 pairs in total. These two colony-groups account for an important percentage of the world total of this falcon. Good views can be obtained on the mainland between Sitía and Piskikefalon, or in the valley of Skopi where the falcons feed every day.

Although these are the major specialities, there are others: Black-headed Bunting, Bonelli's Eagle, Marsh and Montagu's Harriers, the occasional Pallid, Red-footed Falcon, Audouin's Gull, Glossy Ibis and Peregrine, are all regular, but frankly there is nothing quite like spring passage.

Lammergeier

SUMMER Black-necked Grebe, Cory's Shearwater, Squacco Heron, Great White and Little Egrets, Sparrowhawk, Buzzard, Booted, Bonelli's and Short-toed Eagles, Lammergeier, Griffon Vulture, Marsh Harrier, Peregrine, Lanner, Hobby, Lesser Kestrel, Eleonora's and Red-footed Falcons, Chukar, Scops Owl, Pallid and Alpine Swifts, Hoopoe, Short-toed Lark, Woodlark, Crag Martin, Tawny Pipit, Blue-headed, Ashy-headed and Black-headed Wagtails, Red-backed, Woodchat and Masked Shrikes, Cetti's, Savi's, Moustached, Great Reed, Icterine, Olivaceous, Olive-tree, Sardinian, Rüppell's, Wood and Bonelli's Warblers, Black-eared Wheatear, Blue Rock Thrush, Spanish and Italian Sparrows, Golden Oriole, Chough, Alpine Chough, Citril Finch, Black-headed and Rock Buntings.
SPRING Great White Egret, Glossy Ibis, Little Bittern, Purple Heron, Black Kite, Mediterranean, Little and Audouin's Gulls, Little Ringed Plover, Little Stint, Ruff, Spotted Redshank, Greenshank, Curlew, Green and Wood Sandpipers, Black-winged Stilt, Tree and Red-throated Pipits, Whinchat, Redstart, Thrush Nightingale, Collared and Semi-collared Flycatchers.
ACCESS The **Lasithi Plateau** is easily reached from Ag. Nick. The steep, twisting climb may produce vultures and the occasional eagle, but the hills on the south side are best for Lammergeier. The valley floor holds Cirl Bunting among others. The village of **Kritsa** (Byzantine church) lies at the mouth of a gorge with breeding vultures, Chough, Buzzard, and is only a short drive or bus ride from Ag. Nick. Just outside the town (to the east) lies the tiny marsh of Almyros, with Penduline Tit. In the far east, the **Sitía** area is good for Eleonora's (*see* above) and the harbour for Mediterranean and Little Gulls. Beyond, the road leads to Kato Zákros via a deep gorge for vultures, raptors, Crag Martin, Alpine Swift and possible Bonelli's Eagle. The shoreline cover often holds migrants and the adjacent agricultural area should be explored for wagtails and pipits. West from Ag. Nick., the main road passes through the **Selinari Gorge** for breeding Griffon Vultures and, in winter, possible Peregrine, Buzzard and even Lammergeier. Beyond, and off to the right, lies the Minoan site of Mallia, and it is worth exploring the fields and wet scrub to the west for Penduline Tit, Wryneck, Red-throated Pipit, Marsh Harrier and Buzzard in season. The **Heráklion** area is quite productive, with the harbour being good for gulls, terns and sometimes shearwaters following the fishing boats. Agia Reservoir and Lake Kournas are not far away and between them offer the best opportunities

for wetland birds: Black-necked Grebe, Great White Egret plus duck, waders and 'wet' warblers. Also in this part of the island the marsh at Georgiopolis is excellent for waders and, in particular, for Little Crake. The marsh lies south of the town by the main road. One other 'major' wetland lies immediately east of the Creta Sun Hotel – a regular haunt of good waders. Farther south lies the site of Phaestos, where in spring a variety of falcons, including Eleonora's, Hobby and Peregrine, can regularly be seen. At one time the adjacent Geros River was the best spot on Crete, but rubbish-dumping and pollution have changed it beyond recognition. Unfortunately, it is impossible to drive far through the remaining marsh owing to the presence of a military base, but a walk along the northern riverbank should still produce Penduline Tit, Marsh Harrier, Buzzard, Woodchat Shrike and warblers. I would be delighted to hear from anyone who persists along this route as far as the sea: Great Snipe may be the reward. An exploration of Mount Ida on minor roads may be rewarding, before heading west to Chania. Along the north coast the rivers have cut deep gorges that offer chances of several birds, especially Bonelli's Eagle. That of the Petres River is excellent, with a small marsh at the coast as well, while the Sfakoriako River, just west of Réthimnon at Prassies, is also good for the same birds. Beyond the village, watch for a farm with chickens and goats and then walk directly east to the gorge for Bonelli's Eagle etc. From Chania, excursions south to the **Omalos Plateau** for larks and pipits and to the **Samaria Gorge** are excellent. Many tourists walk the gorge, the birder can stay at the café at the top for Lammergeier, Peregrine, etc, and walk only a few hundred metres and get charged an entrance fee for the privilege of Bonelli's Warbler, Crossbill, Citril Finch, etc. **Chóra Sfakíon** on the south coast is first-class for spring migrants, and Frankokastelo to the east has a few damp pools, excellent bush cover and is a regular Isabelline Wheatear spot. ROUTE Heráklion has an international airport with scheduled flights from Athens and summer charters from northern Europe. Accommodation is plentiful and seldom fully booked outside the main holiday period.

DADIA FOREST

Although this superb raptor area was known to us, it was intentionally omitted from earlier editions of *WWBE*. Today the hills and extensive pine forests form a Special Protected Area and we are able to include Dadia for the first time. Meanwhile the area has been visited by several crews of north European birders, most of whom refer to it as 'Lefkimi' after the village that forms the best gateway to the area.

Dadia Forest is arguably the best area in Europe for birds of prey. Where else can 25 species of these birds be found breeding? These include three pairs of Imperial Eagle; twelve pairs of Golden Eagle; twenty plus pairs of Booted Eagle as well as Lesser Spotted, Short-toed and White-tailed Eagles. All three vultures can be found, with Egyptian and Black both outnumbering Griffon. Long-legged, Honey and Common Buzzards are all well represented and there are Peregrine and Lanner for good measure. Such a list of raptors would doubtless be enough to send anyone in northern Greece hotfoot to Dadia, but there's more. Black Stork, Eagle Owl, Roller, Olive-tree Warbler, Lesser Grey and Masked Shrikes and Semi-collared Flycatcher may also be found.

In winter resident raptors are joined by good numbers of Spotted, White-tailed and mostly juvenile Imperial Eagles. Even the occasional Steppe Eagle may appear. There is a single Lammergeier, but it is doomed unless a sophisticated reintroduction programme can produce a mate.

SUMMER Black and White Storks, Black, Egyptian and Griffon Vultures, Imperial, Golden, Booted, Short-toed, Lesser Spotted and White-tailed Eagles, Buzzard, Long-legged and Honey Buzzards, Black Kite, Goshawk, Levant Sparrowhawk, Lanner, Peregrine, Chukar, Eagle and Scops Owls, Roller, Bee-eater, Syrian Woodpecker, Olive-tree, Orphean and Barred Warblers, Semi-collared Flycatcher, Sombre Tit, Golden Oriole, Masked, Red-backed and Lesser Grey Shrikes, Ortolan and Black-headed Buntings, Spanish Sparrow.
WINTER Steppe, Golden, Imperial, White-tailed and Spotted Eagles, Red Kite.
ACCESS Dadia is reached on the E5 north from Alexandroupolis. After 58 km turn left in Soufli. Alternatively, and probably better, turn left off the E5 after 47 km at Provaton. In Lefkimi, which is confusing, continue straight west ignoring a poor road to the left and a better road to the right. If in doubt ask for the 'Radio Mast' in Greek! After several kilometres take a right at a fork and climb an Alpine zigzag road to the radio mast at Kapsala. A deep valley to the east is worth a few hours watching soaring raptors. The open area around Lefkimi is best for Masked Shrike and the more interesting smaller birds. A vulture feeding station has been established in Dadia and a comfortable hide now facilitates views of feeding Black Vulture and others. A small visitor centre and a guest house are also available. Details may be had from the Community of Dadia (Tel. 0554–32208) or the Forestry Dept (Tel. 0554–22221).
ROUTE The nearest international airport is at distant Thessaloníki, but there are daily internal flights between Alexandroupolis and Athens.

Delphi

Twenty years ago it would have been unthinkable to miss Delphi. Today it is full of tourists and seemingly one of the most unlikely birding spots in this book. Yet, by finding accommodation nearby and entering the site at opening time, the delightful open-air theatre, the Temple of Apollo, the stadium and other wonders of Ancient Greece can be enjoyed along with Sombre Tit, Rock Nuthatch, Cretzschmar's Bunting and even Rüppell's Warbler. Other warblers include Orphean, and other buntings Ortolan, Rock and Cirl. Crag Martins are abundant and Alpine Swifts should be seen. This is a quite delightful place provided that an early-morning visit is arranged. Once the coaches have arrived – forget it.

Above Delphi lies Parnassós, which can be explored by road. Stops can be made to watch for the birds of prey that still inhabit this splendid area. The vultures formerly found here have declined rapidly in recent years, but there is still one pair of Lammergeier, and Short-toed and Golden Eagles are still seen along with Lanner and Peregrine.

SUMMER Lammergeier, Griffon Vulture, Golden and Short-toed Eagles, Lanner, Peregrine, Rock Partridge, Alpine Swift, Lesser Grey and Woodchat

Shrikes, Crag Martin, Red-rumped Swallow, Rock Nuthatch, Blue Rock Thrush, Black Redstart, Sardinian, Rüppell's, Orphean, Olive-tree and Olivaceous Warblers, Sombre Tit, Cretzschmar's, Rock, Ortolan and Cirl Buntings, Rock Sparrow.

ACCESS Delphi lies west of Athens along the north shore of the Gulf of Corinth. The ruins are worth thorough exploration and above the Arena, after a bit of a scramble, is the boundary fence. This is broken in several places (presumably by impecunious tourists) and gives access to a track leading north-eastwards. By climbing up to where the ruins are just about to disappear you enter Rüppell's Warbler territory. It is possible to reach this track north and then east of Delphi town. Below the entrance to the ruins, a track leads downhill to the south-west and joins a major track south of the town. This is worth a walk for Red-rumped Swallow, Rock Partridge and Cretzschmar's Bunting. South-west of Delphi, around Itéa, olive groves offer a variety of species, including Olivaceous and particularly Olive-tree Warbler. Watch for a BP garage less than 1 km east of Itéa. Continue east past a track and a small church and stop just beyond a small spur of rocky terrain. A track leads north among excellent groves. For **Parnassós** and the higher-altitude species, take the road north from Arákhova and explore as you climb. A large plateau is worth a stop, and a right turn soon after leads to the mountain for Shore Lark, Alpine Accentor, etc.

ROUTE Via Athens.

ÉVROS DELTA AND ÁVAS GORGE

The Évros Delta has caused me more problems than any other site. Since the first edition, I have received a succession of letters telling of woes that have befallen those who have followed my directions only to find that permits are unavailable, or to be turned away from areas of 'free' access.

In this revision I determined to omit the Évros altogether and it is only in response to direct pleas from George Handrinos, the foremost Greek ornithologist and my guide to all things Hellenic, that I reluctantly changed my mind. So, be warned, the Évros is an outstanding bird haunt, but *do not* write to me if you have problems getting permits or exploring it. Instead write to George at 44 El. Venizelou Str., 166 75 Glyfada, Greece.

If the Évros did not form the frontier between Greece and Turkey, its delta would be one of the most popular bird resorts in Europe. As it is, it is an outstanding wetland, despite the inroads made by continual drainage programmes. Much is now arable or grazing, but there are still lagoons with areas of reed and it is among these that the best birds can be found. Spur-winged Plover, White Stork, Black Kite, Rufous Bushchat, Spanish Sparrow and Isabelline Wheatear can all be seen and there are often many migrating waders, including the essentially eastern Marsh, Broad-billed and Terek Sandpipers, Greater Sand and Sociable Plovers. The Évros is also the best site in Europe for Slender-billed Curlew; mid-April is the best time. There are Bee-eater, Lesser Grey Shrike, Sombre Tit, Olive-tree Warbler, Masked Shrike and often impressive formations of migrating raptors. Spotted and Lesser Spotted Eagles, Honey and Long-legged Buzzards, Levant Sparrowhawk, Goshawk and Red-footed Falcon put in an appearance. There is a chance of White-tailed and Steppe Eagles, Great Black-headed Gull, Laughing Dove and even Rufous Turtle Dove and Black Lark.

In winter the 100,000 wildfowl include smallish numbers of Lesser Whitefronts and Red-breasted Geese and the occasional Bewick's Swan, as well as Saker.

To the north lies the Ávas Gorge, an impressive ravine beloved of Griffon and Black Vultures, Booted, Golden, Imperial and Short-toed Eagles and three species of buzzard. There is a pair of Eagle Owls here, as well as species such as Blue Rock Thrush, Crag Martin and Dipper. Among the olive groves below the gorge there are Isabelline Wheatear along a railway embankment and Masked Shrike – this is the number one European spot for this bird. Some 12 km beyond Ávas village the road ends at Essimi. Beyond is military territory.

SUMMER White and Dalmatian Pelicans, White and Black Storks, Little Egret, Squacco and Purple Herons, Ruddy Shelduck, Garganey, Ferruginous Duck, Egyptian, Griffon and Black Vultures, White-tailed, Booted, Bonelli's, Short-toed, Spotted, Lesser Spotted, Golden and Imperial Eagles, Marsh Harrier, Buzzard, Honey and Long-legged Buzzards, Goshawk, Levant Sparrowhawk, Lanner, Peregrine, Hobby, Red-footed Falcon, Stone-curlew, Spur-winged Plover, Black-winged Stilt, Avocet, Collared Pratincole, Caspian and Gull-billed Terns, Eagle Owl, Hoopoe, Bee-eater, Roller, Grey-headed and Syrian Woodpeckers, Masked, Red-backed and Lesser Grey Shrikes, Golden Oriole, Blue Rock Thrush, Isabelline and Black-eared Wheatears, Rufous Bushchat, Subalpine, Barred, Orphean and Olive-tree Warblers, Collared Flycatcher, Sombre Tit.

SPRING AND AUTUMN Little Stint, Curlew, Broad-billed, Wood, Marsh and Terek Sandpipers, Spotted Redshank.

ACCESS There are three routes into the **Évros Delta**. The two southern ones (to the best areas, naturally) require permits. These may be obtained at least two or three days in advance from either the police or the military HQ in the boulevard near the lighthouse in Alexandroúpolis. Several groups have found that they have applied for a four-hour permit and needed more time. Alternatively you can obtain a permit in advance (allow eight weeks) from Gareth Trewartha, Charioteer Ltd., PO Box 400, 10 Agias Sophias St., Thessaloníki, Greece (Tel. 031-284373; Fax 031-228968). A fee of some £25 was payable in 1993. Armed with a piece of paper, one can then enter the delta from the Town Hall in Ferrai where an earth road leads to a military post and then along the main dyke to the Palukia Lagoon. The public (no permit) route involves leaving the E5 north of Monastiraki where a track leads east just after a small hill. After crossing the railway, there is a good chance of Isabelline Wheatear, Rufous Bushchat and more or less certain Spanish Sparrow. The track continues on the north side of a river to the pumping station, turning right past Drana Lagoon back to the E5. This route can be reversed by leaving the E5 on the east side of the Loutros Bridge on a track to the south where there are small hotels on either side of the road. The advantage of this southern route is that by the time you reach the military post near Monastiraki you are ready to leave. Those with permits on the Monastiraki route can cross the river and turn right to the pumping station, then south to Palukia Lagoon. The **Ávas Gorge** is reached on a minor road crossing the railway north of Alexandroúpolis and leads toward Aisymi. A few kilometres north of Alexandroúpolis and 2–3 km south of Ávas village, take a left turning just past some ruins.

Park where a track leads right and walk northwards for Masked Shrike, Olive-tree Warbler and Syrian Woodpecker. Continue through Ávas to the gorge to and beyond the bridge for Eagle Owl. Higher still, watch for Imperial Eagle two hours after dawn.

ROUTE Nearest international airport is at distant Thessaloníki, but Alexandroúpolis has daily flights from Athens.

IOÁNNINA

The area of north-west Greece around Ioánnina is in almost every way a backwater and remains little explored by international birders. Those intent on the wonders of Porto Lágo and Évros may make a detour to Préspa and those exploring the whole of Greece find their high-altitude birds at Mount Olympus, so Ioánnina is underworked. This is a pity, for it has an excellent lake noted for passage of waders and terns, as well as reedbed species, and the nearby mountains have an excellent raptor population.

The town itself has a strong colony of Lesser Kestrels, good numbers of White Stork, and a rubbish tip that attracts vultures and other scavengers. The lake has Little Bittern, Squacco and Purple Herons and regular Glossy Ibis. There are often Gull-billed Terns and sometimes Caspian, along with Great Reed, Moustached and other marshy warblers.

To the north, Mount Astraka, with Snow Finch, Alpine Accentor and Alpine Chough, rises over 1500 m, while the whole of the area can produce most of the more widespread Greek birds. There is even Wallcreeper for those with patience, and Lammergeier may put in an appearance.

SUMMER White Stork, Griffon Vulture, Golden, Short-toed and Booted Eagles, Long-legged Buzzard, Lesser Kestrel, Water Rail, Rock Partridge, Roller, Hoopoe, Alpine Accentor, Rock Nuthatch, Wallcreeper, Dipper, Alpine Chough, Sombre and Bearded Tits, Snow Finch, Spanish Sparrow.
AUTUMN Purple and Squacco Herons, Little Bittern, Glossy Ibis, Long-legged Buzzard, Black-winged Stilt, Gull-billed and Black Terns.
ACCESS Ioánnina is reached by the major road, the E19, that runs northwards through western Greece north of Árta. Alternatively, it may be reached from Athens via Tríkkala and the E87. The lake lies east of the town, and the excellent southern shore is reached by heading southwards on the E19 and then turning eastwards on a rough lakeside track. After 1 km park and walk to the lakeside reedbeds, which may, at times, make open-water viewing impossible. For Astraka, take the road northwards out of Ioánnina and turn right after about 45 km to Aristi. Continue to Papingon and then walk the mule track to the cliff face of Astraka.

KASTORÍA LAKES

About 150 km north of Metéora and at no great distance from the famed Lake Préspa, in north-western Greece, lies a series of four large lakes, at the western end of which is Kastoría. These lakes have been largely ignored by visiting birders and are, therefore, little known. Yet what we do know is enough to show their potential. Lake Kastorías lies immediately east of the town of the same name and is strangely the most awkward of access. To the east is Lake Cheimaditis, with a smaller subsidiary lake 1 km to the north. Next eastwards is Lake Petron, which is too deep for waders, but has pelicans, grebes and other 'swimming' birds. Here, near the border, there are notices prohibiting photography, so use telescopes and binoculars with discretion. Farthest east is Lake Vegorítis, the largest of the four. This is a deep water, little used by birds, and not as yet fully explored.

Birds in spring have proved quite outstanding, with good numbers of many species. White Pelican, Little Egret, Squacco and Purple Herons, Little Bittern, Spoonbill, Ferruginous Duck, Black-winged Stilt, Little Stint, Water Rail, Bearded Tit, together with Black, White-winged Black and Caspian Terns, are regularly present. The surrounding land has Rock Nuthatch, Hoopoe, Black-eared Wheatear, Lesser Grey and other shrikes, together with raptors and the usual warblers and buntings. A small colony of Pygmy Cormorants has recently become established at Lake Petron.

SPRING Black-necked Grebe, Dalmatian and White Pelicans, Little Egret, Squacco and Purple Herons, Little Bittern, Spoonbill, Gadwall, Ferruginous Duck, Marsh Harrier, Long-legged Buzzard, Water Rail, Kentish Plover, Black-winged Stilt, Sanderling, Ruff, Little Stint, Collared Pratincole, Black, White-winged Black and Caspian Terns, Hoopoe, Roller, Wryneck, Red-backed, Woodchat and Lesser Grey Shrikes, Black-eared Wheatear, Cetti's, Great Reed and Fan-tailed Warblers, Rock Nuthatch, Tree Sparrow.

ACCESS For **Lake Kastorías**, leave Kastoría to the south-east and turn left signposted to the border. Some 100 m before the Marrokórion turn a small bridge with a track to the left leads to the lake. **Lake Cheimaditis** lies south of the 'Yugoslavia' road: turn right before the E90. Do not ignore the smaller, shallow lake to the north. **Lake Vegorítis** lies south of the road to Petron and is best at the shallow southern end. The E90 to Ptolemaís often has huge flocks of Rollers, shrikes and Kestrels on passage.

ROUTE The international airport at Thessaloníki is ideally suited for visiting this area on the way to Préspa.

KERKINI LAKE

The damming in the late 1950s of the Strimón near the Bulgarian border created one of the most important wetlands in Greece. As a result of previous editions of this book it features on most schedules of crews working the coast of Macedonia. Kerkini has shallow northern margins with extensive reeds and other emergent vegetation which have attracted a wide range of species, including Pygmy Cormorant, Glossy Ibis, Spoonbill, several herons, Penduline and Bearded Tits and Whiskered Tern. Nearby breeders, and regular visitors, include White-tailed, Lesser Spotted and Imperial Eagles, a variety of other raptors and a host of smaller birds typical of the region.

White Pelican, Marsh Sandpiper, Caspian and Black Terns, shrikes, etc., can be seen on passage. In winter there are 30,000–40,000 duck, up to 300 Dalmatian Pelicans, 4000 Pygmy Cormorants, 1000 Great White Egrets and Spotted Eagle and Black-necked Grebe. At all seasons Kerkini is full of birds and is a must for visitors to this part of the country.

SUMMER Night, Squacco and Purple Herons, Little Egret, White and Black Storks, Spoonbill, Glossy Ibis, Greylag Goose, White-tailed, Lesser Spotted, Imperial, Short-toed and Booted Eagles, Long-legged Buzzard,

Black Kite, Black-winged Stilt, Collared Pratincole, Gull-billed and Whiskered Terns, Bee-eater, Roller, Syrian Woodpecker, Red-rumped Swallow, Penduline and Bearded Tits.
PASSAGE White Pelican, Marsh and Wood Sandpipers, Caspian and Black Terns, Golden Oriole, Lesser Grey and Woodchat Shrikes.
WINTER Black-necked Grebe, Dalmatian Pelican, Cormorant, Pygmy Cormorant, Great White Egret, Spotted Eagle, Sandwich Tern.
ACCESS From Sérrai head north to Sidhirókastron and continue, taking a left to Vironeia on the Kilkis road. From Vironeia railway station, a track leads to the Strimón. Immediately after crossing the bridge, turn right on the main dyke through a large poplar wood. On the western shore a track leaves Kerkini village to create a lakeside 'loop', which is an excellent vantage point for many species. Turn left on rejoining the road and take the next track left alongside the south-western shore. Some wooded hills on the right have many raptors and White-tailed Eagle may be seen on lakeside mounds. There are good tracks right around the lake except on the northern shoreline. Also, try the old bed of the Strimón for waders.
ROUTE From Thessaloníki on the E20 to Sérrai.

LAKE KORÓNIA

Lake Korónia, or Vassilios, lies a short distance from Thessaloníki and is a shallow, reed-fringed lagoon. Along with Porto Lágo, Korónia is regarded as one of the prime migration sites in this part of Europe and regularly produces excellent passage of both waders and terns. Though over 10 km long and 5 km wide, most of the action is concentrated at the margins. As the lake is so shallow, a slight difference in water level can move the margin from well beyond the fringing reeds when levels are low, to the grassy surroundings when levels are high. In either case waders will be found. Problems start when the margin is actually among the reeds and waders may then be concentrated out of sight tight against the vegetation. The surrounding land is mainly agricultural, with occasional clumps of bushy cover that can hold good numbers of migrating warblers.

Though a good variety of birds breed here, the main attractions are migrants. These include Dalmatian and White Pelicans, Booted Eagle, Marsh Harrier and Night and Purple Herons. There are often Glossy Ibis, occasionally Black Stork and invariably a good variety of waders.

Nearby, Lake Vólvi is too deep for many birds, but the Apollonia woods have both storks and the Rentina Gorge, to the east, has Eagle Owl, Booted Eagle and Lanner.

SUMMER Little Egret, Night and Purple Herons, Pygmy Cormorant, White and Dalmatian Pelicans, Glossy Ibis, Buzzard, Marsh Harrier, Kentish Plover, Black-winged Stilt, Avocet, Collared Pratincole, Calandra, Short-toed and Crested Larks, Tawny Pipit, Hoopoe, Bearded Tit, Cetti's, Savi's, Orphean and Subalpine Warblers, Spanish Sparrow.
PASSAGE Black Stork, Osprey, Little Ringed Plover, Green Sandpiper, Greenshank, Slender-billed Gull, Black, Whiskered and Caspian Terns.
ACCESS The lake is obvious from the main road east from Thessaloníki, and can be explored along its southern shore. At the eastern end is Langadikia, reached via a rough road that continues to a stream (fordable)

and then out to the lake. This area has some of the largest reedbeds at Korónia. In the north-west an excellent sand spit holds waders, and can be reached via minor roads through Langadas and Loutra Langada.

ROUTE Thessaloníki has an international airport with car-hire facilities and a variety of accommodation to suit most pockets.

LAKE MIKRÍ-PRÉSPA

Préspa lies on the borders of Greece, the former Yugoslavia and Albania and consists of two lakes, Magalí (great) and Mikrí (lesser) Préspa, separated by a narrow strip of land. Mikrí Préspa lies almost entirely in Greece and is a National Park. Préspa was once regarded as devoid of birds and few visitors bothered with it, but many birds were displaced when Albania drained Lake Malik and the pelicans, in particular, moved to Préspa. Today it is acknowledged as one of the most important wetlands in Greece.

Both White and Dalmatian Pelicans now breed in reasonable numbers. There are good colonies of Spoonbill, Purple and Grey Herons, Little and Great White Egrets, Cormorant and Pygmy Cormorant and the most southerly Goosanders in Europe.

Marsh Harriers are numerous, but the surrounding countryside holds Golden Eagle, and occasionally White-tailed Eagles appear at the lake. In fact, if the surrounding woods and hills are included Préspa boasts a formidable list of breeding species. The plain of Florina is one of only two breeding areas for Montagu's Harriers in Greece. Migrants have not been as fully documented as the more obvious breeding birds, but a decent collection of waders and terns passes through and there is much scope for recording new species for the park, particularly among the passerines.

SPRING Black Kite, Red-footed Falcon, Little Stint, Curlew Sandpiper, Collared Pratincole, Black, White-winged Black and Whiskered Terns.

SUMMER Black-necked Grebe, Pygmy Cormorant, White and Dalmatian Pelicans, Great White and Little Egrets, Purple, Squacco and Night Herons, Little Bittern, White Stork, Spoonbill, Glossy Ibis, Greylag Goose, Ferruginous Duck, Goosander, Egyptian Vulture, Golden, White-tailed, Booted and Short-toed Eagles, Marsh Harrier, Hobby, Peregrine, Lesser Kestrel, Rock Partridge, Little Crake, Eagle and Scops Owls, Alpine Swift, Bee-eater, Roller, Hoopoe, Syrian and Black Woodpeckers, Shore Lark, Crag Martin, Red-rumped Swallow, Tawny Pipit, Lesser Grey Shrike, Alpine Accentor, Golden Oriole, Great Reed, Moustached, Marsh, Olivaceous, Barred, Orphean, Subalpine and Bonelli's Warblers, Black-eared Wheatear, Rock Thrush, Bearded, Sombre and Penduline Tits, Rock Nuthatch, Black-headed and Rock Buntings, Rock Sparrow.

ACCESS Lake Préspa lies in the north-west of Greece. Approach on the road north from Kastoría. Before reaching Agios Germanos, turn left (west) to the isthmus that separates Mikrí from its larger neighbour. Much of the shoreline can be explored via small roads, or on foot, and the best birding areas are along the isthmus itself (tower hide); at Pyli on the western shore; along the eastern shore between the isthmus and Mikrolimni (hide); and in the south adjacent to the Albanian border. A general impression of Préspa can be obtained from Hill '903' south of the isthmus on the eastern shore and from the hills beyond Krania in the south-east.

ROUTE Via Athens.

LESBOS

Lesbos (Mytilene) lies just off the coast of Turkey. The fourth largest Greek island, it was until recently largely untouched by tourism. Today some package-tour operators offer the island and this is an ideal way of getting its special birds. Lesbos is a rugged island, with scrub-covered hillsides broken by valleys with olive groves and small-scale agriculture. Mitilíni is the capital and the only town of any size. The airport is nearby.

There are considerable eastern influences on its avifauna. Most visitors want Krüper's Nuthatch and Cinereous Bunting, but there is more and certainly sufficient for a good week. Both storks, Levant Sparrowhawk, Eleonora's Falcon and Lanner, and Cretzschmar's Bunting, Rock Nuthatch, Masked Shrike, Middle Spotted Wood-pecker and Olivaceous and Olive-tree Warblers are all regularly seen.

Unfortunately, the best birding sites are scattered throughout the island and a hired car or motorbike is essential. There is thus no ideal centre. A bus service goes almost everywhere each day.

SUMMER White and Black Storks, Ruddy Shelduck, Long-legged Buzzard, Levant Sparrowhawk, Bonelli's Eagle, Hobby, Lanner, Eleonora's Falcon, Chukar, Black-winged Stilt, Avocet, Bee-eater, Scops Owl, Middle Spotted Woodpecker, Krüper's and Rock Nuthatches, Masked and Woodchat Shrikes, Blue Rock Thrush, Subalpine, Olivaceous and Olive-tree Warblers, Cretzschmar's and Cinereous Buntings, Rock Sparrow.

ACCESS Saltpans lie at the head of the huge sea inlet in the south-west and can be seen from the road south of Kallíní. There is a garage opposite the turning to Agios Paraskevi and a track leads to the beach some 200 m farther west. Take this and walk around the pans to buildings, from where access can be achieved. **Míthimna** is a good base for exploration east-ward along the north coast (follow signs to Eftalou). After 3 km the olive grove on the right (opposite Hotel Alceros) has Masked Shrike. Continue

Sombre Tit

as far as possible for Eleonora's at the cape. **Eressós** lies in the west of the island, about 50 km from Kalloní. Above the town is a farm lying beside (but below) a ridge. To the north-west of this is a twin-peaked hill. From the northern peak to the ridge above the farm is the best area for Cinereous Bunting. There are also Cretzschmar's Bunting and Rock Nuthatch here. **Agiássos** lies due west of Mitilini, in the hills. Before reaching the village from the north there is a major fork, with Agiássos signposted 4 km in each direction. Take the left and turn left again immediately on entering the village (the road straight on becomes cobbled); continue out of the village with pines on the left. After 2 km there are pines on both sides. Stop and explore for Krüper's Nuthatch.

ROUTE Fly on a package tour or from Athens, or sail from Piraeus.

MESOLÓNGION

Since this area appeared in an earlier edition, reports have been more or less balanced between pros and cons. Some rated Mesolóngion as high as anywhere in Greece; others found it virtually birdless. Clearly it is an area to be visited at the correct time – mid-April into May, or in winter.

These lagoons and marshes lie on the north shore at the mouth of the Gulf of Corinth on the west coast. South of the town a raised causeway extends seawards, giving excellent views west over lagoons and east over saltpans. The latter are excellent, with Avocet, Stilt, Kentish Plover, Greenshank, Wood Sandpiper and Temminck's Stint. There is a chance of Broad-billed and Terek Sandpipers as well and the really fortunate may see Slender-billed Curlew in April. Pratincole, Black-tailed Godwit, Little Egret, Dalmatian Pelican and a host of small birds can all be found.

To both east and west splendid delta areas probably rival the main Mesolóngion lagoons and may even surpass them in terms of breeding birds. The delta of the Évinos to the east and that of the Akhelóös to the west are, however, difficult of access and remain little known. Most visitors work the causeway and then move quickly on to the Gulf of Arta.

SPRING Dalmatian Pelican, Glossy Ibis, Squacco Heron, Little Egret, Garganey, Griffon Vulture, Marsh Harrier, Lesser Spotted Eagle, Black-winged Stilt, Avocet, Kentish Plover, Broad-billed, Marsh, Wood and Terek Sandpipers, Greenshank, Collared Pratincole, Gull-billed, Black, White-winged Black, Little and Common Terns, Mediterranean Gull, Eagle Owl, Kingfisher, Great Reed, Fan-tailed and Olive-tree Warblers, Lesser Grey Shrike, Black-eared Wheatear, Hoopoe, Red-rumped Swallow, Black-headed Wagtail.

ACCESS Mesolóngion lies west of Athens at the mouth of the Gulf of Corinth, and is reached on the E19. From the town the causeway runs due south to the sea, where there is a taverna. A walk east along a dusty road is also productive, with decent reedbeds and the occasional lagoon. To explore the delta areas, Krionéri (Évinos) and Oeniadae (Akhelóös) are good starting points. Indeed, from Oeniadae there is a motorable track that runs alongside a canal into the delta. This has produced some birds, including Short-toed Eagle and good passerines. Lake Aitolikón, north of Mesolóngion, is worth a look, but usually requires a telescope.

ROUTE Via Athens northward on the E92, then westward.

NÉSTOS DELTA

Only a shadow of its former self, with rubbish tips, fish factories and flat agricultural land where once there was prime bird habitat, Néstos does still attract passing birders by being among Europe's best places for Spur-winged Plover. Despite its degradation, birders still find a good collection of migrants and breeding birds. The latter include Lesser Spotted and Syrian Woodpeckers, Golden Oriole, Reed and Marsh Warblers and Scops Owl. Migrants include herons, harriers and Hobby together with a good collection of waders.

SUMMER Squacco and Purple Herons, Marsh and Montagu's Harriers, Hobby, Spur-winged and Kentish Plovers, Snipe, Little Stint, Ruff, Curlew Sandpiper, Collared Pratincole, White-winged Black Tern, Scops Owl, Red-rumped Swallow, Golden Oriole, Syrian and Lesser Spotted Woodpeckers, Woodchat Shrike, Black-eared Wheatear, Reed and Marsh Warblers, Black-headed Bunting.
ACCESS Leave the E5 27 km east of Kavala to Krisoúpolis. Continue towards Keramoti but at Haidefto turn left (east). This track passes through a huge poplar wood and thence onwards to the river mouth. Though rough, this track is driveable and is about 10 km overall.
ROUTE Thessaloníki airport.

PORTO LÁGO

Porto Lágo is a small village, marked by a Genoese fortress, on the north-east coast, but is one of the great spots for breeding and migrating birds and is the best-known bird spot in Greece. The village is on a narrow sand spit between the sea and a large lagoon – Lake Vistonís. Just east is the narrow channel between the lake and the sea, while to the west lies an area of saltpans that is the main reason for Porto Lágo's reputation.

In winter Lake Vistonís has excellent numbers of duck, but in summer it holds only Black-necked Grebe, Pygmy Cormorant and Caspian Tern. The beach may be good for other terns and gulls, along with Kentish Plover and other shorebirds including Slender-billed Curlew.

The saltpans lie south of the main coast road and extend as far as the beach. They are of variable attraction to birds, but Avocet and Spur-winged Plover breed and passage can be simply fantastic. Among the sandpipers, Marsh is regular, Broad-billed almost so, and Terek as regular here as anywhere in Europe away from its breeding grounds. White-tailed Eagle appears from time to time and other species include White Pelican, Slender-billed Gull, Roller, Bee-eater, Collared Pratincole, Calandra Lark, Tawny Pipit and possible Cretzschmar's Bunting. There are more lagoons to the east and the Porto Lágo area offers a wide variety of habitats in a small, easily worked area – perfect for migration though in winter it is the best place in Greece for Flamingo and White-headed Duck.

SUMMER Black-necked Grebe, Great White Egret, Glossy Ibis, Pygmy Cormorant, Red-footed Falcon, Marsh and Montagu's Harriers, Spotted Crake, Stone-curlew, Kentish and Spur-winged Plovers, Avocet, Black-winged Stilt, Collared Pratincole, Caspian Tern, Slender-billed Gull,

Roller, Bee-eater, Tawny Pipit, Calandra and Crested Larks, Rufous Bushchat, Great Reed, Savi's, Orphean, Sardinian and Subalpine Warblers, Black-headed and Blue-headed Wagtails.

PASSAGE Ruff, Greenshank, Marsh, Wood, Broad-billed and Terek Sandpipers, Slender-billed Curlew.

ACCESS Porto Lágo lies along the main road between Kaválla and Turkey. The saltpans and adjacent lagoon lie 5 km west of the town, between the road and the sea. They can be freely explored. Lake Vistonís is north of the road. The area either side of the channel connecting the lake to the sea is worth exploring. Egrets breed on the spit of wooded land opposite the town next to the camp site. South of Mesi (signs to Mesi Beach) are three lagoons that should be explored. The two so-called 'Mesi Lagoons', (the western one is called Karatza) regularly boast spring Flamingoes, sometimes in large numbers, as well as many waders. Surrounding land has Montagu's Harrier, Quail, Calandra and Short-toed Larks and Black-headed Bunting. Fanari (Xirolimni) Lagoon, west and just north of the campsite, often has Great White and Little Egrets, with Syrian Woodpecker and Black-headed Bunting nearby. Farther east, south of Pagouria, Lake Mitrikou and many small pools usually do have definite interest. Ferruginous Duck, Ruddy Shelduck, Marsh Harrier and Penduline Tit have been seen. Follow signs to Molivoli Beach, bear left, cross a bridge and turn right on an embanked but driveable track to the lagoon. Do not ignore Penduline Tit in riverside scrub *en route*! Small pools line the east bank.

ROUTE The nearest international airport is at Thessaloníki and there are decent hotels at Kaválla and Alexandroúpolis. This is not a tourist area and there are few of the usual amenities, though the hotel at Fanari is cheap, cheerful and regularly used by birders.

STRIMÓN DELTA

The Strimón Delta (once referred to as Aspróvalta), along with the Néstos Delta, is a stop-over between Lake Korónia and Porto Lágo. Development of this coastline is concentrating bird interest on the course and mouth of the Strimón. Here there are still good waders, gulls and terns on passage, particularly at the mouth at Limin. Inland riverside marshes hold Squacco and Purple Herons; surrounding sandy areas hold Stone-curlew, Short-toed and Calandra Larks. Drying pools often boast Collared Pratincole and waders. Offshore, regular gulls include Slender-billed, and shearwaters include Cory's and Mediterranean. To the north a hill east of the river may produce raptors, including Short-toed and Golden Eagles.

SUMMER Cory's and Mediterranean Shearwaters, Little and Great White Egrets, Golden and Short-toed Eagles, Levant Sparrowhawk, Hobby, Red-footed and Eleonora's Falcons, Stone-curlew, Black-winged Stilt, Kentish Plover, Mediterranean, Slender-billed, Audouin's and Little Gulls, Scops Owl, Pallid Swift, Roller, Crested Lark, Golden Oriole, Red-rumped Swallow, Masked, Woodchat and Lesser Grey Shrikes, Rufous Bushchat, Olivaceous and Orphean Warblers and Black-headed Bunting.

ACCESS The E5 crosses the Strimón north of the delta and an exit on the eastern bank gives access along it to Limin. Although there is a maze of tracks here, it is relatively easy to reach the coast and the best area which

lies between Limin and the sea. Also explore the sandy area to the east between sea and the E5 and the pools adjacent to the road. From here it is worth casting an eye over the hill to the north-east.
ROUTE Thessaloníki has an international airport.

THESSALONÍKI

Near Thessaloníki several deltas and saltpan areas form one of the most important birding sites in Greece. Sadly, the Axios delta, has become a sea of polythene. Birds are found here, but not in their former abundance and variety. The Loudhias Delta has also been developed.

Less spoilt and now probably the best area for birds is the Aliákmon delta which, south to Nea Agathoúpolis, is much better preserved. Farther south is the excellent Alyki lagoon with surrounding saltpans. This is the only regular spot in Greece for Cattle Egret, while Marsh and Terek Sandpipers often appear along with Flamingo, White-tailed Eagle, Lanner and occasionally Saker. Breeding birds include Slender-billed Gull, Gull-billed and several other terns, Avocet, Stilt, Stone-curlew, Pratincole. Non-breeding summer visitors include Glossy Ibis and Spoonbill, passage brings hosts of waders and winter up to 20,000 duck. At this time of the year divers and grebes, egrets, harriers, Spotted Eagle and Saker are present.

Across the gulf lies the promontory of Angelohori, with more saltpans and a substantial lagoon. Species here include migrant waders: Black-tailed Godwit, Ruff, Curlew Sandpiper, Little Stint and odd Slender-billed Curlew. Black and White-winged Black Terns occur, and plentiful small birds include good numbers of Red-backed Shrike and Black-headed Bunting.

SUMMER Glossy Ibis, Spoonbill, White Stork, Avocet, Black-winged Stilt, Stone-curlew, Slender-billed Gull, Gull-billed, Common and Little Terns, Calandra Lark.
PASSAGE Pygmy Cormorant, Flamingo, Great White, Little and Cattle Egrets, Glossy Ibis, Marsh Harrier, White-tailed Eagle, Lanner, Red-footed Falcon, Hobby, Garganey, Ferruginous Duck, Kentish and Little Ringed Plovers, Avocet, Black-winged Stilt, Little Stint, Ruff, Curlew and Marsh Sandpipers, Slender-billed Curlew, Collared Pratincole, Gull-billed, Caspian, Black and White-winged Black Terns, Mediterranean and Slender-billed Gulls, Red-backed Shrike, Red-rumped Swallow, Great Reed and Icterine Warblers, Tawny Pipit, Black-headed Wagtail, Black-headed Bunting.
ACCESS Angelohori Take the road east past the airport, turn right to Agios Trias and continue to a taverna. A track goes into the saltpans to the major lagoon and beach. The **Axios** is between Thessaloníki and Kateríni. There is no access off the toll motorway here so take the nearest exit and follow the old road to Halastra east of the river or Kimina west of it. Tracks lead from both under the motorway and by the riverside scrub to the shore, giving access to marshy pools near the sea: a regular spot for Mediterranean and Slender-billed Gulls. The surroundings have Tawny Pipit, Calandra and Short-toed Larks and Stone-curlew. The **Aliákmon** is best from Nea Agathoúpolis close to the E92 20 km south of Thessaloníki. For **Alyki** go via Kítros, 28 km north of Kateríni. Where the old Kateríni–Thessaloníki road crosses Kítros, turn east onto a track to the shore.
ROUTE Via Thessaloníki airport; take the bypass and avoid the city.

HOLLAND

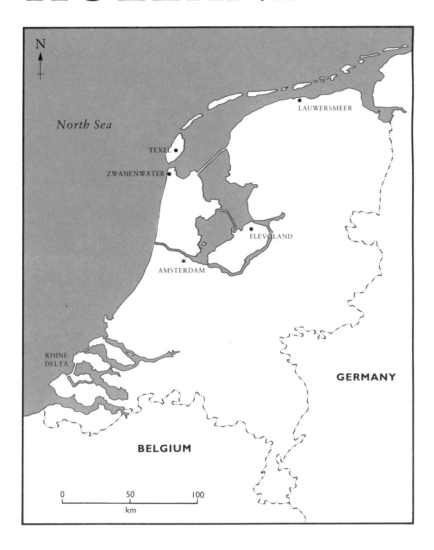

N

North Sea

LAUWERSMEER

TEXEL

ZWANENWATER

FLEVOLAND

AMSTERDAM

RHINE
DELTA

GERMANY

BELGIUM

0   50   100
km

AMSTERDAM

Visitors to Holland with only a few hours at their disposal need not
despair because they do not have the time to visit the Friesian Islands or
the Polders. Some of the best Dutch birding areas are no more than a few
kilometres from the city of Amsterdam and are served by an excellent
network of motorways. Most famous of these is the Naardermeer
reserve, which should be on the itinerary of any visitor to Holland, but
there are the Westzaan reserve to the north and the lakes at Botshol and
Nieuwkoop to the south. Each offers splendid birding.

The Naardermeer is a totally protected area that cannot be seen from the surrounding roads. It lies 16 km east of the city and has been a reserve since 1906. There are Spoonbill colonies, and the surrounding reedbeds and willow thickets hold a wealth of otherwise scarce species. These include Purple Heron, Bittern, Marsh Harrier, Black Tern, Bearded Tit and various warblers.

To the south the lake at Botshol has, with the exception of Spoonbill, much the same range of species. It does, however, often have Red-crested Pochard as well as Little Bittern; the former is not often present at Naardermeer and the latter cannot be relied on there. Farther south still the lakes at Nieuwkoop offer similar habitat, with extensive reedbeds holding Bittern, Little Bittern and Purple Heron, plus Black Tern and warblers.

To the north of Amsterdam lies the area of Zaanstreek, often marked on maps as 'Waterland'. Here Black-tailed Godwit abound. In the west of this area is the reserve of Westzaan, with most of the Dutch specialities of meadow and marsh including Black Tern and Ruff. There are also Bittern, Spotted Crake, Snipe, Redshank, Bluethroat and so on.

SUMMER Cormorant, Purple Heron, Spoonbill, Bittern, Little Bittern, Garganey, Red-crested Pochard, Marsh Harrier, Hobby, Black-tailed Godwit, Ruff, Black Tern, Bearded Tit, and Savi's and Great Reed Warblers.

ACCESS It is essential to book permits for the **Naardermeer** reserve well in advance. Write to Vereniging tot Behoud van Natuurmonumenten, Herengradt 540, Amsterdam, giving proposed date of visit (and an alternative) and numbers of permits required. The reserve is reached by taking the A1 eastwards from Amsterdam and taking the exit to Muiderberg (not Muiden). Take the road to the right that runs parallel with the motorway and after 1 km turn right to a fisherman's house called 'Visserji'. **Botshol** is reached by taking the A2 southwards to its junction with the N201. Turn right (west) and then right again after 3 km to Botshol. For **Nieuwkoop**, return to the N201 and continue westwards to the junction with the N212. Turn left (south) for 6 km then turn right to Noorden. Much of the area can be seen by turning right and viewing from the road along the northern edge. **Westzaan** is reached by taking the A7 northwards to Oostzaan and forking left on the motorway to Westzaan. There is a dyke to the west along which a footpath offers good views over the reserve. Most of this area has interesting waders on the fields and other species on or around the lakes.

ROUTE Schiphol is one of the world's busiest airports and the adjacent A9 can have you birding within a few minutes of clearing customs and hiring a car.

FLEVOLAND

The former Zuiderzee was enclosed in 1932 to form the huge shallow inland lake the Ijsselmeer. Over the years parts of this new lake have themselves been enclosed and subsequently drained to form polders. The largest and most famous of these is Flevoland. Flat, criss-crossed by dykes, rich, fertile and quite outstanding for birds at all seasons,

Flevoland has become one of Europe's top birding spots. Though agriculture dominates the landscape, there are quite extensive areas of woodland, many windbreaks and several lakes and reedbeds that have been specially maintained as nature reserves. In winter Flevoland is alive with geese; in summer the meadows echo with the cries of Black-tailed Godwits.

Lelystad is a completely modern town on Flevoland itself, though most visitors prefer the more traditional delights of Hardewijk, which formerly bordered the Zuiderzee. In either case it is a simple matter to drive over fast roads to the main areas of bird interest.

Best of all is Oostvaardersplassen in the north, where huge lagoons are separated by equally huge reedbeds. Here, all of the species for which Flevoland is best known breed abundantly. There are Black-tailed Godwit, Avocet, Marsh and Hen Harriers, Bittern, Purple Heron, Spoonbill, Spotted Crake and Water Rail, Bearded Tit and White-spotted Bluethroat, as well as Sedge, Great Reed, Reed, Marsh and Cetti's Warblers. Occasional summer visitors include Great White Egret, but in winter this same area is excellent for duck and raptors.

A similar, though less extensive, marshland lies in the south at Harderbroek. This holds many of the same species, but is the best place for Little Bittern. The woods to the north-east have Goshawk and Honey Buzzard, while those immediately east of Oostvaardersplassen have Golden Oriole. In the south-west at Hulkesteinse is a bushy plantation area alive with Icterine and Marsh Warblers.

Winter geese are widespread, but may be difficult to locate. Bean are usually to be found in the area between Lelystad and Harderwijk, and there are usually Hen Harrier and Rough-legged Buzzard here too. Smew number 10,000 and there are thousands of other duck on the Ijsselmeer at this season, with good watchpoints to the north and south of Lelystad. The bridge across the Ketelmeer is a good spot for duck and, in any case, leads to the Noordoostpolder, where the coastal road north of Urk produces both wild swans, more geese, harriers and Merlin. Farther north still lies Friesland, arguably the best goose area in Europe. The area between and around Balk and Koudum is full of these birds, with totals of 20,000 Barnacles and a similar number of Whitefronts laced with other species, often including Red-breasted Goose. The coast to the west is a noted haunt of White-tailed Eagle.

SUMMER Great Crested Grebe, Wigeon, Shoveler, Garganey, Pintail, Gadwall, Greylag Goose, Marsh and Montagu's Harriers, Buzzard, Honey Buzzard, Spoonbill, Great White Egret, Bittern, Little Bittern, Purple Heron, Water Rail, Spotted Crake, Black-tailed Godwit, Ruff, Avocet, Common Tern, Short-eared Owl, Golden Oriole, Bearded Tit, Blue-headed Wagtail, Bluethroat, Savi's, Marsh and Icterine Warblers.
WINTER Red-necked Grebe, Wigeon, Teal, Tufted Duck, Pochard, Goldeneye, Smew, Goosander, Red-breasted Merganser, Bean, White-fronted and Barnacle Geese, Hen Harrier, Buzzard, Rough-legged Buzzard, Goshawk, White-tailed Eagle.
ACCESS Hardewijk is easily reached via the A28 and Lelystad is well signposted from there on the N302. This road crosses Flevoland and produces geese and raptors in winter. In Lelystad turn left along the coastal

embankment to **Oostvaardersplassen** – a fast road with few stopping places. The eastern side of the reserve can be reached by turning left just outside Lelystad. This is quite excellent at all seasons. At the end of the marsh turn left at Torenvalk for Oriole woods and later some fine harrier scrubland. The marsh at **Harderbroek** is reached by turning left as soon as the Harderhaven Bridge is crossed, and by following along this road (and aided by a local map) the **Hulkesteinse** area can be found. North of Lelystad is a power station-factory area with water outlets that attract winter duck, and the main A6 leads on to the Ketelmeer for duck and north to Balk in Friesland for geese. Return via the Noordoostpolder coastal road for swans. Flevoland and Friesland are both deserving of exploration; apparently aimless motoring of country roads quickly produces birds.

ROUTE Amsterdam has one of the world's best connected airports and the Dutch motorway system makes travel fast and simple. Motorway restaurants and cafés are excellent.

LAUWERSMEER

The Waddensee is acknowledged as the most important single intertidal area in Europe, with outstanding populations of wildfowl and waders in internationally important numbers. As with all such areas, from Morecambe Bay to the Tagus estuary, there are many other birds attracted by the wildness of the landscape and some of these may have an extra appeal. The problem is how to get to grips with such a large area. As elsewhere, it a matter of timing and placing. The best time is around high tide, and one of the best places is Lauwersmeer. Until 1969 this was an estuary draining into the Waddensee south of the island of Schiermonnikoog. Then a barrage was built and drainage plans put into operation. Fortunately, this scheme has not been entirely successful and the area remains rich in wildfowl and waders. It is one of the major European wintering grounds of Bewick's Swan and Barnacle Goose, and Rough-legged Buzzard, Hen Harrier and often White-tailed Eagle can be seen at this season. Both Marsh and Hen Harriers breed and there are hundreds of pairs of Avocet, Godwit and Ruff as well. Passage brings a wide variety of waders and terns.

SUMMER Marsh and Hen Harriers, Bittern, Avocet, Black-tailed Godwit, Ruff, Little Gull, Black, Common and Arctic Terns, Short-eared Owl.
WINTER Bewick's and Whooper Swans, Barnacle Goose, Wigeon, Teal, Pintail, Shoveler, Marsh and Hen Harriers, White-tailed Eagle, Rough-legged Buzzard, Merlin, Grey Plover, Bar-tailed Godwit, Knot, Curlew, Shore Lark, Snow Bunting.
ACCESS The whole area can be explored from the surrounding roads, several of which overlook areas designated as nature reserves. The road across the dam to Lauwersmeer Harbour is a good starting place, while the minor roads that give access to the eastern shore are excellent. Do not ignore the surrounding woods at any season.
ROUTE Take the N361 from Groningen, which is an excellent base and an attractive university town.

RHINE DELTA

After the spending of a staggering amount of money and effort, the delta works at the mouth of the Rhine are now complete. The exact benefits to the economy of southern Holland (and the European Community) do not concern us here. What was once a maze of channels and mud-banks, islands and marshes has been changed by the construction of several major dams across the mouths of the various Rhine channels, effectively cutting them off from the sea. This has created a series of major lakes with marshy shorelines and some quite excellent bird habitats, some of which have, in traditional Dutch manner, been declared reserves. Whether the transformation has been beneficial or detrimental to bird populations is not the point; what is important is where to watch birds now.

Today the Rhine delta is still a major bird haunt. In winter there are vast flocks of wildfowl, including good numbers of both Barnacle and Brent Geese. Duck populations are often quite staggering and many can be approached quite closely. Off the Brouwersdam there is one of the greatest concentrations of Great Crested Grebes to be found anywhere – guesstimates talk of tens of thousands. Winter also brings a multitude of common waders, with a major high-tide roost on Duiveland on the southern shores of Schouwen. Harriers, Merlin, Peregrine and Rough-legged Buzzard are regular visitors at this season.

Passage brings excellent numbers of waders, with Little Stint, Curlew Sandpiper and Golden Plover along with almost every other wader that regularly occurs in north-western Europe. In summer there are colonies of all the usual terns, including Arctic, plus excellent populations of Black-tailed Godwit, Avocet, Kentish Plover and, in the Schaelhoek reserve, Marsh Harrier, Bittern, Bearded Tit and, at Biesbosch alone, some 1000 pairs of Bluethroat.

This is an outstanding area with plenty of places to visit that has largely been ignored by foreign birders. Perhaps this account will do something to change this apparent lack of effort.

SUMMER Great Crested Grebe, Marsh Harrier, Bittern, Shelduck, Greylag Goose, Kentish Plover, Black-tailed Godwit, Avocet, Common, Arctic and Sandwich Terns, Bearded Tit, Bluethroat.
WINTER Red-throated and Black-throated Divers, Red-necked, Slavonian and Great Crested Grebes, Marsh and Hen Harriers, Rough-legged Buzzard, Merlin, Peregrine, Brent and Barnacle Geese, Wigeon, Gadwall, Pintail, Shoveler, Teal, Eider, Scaup, Long-tailed Duck, Scoter, Goosander, Smew, Golden and Grey Plovers, Knot, Curlew, Redshank, Short-eared Owl.
PASSAGE Golden Plover, Little Stint, Curlew and Wood Sandpipers, Spotted Redshank, Greenshank, Black Tern.
ACCESS There are excellent birding spots throughout the delta and a week of exploration would be very rewarding. Four major areas are outstanding and are detailed. **Brouwersdam** encloses Grevelingen Lake between the islands of Goeree-Overflakkee and Schouwen-Duiveland in the north of the delta. This is superb at all seasons, but in winter has divers and duck in fine numbers plus the outstanding concentrations of grebes. There are roads along the dam that make perfect vantage points.

Flauwers and Weversinlagen lie on the south side of Schouwen with the excellent marshy area of Duiveland. The meadows behind the Inlagen are a major wader roost. The reserve lies west of Zierikzee and can be viewed from the road 8 km to the west, south of the main road to Haamstede. **Veerse Meer** was one of the first arms of the delta to be cut off and forms a brackish lake with adjacent marshes. This is now an outstanding winter wildfowl haunt, with excellent passage waders and most of the good breeding birds at the reserve of Middleplaten. The whole area can be viewed from the road along the south side, but the area east of Veere is the best. This is remarkably convenient for anyone using the port of Vlissingen (Flushing), being only a few kilometres to the north. **De Scheelhoek** is on the island of Goeree-Overflakkee just east of the village of Stellendam. This river, meadow and reedbed area has excellent breeding birds, but is of interest throughout the year. The whole can be seen from adjacent roads. To the west of Stellendam, close to the dyke that leads to Voorne, is **Kwade Hoek**, a bay with superb wader habitat and a lake behind the dunes. All can be seen from Stellendam port.

ROUTE Excellent communications via nearby Rotterdam or Vlissingen.

TEXEL

Texel (pronounced 'Tessel') is the largest and most southerly of the Friesian islands and therefore the easiest to reach and explore. This is highly fortunate, for it is also the best for birds. Being only 15 km long by 11 km wide, it is relatively easy to cover, and virtually every major birding spot is a nature reserve. In the west the coast comprises a huge dune system, broken here and there by lagoons, slacks and inlets; here, from north to south, lie the reserves of Krim, De Slufter, Muy, Westerduinen, Bollenkamer and De Geul. In the east the shoreline is more broken,

Spoonbill

muddy and lies adjacent to the Waddensee, the most important intertidal zone in Europe; here lie (again north to south) the bird spots of Cocksdorp, Shorren, De Bol, Dijkmanshuizen and Mok. Between the two lies an island of meadows centred on Waalenburg, which is damp grazing land with abundant Black-tailed Godwit and a fine population of Ruff. There are also areas of woodland, at Dennen for example, with Golden Oriole, Icterine Warbler and Short-toed Treecreeper.

The ultimate Texel experience, however, is reserved for those who visit Muy, where there is a colony of Spoonbills together with Marsh and Montagu's Harriers. At the Slufter there are Avocet, Kentish Plover and terns, while at Geul there are more Spoonbills, plus Avocet, harriers and Godwit. A week is just long enough to visit all the reserves and other major sites and provide one of the best birding holidays to be had in northern Europe.

SUMMER Black-necked Grebe, Bittern, Spoonbill, Garganey, Eider, Marsh and Montagu's Harriers, Water Rail, Kentish Plover, Black-tailed Godwit, Ruff, Avocet, Common and Sandwich Terns, Long-eared and Short-eared Owls, Grasshopper, Great Reed, Marsh and Icterine Warblers, Short-toed Treecreeper, Golden Oriole.

ACCESS Permits to visit the various reserves can be obtained locally or in advance. The best contact is the Tourist Office, VVV Texel, Den Burg, Texel, Netherlands, which has leaflets giving up-to-date details of access and permits. Not all the reserves are administered by the same organization. Vereniging tot Behoud van Natuurmonumenten, Herengradt 540, Amsterdam, may also prove helpful as they administer most of the reserves in the east of Texel.

ROUTE Texel is reached by frequent ferry from the mainland and is only a short drive from Amsterdam. Most villages offer some form of accommodation and there are several hotels that understand birders' proclivities.

ZWANENWATER

This is a dune lake lying south of Den Helder that is still largely overlooked by those heading northwards to Texel. Yet its shallow waters, with their strong growth of reeds, can be compared, not unfavourably, with any other of the many marshlands of the Netherlands. Lying among the dunes near the shore, its breeding birds include Avocet and Kentish Plover. This is also the site of another Spoonbill colony and these birds can often be seen at the tiny reserve of Houdsbossche a little way south near Petten.

As well as having its breeding birds, by virtue of its position the Zwanenwater is also attractive during passage periods, and terns, gulls and waders are often interesting. There are some useful pines among the dunes.

SUMMER Bittern, Spoonbill, Garganey, Hobby, Marsh Harrier, Water Rail, Spotted Crake, Kentish Plover, Avocet, Common Tern, Long-eared and Short-eared Owls, Crested Lark, Reed and Marsh Warblers.

ACCESS Via Callantsoog and minor roads. This is a reserve, but much can be seen from the adjacent dunes.

ROUTE Via Amsterdam to Callantsoog.

HUNGARY

BALATON

Lake Balaton is the primary holiday resort of land-locked Hungary and much of its shoreline is not worthy of the birder's attention, although in winter there are important concentrations of ducks. There is, however, one of Europe's greatest bird reserves here, as well as various marshes and ponds nearby that attract a superb collection of birds. As with other East European countries it is difficult to understand why there are not more carloads of western birders seeking out the delights of what are usually rather better places than in the more populous west. Things are, of course, changing and there are now several organized bird tours here every year.

The gem and centrepiece of this area is the Kisbalaton reserve at the south-western end of Balaton. Here open water has been colonized by reeds and scrub, creating the perfect environment for breeding marsh birds. Red sedge grows here and nowhere else in Europe. Despite the fact that enormous colonies of Cormorants are slowly, but surely, killing off the trees, there are still good numbers of breeding herons. Night Heron (200 pairs), Squacco Heron (20 pairs), Little Egrets (35 pairs), Great White Egret (130 pairs), Purple Heron (40 pairs) and Spoonbill (35 pairs) make this site one of the most varied and important in the whole of Europe. The occasional Glossy Ibis may stay to breed, but there are also White-tailed Eagle, both of the smaller crakes, Whiskered Tern, Black Woodpecker and Moustached Warbler here. Passage brings hordes of wildfowl, plus a number of other species including reasonably regular Pygmy Cormorant.

Along the shores of Lake Balaton itself there are a few areas that should not be missed. The fish-ponds around Badacsony are also good for herons as well as passage waders and terns as is Lake Kulso, on the Tihany Peninsula along the opposite shore. This lake also has breeding herons and warblers among its reedbeds. The peninsula itself has Scops Owl, Nightjar and Golden Oriole among its scrub-covered interior.

To the north of Balaton, the western end of the Bakony Hills attracts birdwatchers based at Kerszthely for Kisbalaton. These are gentle hills rising to no great height and are mostly wooded, offering a chance of interesting woodland species. The beech woods around Sümeg are excellent for woodpeckers and there is even Rock Thrush at the ruined tower on the hill above the town. There is another ruin at Tatika near Bazsi, where the surrounding woods have Red-breasted Flycatcher and Black Woodpecker. Between Sümeg and Tapolca, there are fish-ponds on the western side of the road that should not be ignored.

SUMMER Black-necked Grebe, White Stork, Purple, Squacco and Night Herons, Little and Great White Egrets, Little Bittern, Spoonbill, Garganey, Ferruginous Duck, Greylag Goose, Marsh and Montagu's Harriers, White-tailed Eagle, Little, Baillon's and Spotted Crakes, Corncrake, Avocet, Black, White-winged Black and Whiskered Terns, Black, Syrian and Grey-headed Woodpeckers, Rock Thrush, Golden Oriole, Lesser Grey Shrike, Penduline Tit, Bluethroat, Red-breasted Flycatcher, Savi's, Moustached, Great Reed, Icterine and Barred Warblers, Serin.
ACCESS Kisbalaton is a nature reserve and permits must be obtained to visit. Contact Nyu-kövizig, 9700, Szombathely, Vorosmarty U.2, Hungary. Alternatively, walk eastward along the river bank from the bridge that crosses the Zala River just north of Kisbalaton village. The observation towers on Kányavári Island need no permits to visit. The fish-ponds at Badacsony lie along Route 7 southward. The **Bakony Hills** lie between Sümeg and Keszthely.
ROUTE Budapest, then south-west on the M7 motorway.

BUDAPEST

The capital of Hungary is recognized as one of the world's most beautiful cities, a fact even acknowledged by birders. There are parks, such as the extensive Varosliget Park in the centre, that have interesting birds, but the visitor to Budapest would be well advised to look just a little farther, for there are several first-class birding areas within a relatively short distance of the city.

To the north lie several areas of wooded hills extending as far as the border with the Slovak Republic. Nearest are the Buda Hills, with mature oaks and a good collection of woodpeckers including Middle Spotted, Syrian and Black, together with Goshawk, Golden Oriole, Red-breasted and Collared Flycatchers and even the occasional Rock Thrush. Farther north, the area around Pilis is important for breeding raptors, including Saker, Lesser Spotted Eagle, Honey Buzzard and Goshawk. Here too there are Bee-eater, Red-breasted and Collared Flycatchers and Rock Bunting.

To the south-west of Budapest is the excellent Lake Velence, which is treated separately, while to the south-east is the Ócsa Reserve with damp alder woodland broken by heath and reed-marsh. The area of marsh and damp meadow lies on one side of the road and holds Roller, Golden Oriole, Marsh and Montagu's Harriers and Black-tailed Godwit. The forest proper is a dense jungle of vegetation and decidedly wet underfoot. Mosquitoes find the conditions here ideal but so do raptors. Species include Lesser Spotted Eagle, Saker and Goshawk, though Buzzard is certainly more numerous. Syrian Woodpecker is common and River Warbler almost so.

SUMMER Black Stork, Bittern, Honey Buzzard, Lesser Spotted Eagle, Red and Black Kites, Goshawk, Marsh and Montagu's Harriers, Saker, Hazelhen, Curlew, Black-tailed Godwit, Corncrake, Great Spotted, Middle Spotted, Syrian, Grey-headed and Black Woodpeckers, Golden Oriole, Roller, Bee-eater, Hoopoe, Rock Thrush, Red-breasted and Collared Flycatchers, River Warbler, Serin, Hawfinch, Rock Bunting.

ACCESS The **Buda Hills** lie immediately outside the city limits and can be reached by public transport. Those with their own transport would be best advised to try Pilis. Take Route 1 to Pilisvörösvar and turn right to the hills. For Borzsony, take Route 2 and then the minor roads left into the hills. Ócsa lies just east of Route 5. Though it is a reserve, visits can be arranged at the visitor centre in the village.

ROUTE Budapest has an international airport.

HORTOBÁGY

The Hungarian Hortobágy (pronounced Hort-o-barge) is one of the most outstanding bird haunts in Europe, to be ranked alongside Spain's Coto Doñana, the French Camargue and the Danube Delta of Romania. It is quite simply the best birding site in central Europe, as a roll call of its breeding birds easily confirms. Red-necked Grebe, Bittern, Little Bittern, Great White Egret (180 pairs), Black Stork, Glossy Ibis, Spoonbill (450

Red-footed Falcon

pairs), Ferruginous Duck, Saker, Red-footed Falcon (400 pairs), Great
Bustard (200 pairs), Little Crake (10 pairs), Collared Pratincole,
Mediterranean Gull, Whiskered Tern (300 pairs), White-winged Black
Tern (200 pairs), Short-toed Lark, Bluethroat and the scarce and rare
Aquatic Warbler (200 pairs) – such a list and such figures speak for
themselves. But there is more.

On passage tens of thousands of geese descend on the plains. Mostly
these are Whitefronts and Bean, but there are always numbers of Lesser
Whitefronts and sometimes Red-breasted Geese as well. Similarly, there
are thousands of Crane, Ruff and Black-tailed Godwit, as well as lesser
numbers of Short-toed Eagle, Long-legged Buzzard, Saker and one or
two Slender-billed Curlew. Even the most hardened birder can be moved
by such quality in quantity. By the way, the winter visitor can expect up
to 25 White-tailed Eagles here.

The Hortobágy is an area of steppe broken by marshes, pasture,
woodlands and ponds. An excellent area of steppe lies immediately east
on the road to Debrecen. Here there are ponds and drying marshes with
Greylag, Pratincole and Great Bustard. To the north-west, an area of
fish-ponds bordered by roads has breeding herons and White-winged
Black Tern.

Much of the area, including Hortobágy-Halastó itself, is incorporated
into the national park of the same name. The heron colonies here contain
Great White Egret, Little Egret, Squacco Heron and Spoonbill. There are
other exciting birds, including Red-necked Grebe, White-winged Black
and Whiskered Terns, plus Mediterranean Gull and both small crakes.

There is a fine area of steppe near Hortobágy village where Great
Bustard have a stronghold. This is also a good area for Tawny Pipit, Red-
footed Falcon and Short-toed Lark – the last a decidedly scarce bird in
Hungary. This same area is particularly important during passage periods when seasonal floods create perfect conditions for passage waders
and terns and, of course, the geese.

SUMMER Red-necked Grebe, Bittern, Little Bittern, Night, Squacco and
Purple Herons, Little and Great White Egrets, Black and White Storks,
Glossy Ibis, Spoonbill, Greylag Goose, Ferruginous Duck, Marsh and
Montagu's Harriers, Saker, Red-footed Falcon, Great Bustard, Little and
Baillon's Crakes, Corncrake, Avocet, Stone-curlew, Collared Pratincole,
Black-tailed Godwit, Mediterranean Gull, Common, Whiskered and White-
winged Black Terns, Short-eared Owl, Short-toed Lark, Tawny Pipit,
Bluethroat, Icterine, Moustached, Aquatic and Barred Warblers,
Penduline Tit, Serin.
PASSAGE White-fronted, Lesser White-fronted and Bean Geese, Crane,
Saker, Ruff, Black-tailed Godwit.
WINTER White-tailed Eagle.
ACCESS Most of the region including the Halastó area north of Route
33 can be explored quite freely though permission to enter the various
fish-pond areas should be sought locally. The more sensitive areas are
strictly protected. Write for permission to: Hortobágyi Nemzeti Park,
4015, Debrecen, Böszörményiút 138, Hungary.
ROUTE Budapest then Route 4 to Debrecen.

LAKE FERTÖ

Lake Neusiedl in Austria has long been the most famous bird resort in central Europe and a favourite resort of generations of western birders. Most have stared longingly at the birds of prey soaring over the Kapuvarer Erlen Wald adding species to their 'life', but not to their Austrian, lists. For long these splendid woods remained out of bounds in Hungary. Today the southern part of Lake Neusiedl, the Hungarian part known as Lake Fertö, is accessible for the first time since the 1930s.

The birds are, of course, similar to those found in the Austrian part, but because of previous restrictions on visiting such a sensitive border zone much of the Hungarian side has remained undeveloped and in remarkably pristine form. Lake Fertö is shallow with a broad growth of emergent vegetation consisting of huge reedbeds, home to Purple Heron, Spoonbill, Bittern, Great White Egret and hosts of Great Reed and Savi's Warblers, as well as Moustached and River Warblers, Marsh Harrier, Black-tailed Godwit and Bluethroat. The rare Red-crested Pochard has bred and Red-necked Grebe does so regularly in small numbers. Local villages and woods hold Icterine Warbler, Syrian Woodpecker and Red-backed Shrike and there is a good population of raptors that includes Marsh Harrier, Black Kite, Honey Buzzard and possible Lesser Spotted Eagle.

To the south and east lie the plains, marshes, ponds and woods of the Hanság, roughly equivalent to the Seewinkel and Tadten Plain in Austria. They have similar birds, with up to ten pairs of Great Bustard, plus variable numbers of Great White Egret, Black Stork, Hen Harrier, Black-tailed Godwit, Black Tern, Roller, Black Woodpecker, Bluethroat and Moustached Warbler. Great Bustard may be more numerous in winter and there are often a few Imperial Eagles at this season.

Passage brings hordes of wildfowl to Lake Fertö, including up to 30,000 Bean Geese, 2000 Whitefronts, up to 6000 Greylags and even the odd White-tailed Eagle in spring.

SUMMER Red-necked Grebe, Bittern, Little Bittern, Great White Egret, Purple Heron, White and Black Storks, Spoonbill, Garganey, Red-crested Pochard, Honey Buzzard, Black Kite, Goshawk, Hen, Montagu's and, Marsh Harriers, Hobby, Great Bustard, Black-tailed Godwit, Black Tern, Roller, Black and Syrian Woodpeckers, Red-backed Shrike, Savi's, River, Moustached, Great Reed and Icterine Warblers, Bluethroat, Bearded and Penduline Tits, Golden Oriole.
PASSAGE Bean, White-fronted and Greylag Geese, Garganey, White-tailed Eagle.
WINTER Great White Egret, Imperial Eagle.
ACCESS Even today some areas are still closed to casual visitors and all visitors to all areas should be prepared to expect police curiosity. Carrying a passport, bird book and a site guide such as this one, should cover most eventualities. But do be polite and *do not* enter restricted zones. Lake Fertö can be viewed from the road between Sopron and Fertöboz and from tracks leading northwards among the reeds. The Hanság is best explored from Route 86 between Csorna and Mosonmagyarovar. For example, take a left 3 km south of the latter on Route 86 opposite a café where a track leads into a splendid area of marshes and woodland.

In Fertö-tó a path leads to a lake that is a nature reserve and an observation tower with many waterbirds. In compiling this account I have been greatly helped by my friend and colleague in 'Birding Holidays', Gerard Gorman. Gerard's book *A Guide to Birdwatching in Hungary* is essential reading for anyone planning to visit his adopted country and has proved helpful in updating the sites mentioned in this chapter.

ROUTE Vienna is the nearest international centre and is only an hour away by road via the border at Klingenbach.

LAKE VELENCE

This famous bird lake lies only 50 km south-west of Budapest and is almost as well known as Balaton. It differs, however, in being considerably smaller and in offering good habitat throughout its area. Its shallow waters are fringed by reeds, which form dense beds in several parts, especially at the western end. Here there are good colonies of Great White Egret and Spoonbill, but both of these, and the other birds of Velence, can be seen at almost any point around the shoreline. The reeds also hold Purple Heron and Little Bittern, plus Savi's, Moustached and Marsh Warblers.

The old Budapest–Székesfehervár road Route 70 runs along the southern shoreline, offering excellent viewing at many points. At Dinnyes, however, the grazing marshes hold Ruff, Black-tailed Godwit and Bluethroat and offer valuable feeding grounds for many of the Velence herons. The small pond near the village is a haunt of Black Tern, as well as of Great Reed and Moustached Warblers. Together with the surrounding agricultural land, Lake Velence offers really first-class birding to anyone with a day or more to spend outside the capital.

SUMMER White Stork, Great White Egret, Spoonbill, Little Bittern, Night, Purple and Squacco Herons, Ferruginous Duck, Garganey, Greylag Goose, Marsh and Montagu's Harriers, Little Crake, Ruff, Black-tailed Godwit, Black Tern, Quail, Roller, Bee-eater, Hoopoe, Golden Oriole, Lesser Grey and Red-backed Shrikes, Bluethroat, Great Reed, Savi's, Moustached, Marsh and Barred Warblers, Bearded and Penduline Tits.

ACCESS There is generally free access off the main road to the lakeside, but nearby hills offer better views over the reedbeds. The marshes at Dinnyes and the Velence Bird Reserve, which together cover most of the best areas, can be visited with permission. Write to: Kdt-Kövizig, 8000, Székesfehervár, Balatoniút 6, Hungary. Much can, however, be seen along the road from Dinnyes station to Pákozd and among the adjacent fish-ponds – ask the workers for permission to birdwatch here either in fluent Hungarian or sign language – whichever comes easiest. The ferry between Agárd and Szúnyog-sziget is worth a trip.

ROUTE Take the M7 from Budapest.

SZEGED AND THE TISZA PLAIN

Just before it crosses the border into the former Yugoslavia, the River Tisza meanders over a wide plain dotted with lakes, marshes and old river courses. In some parts there are excellent reedbeds, though others have been converted to fish-ponds. The whole area has been recognized as an internationally important wetland and is often referred to as the Pusztaszer Conservation Area.

Within this area near Szeged is Lake Fehértó, which has been extensively modified to provide areas of fish-ponds, as well as lakes for extracting soda. Even today the reedbeds hold good numbers of marsh birds, including Little Bittern and Penduline Tit. There is a large colony of Black-headed Gulls here among which one or two pairs of Mediterranean can be found. The centrepiece of the whole area is the island of Sasér, part of which forms the Mártély Reserve, where the marshes hold one of the best heronries in Hungary. There are Great White and Little Egrets, Squacco Heron, Spoonbill, Little Bittern, and a good population of breeding waders including Avocet and Black-tailed Godwit. Stone-curlew and 40 pairs of Red-footed Falcon also breed, along with Black Stork. Here too are Moustached and Barred Warblers together with Red-backed and Lesser Grey Shrikes. Passage brings thousands of Whitefronts and Cranes together with equally large numbers of Ruff and Black-tailed Godwits. Winter brings White-tailed Eagle. This is a superb and often overlooked area that would repay a visit at any time of the year.

SUMMER Black-necked Grebe, Red-necked Grebe, White Stork, Black Stork, Bittern, Little Bittern, Night Heron, Purple Heron, Little Egret, Great White Egret, Squacco Heron, Spoonbill, Ferruginous Duck, Greylag Goose, Marsh Harrier, Red-footed Falcon, Stone-curlew, Avocet, Black-tailed Godwit, Mediterranean Gull, White-winged Black Tern, Spotted Crake, Penduline Tit, Red-backed Shrike, Lesser Grey Shrike, Roller, Hoopoe, Barred Warbler, Moustached Warbler.

PASSAGE White-fronted Goose, Crane, Ruff, Black-tailed Godwit.

ACCESS The reserves at Lake Fehértó and Sasér can be entered with permits from Ati-Kövizig, 6720, Szeged, Tanácsköztársaság U4, Hungary. A considerable amount can, however, be seen in the area without entering the reserves, including from the local roads, a public observation platform and river bank footpaths.

ROUTE Southwards from Budapest on Route 5.

ICELAND

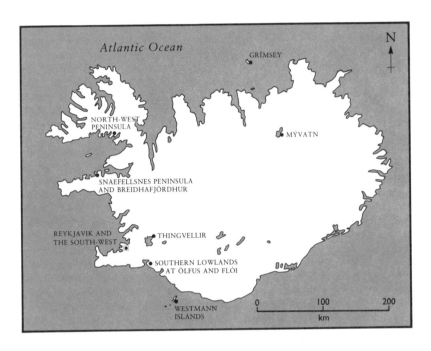

GRÍMSEY

The island of Grímsey, the most northerly point of Iceland, is situated in a volcanically active zone, and the Arctic Circle passes through it. The island is less than 4 km long and half that wide. Its population is little more than a hundred and fowling and egg-collecting have been practised for centuries. About 36 species breed including the only remaining Little Auk still breeding in Iceland (2–3 pairs). It is far from certain that visitors will see them as they are strictly protected and photography is forbidden.

Huge numbers of other auks breed on Grímsey including Brünnich's Guillemot, Razorbill and Puffin. Both Kittiwake and Fulmar breed on the cliffs, the latter sometimes in the rare dark phase. The oldest known Fulmar colony in the world is on Grímsey, first mentioned in 1713. On small pools, Red-necked Phalarope may be found and Snow Bunting is widespread. In winter, especially with drift ice, Little Auk is common and Ivory Gull occasionally seen, though, to be fair, this is not a very popular birding spot at this season.

SUMMER Fulmar, Kittiwake, Razorbill, Brünnich's Guillemot, Guillemot, Little Auk, Red-necked Phalarope, Snow Bunting, Raven.
ACCESS In the summer there are daily tours by ferry and by air from Akureyri. There is a guest house and camping site on the island.
ROUTE From Reykjavík to Akureyri by air.

MÝVATN

Mývatn – literal translation 'Lake of Midges' – is the greatest duck breeding centre in Europe and an absolute must for anyone visiting Iceland. For the birder it holds all of the special species that make the country so appealing, and for the ordinary tourist its muddy sulphur pools, lava formations and volcanic craters are an irresistible attraction.

Mývatn is some 37 km square in area, but its coastline is so indented and broken that long-distance views are almost impossible. It varies in depth from 2–4 m and holds an amazing 50,000 breeding pairs of 15 species of duck. Among these are several Nearctic species otherwise unobtainable for Euro-listers. Barrow's Goldeneye number some 800 pairs, while Harlequin Duck are especially numerous along the turbulent waters of the Laxá River. American Wigeon and Ring-necked Duck are regular, though they have not yet been proved to breed. Great Northern Divers do breed here, usually on remote upland lakes, but are frequently to be seen on Mývatn. Scoter, Long-tailed Duck, Merganser, Goosander and even non-breeding Goldeneye and Whooper Swan are all regular. Pinkfeet and Greylags breed, as do some 140 pairs of Slavonian Grebe, Red-necked Phalarope, Arctic Skua, Whimbrel, Black-tailed Godwit, Redwing, Snow Bunting and Merlin.

Gyrfalcon breed at a few places around Mývatn, though these birds may be seen anywhere in the area.

SUMMER Great Northern and Red-throated Divers, Slavonian Grebe, Whooper Swan, Greylag and Pink-footed Geese, Teal, Gadwall, Wigeon, American Wigeon, Pintail, Shoveler, Scaup, Scoter, Harlequin Duck, Long-tailed Duck, Barrow's Goldeneye, Goldeneye, Goosander, Red-breasted Merganser, Gyrfalcon, Merlin, Whimbrel, Red-necked Phalarope, Arctic Skua, Redwing, Wheatear, Snow Bunting.

ACCESS The whole of Mývatn can be explored by road, and one of the best places to start is on a bridge over the Laxá River in the west where the river runs from the lake. The road northwards to the coast crosses the Laxá lower down, and here there are Harlequin and Eider. The sulphur pools and the most beautiful lava formations lie to the east. From 15 May to 20 July all the islands, plus the shoreline in the north-west, are out of bounds. Otherwise one can explore at will.

ROUTE Plane and bus services connect with Reykjavík several times a day. The plane takes about an hour; the bus about eight times longer. Bicycles, motorbikes and cars can be hired in Reykjahlíd and there are two hotels and a wide variety of other types of accommodation, but do book in advance – even a few days in advance from Reykjavík.

NORTH-WEST PENINSULA

The remote north-western corner of Iceland is all but cut off from the rest of the country by the huge inlets of the Breidhafjördhur and Húnaflói. Its harsh landscape and sheer inaccessibility have made it the last real stronghold of Iceland's most famous birds of prey, the Gyrfalcon and the White-tailed Eagle. Special fines protect them both even from disturbance.

The north-west has three monumental bird cliffs at Látrabjarg, Hornbjarg and Haelavikurgbjarg. From the sea these monoliths rise

Gyrfalcon

500 m and are packed with Guillemot, Brünnich's Guillemot, Razorbill, Puffin, Fulmar and Kittiwake. Látrabjarg is probably Europe's largest seabird colony with about a million pairs of auks including the largest Razorbill colony (400,000 pairs) in the world.

SUMMER Great Northern and Red-throated Divers, Whooper Swan, Eider, Long-tailed Duck, White-tailed Eagle, Gyrfalcon, Red-necked Phalarope, Purple Sandpiper, Arctic Skua, Glaucous Gull, Guillemot, Brünnich's Guillemot, Razorbill, Puffin, Ptarmigan, Snow Bunting.

ACCESS Ísafjórdhur can be reached by road and has regular buses and flights from Reykjavík, and a variety of accommodation. Other fishing villages in the western part of the peninsula also have hotels or guest houses that can be reached by road. A ferry service across Breidhafjördur runs from Stykkishólmur to Brjánslaekur. Látrabjarg can be reached by car or bus. But to get to the twin 'Hs' a boat is necessary. A mixture of bus and boat may be the best method of exploring this splendid wilderness.

ROUTE Bus or plane from Reykjavík.

REYKJAVIK AND THE SOUTH-WEST

Reykjavík is a substantial city of 100,000 inhabitants and the obvious starting point for an exploration of Iceland. Most travellers have a day here at the start or end of a holiday, and birders should take the opportunity of getting out to enjoy its rather special appeal. Lake Tjornin, in the city centre, has a small remnant colony of Arctic Terns as well as breeding Greylag, Gadwall, Scaup and Eider. In winter, the lake is a haunt of

Barrow's Goldeneye, Wigeon and Eider, as well as gulls and feral Greylag Goose. Coastal areas have waders. Glaucous Gull is common in summer and Iceland Gull common in winter. King Eider are regular among the huge Eider flocks in Reykjavík harbour and elsewhere in late winter.

A short trip across the lava flows to Keflavík and beyond on the Reykjanes peninsula brings one to the massive cliffs of Hafnarberg and Krisuvikurberg, which hold excellent numbers of seabirds, including Brünnich's Guillemot and Glaucous Gull, while Purple Sandpiper and Snow Bunting breed nearby. The pointed 'toe' of Reykjanes, north of Keflavík, is favoured by local birders looking for American vagrants as well as passage migrants such as Pomarine Skua and Sooty Shearwater in autumn. Two or three species are being added to the Icelandic list each year.

Even totally dude birders, who would rather spend their time on the links, are well catered for hereabouts. The course on the Seltjarnarnes peninsula is a noted haunt of an aggressive colony of Arctic Terns, as well as of summering Glaucous Gull, Purple Sandpiper and Red-necked Phalarope.

For the ornitho-affluent, boats may be chartered to sail around the island of Eldey, with its massive gannetry. Over 16,000 pairs breed on the dramatic stack, but landing is not allowed and all but impossible anyway. The boat-trip will certainly be as near as anyone will ever get to 'ticking' the Great Auk, which became extinct here in 1844.

SUMMER Manx Shearwater, Gannet, Whooper Swan, Greylag Goose, Ringed Plover, Purple Sandpiper, Turnstone, Red-necked Phalarope, Kittiwake, Glaucous Gull, Arctic Tern, Guillemot, Brünnich's and Black Guillemots, Razorbill, Puffin, Redwing, Snow Bunting.
ACCESS The lake, harbour and golf course are all easily found, and there is a regular bus service to Keflavík and on to the smaller villages on the Reykjanes peninsula.
ROUTE Reykjavík has a domestic airport, and Keklavík an international one.

SNAEFELLSNES PENINSULA AND BREIDHAFJÖRDHUR

Snaefellsnes and Breidhafjördhur are the kind of names that at first sight seem awkward to pronounce, but which roll off the tongues of birders with the same ease as the Camargue. Their fame rests on a single species: the White-tailed Eagle. Altogether there are some 40 pairs in Iceland, giving a total population of about 120–150 individuals. The recent increase is due to a solid conservation policy by the Icelandic government backed by the Icelandic Society for the Protection of Birds, which probably saved the species from extinction in Iceland. The nests of both White-tailed Eagle and Gyrfalcon are completely protected from disturbance. The Eagle stronghold has always been the Breidhafjördhur area and when the population was at its lowest at about 20 pairs between 1940 and 1960 the birds survived almost entirely here. The cliffs are superb and on the North-west Peninsula hold most of the Glaucous Gull colonies in Iceland. The islands are equally splendid with huge colonies of Puffin, Kittiwake and Eider. Black Guillemot and Snow Bunting are also commonly found on the islands which are now the stronghold of the Grey

Phalarope. Many waterfowl, including Greylag, Harlequin and Eider, moult in Breidhafjördhur.

The island of Flatey (Flat Island) is the largest inhabited island in Breidhafjördhur. It is a unique place to visit and the old town has been virtually unchanged for one hundred years. Arctic Tern, Black Guillemot and Snow Bunting are numerous among the houses.

SUMMER Great Northern and Red-throated Divers, Fulmar, Whooper Swan, Greylag Goose, Harlequin, Eider, White-tailed Eagle, Gyrfalcon, Merlin, Grey and Red-necked Phalaropes, Glaucous Gull, Brünnich's and Black Guillemots, Razorbill, Puffin, Arctic Skua, Arctic Tern, Ptarmigan, Snow Bunting.

ACCESS There are roads along the shore of Breidhafjördhur and around Snaefellsnes. The ferry that crosses Breidhafjördhur stops in Flatey in both directions. It sails twice a day in summer and once a day in winter. It is possible to take longer or shorter boat-trips among the islands, mainly from Stykkishólmur but also from Flatey and elsewhere. There is a wide variety of accommodation in this area, including Flatey, but book in advance.

ROUTE An easy drive from Reykjavík.

SOUTHERN LOWLANDS AT ÖLFUS AND FLOI

For those visitors who cannot take in Mývatn, but who wish to see waterfowl and other wetland birds, the Southern Lowlands offer excellent opportunities. Only 40–50 km from Reykjavík is the Ölfusá Delta. The Ölfusforir and Kaldadharnes wetlands hold the highest breeding density of Black-tailed Godwit and Dunlin in Iceland. On passage there are thousands of geese, duck and waders and in winter there are Teal, Goosander and Grey Heron. The mouth of the Ölfusá River eastwards to the Thjórsá River – the Flói district – is very popular with birders. Whooper Swan breeds and one or two pairs of Grey Phalarope are seen occasionally. The broken shoreline with skerries, inlets and pools, is the edge of the largest lavaflow known from a single eruption, about 8000 years ago. Many migrants use it as a stop-over and seabirds find a fine feeding ground offshore. The River Sog with Barrow's Goldeneye and Harlequin is only a few minutes' drive from Selfoss, the main town of the area. The Southern Lowlands are one of the main agricultural regions of Iceland but some fine wetlands still remain.

SUMMER Red-throated Diver, Fulmar, Gannet, Whooper Swan, Greylag Goose, Mallard, Gadwall, Teal, Wigeon, Pintail, Shoveler, Tufted Duck, Scaup, Long-tailed Duck, Eider, Red-breasted Merganser, Golden and Ringed Plovers, Whimbrel, Black-tailed Godwit, Red-necked and Grey Phalaropes, Arctic and Great Skuas, Glaucous Gull, Kittiwake, Wheatear, Redwing, Raven, Snow Bunting.

PASSAGE Slavonian Grebe, Whooper Swan, Greylag, White-fronted, Pink-footed and Brent Geese, Scaup, Black-tailed Godwit, Purple Sandpiper, Knot, Sanderling, Red-necked Phalarope, Arctic Tern.

ACCESS A good network of roads covers the whole area. However, the Ölfusá Delta is best reached by foot and it is advised to get permission and guidance from local farmers before penetrating the area. The shore is open to all and the wetlands of Flói, close to Stokkseyri and Eyrarbakki, are easily accessible.

ROUTE By bus from Reykjavík, less than an hour away.

THINGVELLIR

Some 50 km east of Reykjavík in a landscape of lava flows, volcanoes and grassy meadows, lies Iceland's largest lake and the seat of the country's parliament. The meadows are reminiscent of Europe and it is not surprising to find breeding Black-tailed Godwit here. Thingvallavatn is not so good as Mývatn (too deep), but it is much easier to get to, has a good hotel and can offer several specialities. Gyrfalcon is reasonably regular and Great Northern Diver breeds in small numbers. The River Öxará has Harlequin, and Barrow's Goldeneye ooccasionally breed at the outlet of the River Sog.

SUMMER Great Northern Diver, Goosander, Harlequin, Tufted Duck, Scaup, Barrow's Goldeneye, Gyrfalcon, Merlin, Whimbrel, Black-tailed Godwit, Arctic Tern, Lesser Black-backed Gull, Snow Bunting.
ACCESS A well-signposted 50-km drive from the capital, with frequent bus services. Good roads all around the lake, but the east side is the best.
ROUTE Via Reykjavík.

WESTMANN ISLANDS

These islands lie off the south-west coast of Iceland and have a world-wide reputation for their seabird colonies. The group consists of 15 islands, only one of which, Heimaey, is inhabited. The second largest island is Surtsey, which emerged from the sea as a result of volcanic activity between 1963 and 1967, and which is now the home of Great Black-backed, Lesser Black-backed and Herring Gulls, a few pairs of Black Guillemot, Fulmar and a pair of Raven.

Four of the smaller islands hold gannetries, but Heimaey has five species of breeding auk, including Brünnich's Guillemot, here hugely outnumbered by its common cousin. Altogether 15 species of seabird breed, the most numerous of which is probably the Puffin.

Manx Shearwater and Leach's and Storm Petrels breed on the outer islands, though they are difficult to locate because of their nocturnal habits. The Leach's colony on Ellidhaey is considered the largest in Europe. Shearwaters can often be seen gathering offshore in the late afternoon. Heimaey has some of the most spectacular cliff colonies in the world.

SUMMER Manx Shearwater, Fulmar, Storm Petrel, Leach's Petrel, Gannet, Cormorant, Shag, Guillemot, Brünnich's and Black Guillemots, Razorbill, Puffin, Glaucous Gull, Kittiwake, Great and Arctic Skuas.
ACCESS The islands can be reached by daily ferry from Thorlákshöfn, itself in contact with the capital by a regular bus service, or by several flights each day from Reykjavík which usually pass over Surtsey. If you take a 'day' trip, take all your luggage as services are often held up somewhat, though it is exceptional for the ferries not to sail.
ROUTE Via Reykjavík.

IRELAND

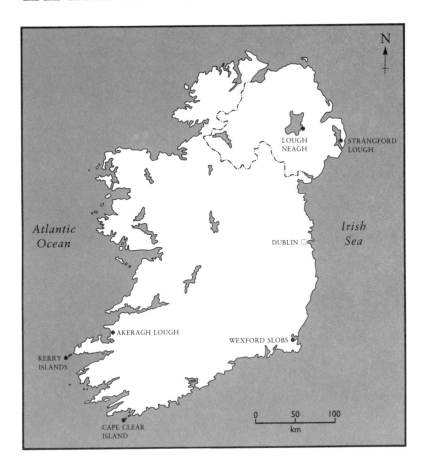

AKERAGH LOUGH

Akeragh Lough lies behind the sand-dune beach at the head of Bally-heighe Bay south of Kerry Head. It is a shallow water of 2.4–2.8 ha, set in a flat landscape. A slight change in water level affects its size considerably. Its marshy surrounds are grassy and typical of those favoured by Ruff, while there are considerable areas of reeds. It is the Irish stronghold of Gadwall, and other duck occur according to water levels. Its position 'across the sea' from America has brought Akeragh ornithological fame as the eastern 'home' of Nearctic waders. Pectoral Sandpipers are annual visitors, and others have included Killdeer, Lesser Golden Plover, dowitchers, Least, Baird's, White-rumped and Western Sandpipers. American duck sometimes turn up as well.

AUTUMN Ruff, Little Stint, Greenshank, rarities.
ACCESS Akeragh Lough, which is private property, lies south of

Ballyheighe village and can be best looked over from Route 105 which passes it on the landward side.
ROUTE Via Dublin, Shannon or Cork have international airports.

CAPE CLEAR ISLAND

Established as a bird observatory in 1959, Clear was in the forefront of the seawatching mania of the 1960s and remains an outstanding site for seabirds today. At the south-western corner of Ireland, it is ideally placed for watching birds blown inshore by the south-westerly gales of late sum mer. It is equally well placed to receive American birds that find their first European landfall here. Clear has had its fair share of rarities, and it is surprising that it has not received more attention from rarity-hunters, especially as Scilly is becoming so overcrowded during the October peak.

Though Clear has a few interesting breeding birds, the migration seasons offer most to the adventurous birder who comes here. August to October is best and seawatchers can expect most of the specials that regularly occur in Europe. Passerines definitely merit more attention than they have so far received. Go for an autumn week and see what turns up.

AUTUMN Great, Cory's, Sooty and Manx Shearwaters, Storm and Leach's Petrels, Gannet, Great Skua, passerines.
SUMMER Black Guillemot, Chough.
ACCESS The best way to arrange a week on Clear is to write to the Bird Observatory. Contact BTO, The National Centre for Ornithology, The Nunnery, Thetford, Norfolk, IP24 2PU for current details of bookings. The observatory will provide up-to-date details of its own accommodation, which is hostel/self-catering type for up to ten people, and can also put prospective visitors in touch with locals offering accommodation.
ROUTE The mailboat sails daily from Baltimore, Co. Cork, at 2.15 p.m. . . more or less.

KERRY ISLANDS

The westernmost points of Ireland are a collection of small, largely uninhabited islands off County Kerry. They lie in three groups as continuations of the peninsulas separated by Dingle Bay and the Kenmare River. All species of breeding British seabirds are found here.

The islands have romantic-sounding names, and part of their attraction lies in reaching them by fishing boat from the charming western Ireland fishing villages. They are: **Inishtooskert** (Storm Petrel, Manx Shearwater); **Inishtearaght** (large colonies of Storm Petrel, Manx Shearwater, Puffin); **Inishabro** (Storm Petrel, Manx Shearwater, Fulmar); **Inishvickillane** (large colonies of Storm Petrel, Manx Shearwater, Fulmar, Puffin, Razorbill); **Puffin Island** (20,000 Manx Shearwater, Fulmar, Puffin); **Little Skellig** (22,000 Gannet); **Great Skellig** (Storm Petrel, Manx Shearwater) and **Bull Rock** (actually in Co. Cork – 500 Gannet, Kittiwake, Razorbill).

ACCESS It is possible to charter boats from the adjacent fishing villages, price by negotiation. Petrels and shearwaters are only about at night so, unless you intend to camp and stay for several days, it is as well to choose

Pectoral Sandpiper

an island where birds such as auks and Gannets can be seen during the day. Landing is difficult and really unnecessary, but can make for a marvellous holiday for birders who organize thoroughly. Camping on the Blaskets is prohibited, except on Great Blasket.

ROUTE Via Dublin or Cork which have international flights.

LOUGH NEAGH

This is the large, empty rectangle shown on so many bird-distribution maps of Ireland. It is a huge wetland of about 40,000 ha, measuring 25 km by 17 km. Lying only a short drive to the west of Belfast, it attracts considerable attention from both resident and visiting birders, particularly in winter when it harbours more duck than any other Irish site.

Lough Neagh is shallow and reed-fringed, offering feeding opportunities to a wide variety of species. Outstanding are the flocks of diving duck, with Pochard and Tufted regularly reaching a combined total of 40,000 birds. Several other species reach four-figure numbers and all three swans find a major stronghold here. Because of its size, Lough Neagh is seldom accurately censused and may, sometimes, prove disappointing to visitors. There is, however, an adjacent water called Lough Beg, which is much smaller, shallower, and offers rich feeding to many wildfowl. It also has the habit of attracting passage waders, including the odd Nearctic species.

In summer a good population of breeding birds includes 1000 pairs of Tufted Duck, the occasional Garganey and regular Goldeneye.

WINTER Mallard, Teal, Wigeon, Pintail, Shoveler, Tufted Duck, Pochard, Scaup, Goldeneye, Mute, Bewick's and Whooper Swans.
SUMMER Great Crested Grebe, Teal, Shoveler, Garganey, Tufted Duck, Goldeneye, Red-breasted Merganser, Scoter, Common Tern.
ACCESS Lough Neagh is easily viewed at many points around its perimeter from public roads. Birds often congregate in the lee shore. Lough Beg is private, but may be approached via public roads from the west.
ROUTE Easily reached westwards from Belfast.

STRANGFORD LOUGH

This virtually land-locked sea lough to the south-east of Belfast acts as a magnet to local watchers. At low tide a huge area of exposed intertidal mud attracts large numbers of wintering and passage waders. The low islands of the north shore form important high-tide roosts, regularly attracting Knot (10,000), Bar-tailed Godwit (1700), Dunlin (10,000), and large numbers of Curlew, Oystercatcher and Redshank. Over half the Irish population of Brent Goose (10,000) winter along with huge flocks of Wigeon. Whooper Swan, Pintail and Merganser all reach three figures.

The only river to enter the lough has been dammed as part of a flood-control scheme and forms a fresh-water pool – the Quoile Pondage – a National Nature Reserve. This is always worth a look. On passage a wide variety of waders and other species put in an appearance and, as elsewhere in Ireland, there is every chance of an American wader or two in the autumn. Breeding birds include terns and gulls, and Merganser.

WINTER Brent Goose, Shelduck, Wigeon, Pintail, Red-breasted Merganser, Whooper Swan, Curlew, Bar-tailed Godwit, Knot, Dunlin.
SUMMER Red-breasted Merganser, Shelduck, Arctic Tern.
ACCESS The largest concentrations of birds are usually in the north-west, north of Mahee Island. There are several shoreline refuges as well as island sanctuaries, though the area can be explored via public roads and pathways.
ROUTE Easily reached south-eastwards from Belfast.

WEXFORD SLOBS

Long famous as the major wintering ground of wildfowl in Ireland, the Slobs have changed quite dramatically since the first *WWBE*. Much of the North Slob has been put to the plough, while the South Slob has changed from a region of grazing to one of mowing. Fortunately, though breeding birds have undoubtedly suffered, the appeal to winter enthusiasts remains the same, while rarity-watchers have the same chances as ever.

About half of the world population of Greenland Whitefronts winter here, along with several hundred Brent. Many duck reach numbers in excess of 1000 and for Lapwing and Golden Plover the damp fields offer a refuge when Britain is ice-bound. Black-tailed Godwits are particularly important in winter, and during passage periods the Slobs become a major staging post to a wide variety of waders.

As this is one of the major wetlands in Ireland, American birds can appear here. Snow Geese are fairly regular, presumably having arrived with the Greenland geese, and transatlantic waders appear every autumn.

WINTER Slavonian Grebe, Bewick's Swan, Brent, White-fronted, Pink-footed and Barnacle Geese, Teal, Pintail, Scaup, Golden Plover, Black-tailed Godwit.
PASSAGE Whimbrel, Spotted Redshank, transatlantic waders, Little Gull.
ACCESS The South Slob is reached from Route 8 south of Wexford. Turn left to Rosslare, past Killinick, and continue to Burrow.
ROUTE Dublin international airport.

ISRAEL

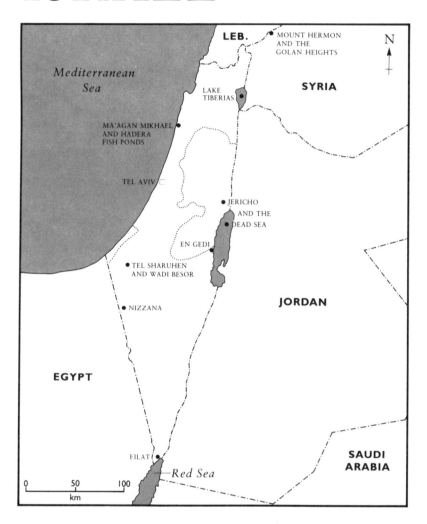

EILAT

Eilat is Israel's resort on the Red Sea and is sited to receive migrants on their way to and from Africa. At first it was regarded simply as a splendid place to watch raptors, especially in the spring, when over 750,000 birds of prey have been counted moving north. This figure is ten times the number over the Bosporus and five times as many as over Gibraltar. Such a dramatic passage inevitably attracted a considerable number of enthusiasts, and it is their work, coupled with that of the local International Birdwatching Centre Eilat that has publicized the area's other attractions.

Migrants of a wide variety of species find refuge among the various habitats in what is otherwise a decidedly inhospitable landscape. The buildings and their gardens offer shelter to small migrants, as do the intensively farmed kibbutz to the north of the town. Such birds include hordes of the common visitors to northern Europe, as well as the more exotic Red-throated Pipit, Thrush Nightingale, Rufous Bushchat, Black-eared Wheatear, Olivaceous and Bonelli's Warblers, Masked Shrike and Cretzschmar's Bunting. Waders pour through, mostly concentrating on the saltpans that lie immediately east of the airport. The sewage canal attracts crakes and rails, while there are common migrants such as Pied and Collared Flycatchers and Wryneck virtually everywhere. There are even records of Wrynecks frequenting a traffic roundabout.

The massive passage of raptors and small migrants would certainly be enough to attract birders from all over Europe, but Eilat's geographical position gives it one more major attraction. As it is on the Red Sea, there is a chance of several seabirds that are otherwise not to be found in the Western Palearctic. Brown Booby and Western Reef Heron fall into this category, along with various gulls and terns that could include Lesser Crested and Bridled Terns and even White-eyed Gull, Eilat is also an 'oasis' for desert birds that live in the surrounding area, and various species of sandgrouse, larks, chats and finches occur that are both decidedly both southern and definitely desert-dwelling.

With good international transport links, a variety of accommodation, easy (if expensive) car hire, absolutely superb birding and good local contacts, it is not surprising that Eilat has proved so popular with birders every spring and autumn. One word of warning: as with other desert areas, the peaks of bird activity are in the early morning and late afternoon. Apart from waders and seabirds, most species simply disappear during the heat of the day and it is unwise to chase around after them.

PASSAGE Brown Booby, Western Reef, Night and Squacco Herons, Cattle, Little and Great White Egrets, White Stork, Black Kite, Egyptian and Lappet-faced Vultures, Short-toed and Steppe Eagles, Honey Buzzard, Buzzard, Long-legged Buzzard, Pallid Harrier, Levant Sparrowhawk, Osprey, Barbary Falcon, Sand Partridge, Spur-winged Plover, Marsh and Broad-billed Sandpipers, Collared Pratincole, Cream-coloured Courser, Slender-billed Gull, Gull-billed and Whiskered Terns, Lichtenstein's and Crowned Sandgrouse, Eagle Owl, Bee-eater, Blue-cheeked and Little Green Bee-eaters, Masked Shrike, Bifasciated and Bar-tailed Desert Larks, Pale Crag Martin, Citrine Wagtail, Red-throated Pipit, Yellow-vented Bulbul, Arabian Babbler, Rufous Bushchat, Hooded and White-crowned Black Wheatears, Thrush Nightingale, Blackstart, Graceful, Scrub and Arabian Warblers, Desert and Trumpeter Finches, Dead Sea Sparrow, Sinai Rosefinch, House Bunting, Tristram's Grackle, Brown-necked Raven.

ACCESS Eilat lies mainly on the western shore of the Gulf of Aqaba, with an area of hotels around the lagoon (marina) on the North Beach. The main birding areas lie to the north between the main road north and the Jordanian border. A good introduction to this area is to join a guided birding tour organized by Hadoram Shirihai (Tel/Fax. 972–7–379326). Hadoram is also co-author of *Birdwatching in the Deserts of Israel* a site guide to most of Israel. The saltpans are reached via the driveable track up the western side of the sewage canal – Flamingo, waders and Dead Sea Sparrow. The ringing station and the Kibbutz Fields – Namaqua Dove,

Little Green Bee-eater, Desert Finch – are approached by driving up the eastern side of the canal, past a palm plantation, and ending up at a pumping station near the main north road. The small pond here regularly attracts desert species to drink, including early-morning Crowned Sandgrouse. Just before the pumping station, a turning on the right leads to the **Northern Fields**. These are good for small birds such as Pale Rock Sparrow and Bimaculated Lark. The **North Beach** itself is the regular seawatch and afternoon meeting place. Gather at the mouth of the sewage canal. The football field lies to the west and is reached by taking the turning opposite the airport terminal. Turn left at the second intersection and take the first right into Jerusalem Street. Watch for a dome on the left and, as the road swings left, take the track on the right. Just over the rise the water-sprinklers keep the pitch in prime condition and attract huge numbers of migrants. Farther along the track, the water-pumping station has a small pool that attracts Trumpeter Finch and House Bunting. At dusk, Lichtenstein's Sandgrouse come to drink. The secret is to park a car about 20 m away facing the pool. Turning headlights on is now banned. Access at dusk is restricted to two nights per week. The **Moon Valley Mountains** are the best spot for raptor-watching, though migrating birds can be seen throughout the area. About 13 km north of Eilat, the Be'er Ora is good for Courser and Bifasciated and Bar-tailed Desert Larks. Though there is no reason to suppose that these birds do not occur throughout this area, a stop at kilometre post 33 gives a chance of Lappet-faced Vulture soaring over the hills to the west at about 7 a.m. There is only one pair in Israel. Desert birds are best to the east of the road. Turn off on a short tarmac road and park at the pumping station. Returning towards Eilat, watch for kilometre post 20 and a track westward signposted 'Amrams Pillars'. Drive along and take a right-hand fork at 5 km to a parking area. Sinai Rosefinch winters here until the third week of March (sometimes into April), frequenting the rubbish bins. Desert Lark and White-crowned Black Wheatear are also seen here regularly. **Yotvata** is an area of bushy scrub just beyond kilometre post 45 on the north road out of Eilat. There is a petrol station and café on the right-hand side of the road, behind which is a rubbish dump among the acacia trees. This is good for migrants and specialities such as Arabian Warbler – an Orphean-type bird with a completely black tail, which is continuously cocked, and a rounded bulbul-type head. Also found here are Scrub and Olivaceous Warblers and Little Green Bee-eater. To the south, at kilometre post 40 the area east of the road holds similar species, and possible Cream-coloured Courser, Bifasciated Lark, Desert Wheatear and sometimes Houbara Bustard. Also check the outflow from the sewage pool to the south.

En Gedi

The Dead Sea lies 394 m below sea-level and is the lowest place on earth. Its waters are highly saline and virtually devoid of life. The most famous birding here is centred on the oasis of En Gedi approximately half-way along the western shore. The main wadi here is a nature reserve and is excellent for small migrants, while along the ridge is the best point for watching raptor-passage. Local specialities include Griffon Vulture, Sand Partridge, Tristram's Grackle and Arabian Babbler. Outstanding, however, is Hume's Tawny Owl, a pair of which frequents the area of the field school north of the wadi entrance. These birds regularly perch on the boundary fence (floodlit!) and can, with a little patience, be seen superbly. It is possible to stay at the field centre or the adjacent youth hostel. The wadi reserve opens at 9 a.m., so early-morning walkers concentrate on the trees and bushes on the south side of the wadi – excellent for migrants.

All of the wadis to the south between En Gedi and Massada are worth exploring. They hold a good variety of species, including both ravens, Blackstart, Scrub Warbler and Trumpeter Finch. Two in particular, Wadi en Zafzafa and Wadi n Ze'elim, are noted as haunts of Lammergeier, while the latter is also a possible Hume's site. A further wadi about 3 km south of Massada is also good for these species plus Bonelli's Eagle.

The En Gedi Kibbutz is run as a hotel, with cottage-style accommodation, swimming pool, etc, and is one of the nicer places to stay. The bushes on the right side of the road are a wintering ground of Cyprus Warbler.

PASSAGE Lammergeier, Griffon Vulture, Short-toed, Steppe and Bonelli's Eagles, Buzzard, Long-legged and Honey Buzzards, Barbary Falcon, Sand Partridge, Hume's Tawny Owl, Bee-eater, Pale Crag Martin, Masked Shrike, Desert Lark, Arabian Babbler, White-crowned Black and Hooded Wheatears, Thrush Nightingale, Blackstart, Scrub and Cyprus Warblers, Trumpeter Finch, House and Cretzschmar's Buntings, Tristram's Grackle, Fan-tailed Raven, Brown-necked Raven.

ACCESS The wadi reserve is easily found, with the field school and youth hostel at the entrance. Hume's Tawny Owl can be seen after dark on the perimeter fence. North of the field centre is an amphitheatre, beyond which is a gate through the fence leading up a path to a raptor-watching spot. The reserve is open at about 9 a.m. and an admission fee is charged but may still be worth visiting. The area south of the wadi is good for migrants. The wadis to the south (*see* above) should all be explored to and beyond Massada. There are no restrictions on access.

ROUTE En Gedi is an hour from Jerusalem and three hours from Eilat.

JERICHO AND THE DEAD SEA

The area around Jericho southwards to the Dead Sea makes an ideal 'day off' for anyone with time on their hands either in Jericho or Jerusalem. To the south of the town, the road crosses the large Wadi Quilt. On the south side of the bridge, a track leads westwards along the rim of the wadi to a monastery and the canyon. This is an excellent spot for a variety of species, including the elusive Hooded Wheatear and Bonelli's Eagle.

Farther south, on the Dead Sea road, the Qayla Fish-ponds are on the right about 0.5 km before the right turn to Qayla. These ponds have Clamorous Reed Warbler, as well as Little Crake and other wetland species.

Roughly half-way between Jericho and En Gedi is the Wadi Darga, a great gorge in the wall of the Rift Valley. This is a splendid area for birds of prey, including Bonelli's Eagle, Lanner and Barbary Falcon and occasional vultures. A turning north of the Wadi leads to Mezokei Dragot, a holiday village. Beyond here a track leads west with a turning left after 1.5 km to a viewpoint overlooking the gorge. Wheatears, larks, Trumpeter Finch, House Bunting, Brown-necked and Fan-tailed Ravens can all be seen, some commonly. This area is a major raptor-migration watch-point in spring.

SUMMER Bonelli's Eagle, Lanner, Barbary Falcon, Black Francolin, Sand Partridge, Little Crake, Pale Crag Martin, Desert Lark, Blackstart, Arabian Babbler, Hooded, White-crowned Black and Mourning Wheatears, Tristram's Grackle, Rock Sparrow, Trumpeter Finch, Cinereous and House Buntings.

ACCESS Wadi Quilt is easily found between Jericho and the Dead Sea–Jerusalem road. Qayla Fish-ponds are nearer the Dead Sea. Follow instructions above for Mezokei Dragot.

ROUTE Less than an hour by road from Jerusalem to Jericho.

LAKE TIBERIAS

Tiberias is a first-class base for exploring several places for a wide variety of species: two areas of fish-ponds, a marshland nature reserve, many wadis and a mountain area. North of Tiberias, on the road to Qiryat Shemona, lies the Huleh reserve. This is approached via a track east off the main road which passes an area of fish-ponds before the car park. Three rather difficult species can be seen, both at the ponds and in the reserve: White Pelican, Marbled Teal and Clamorous Reed Warbler. Dead Sea Sparrow may be here, and herons, egrets and Smyrna and Lesser Pied Kingfishers are always on the reserve. Penduline Tit, Moustached Warbler and small crakes can be seen. North of the reserve, where the swamp has been drained, is a regular wintering ground of Spotted Eagle. Raptors come in to roost at dusk.

To the south, westwards off the main road, is Wadi Amud, a wadi that leads into a deep canyon with some very good birds. Eagle Owl is found throughout the year. Little Swift and Blue Rock Thrush both breed. Syrian Woodpecker may be found, and this is one spot for Long-billed Pipit. On the way check Lake Tiberias at its north-western corner, which is good for kingfishers. A little way to the south there is a road to Maghar where, just south of the town, another canyon leads into Arbel Mountain. This has Alpine Accentor and Wallcreeper, and has produced Finsch's Wheatear.

Along the eastern shore of the lake is Wadi Sumakh. This is the only site in this book for Brown Fish Owl and a special trek is required even for a chance of this bird. Access is along the wadi, which lies 750 m north of the turning to Ramat Mogshimm, for about an hour. Despite bushes and thickets, stay close to the stream and look for an obvious rock in the middle covered with crab shells and droppings. Some have said that the rock is not obvious! Settle down for a long wait, or return at dusk. This is the owl's feeding post. When it is quite clear that the bird is present, point a powerful torch skywards, turn it on and slowly bring it down to point at the rock. Good luck is needed, for the bird is decidedly erratic even here.

Southwards from Tiberias, there are fish-ponds north of Bet She'an on the left-hand side of the road. Take a left and park after 100 m. These ponds cover a substantial area, but should produce Barbary Falcon, Clamorous Reed Warbler, Penduline Tit and possible Great Snipe.

SUMMER White Pelican, White Stork, Glossy Ibis, Night, Purple and Squacco Herons, Cattle Egret, Little Bittern, Barbary Falcon, Griffon Vulture, Marbled Teal, Little Crake, Black-winged Stilt, Great Snipe, Brown Fish Owl, Eagle Owl, Little Swift, Alpine Accentor, Wallcreeper, Syrian Woodpecker, Long-billed Pipit, Penduline Tit, Blue Rock Thrush,

Smyrna Kingfisher

Finsch's Wheatear, Moustached and Clamorous Reed Warblers, Orange-tufted Sunbird, Dead Sea Sparrow, Rock Bunting.
WINTER Spotted Eagle.
ACCESS The **Huleh Swamp** is reached 10 km north of Rosh Pinna, beyond Yesud Hama'ala. The track to the fish-ponds and the reserve is on the right, but poorly signposted. For **Wadi Amud**, leave Tiberias northward and take the small turning left to Huqoq. After 6–7 km a large wadi, with a bridged river, runs beneath the road. There is a car park, with a footpath leading north (right) along the wadi and canyon. Take this until the canyon becomes less steep and you can scramble up the left side to the top. Eagle Owl starts calling before dusk. Long-billed Pipit is found in grass-covered areas broken by gorse bushes. Syrian Woodpecker haunts the trees on the west of the wadi on the south side (left) of the road. For **Arbel Mountain**, take the Maghar road, which is closer to Tiberias than the Huqoq road. Just before Maghar, turn left into a deep gorge with cliffs holding Wallcreeper and (possibly) Finsch's Wheatear. The Fish Owl site is detailed above.
ROUTE Tiberias is easily reached by road from the south. Hotels are a little simple, but decidedly cheap.

MA'AGAN MIKHAEL AND HADERA FISH-PONDS

These two areas of fish-ponds lie adjacent to the Mediterranean coast, only a short drive north from Tel Aviv, and are thus excellent for those with only a day free for birding. The first attracts those with more time by virtue of being a winter (late-spring?) haunt of Great Black-headed Gull. Other regulars include Flamingo, Greater Sand and Spur-winged Plovers, Glossy Ibis, Smyrna and Lesser Pied Kingfishers and Slender-billed Gull.

WINTER Great Black-headed and Slender-billed Gulls.
SUMMER White Pelican, White Stork, Glossy Ibis, Little and Great White Egrets, Night and Squacco Herons, Greater Sand and Spur-winged Plovers, Black-winged Stilt, Slender-billed Gull, Water Rail, Little and Baillon's Crakes, Smyrna and Lesser Pied Kingfishers, Clamorous Reed and Rüppell's Warblers.

ACCESS **Ma'agan Mikhael** is reached on the old road north of Tel Aviv (not the motorway) after 50 km. Turn left (signposted) and then right opposite the football pitch. After 200 m turn right to the cemetery, where a rocky area to the north holds Rüppell's and other warblers. Return and continue northwards along the road to the 'No Entry' sign. Park and continue on foot, turning left to the beach then north again, checking all the gulls. There is another entrance off the main road north of the fishponds. The fish-ponds can be explored on foot by returning to the football pitch and turning right (west) towards the sea. There are ponds to the left and right. At the coast, turn right and watch over a marshy ditch for crakes. **Hadera fish-ponds** lie north of Tel Aviv, a little way north of the town of Hadera to the east of the main road. They offer similar species to the more famous Ma'agan Mikhael area, while lacking some of the specialities. A ditch running along the southern edge of the ponds may sometimes hold Painted Snipe.

ROUTE About an hour's drive northward from Ben Gurion Airport.

MOUNT HERMON AND THE GOLAN HEIGHTS

The Golan Heights are etched on the memory of anyone with even the slightest awareness of Israel's history. Strategically of critical significance, the area is now settled and developed into a holiday area for skiing. It is also remarkably good for birds, with several species that are otherwise almost impossible to find in the country. This is an alpine area with woods, meadows and high screes, where snow is regular and may still fall as late as April. Warm protective clothing is essential at all times.

At the top of Mount Hermon, Crimson-winged Finch is the speciality. Lower down, species such as Syrian Serin, Rock Sparrow, Sombre Tit and Orphean Warbler are found around the area of the ski-lift base station, as well as along the approach road. The Serin also occurs as low as Majdal Shams, and there are also Rock Nuthatch, Black-eared Wheatear, Rüppell's and Upcher's Warblers and Cretzschmar's Bunting.

Lower still, on the approach road south of Masada, are Calandra and Bimaculated Larks and Isabelline Wheatear. Even Finsch's Wheatear may be seen here, and in late summer White-throated Robin occurs. Raptors, including Griffon and Egyptian Vultures and Bonelli's and Short-toed Eagles, are present throughout the area. Anyone wishing to see as wide a variety of species as possible in Israel cannot afford to miss this area.

SUMMER Griffon and Egyptian Vultures, Short-toed and Bonelli's Eagles, Long-legged Buzzard, Little Swift, Rock Nuthatch, Calandra, Bimaculated and Short-toed Larks, Woodlark, Sombre Tit, Rock Thrush, Black-eared, Finsch's and Isabelline Wheatears, White-throated Robin, Orphean, Rüppell's and Upcher's Warblers, Syrian Serin, Crimson-winged Finch, Rock and Pale Rock Sparrows.

ACCESS There is an army checkpoint on the final approach to **Mount Hermon** that does not permit access until 9.30 a.m. Continue northwards after this time to the end of the road at the ski-lift base station. Check that you are allowed out at the top; it is pointless to waste money and time if you are not. Crimson-winged Finch is the only reason for going so high. The area around the base station is good, especially the rubbish tip,

Bimaculated Lark

and, on the drive down, a small lake on the right has two mounds with Rock Nuthatch, Rock Sparrow and Rock Thrush. Lower still, a car park with a monument on the right has similar birds. Below this, there is a one-way system below Majdal Shams. At the T-junction turn right, and watch for a car park with a wrecked coach on the left after a few hundred metres. Syrian Serin, Sombre Tit, Cretzschmar's Bunting and Rüppell's and Upcher's Warblers can be found in the area north and south of the road. Just south of Masada, soon after the turning to Bu'Qata, there are some tin sheds to the right of the road. A track alongside them leads into a stony area for three larks and Isabelline Wheatear. If time permits, the area of **Caesarea Philippi** will produce Griffon Vulture and other raptors, Rock Thrush and Little Swift.

ROUTE North from Tiberias through Rosh Pinna to Majdal Shams.

Nizzana

The castle of Nizzana lies right against the Egyptian border in the Negev Desert, south of Beersheba. It takes little knowledge of recent history to realize that this is a sensitive area, full of military, tanks and personnel-carriers. Birders have been asked to leave, had their films confiscated and even been detained and interrogated. It is for each to calculate whether or not it is worthwhile to explore what is the only area in the country that may produce Houbara Bustard and Temminck's Horned Lark.

The approach is via Beersheba southwards; the old road to Nizzana is closed, so an up-to-date map is essential. Beyond the Zeelim turn-off, the area of pools at Ashalim has three species of sandgrouse soon after dawn; but beware, for they are often dry by mid-April. A wadi here has produced Houbara, Cream-coloured Courser and Lesser Short-toed Lark.

Continuing southwards, a flat plain is noted for Bifasciated and Lesser Short-toed Larks and possible Houbara. A turning to the left leads to the castle itself, where Desert Wheatear, Courser and Pin-tailed and Spotted Sandgrouse have been seen. After passing the castle take the first right on a track to Keziot sewage ponds. In the early morning this is a major sandgrouse drinking station with Spotted, Black-bellied, Pin-tailed and even a few Crowned. Scrub Warbler is also here among the surrounding bushes. Another excellent area is the Wadi Beerotayim, which is crossed by the Nizzana–Izuz road just a few hundred metres north of the latter. This is excellent for Houbara, sandgrouse and Courser.

SUMMER Lanner, Long-legged Buzzard, Houbara Bustard, Black-bellied, Pin-tailed and Spotted Sandgrouse, Cream-coloured Courser, Bifasciated, Desert, Lesser Short-toed and Temminck's Horned Larks, Desert Wheatear, Desert and Trumpeter Finches.
ACCESS Take the new Nizzana road southwards from Beersheba and watch for the roadside pools and adjacent ridge after the turning (right) to Ashalim. Some 15–20 km farther and you are in the Nizzana area.
ROUTE Beersheba can be reached from Tel Aviv or Jerusalem in a day. There is an Educational Settlement at Nizzana that offers accommodation, and a camp site at Izuz.

TEL SHARUHEN AND WADI BESOR

These adjacent areas lie in the Nahal Habosar Nature Reserve on the edge of the Negev Desert. Wadi Besor is huge, extending from the desert to the coast, while the Tel is an obvious, rounded hill with a deep quarry on its south side. Though much of the surroundings is arid, irrigation has made large areas fertile. There are some trees and bushes with Scops Owl and Syrian Woodpecker, while the fields have Courser, Stone-curlew and Pin-tailed Sandgrouse. Raptors present include Imperial Eagle, Pallid Harrier and Lanner, but above all the quarry is an excellent Eagle Owl spot.

In winter the area around Urim has Sociable Plover, while south, nearer the border, around Yevul and Deqel is a haunt of Houbara Bustard and Courser. To the east, between this area and Ofaqim, between Maslul and Hippushit and, in particular the line of pylons south of Urim, make up one of the best places for winter raptors in Israel. Imperial Eagle, Saker, Lanner and Hen and Pallid Harriers are regular. Sandgrouse are often abundant and Sociable Plover and Dotterel are regular every winter.

SUMMER Long-legged Buzzard, Pallid Harrier, Lanner, Chukar, Stone-curlew, Cream-coloured Courser, Eagle and Hume's Tawny Owls, Pin-tailed Sandgrouse, Bifasciated and Calandra Larks.
WINTER Imperial Eagle, Saker, Lanner, Sociable Plover, Dotterel, Little and Houbara Bustards, Pin-tailed Sandgrouse.
ACCESS Leave Beersheba northwards and turn left for Ofaqim. Some 18 km farther, there is a car park on the left side of the road just before Wadi Besor. Walk down the western side of the wadi to the Tel. At dusk, Eagle Owl may be seen from the southern edge of the hill. Examine fields and the wadi for other species. Follow the road to Kelem Shalom and turn southwards towards Dekel. Ignore the Dekel turning and continue past the Isra-Beton factory to a sandy plain for Houbara and Courser.

East of Ofaqim, watch for a minor turning to Maslul on the north side of the road. Opposite this is a track. Motor about 2 km to a line of pylons and explore. These same pylons extend to Urim and beyond.
ROUTE Beersheba can be reached from Tel Aviv/Jerusalem in a day.

ITALY

Circeo National Park

While most Italian national parks are centred on the high mountains of
the Alps and the Appennines, Circeo is a coastal wilderness on the west
coast half-way between Rome and Naples. It is, inevitably, something of
a playground for city-dwellers, but the extensive forests of evergreen oaks
together with coastal lagoons and marshes swallow them up and have
plenty of fine sites for birding. Breeding birds include Great Spotted Cuckoo
and Golden Oriole, but on passage and in winter there may be impressive
gatherings of a wide range of birds. Glossy Ibis, Spotted Eagle and

Red-footed Falcon may whet the appetite, but Marsh Sandpiper and Audouin's Gull are among other reasonably regular birds here.

Winter brings some wildfowl, including Ferruginous Duck, but the park is said to be a good Wallcreeper spot at this time of the year.

SUMMER White Stork, Marsh Harrier, Great Spotted Cuckoo, Golden Oriole, Hoopoe, Grey-headed Woodpecker, Moustached, Subalpine and Sardinian Warblers, Serin, Cirl Bunting.
WINTER Black-throated Diver, Peregrine, Great White Egret, Pintail, Gadwall, Ferruginous Duck, Sandwich Tern, Wallcreeper.
PASSAGE Little and Great White Egrets, Spoonbill, Glossy Ibis, Osprey, Red-footed Falcon, Crane, Marsh Sandpiper, Avocet, Little Stint, Great Snipe, Spotted Redshank, Collared Pratincole, Audouin's Gull, Caspian and Whiskered Terns, Woodchat Shrike.
ACCESS The coastal road south between Latina and Sabaudia and beyond passes the main lagoons and gives access to the major areas of woodland.
ROUTE Southwards along the main coastal road from Rome.

CONERO PROMONTORY

The Conero coastline is one of the few as yet untouched areas on the Adriatic coast between Gargano and the Po Delta. Although relatively small, the wide variety of vegetation includes areas of evergreen and deciduous woodland along with typical Mediterranean scrub. There are a couple of brackish ponds and some cliffs called the 'Two Sisters'. Such a variety of habitats naturally holds a good selection of birds, including breeding Peregrine, Alpine Swift, Blue Rock Thrush and Sardinian, Fantailed and Melodious Warblers, and Cirl Bunting. It is, however, the strategic siting of the Conero Promontory that is responsible for its ornitho-fame. This is quite simply the best viewpoint for watching the spring passage of birds of prey on the Adriatic coast. As elsewhere in Italy, May is the best month and Honey Buzzard (up to 1000 a day) the most abundant species. There are, however, regular White and Black Storks, Marsh and Pallid Harriers, Kestrel and Lesser Kestrel, Hobby and Eleonora's Falcon and even the occasional Lesser Spotted Eagle. The area is also good for migrating small birds with Red-throated Pipit and Black-eared Wheatear regular.

SUMMER Peregrine, Alpine Swift, Blue Rock Thrush, Sardinian, Fantailed and Melodious Warblers, Cirl Bunting.
PASSAGE White and Black Storks, Marsh and Pallid Harriers, Lesser Kestrel, Hobby, Eleonora's Falcon, Honey Buzzard, Lesser Spotted Eagle, Golden Oriole, Red-throated Pipit, Wheatear, Black-eared Wheatear, Yellow Wagtail, Pied Flycatcher.
WINTER Red-throated Diver, Slavonian Grebe, Cormorant, Eider, Mediterranean and Little Gulls.
ACCESS Ancona lies just north of Conero and the coast road toward Sirolo leads to the area. There are two small brackish pools at Porto Novo, just below Mount Conero. A path leads from Poggio di Ancona to Pian Grande, while the 'Two Sisters' are adjacent to Badia San Pietro.
ROUTE The coastal autostrada from Bologna passes just inland.

GARGANO

The Gargano peninsula forms the spur on the boot of Italy on the Adriatic coast, and is a splendid birding area to be ranked with any in the country and alongside many better known sites elsewhere in Europe. Indeed, the variety of habitats is quite exceptional and there are many outstanding birds to be seen. To the south lies Brindisi, with its ferries offering an alternative route to Greece (at the time of writing undoubtedly the best and safest route) and several crews have (and doubtless will) stopped off here and been surprised by what they found.

To the north the Tremiti Islands are large enough to be a home to farmers and a growing tourist industry. They are also home to colonies of Cory's and Mediterranean Shearwaters, and two or three pairs of Peregrine. Their potential as migration watch-points has yet to be explored.

Along the northern shores of the Gargano peninsula lie two huge lakes. Lake Lesina is shallow with an extensive growth of reeds along its shoreline. Lake Varano, in contrast, is deep and has steeply banked artificial and rocky shores. Both hold excellent winter populations of wildfowl, including thousands of Pintail, Wigeon and Cormorant together with hundreds of Red-breasted Merganser. Lesina is generally the better of the two, especially in spring and summer when Marsh Harrier, Bittern, Little Bittern and Great Reed Warbler can all be found.

The mountains of Gargano itself are limestone and relatively bare on their lower slopes. Higher up are extensive areas of forest and it is here that Black, Middle Spotted and White-backed Woodpeckers can be found. Among inland cliffs and gorges there are Egyptian Vulture, Peregrine, Short-toed Eagle and seven or eight pairs of Eagle Owl, as well as both kites, Roller, Lesser Grey Shrike and Dartford Warbler.

South of the peninsula the Bay of Manfredonia is backed by marshes, fish-ponds and saltpans reclaimed from what, at one time, was an outstanding wetland. Even today the area is superb, with many excellent birding sites. In the north the remains of the Lago Salso and Lago di Diana offer mud-flats and reedbeds that hold Bittern, Little Egret, Squacco, Purple and Night Herons plus a small nucleus of breeding Glossy Ibis. On passage Glossy Ibis, Spoonbill and Crane are regular. The Daunia Risi area is the centrepiece of this wetland. Farther south the marshes around Carapelle and San Floriano are primarily a winter haunt with tens of thousands of Wigeon plus Lanner and Peregrine both relatively easy to see.

Finally, the saltpans of Margherita di Savoia are the largest in Italy and the Lagoon of Alma Dannata to the north is used for fish farming. Breeding birds here include Stilt, Avocet, Kentish Plover, Slender-billed Gull, and an important colony of 150 pairs of Little Tern. The surrounding fields are good for Calandra and Short-toed Larks and passage, especially spring, brings more than 10,000 Black-tailed Godwit and over 25,000 Ruff, as well as other waders.

SUMMER Cory's and Mediterranean Shearwaters, Cormorant, Bittern, Little Bittern, Night, Squacco and Purple Herons, Little Egret, Glossy Ibis, Black Kite, Egyptian Vulture, Short-toed Eagle, Marsh Harrier, Goshawk, Hobby, Peregrine, Quail, Black-winged Stilt, Avocet, Kentish Plover, Slender-billed Gull, Little Tern, Eagle Owl, Alpine Swift, Roller,

Hoopoe, Black, Middle Spotted and White-backed Woodpeckers, Calandra and Short-toed Larks, Great Reed and Dartford Warblers, Lesser Grey Shrike, Bearded Tit, Rock and Black-headed Buntings.
PASSAGE Crane, Spoonbill, Glossy Ibis, Black-tailed Godwit, Ruff, Little Stint, Black Tern,
WINTER Black-throated Diver, Black-necked Grebe, Wigeon, Shoveler, Pintail, Red-breasted Merganser, Goosander, Eider, Lanner, Peregrine, Avocet.
ACCESS The Tremiti Islands can be reached by regular ferries from Termali and Rodi Garganico. Lake Lesina has the largest reedbeds at the eastern end, but is rather awkward to work. The pumping station at the eastern end of the Torre Mileto–Sannicandro road is worth a try. Gargano itself can be explored on several small roads and the marshes south of Manfredonia can be worked from the coastal road, SS159. For the Margherita di Savoia saltpans continue on this road to near the mouth of the Carmosina and take the track on the left just after the canal. Once on this track it is possible to drive along the canal bank. For information on the saltpans, which are a state nature reserve contact the Forester's office in Trinitapoli: Tel. 039–883–732160.
ROUTE Naples is the nearest major airport, with a good road to Foggia.

GRAN PARADISO

The Gran Paradiso National Park lies against the French border in north-western Italy and covers 60,000 ha of high mountain. There are 57 Glaciers and some 60 lakes, surrounded by forests of fir and larch, and over three-quarters of the park lies above the 3000 m contour. The actual park boundary also follows the contours, thus excluding most of the deep valleys and meadows. This is an area of superb scenery with many typical alpine birds, including Golden Eagle, Ptarmigan, Alpine Accentor, Snow Finch and Alpine Chough. It is, however, best explored at a leisurely pace with considerable walking, preferably from one refuge to the next.

Across the French border lies the Vanoise National Park, offering the same sort of landscape and similar birds. The whole area is best known for its ibex, but those prepared to spend time among the peaks and forests may be rewarded with some of the best birding in Italy.

SUMMER Golden Eagle, Ptarmigan, Black Grouse, Hazelhen, Eagle and Tengmalm's Owls, Black and Three-toed Woodpeckers, Alpine Swift, Crag Martin, Alpine Accentor, Ring Ouzel, Crested Tit, Snow and Citril Finches, Nutcracker, Alpine Chough.
ACCESS Aosta is a pleasant town that makes an excellent base. The valley has several camp sites and a variety of accommodation. From the road that runs between Aosta and the Mont Blanc Tunnel, several minor roads lead southward into the park. The villages of Cogne and Valnontay are the starting points of several paths toward refuges, but do not ignore the roads on the way. Other areas worth exploring are from Degioz towards Alpe Djuan and from Cretaz towards Pousset. In the south-east of the park, the road through the Col di Nivolet is a little rough, but well worth the effort.
ROUTE South of the main road between Mont Blanc and Milan.

ISONZO DELTA

The shores of the Gulf of Venice are lined by exciting marshes and deltas right at the head of the Adriatic. Most famous of these are the marshes at the mouth of the River Po, but against the former Yugoslavian border are the little known lagoons of Marano, the islands and causeway at Grado and the delta of the River Isonzo. The eastern end of this large intertidal complex is more shallow than the west with large areas of saltings, mud-flats and emergent islands. This is the former delta of the Isonzo, a river that now reaches the sea even farther to the east. Much of the landscape has been reclaimed for agriculture and more to fish farming, but there are still large areas of marsh, reed and mud that offer a home to a good collection of breeding birds, some excellent winter wildfowl, and monumental numbers of passage waders, among which the numbers of Ruff and Curlew are most impressive. There are good numbers of Garganey, and the local ringing station regularly turns up a variety of passerine migrants that has included Aquatic Warbler, Thrush Nightingale and Little Bunting.

Winter is also good here with hundreds of Bean, White-fronted and Greylag Geese, thousands of ducks, good numbers of Little Egret and even a handful of Great White Egret. Summer is less productive, but Purple Heron, Little Bittern, Marsh Harrier and Bearded Tit all breed and a small flock of Eider spends the summer.

SUMMER Purple Heron, Little Bittern, Marsh Harrier, Water Rail, Black-winged Stilt, Bearded Tit.
PASSAGE Garganey, Ruff, Curlew.
WINTER Red-throated and Black-throated Divers, Great Crested, Red-necked and Black-necked Grebes, Bean, White-fronted and Greylag Geese, Scoter, Velvet Scoter, Goldeneye, Eider, Red-breasted Merganser, Curlew.
ACCESS Leave Monfalcone westwards on the old road (not the Autopista) and turn left (south) on Route 352 towards Grado. Before the bridge turn left (east) on the Primero Canal and explore towards the mouth of the Isonzo River. There is a visitor centre, an observation post, a small hide and a ringing station – part of the area forms the Isola Cona Nature Reserve. LIPU has a reserve near Punta Spigolo at the river mouth.
ROUTE Venice and Trieste are joined by an Autopista and both have good air connections. A fly-drive winter city-break in Venice is recommended for ornitho-culture freaks.

ORBETELLO

Mount Argentario is a substantial rocky promontory along the western coast of Italy, north of Rome, best known for its picturesque sixteenth-century Spanish forts. It is joined to the mainland by three sandbars that enclose two large lagoons, Burano and Orbetello. Though these are popular resorts, the WWF has now converted 2600 ha of Orbetello into a nature reserve and dramatically increased the population of breeding birds. Here the combination of marshy edges, open water, scrub and pine woods holds a good variety of Mediterranean species, including Montagu's Harrier, Stilt, Stone-curlew and Bee-eater. Not so long ago, one could find only a few Kentish Plovers trying to hatch out their eggs among the sunbathers.

Passage birds, arriving out of season, always fared rather better, but Ferruginous Duck, Crane, Osprey and Marsh Sandpiper are now regular, indicating the possibilities of other considerably scarcer species that might reasonably be expected to pass through. As this is a winter haven, the lack of shooting over the reserve has significantly affected the variety and number of birds that can be expected. Reasonably regular species include Spoonbill, Great White Egret, Greylag Goose, duck and Moustached Warbler. All in all, the Orbetello area has been converted from a good place where something might appear to a regular haunt of a splendid variety of Italian birds. It is the prime example of what can be achieved with control and protection. Flamingoes are now non-breeding visitors.

SUMMER Montagu's Harrier, Kentish Plover, Black-winged Stilt, Stone-curlew, Hoopoe, Bee-eater, Short-toed Lark, Reed, Cetti's, Melodious and Sardinian Warblers.
PASSAGE Ferruginous Duck, Osprey, Crane, Flamingo, Marsh Sandpiper, Red-necked Phalarope, Black and White-winged Black Terns, Bluethroat.
WINTER Black-throated Diver, Shelduck, Pintail, Long-tailed Duck, Smew, Eider, Greylag Goose, Spoonbill, Great White Egret, Sandwich Tern, Moustached Warbler.
ACCESS Much of the lagoon can be seen from the road along the isthmus that holds the town of Orbetello. The WWF reserve may be entered by permit, for which there is a small charge. Contact the WWF for current details prior to departure.
ROUTE Orbetello is 148 km north of Rome on the Via Aurelia.

PO DELTA AND VENICE

The River Po reaches the sea between Venice and Ravenna and a glance at a map should be sufficient to convince anyone that this is a good birding area. In fact, the whole of the coastline from the Slovene border is broken by lagoons and marshes, though those in the south are generally regarded as the best. Thus the Venetian lagoons, the Valli di Comacchio and the delta itself are treated here as one huge birding centre.

Everyone, they say, should see Venice before they die; and it is a most beautiful place, despite shark-like gondoliers, rip-off restaurants and too many tourists. The family birder can also lace culture with some excellent birding. Venice stands on islands on the landward side of a huge lagoon, almost cut off from the sea by sandbars. Regular boat services connect the various islands and the main beach resorts, and offer easy access to many of the better spots, plus the chance of viewing passage Black Tern. Much can, however, be seen from the network of surrounding roads.

This is still a major staging post for duck, with Garganey often abundant in spring, and a large and varied wintering population. Waders too are regular migrants, though breeding birds suffer from excessive disturbance.

To the south, the Po delta is a huge maze of channels, islands and marshes and one of the most important wildfowl wintering grounds in Europe. Some areas have been given reserve status, but the only restrictions on access are to the private fishing reserves. In 1981 Pygmy Cormorants bred, but the more usual breeding population includes Bittern, Avocet and Stilt. A wide variety of species on passage includes Spoonbill, Lesser

Spotted Eagle and Terek and Marsh Sandpipers (there is no information about the regularity (or otherwise) of the eagle). Winter brings divers, Great White Egret and a splendid and varied duck population. The delta can be penetrated by various routes, via Porto Talle, Bonelli, Goro and Pila Contarina. Boat exploration (easily rented) is recommended, though personally I find boats a frustrating form of birding transport.

Farther south, the Valli di Comacchio is a huge, salty-brackish lagoon surrounded by marshes and smaller waters. It is a primary resort of duck, and regularly attracts a good collection of passage waders and terns. In summer, there are Stilt, Avocet and Pratincole here. The lake can be worked from the road between Ostellato and Porto Garibaldi, and south off this from the road that crosses the lagoon from Spina to Alfonsine.

There are so many marshes and lakes along this coast that the area would repay an intensive survey. Full checklists for any site would be welcome.

SUMMER Bittern, Avocet, Black-winged Stilt, Collared Pratincole, Mediterranean Gull, Common, Gull-billed, Sandwich and Whiskered Terns.

WINTER Red-throated and Black-throated Divers, Great White Egret, Wigeon, Pintail, Shoveler, Pochard, Tufted and Ferruginous Ducks, Scaup, Eider, Goldeneye, Red-breasted Merganser.

PASSAGE White Stork, Spoonbill, Garganey, Osprey, Ruff, Lesser Spotted Eagle, Spotted Redshank, Terek and Marsh Sandpipers, Temminck's Stint, Jack Snipe, Stone-curlew, Grasshopper and Aquatic Warblers, Bluethroat.

ACCESS As detailed above under individual sections. Outside Venice, accommodation is available at reasonable prices.

ROUTE Venice airport or package holidays to the Lido.

RIVER TELLARO

Sicily, even more than the rest of Italy, has been largely ignored by birders. At first sight this may not seem surprising. The idea of wasting a holiday looking for non-existent birds does not have a great deal of appeal. Yet Sicily is rugged, mountainous country, with large unfrequented areas of countryside, and is on a migration route, particularly of birds of prey.

Fortunately, one area of the island has been worked in spring and produced a good collection of both local and migrant species. The Tellaro rises in the mountains and reaches the sea at the south-east corner of Sicily on the Gulf of Noto. For the last few kilometres it is reed-fringed, while at the mouth there are a few small pools used by migrant waders in the mornings before the nude bathers arrive. Behind the beach are areas of scrub and stony fields, with some olive and almond groves farther inland.

Squacco and Purple Herons regularly use the river; Little Egret, Spoonbill and Little Bittern also occur. If you are lucky, a flock of Glossy Ibis that have wintered in Tunisia may pass through. Raptors vary daily; harriers are regular and other species occur. Waders are regular in small numbers (perhaps the lagoons 10 km south might produce more?), gulls include regular Little and terns regular Sandwich. Warblers and chats pass through and local species include Cetti's. Sardinian, Fan-tailed and Nightingale.

SPRING Cory's Shearwater, Little Bittern, Little Egret, Squacco and Purple Herons, Glossy Ibis, Spoonbill, Garganey, Black Kite, Montagu's and Marsh Harriers, Osprey, Little Ringed and Kentish Plovers, Little

Stint, Green, Wood and Common Sandpipers, Little Gull, Sandwich and Common Terns, Pallid Swift, Hoopoe, Short-toed and Crested Larks, Tree and Red-throated Pipits, Woodchat Shrike, Hooded Crow, Cetti's, Great Reed, Sardinian, Subalpine and Fan-tailed Warblers, Black-eared Wheatear, Nightingale, Short-toed Treecreeper, Serin, Cirl Bunting.

ACCESS A road runs southward from Avola as far as the Hotel Eloro, then turns inland to join the Pachino road. A path leads from the Eloro to the mouth of the Tellaro where the wader pools are located. Walk inland along the river, with tracks to the right through scrub, fields and groves.

ROUTE Catania, to the north, has an airport.

SAN ALESSANDRO AND THE PO HERONRIES

Directly east of Turin the Po meets the Sesia in the border region between Piemonte and Lombardia. Here, the two rivers meander through an essentially agricultural landscape broken by marshy backwaters and isolated riverine woods. It is in these woods and marshes that the greatest heronries of Italy are found. Little Egret, Night, Purple and Grey Herons are the dominant species, but there are also Bittern, a growing number of Cattle Egret and a regular pair or two of Glossy Ibis. The larger wetland areas hold Marsh Harrier, Savi's, Great Reed and Icterine Warblers.

SUMMER White Stork, Glossy Ibis, Little and Cattle Egrets, Night, Squacco, Purple and Grey Herons, Little Bittern, Bittern, Marsh Harrier, Reed, Savi's and Great Reed Warblers.

ACCESS One of the best of the heronries is that of San Alessandro. From Pavia, south of Milan, take the N596 westwards to Mortara. Continue on the N596 to Zeme Lomellina. In this village follow directions for Cascina San Alessandro and the heronry. Other heronries nearby include those at Villarboit, Isolone di Oldenico, Morghengo, Isola Langosco and the Lago di Sartirana Lomellina. There are many others in the region.

ROUTE Turin and Milan are served by international transport systems.

SARDINIA

Sardinia may be a Mediterranean island but a week at a single resort is insufficient for a thorough exploration. This is a big island. There are splendid marshes and saltpans, excellent mountain areas and rocky coasts that deserve more attention than they get. Though much of the recent holiday development in Sardinia has taken place in the north-east, the main airport and capital lies in the south at Cagliari. In many ways this is fortunate, for it is the southern half of Sardinia that holds the best birds.

Oristano, on the west coast 92 km north of Cagliari, is an old town with excellent wetlands nearby. There are lagoons and saltpans at Cabras, reached from the coast at Marina di Torre Grande – the ideal base. Avocet, Stilt and wildfowl make this an internationally important wetland; there are even Purple Gallinule and Red-crested Pochard. Passage brings wider variety, including good numbers of waders, Eleonora's Falcon, Flamingo and Spoonbill, while in winter Peregrine is more or less regular.

Inland, there are two major areas of interest: the Giara di Gesturi and Monto del Gennargentu. The latter is the highest point of Sardinia and has Griffon Vulture and Golden and Bonelli's Eagles, while the former is a plateau with wild ponies and Little Bustard.

Visitors will hope for two Mediterranean island specialities, Marmora's Warbler and Eleonora's Falcon. There are some 200–300 pairs of falcons grouped in two main sites: in the east around the Capo di M. Santu and in the south near Carbonia. The latter is easiest of access, with good colonies on San Pietro. This large island is, in fact, worth more than a cursory once-over. It has huge sea cliffs and a hinterland of scrub with considerable areas of pine woodland. Eleonora's Falcon is easily found, but there are also Peregrine here, along with Audouin's Gull, Marmora's Warbler and Storm Petrel. The more widespread Scops Owl, Alpine Swift, Woodchat Shrike, Spectacled Warbler and Blue Rock Thrush make San Pietro a good holiday base. The lagoons and saltpans at the head of the Golfo di Palmas are good for marsh birds, including Flamingo.

One of the best areas of Sardinia is, however, centred on Cagliari itself. Here, within a few kilometres of the airport and town, are extensive areas of saltpans to the west and the remarkable pool of Molentargius to the east. The latter covers some 500 ha of reed-marsh and open water and has been recognized as a wetland of international importance. As a result, hunting is banned, and both Cattle Egret and Glossy Ibis bred in 1986. Flamingo, Purple Gallinule, Stilt, Avocet, Slender-billed Gull, Pratincole and a variety of warblers all occur. There are often arriving and departing Eleonora's here, and in winter Spotted Eagle is not unknown.

Sardinia has some of the best birding places in Italy and is certainly worthy of more attention that it has received to date.

SUMMER Storm Petrel, Flamingo, Little Egret, Purple Heron, Glossy Ibis, Purple Gallinule, Griffon Vulture, Golden and Bonelli's Eagles, Peregrine, Eleonora's Falcon, Avocet, Black-winged Stilt, Kentish Plover, Collared Pratincole, Slender-billed and Audouin's Gulls, Scops Owl, Bee-eater, Hoopoe, Pallid and Alpine Swifts, Blue Rock Thrush, Marmora's, Sardinian, Cetti's and Great Reed Warblers, Cirl Bunting, Citril Finch, Spanish and Rock Sparrows.
WINTER Flamingo, Spotted Eagle, Osprey.
PASSAGE White Stork, Spoonbill, Shelduck, Red-crested Pochard, Ferruginous Duck, Osprey, Pallid Harrier, Red-footed and Eleonora's Falcons, Crane, Caspian Tern.
ACCESS Oristano 92 km north-west of Cagliari on Route 131. A minor road leaves to Cabras and to Marina di Torre Grande. The lagoons and saltpans can be seen from the road between the two. **Golfo di Palmas** South of Carbonia to the east of the road to San Antioco. The lagoons and saltpans are adjacent. Local exploration to San Pietro for Eleonora's Falcon, etc., via the ferry between Calasetta and Carloforte. Cagliari is the main town of Sardinia, and lagoons and saltpans to the west are viewed from the main coast road towards Pula. The pool of Molentargius is reached via a footpath near the IP petrol station in Cagliari, or along the drainage canal adjacent to Quartu S. Elena. **Giara di Gesturi** Reached by turning eastwards off the A131 south of Oristano at Uras. Continue through Ales to Esdovedu and Senis. Gennargentu is found by continuing eastwards after Gesturi to Laconi and then turning northward. After several kilometres turn right on to Route 295 to Aritzo, then exploring to

the south (right). **Monte Limbara** In the north-east, this can be reached via roads towards the radar station. It holds many altitude birds including Blue Rock Thrush and Cirl Bunting, as well as Marmora's Warbler.

STRAIT OF MESSINA

There is a considerable passage of birds of prey across the Strait of Messina, between Sicily and the toe of Italy. Sadly, the local hunters shoot them and are vehement and sometimes aggressive in defence of their 'sporting rights'. Italian conservationists deserve the support of all European conservationists in their attempts to stop them. The hills above Messina, the Monti Peloritani, are covered with Mediterranean scrub and bush, broken here and there by small woods. The Montagne delle Madonie offers a home to a good population of raptors among its woods, scrub and inland cliffs. These include Golden and Bonelli's Eagles, Egyptian Vulture, Red Kite and eight pairs of Peregrine. There are also Rock Partridge and Chough here. It is, however, the spring passage of birds of prey that makes this area so important. In April there are good numbers of Marsh and Montagu's Harriers and Black Kite. But in May a wider variety of species includes Black Stork, Egyptian Vulture, Booted Eagle, Hobby, Lesser Kestrel and Red-footed Falcon. Outstanding, however, are the numbers of Honey Buzzards with a peak of 3000 birds in one day.

PASSAGE White and Black Storks, Golden and Booted Eagles, (Bonelli's Eagle), Black Kite, (Red Kite), Egyptian Vulture, Honey Buzzard, Hobby, Lesser Kestrel, Red-footed Falcon, (Rock Partridge), (Chough).
ACCESS Take the Palermo road from the centre of Messina and continue uphill for 5 km until you reach the crossroads at Portella Castanea. This is a fine viewpoint, especially with northerly winds. From here, walk to Monte Ciccia which offers an impressive view over the Strait of Messina.
ROUTE Ferries run between Reggio Calabria on the mainland and Messina in Sicily about every hour.

Eleonora's Falcon

JORDAN

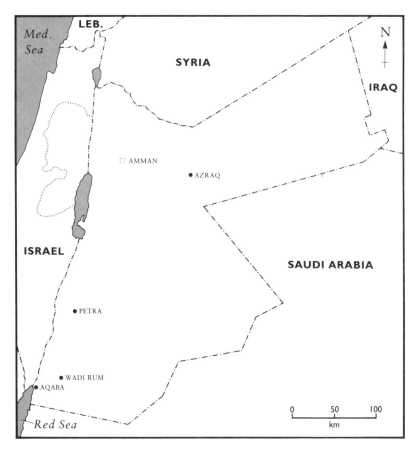

AQABA

Aqaba is Jordan's port on the Red Sea and lies virtually alongside Israel's more famous Eilat. Not surprisingly, at migration times, it can produce many of the same birds and in similar dramatic numbers. There, however, the similarity ends. For Aqaba is a port, not a holiday resort. Its hotels are mostly acceptable, rather than pleasurable and the landscape lacks the intensive agriculture and 'greenness' of its neighbour. Nevertheless, it does produce birds with many species not found elsewhere in the country. Firsts for Jordan have included Sooty Shearwater, Long-tailed and Arctic Skuas, and Bridled and White-cheeked Terns. More regular birds include Black Stork, Black Kite, Buzzard and Long-legged Buzzard and Steppe Eagle on spring migration. Laughing Dove, Rose-ringed Parakeet, Bulbul, Orange-tufted Sunbird, House Crow and Tristram's Grackle are among the Jordan specialities that can be found in and around the town.

SPRING/SUMMER Black Stork, Black Kite, Buzzard, Honey and Long-legged Buzzards, Steppe Eagle, Laughing Dove, Rose-ringed Parakeet, Bee-eater, Red-rumped Swallow, Common Bulbul, Orange-tufted Sunbird, Masked Shrike, House Crow, Tristram's Grackle, Cretzschmar's Bunting.
ACCESS Almost any area away from the docks and town produces birds and the main effort is to find an area without inquisitive people.
ROUTE Aqaba has its own airport.

AZRAQ

Azraq has been one of the most famous bird areas in the Middle East for longer than most birders can remember. It was brought to popular attention during the 1960s by Guy Mountfort's *Portrait of a Desert* which described two expeditions to Jordan and the resulting conservation initiatives.Azraq is an inland drainage basin where fresh water comes to the surface to maintain a wetland, or oasis, surrounded by hostile desert. It is the most significant wetland for hundreds of miles and acts as a 'Heligoland' or 'Fair Isle' of plenty in a sea of desert. Its effect on migrants, especially in spring when it is lush and green, is often dramatic, with hordes of a wide variety of birds finding in its cool and shade a respite from their migrations from Africa to the Palearctic. Chats, warblers and flycatchers, swallows and buntings, waders and raptors all pass through in numbers and inevitably include a number of sought-after species.

If migrants are the speciality, the winter wildfowl are often equally attractive, with over 100,000 duck present at peak seasons. However, the visiting birder will probably find the resident birds as attractive as any, using the oasis as a splendid base for exploring the surrounding desert. Here Houbara Bustard, Cream-coloured Courser, Spotted and other sandgrouse, a wonderful collection of larks and wheatears, plus Graceful and Streaked Scrub Warblers can all be found.The Shaumari Wildlife Reserve is within easy range to the south-west and, though not strictly a bird place, most visitors to Azraq will enjoy seeing the endangered Arabian oryx in something like its natural habitat.The bushes just before the reserve entrance may be alive with migrants.

SPRING Black Stork, Honey Buzzard, Levant Sparrowhawk, Short-toed, Booted, Steppe, Spotted and Lesser Spotted Eagles, Hen Harrier, Red-footed Falcon, Lesser Kestrel, Temminck's Stint, Spotted Redshank, Marsh, Green and Wood Sandpipers, Gull-billed, Whiskered and White-winged Black Terns, Pied Kingfisher, Bee-eater, Roller, Red-throated Pipit, Yellow Wagtail, Isabelline, Masked and Lesser Grey Shrikes, Marsh, Barred and Booted Warblers, Collared Flycatcher, Isabelline Wheatear, White-throated Robin, Thrush Nightingale, Bluethroat, Ortolan and Black-headed Buntings.
SUMMER Houbara Bustard, Greater Sand and Spur-winged Plovers, Black-winged Stilt, Stone-curlew, Cream-coloured Courser, Collared Pratincole, Egyptian Nightjar, Blue-cheeked Bee-eater, Dunn's, Lesser Short-toed, Thick-billed and Temminck's Horned Larks, Moustached, Clamorous, Streaked Scrub and Graceful Warblers, Mourning, Desert and Red-rumped Wheatears, Rufous Bushchat, Rock Sparrow, Trumpeter and Desert Finches.

Masked Shrike

ACCESS Exploring the marshes and ponds is not always easy simply because of the size of the area. A mixture of driving and walking should, however, produce the migrants that are likely to turn up anywhere. Thus visiting the same place on consecutive days may produce quite different species. There are two villages, a few cafés and a lodge run by the Royal Society for the Conservation of Nature, PO Box 6345, Amman (Tel. 811689). To find the desert birds use the good roads to reach suitable habitat and explore on foot. Do not get lost. Inevitably, any particular recommended sites are, more than perhaps elsewhere, just places that others have found birds. The Lodge (Rest House) complex has a wet patch that produces Thrush Nightingale and Clamorous Warbler, while White-throated Robin may be beside the buildings. A pool to the south may have Little Crake and Great Snipe. A little to the north a track leads eastwards from Azraq village to an oasis with waders, terns, Rufous Bushchat and even the occasional Pallid Harrier. At Shaumari the area to the left of the entrance track has Bifasciated Lark, while a stop at the castle of Qasr Amra, on the southern Amman road may produce the elusive Desert Finch. Farther west at Qasr al Kharana a track leading southwards east of the castle compound leads to a wadi with Cream-coloured Courser *en route* and Red-rumped Wheatear at the end.

ROUTE Amman has an international airport and Azraq is an easy one-day drive with plenty of time for birding along the way.

PETRA

Carved from the living rock by the Nabateans 2000 years ago, Petra is one of the most famous and beautiful historical sites in the world and is visited by tens or hundreds of thousands of visitors every year. Like India's Taj Mahal, it is just so important that even birders should not miss the experience. It is, however, also good for birds and it is a relatively simple matter to walk away from the trippers and get to grips with some good species. Barbary Falcon, Sand Partridge, Pale Crag Martin, Mourning Wheatear, Orange-tufted Sunbird, Rock Sparrow, Sinai Rosefinch and Tristram's Grackle could all oblige. As the sun goes down in the late afternoon the rose-red rock is simply beautiful. But it also colours the birds!

SUMMER Barbary Falcon, Sand Partridge, Laughing Dove, Pallid Swift, Desert and Temminck's Horned Larks, Pale Crag Martin, Common Bulbul, Blackstart, Mourning Wheatear, Rock Thrush, Blue Rock Thrush, Scrub Warbler, Orange-tufted Sunbird, Fan-tailed Raven, Tristram's Grackle, Spanish and Rock Sparrows, Sinai Rosefinch.
ACCESS Petra lies between the two north–south routes that link Amman and Aqaba and considerably nearer the latter. However, Amman has better flights and most birders start (and end) there. Petra itself can easily be reached in a day from the capital and the Azraq–Petra route is regularly travelled by birders. Although there is a wide variety of accommodation at Petra, it is heavily booked by tourists and advance reservations are essential and even then not certain. Be prepared to 'rough it' and you will adore the place.
ROUTE Amman or Aqaba airports.

WADI RUM

Situated in the south and within easy reach of Aqaba, this is Jordan's answer to the Grand Canyon, with spectacular cliffs, isolated pillars and wonderful colours. There is even a 'Beau Geste' police post to heighten the feeling of the last frontier. Inevitably, such a landscape attracts tourists, but it is easy enough to explore the unfrequented wadis and pick up some really fine birds including Barbary Falcon, Hooded Wheatear, Trumpeter Finch, Scrub Warbler and Bifasciated Lark. Given time and a little good fortune it is even possible to pick up both of the specialities – Verreaux's Eagle and Sooty Falcon. Both are usually seen to the east of the Bedu village that lies in Wadi Rum near the Desert Police HQ. This village also has Tristram's Grackle, Sinai Rosefinch, Masked Shrike and House Bunting. Between the village and the main road the road passes through agricultural land with more Trumpeter Finch and both Desert and Bar-tailed Desert Larks. Farther east lies the man-made oasis of Disi, where the fields attract hordes of migrants including Wryneck, Thrush Nightingale, Rufous Bushchat plus many waders.

SPRING/SUMMER Long-legged Buzzard, Verreaux's Eagle, Barbary and Sooty Falcons, Sand Partridge, Black-headed and Lesser Black-backed Gulls, Laughing Dove, Desert, Bar-tailed Desert and Calandra Larks, Pale Crag Martin, Common Bulbul, Black-eared, Mourning and White-crowned Black Wheatears, Rock Thrush, Blue Rock Thrush, Orange-tufted Sunbird, Fan-tailed and Brown-necked Ravens, Tristram's Grackle, Spanish and Rock Sparrows, Trumpeter Finch, Sinai Rosefinch, House, Ortolan and Cretzschmar's Buntings.
ACCESS Leave Aqaba northwards on Route 53 and turn right to Wadi Rum. Stop and explore wadis without tourists, plus the Bedu village. Continue eastwards to Disi.
ROUTE Aqaba has an airport with some international flights.

LATVIA

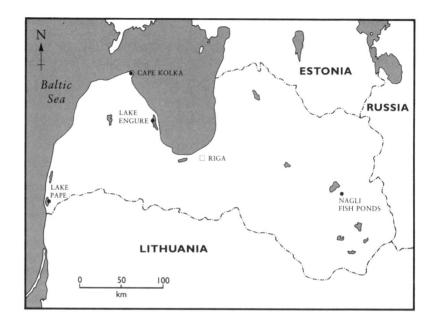

CAPE KOLKA

Cape Kolka is a migration bottleneck for northbound migrants in spring that has already attracted the more dedicated Scandinavian birders and will doubtless soon be added to the list of 'high value' places by British, German and other western birders. However, before we all set out in April and May it may be appropriate to outline the other attractions of this outstanding area. Away from the sand-dune beach there is a mosaic of bogs, farmland and dunes mostly covered with woodland that boasts a really excellent population of breeding birds that should not be ignored. Black Stork, Honey Buzzard, Short-toed and Golden Eagles, Osprey, 150 pairs of Hazelhen together with smaller numbers of Capercaillie and Black Grouse is pretty good for starters. But there are also Crane, Golden Plover, woodpeckers and good numbers of Red-breasted Flycatcher.

In spring between 12,000 and 20,000 raptors pass through including Buzzard (8500), Sparrowhawk (3500) and Honey Buzzard (500), and Rough-legged Buzzard, Osprey, Golden Eagle and White-tailed Eagle, Though these are the stars of the show, there are also vast flocks of Woodpigeon and hundreds of thousands of finches heading northwards.

PASSAGE Osprey, Buzzard, Rough-legged and Honey Buzzards, White-tailed and Golden Eagles, Sparrowhawk, Woodpigeon, waders, finches.
SUMMER White and Black Storks, Honey Buzzard, Short-toed and Golden Eagles, Osprey, Hazelhen, Black Grouse, Capercaillie, Crane,

Corncrake, Golden Plover, Common Tern, Eagle and Tengmalm's Owls, Nightjar, Black and Three-toed Woodpeckers, Woodlark, Red-breasted Flycatcher, Red-backed Shrike.

ACCESS The village of Kolka can be reached quite easily and roads offer access to local woodlands. However, it would be sensible to contact the Nature Reserve Office in Mazirbe village for a permit and to arrange for camping and visits to the observation tower: Slitere Nature Reserve, Mazirbe, Talsu raj. LV-3273, Latvia. Latvian ornithologists need support and recording your visit is a simple way of doing so.

ROUTE There is a bus service from Riga to Kolka village, or drive to Kolka via Mazirbe.

LAKE ENGURE

This shallow lake lies on the Latvian shore of the Gulf of Riga and is separated from the sea by a narrow strip of land about 1 km wide. About a third is covered with reeds and other emergent vegetation which makes it one of the most important waterfowl breeding sites in the Baltic. The surrounding land has mixed and pine forests which should not be ignored. Although its main attractions are in the summer, there is also a strong population of winter wildfowl, plus 12,000 Coot.

Breeding species include all five European grebes with 200 pairs of Red-necked and 100 pairs of Slavonian. Both bitterns breed, as do both storks. Raptors include White-tailed and Lesser Spotted Eagles, and Merlin and Marsh Harrier. Hazelhen and Black Grouse can be found in the woods, while the marshes echo to the calls of Crane, and Spotted and Little Crakes. A huge Black-headed Gull colony has associated colonies of Little Gull and Common and Black Terns. Eagle and Tengmalm's Owls are in the woods, with Short-eared Owl among the marshes. Savi's Warbler and Red-breasted Flycatcher are common and there are also numbers of Bearded and Penduline Tits.

Tengmalm's Owl

SUMMER Great Crested, Red-necked, Little, Slavonian and Black-necked Grebes, Bittern, Little Bittern, Black and White Storks, Greylag Goose, Pochard, Tufted Duck, Honey Buzzard, Marsh Harrier, Lesser Spotted and White-tailed Eagles, Merlin, Hazelhen, Black Grouse, Crane, Spotted and Little Crakes, Corncrake, Ruff, Little Gull, Common and Black Terns, Eagle, Short-eared and Tengmalm's Owls, Nightjar, Savi's Warbler, Red-breasted Flycatcher, Red-backed Shrike.

PASSAGE Wildfowl, waders.

ACCESS Though the lake is closed to the public during the breeding season, there is limited camping allowed at the Ornithological station 2 km east of Bérzciems, with access to the observation tower. Permits can be obtained from the Ornithological Station. The best time is from May to July.

ROUTE There is a bus service from Riga to Bérzciems, but car travel is recommended.

Lake Pape

This fresh-water lake lies close to the Lithuanian border and adjacent to the Baltic. Its indented shoreline is lined by a strong growth of reeds and scrub, while the surrounding meadows are broken equally by patches of thorn and willow. The narrow beach is composed of sand dunes covered with pines of varying age. Because of its strategic position, Lake Pape has become a major migration watch-point, with concentrations of raptors, pigeons, owls and many small birds, especially visible movements of pipits and finches. However, it is also a stop-over for many wildfowl and other waterbirds both in spring and autumn. The best migration seasons are April–May and September–October.

There is, however, considerably more to Pape than migration. It has an interesting population of breeding species including Bittern, two harriers, Water Rail, Tawny Pipit, a variety of warblers, plus both Bearded and Penduline Tits. The recent breeding of Paddyfield Warbler should not encourage visitors to expect to see this very rare species here. Though few in number, there are also breeding Crane both here and at Lake Liepaja a short distance to the north. As important as any are the 500 pairs of Pochard that nest.

SUMMER Bittern, Greylag Goose, Pochard, Marsh and Montagu's Harriers, Water Rail, Corncrake, Crane, Whimbrel, Hoopoe, Tawny Pipit, Savi's, Reed, Great Reed and Paddyfield Warblers, Bearded and Penduline Tits, Serin.

PASSAGE Geese, duck, raptors, Crane, pigeons, owls, passerines.

ACCESS Though the lake and its surroundings can be worked from roads and tracks, especially in the south-east, visitors would be well advised to drive to Pape village (no public transport beyond Rucava which is 12 km to the east) and continue to the Ornithological Station 3 km north. Here it is possible to camp, hire a local guide and use the observation tower. Permits to explore the area can be obtained from local government offices at Rucava.

ROUTE Drive from Riga via Jelgava to Liepája then southward to Rucava. Riga has ferry services and an airport.

Nagli Fish-ponds

These extensive fish-ponds lie to the east and south-east of Lake Lubána in the east of Latvia and are generally regarded as one of the richest bird areas in the country. There are some 3000 ha of ponds here divided into three major groups. The southern two lie either side of the village of Nagli, while the third is situated either side of the Lubána–Gaigalava road. Perhaps the outstanding species are Marsh Sandpiper, some ten pairs of which breed annually, and Terek Sandpiper, one or two pairs of which breed most years. While seeing these species could be decidedly tough, there should be no difficulty with the five species of grebe, ten species of duck, two species of bittern, fifteen species of wader and ten species of gulls and terns. Other, perhaps scarcer, breeders include Black Stork, White-tailed Eagle, and outstandingly, both Lesser Spotted and Spotted Eagles. This is the only site in Latvia for the latter, but this nevertheless makes it one of the very few known sites for this very elusive European bird. Among smaller birds Blyth's Reed Warbler is increasing in numbers and no fewer than seven species of woodpecker breed. The general area of bogs, meadows and woodland should be explored as well as the fish-ponds.

SUMMER Great Crested, Little, Red-necked, Slavonian and Black-necked Grebes, Cormorant, Bittern, Little Bittern, Black Stork, duck, Osprey, White-tailed, Lesser Spotted and Spotted Eagles, Marsh Harrier, Hobby, Little Crake, Marsh, Terek, Green and Wood Sandpipers, Black-tailed Godwit, Little Gull, Black Tern, Black, White-backed, Lesser Spotted and Great Spotted Woodpeckers, Savi's, Blyth's Reed, Marsh and Icterine Warblers.

PASSAGE Swans, geese, ducks, waders.

ACCESS This is very much a breeding season site, though passage should not be ignored. In September many of the ponds are drained to harvest the fish and access may then be restricted. At other times much can be explored quite easily, though a permit from the local Fishermen's Department in Nagli would save any problems. Advice and uncomfortable camping can be obtained from the Orenisi Ornithological Station, which is situated among the pond group east of Nagli. From Lubána take the road south then east towards Grigalava. This passes the northern shore of Lake Lubána and then turns south then east away from the lake. The first fish-ponds are here on either side of the road. Stop and explore. A turning to the right (south) leads to Nagli where there are ponds on either side of the village. Explore. Turn left and then left between the last group of ponds. The Orenisi camp is on the right. The Teiči Nature Reserve to the west of Nagli is the largest raised bog in Latvia and is a maze of marshes, bogs and lakes with islands, all with a varying cover of forest. Although it boasts some excellent birds, including Black-throated Diver, Lesser Spotted Eagle, Willow Grouse, Crane and White-backed Woodpecker, the area is so vast and difficult to work that (for the time being) it cannot sensibly be treated as a separate site. Anyone wishing to explore the area should contact Teiči Nature Reserve, Laudona, Madonas raj. LV-4862, Latvia. Laudona village lies some 30 km south of Madonna.

MOROCCO

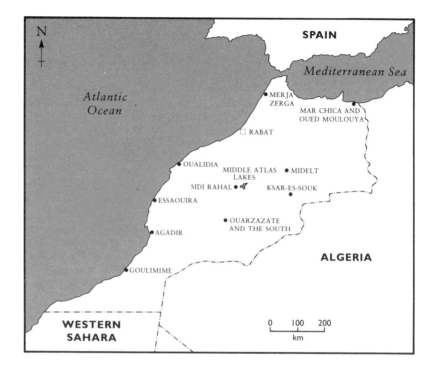

AGADIR

Agadir is a modern city and resort. Fortunately, there are several excellent birding areas within reach of the city and many south Moroccan specialities can be located. Without leaving Agadir, it is possible to see Little Swift, Bulbul, Moussier's Redstart and House Bunting, but excursions northwards to Cap Rhir and the Tamri estuary, inland to Taroudannt, and south to the Oued Sous and the Oued Massa will prove rewarding.

Likely species include Lanner and Barbary Falcon, Flamingo, Audouin's Gull, Ruddy Shelduck, waders and warblers and the chance of Chanting Goshawk, Black-headed Bush Shrike and Red-necked Nightjar. Since 1988 colonies of Plain Swift have been discovered among the sea cliffs south of the Tamri estuary and the cliffs between Agadir and Cap Rhir. This species is otherwise confined to the Canaries and Madeira.

For those who do not mind long journeys in search of their birds, a drive inland to Aoulouz leads to one of the few remaining colonies of Bald Ibis left in the world. To the north lies the rugged Tizi-n-Test pass, with Lammergeier, Long-legged Buzzard and Short-toed Eagle.

SUMMER Cory's Shearwater, Flamingo, Little and Cattle Egrets, Glossy and Bald Ibises, Spoonbill, White Stork, Ruddy Shelduck, Marbled Teal, Black Kite, Short-toed, Bonelli's and Tawny Eagles, Lammergeier, Lanner,

Barbary Falcon, Peregrine, Chanting Goshawk, Barbary Partridge, Black-winged Stilt, Avocet, Audouin's Gull, Black Tern, Roller, Bee-eater, Bulbul, Plain and Little Swifts, Brown-throated Sand Martin, Black-headed Bush Shrike, Black-eared Wheatear, Moussier's Redstart, House Bunting.

ACCESS The road north from Agadir to Cap Rhir passes several small beaches where gulls and terns should be checked – Audouin's Gull is regular. Cap Rhir may produce interesting seabirds and the Tamri estuary is easily viewed from the road: egrets, waders, more Audouin's, Moussier's and possible Lanner or Barbary Falcon. It is an hour back to Agadir. **Oued Sous**, a few kilometres to the south, is the estuary of the Sous which runs inland to Taroudannt and beyond. Flamingo, Spoonbill and waders are good here, and Brown-throated Sand Martin and Bush Shrike can be found. About 1 km south of the airport, a track leads to Hotel Pyramid and the estuary. About 30 km to the south is the **Oued Massa**, a large lagoon next to the sea, with a reputation for building a big bird list, with Ruddy Shelduck, Marbled Teal, Bonelli's Eagle, Flamingo, Spotted Crake, Black-bellied Sandgrouse and masses of waders, and Bush Shrike among the eucalyptus. Approach via the main road, turning right towards Massa village at Tiferhal and continuing along the valley to the sea. Inland the grove-like countryside around **Taroudannt** is the most reliable area for Chanting Goshawk, as well as a possible one for Tawny Eagle. Some 5 km south of Taroudannt, the main road crosses the Oued Sous. Soon after this a track leads left past a rubbish tip, and after 1.5 km a row of trees on the left has Red-necked Nightjar and Bush Shrike. Continue for 80 km to **Aoulouz** for Bald Ibis, Lanner and Barbary Falcon. Stop at the bridge and walk northwards along the western edge of the gorge for 2 km to the colony of Bald Ibis, or turn left 30 km earlier to Tizi-n-Test for mountain species.

ROUTE Agadir airport.

ESSAOUIRA

Under colonial rule Essaouira was called Mogador and the long, low island offshore is still referred to as Mogador Island. It was famous as the only non-Mediterranean breeding site of Eleonora's Falcon, though another colony has been discovered farther south. From May to October, they can be seen hawking over the island. Boat-trips can be arranged . . . but let's try to discourage the practice. In any case, the falcons regularly frequent a wadi just south of the town, where they bathe among the mass of gulls that loaf in the area. This wadi is actually a little gem, with open water and muddy edges encouraging a good variety of waders to pause on passage, along with egrets and the occasional Spoonbill. In the upper parts of the wadi there are areas of dense thorn scrub, and here are many warblers plus Rufous Bushchat and Black-crowned Bush Shrike. Another area for the latter species is 12 km north of the town on the main road.

AUTUMN Little Egret, Spoonbill, Eleonora's Falcon, Osprey, Barbary Partridge, Little Ringed Plover, Green Sandpiper, Greenshank, Little Stint, Mediterranean Gull, Black Tern, Crested Lark, Red-rumped Swallow, Little Swift, Rufous Bushchat, Hoopoe, Great Grey, Woodchat and Black-crowned Bush Shrikes, Cetti's and Melodious Warblers, Pied Flycatcher, Serin, House Bunting.

ACCESS Essaouira lies on the main coast road 192 km north of Agadir. The old town is picturesque and, from the quay, views of Mogador Island (and falcons) can be had. The wadi lies 2 km south of the town and is easily found on tracks leading to the beach.
ROUTE Agadir airport.

GOULIMIME AND THE SOUTH

Beyond Goulimime (Guelmine) the landscape becomes more arid and the roads worse. At Tan-Tan Plage the road reaches the sea, and sticks close to it until Tarfaya and the border with Spanish Sahara. Though a border crossing is shown on maps, it is not easy to Spanish Sahara, and simply turning up is unlikely to do much good. Road conditions apart, there is no problem in motoring south as far as Puerto Cansado; indeed, there is much to recommend it. Here there are otherwise awkward, decent birds. Typical larks are Bar-tailed Desert, Thick-billed, Bifasciated and Temminck's Horned, and wheatears include Desert, Black and Red-rumped. The only other area for many of these birds lies east of Ouarzazate. Sandgrouse of three species, Cream-coloured Courser, Trumpeter Finch, Brown-necked Raven and the elusive Scrub Warbler await the intrepid in this area.

There are also two fine wetlands, the Oued Chebeika and the lagoon of Puerto Cansado, which offer a wide variety of birds at all seasons. The latter is particularly important for waders, with over 100,000 birds in winter including huge flocks of Knot, Dunlin and Redshank together with a staggering 8000 Little Stint; it is also one of the most reliable world spots for the endangered Slender-billed Curlew. Oued Chebeika too holds many wintering waders, but is also known as the stronghold of Flamingo and Scrub Warbler.

PASSAGE Sooty Shearwater, Little Egret, Flamingo, Bonelli's Eagle, Long-legged Buzzard, Osprey, Lanner, Whimbrel, Slender-billed Curlew, Black-tailed Godwit, Wood Sandpiper, Spotted Redshank, Little Stint, Curlew Sandpiper, Ruff, Avocet, Collared Pratincole, Cream-coloured Courser, Audouin's and Slender-billed Gulls, Caspian Tern, Pin-tailed Sandgrouse, Black-bellied and Spotted Sandgrouse, Bar-tailed Desert, Thekla, Bifasciated and Thick-billed Larks, Brown-necked Raven, Desert, Red-rumped and Black Wheatears, Scrub and Fan-tailed Warblers, Trumpeter Finch, House Bunting.
ACCESS The road from Bou-Izakarn southward produces desert birds, with best numbers over the long stretch (120 km) between Goulimime and Tan-Tan. For sandgrouse, larks and wheatears there are no particular places, but Brown-necked Raven is often on the Goulimime rubbish tip and Coursers are most frequently seen around this town. Scrub Warbler is a Chebeika speciality, though it has been found elsewhere, while the waders and seabirds are confined to the two wetland areas.
ROUTE The nearest airport is Agadir, and it is quite possible to drive to Puerto Cansado in a day. However, this is desert country and it is fool-hardy to go ill-prepared and ill-equipped. Some birders have done the Chebeika estuary in a family saloon with camping equipment; it would seem a better idea to take a four-wheel drive and preferably two vehicles. Camping is essential, and food, water and spare petrol should be carried.

KSAR-ES-SOUK AND THE SOUTH

Ksar-es-Souk is a major crossroads, with roads leading to the four cardinal points. Birders on the Moroccan tour inevitably pass through: to the north lies Midelt with Dupont's Lark; to the west lies Boulmane and all the larks and chats; to the south lies Erfoud with real desert species; while the road to the east to Boudenib remains unexplored. It is the road into the desert with which we are concerned here. This route follows the line of a major wadi, with palms and occasional oases. Throughout the area are most of the larks, chats, birds of prey, sandgrouse, etc., but the really intrepid drive south through Erfoud to Rissani and Merzouga. This oasis is impossible to find without a guide; hire one in Erfoud. Even then, there is no guarantee that your vehicle will not get bogged down in sand. Surprisingly enough, there is a hotel at the end of the trek – Hotel Merzouga.

SUMMER Houbara Bustard, Arabian Bustard, Eagle Owl, Egyptian Nightjar, Blue-cheeked Bee-eater, Bar-tailed Desert and Bifasciated Larks, Fulvous Babbler, Desert and White-crowned Black Wheatears, Desert and Scrub Warblers, Desert Sparrow.

ACCESS On the way south, watch for Brown-necked Raven, Fulvous Babbler (at Source Bleue de Meski), Mourning Wheatear and Blue-cheeked Bee-eater. From Erfoud a road leads west to Jorf, and 10 km beyond passes through an area of heavily broken, scrub-covered land. This has Desert and White-crowned Black Wheatears, Bar-tailed Desert and Bifasciated Larks, Scrub and Desert Warblers plus Houbara Bustard and Eagle Owl. Also starting at Erfoud is the track direct to Merzouga running alongside the dunes. The first café among the dunes has a birders' log which, according to one group, is 'a gripping read'. This is a site for Desert Sparrow. There are also irregular sites for this high-value species 300 m north of Merzouga (there are two villages – try both), and another in an isolated palm 1 km east of the road, 7 km north of Merzouga. Desert Warbler may be found where the tarmac road ends between Erfoud and Merzouga, and two other high-value species – Egyptian Nightjar and Arabian Bustard (as well as Houbara) – are also worth searching for. The nightjar is best located in headlights at night, while the bustards require hard work and luck. Even if the specialities do not appear, the town is excellent for migrants and has been thoroughly enjoyed by all who have braved the trek.

ROUTE Via Ksar-es-Souk or from Tinedad on Route 3451.

MAR CHICA AND OUED MOULOUYA

A large lagoon, virtually separated from the sea, on the Mediterranean coast not too far from the Algerian border. The Oued Moulouya reaches the same coast about 70 km to the east, after rising high in the Middle Atlas. Between the two is a virtual desert of sandy scrub that is difficult to penetrate and which remains largely unexplored by birders. The resort of Nador lies on the Mar Chica and is an excellent base for exploring.

Mar Chica attracts gulls, terns and waders and is a regular stop-over for Osprey. All the passage species one would expect over the Mediterranean appear, often in good numbers. Black-winged Stilt is often the dominant wader, followed by Black-tailed Godwit, Greenshank, Wood Sandpiper and

Houbara Bustard

Little Stint. Black and Caspian Terns also appear regularly. At the eastern end of Chica an area of saltpans at Arkmane has all of these species.

The mouth of the Oued Moulouya is marked by a series of lagoons with reeds, making a fresh-water complement to the saline habitats of Chica. Here Purple Heron and Little Bittern can be added to the list, along with Purple Gallinule, Marbled Teal and a good selection of warblers. Just offshore lie the Chafarinas Islands, a noted breeding site of Audouin's Gull. These birds are regular along the adjacent beach.

PASSAGE Purple Heron, Little Egret, Little Bittern, Marbled Teal, Pintail, Shoveler, Marsh Harrier, Osprey, Water Rail, Purple Gallinule, Bar-tailed and Black-tailed Godwits, Wood Sandpiper, Spotted Redshank, Greenshank, Ruff, Little Stint, Curlew Sandpiper, Black-winged Stilt, Slender-billed and Audouin's Gulls, Black and Caspian Terns, Kingfisher, Great Grey Shrike, Bulbul, Rufous Bushchat, Cetti's and Fan-tailed Warblers.

ACCESS Terns and Osprey can be seen from Nador. About 6 km to the south, a road to the left leads to Kariet-Arkmane and the saltpans. From here, a track leads east for 40 km to Ras-el-Mar, opposite the Chafarinas Islands. This track may or may not be passable, or it may now be a proper road. It is simple to detour via Selouane to the mouth of Oued Moulouya.

ROUTE Melilla airport is near Nador and there are ferry connections to Malaga and Almería in Spain.

MERJA ZERGA

A large shallow lagoon surrounded by damp grassland and marshes on the coast between Tangier and Rabat. At the heart of the seasonally flooded Rharb, it is connected to the sea by a narrow channel through the dunes at Moulay-Bou-Selham. Though the wetlands are noted mainly for their wildfowl and waders, Merja Zerga is attractive at all seasons. It has a wide range of breeding birds, is exciting during migration and has other outstanding sites in striking distance. Egrets, storks and Flamingo are regular, and the waders can be outstanding: 5000 Black-tailed Godwit, 1000 Little Stint, 400 Greenshank, 250 Spotted Redshank, 50 Wood Sandpiper and thousands of the more common species on one autumn day shows the possibilities here. Terns regularly include Lesser Crested and

Caspian – both sometimes into double figures. Slender-billed Curlew occurs regularly in small numbers – this is a prime spot for this rare bird.

To the north, beyond Larache, an area of cork groves covers rolling countryside where Black-shouldered Kite is regularly seen, along with other typical species. African Marsh Owl has even been seen in this area.

South, beyond Mehdiya Plage, lies the small coastal lagoon of Sidi Bourhaba. As well as being a haunt of Marsh Owl, Marbled Teal and Crested Coot, this delightful water regularly collects good numbers of migrants.

PASSAGE Little and Cattle Egrets, White Stork, Glossy Ibis, Flamingo, Shoveler, Pintail, Marbled Teal, Black-shouldered Kite, Long-legged Buzzard, Osprey, Hobby, Little Ringed and Kentish Plovers, Slender-billed Curlew, Black-tailed Godwit, Wood Sandpiper, Spotted Redshank, Greenshank, Ruff, Little and Temminck's Stints, Curlew Sandpiper, Black-winged Stilt, Avocet, Little Gull, Black, Whiskered, Gull-billed, Caspian and Lesser Crested Terns, Fan-tailed and Subalpine Warblers, Short-toed Lark.
ACCESS Moulay-Bou-Selham is a good base, giving access to the north of the lagoon and the river exit to the sea. Boats can be hired, but are not rewarding. A road inland and a turn right (south) towards Kenitra, lead to marshes. Continuing south, a village with a line of tall trees appears on the right. A sharp right leads into this and continues on a track to the south of the lagoon and probably the best viewpoints. Don't stop in the village.

The cork woods north of Larache are best watched where the road rises 20–23 km to the north. The Lac di Sidi Bourhaba lies on the coast south of Mehdiya Plage, itself just west of Kenitra. Watch for Marsh Owl at dusk from the causeway across the marsh at the northern end of the lake.
ROUTE Rabat has an airport, but Tangier is nearer.

MIDDLE ATLAS LAKES

North-east of Ifrane lies a series of mainly small, shallow lakes with a narrow band of vegetation which shelters a number of breeding birds. The lakes also attract an interesting population of duck on passage and in winter, with good numbers of waders and terns. Outstanding are the small numbers of breeding Crested Coot, though they can be difficult to spot among their more common relatives. Ruddy Shelduck and Marbled Teal are more numerous and can usually be located without too much difficulty. The main lakes are Dayet Aaoua, Dayet Hachlaf with its reedbeds, and Dayet Afourgan. There are others in the same area, but these are the most visited. Demoiselle Crane is a speciality, if difficult.

The best lake is much farther north just west of Fès at Douyiet. This excellent water has all the attributes of the others, but is also very near a major city. Fès itself is notable for the huge colony of Alpine Swift that nests in the walls of the old city: tens of thousands (?) at dusk.

PASSAGE Great Crested and Black-necked Grebes, Purple and Night Herons, Cattle and Little Egrets, Ruddy Shelduck, Marbled Teal, Marsh Harrier, Barbary Partridge, Crested Coot, Demoiselle Crane, Little Ringed Plover, Black-tailed Godwit, Greenshank, Black-winged Stilt, Avocet, Black and Whiskered Terns, Alpine Swift, Levaillant's Woodpecker, Woodlark, Bluethroat, Fan-tailed Warbler, Spanish Sparrow, Raven.

Bald Ibis

ACCESS Leave Fès on the Mèknes road and stop at Douyiet after 20 km. The other lakes are worked from Ifrane; all are passed by roads. If short of time, Dayet Aaoua is off the main road (P24) towards Fès. Turn right at the junction with Route 4630 and right again beside the lake. The trees along this track and the woods to the right have Levaillant's Woodpecker, which can also be seen in the woods around Mischliffen. The Demoiselle area lies between the P20 and Route S309 south-east of Ilfrane.

ROUTE Fès has an airport, but the area is usually worked on the way to or from the area south of the Atlas via Gorges du Ziz. See Midelt.

MIDELT

Midelt is a convenient centre for a number of bird spots that do not merit separate entries. They are not unimportant, simply highly specific. To the south lies Tizi-n-Talrhenit, the pass leading to Ksar-es-Souk. Tristram's Warbler can be seen 2 km north of the summit, along with Crimson-winged Finch. Most will explore this on their way, rather than make an excursion from Midelt, but it should not be ignored. Here there are Lammergeier, Lanner, Long-legged Buzzard, Chough, Moussier's Redstart and others.

To the west, Cirque de Jaffar, has a strangely north European fauna including Woodpigeon, Great Spotted Woodpecker, Woodlark, Magpie, Jay and Robin, but there are also Moussier's Redstart and Tristram's Warbler. Among others there are often good flocks of Rock Sparrow.

North of Midelt, the countryside becomes a gently rolling steppe with clumps of halfa grass. The Plateau de l'Arid is the best spot for Dupont's Lark. Sit in a vehicle and watch carefully. In despair, some have walked up the hill to catch a glimpse. Try kilometre stone 26 or the track running west signposted to Ait Illousen 3 km south of Zeida. About 1 km down this track is a quarry. Turn south and wait. Cream-coloured Courser, sandgrouse, Red-rumped Wheatear and Thick-billed Lark are also possible.

Farther north the road to Azrou leads through the Col du Zad before passing along the Foum Kheneg toward Timhadite. This is another Bald Ibis spot, though the recent decline may have put an end to the colony.

SUMMER Lammergeier, Red Kite, Long-legged Buzzard, Lanner, Black-bellied Sandgrouse, Bald Ibis, Woodlark, Thekla, Lesser Short-toed and Dupont's Larks, Great Grey Shrike, Moussier's Redstart, Tristram's Warbler, Tawny Pipit, Serin, Crimson-winged Finch, Rock Sparrow.

ACCESS All of the areas are easily found along the roads in the directions indicated, except the Cirque de Jaffar which lies south-west of Midelt on a well-marked minor road. Dupont's can be looked for anywhere about 26 km north of Midelt, but patience is a necessity.

ROUTE The area lies on the road between Ifrane and Ksar-es-Souk. It is thus somewhat divided from the lakes of the Middle Atlas near Ifrane.

OUARZAZATE AND THE SOUTH

Ouarzazate is a large 'oasis' town south of the High Atlas and an excellent headquarters for exploring along the northern edge of the Sahara. Good roads in several directions, give access to a wide range of habitats and offer the chance of finding many species typical of the area. For our purposes, the most important areas lie to the south-east, east and north-west along the roads to Zagora, Tinehir and Marrakech. All three can be worked from Ouarzazate, though the distances are significant. Many species here are widespread and easily found throughout the area: Desert and Bar-tailed Desert Larks, Mourning Wheatear, White-crowned Black Wheatear, Black Wheatear and House Bunting can be found without difficulty. Other species are more localized and must be more definitely sought after.

The main areas to visit are Tizi-n-Tichka, the high pass through which the Ouarzazate-Marrakech road winds its way and where Lammergeier is a possibility; riverside palms hold Fulvous Babbler and Scrub Warbler; Boulmane, where sandgrouse and wheatears abound and where there is access to Houbara Bustard country; and the Gorge du Todra, which has Pale Crag Martin among its specialities. Ouarzazate itself has areas of tamarisk and a rubbish tip, neither of which should be ignored.

Though the breeding birds of the area and the possibilities of seeing all the wheatears and larks are the main attraction, the passage of warblers and chats through the area cannot be ignored in either spring or autumn.

SUMMER Cattle Egret, Black Kite, Long-legged Buzzard, Booted Eagle, Egyptian Vulture, Lammergeier, Lanner, Houbara Bustard, Cream-coloured Courser, Crowned Sandgrouse, Rock Dove, Little Swift, Bee-eater, Blue-cheeked Bee-eater, Roller, Hoopoe, Shore, Temminck's Horned, Short-toed, Bifasciated, Lesser Short-toed, Desert, Bar-tailed Desert, Thick-billed and Thekla Larks, Pale Crag Martin, Bulbul, Scrub Warbler, Blue Rock Thrush, Wheatear (including Seebohm's), Desert, Black-eared, Mourning, Red-rumped, White-crowned Black and Black Wheatears, Moussier's Redstart, Rufous Bushchat, Fulvous Babbler, House and Rock Buntings, Trumpeter Finch, Chough, Alpine Chough, Raven.

ACCESS The Tizi-n-Tichka is the major pass across the High Atlas. Just below the pass on the southern side, a road leads eastward to Telouet, which is a beautiful valley complete with palace and frequented by tourists. Bald Ibis has been recorded and White Storks breed. Lammergeier, Chough and Alpine Chough, Blue Rock Thrush and Shore Lark may be seen on or near the pass. North of the pass there is a cluster of shops, with a hairpin bend 400 m beyond. Walk left along the ridge for Crimson-winged Finch. **Zagora** and the **Drâa valley** are easily reached, and a good exploration of the Agdz area should produce Babbler, Bulbul, Scrub Warbler and Blue-cheeked Bee-eater. **Boulmane** lies east. Beyond the town and just past a garage there is a track which leads south towards Tagdilt. After a few kilometres there is a major fork, between the arms of which are major concentration of Red-rumped Wheatear, Temminck's Horned Lark and Crowned Sandgrouse. Continue south on the left track for 25 km in the search for Houbara. Along the way, stop at a small oasis for Trumpeter Finch. A further Houbara area lies 20 km west of El Kelaa (west of Boulmane) at telegraph pole no. 1421, where the wadi should be explored. **Gorge du Todra** lies above Tinehir in a steep escarpment. It can be driven (by the intrepid), and the palm groves and rocky cliffs hold a good variety of species including Pale Crag Martin, Rock Dove, Black Wheatear and Grey Wagtail. Higher up, the road crosses the river from right to left. Some 2.5 km farther is an area of scrub for Tristram's Warbler, as well as Bonelli's Eagle and Lanner.

Several specialities are awkward to find and have not yet been mentioned under specific places: Trumpeter Finch and Thick-billed and Bifasciated Larks will be found by stopping a few kilometres east of Ouarzazate and walking out in a large loop over the surrounding plains and broken wadis. Of the three, Thick-billed often proves the most elusive. Moussier's Redstart can be found along the road between Tichka and Ouarzazate, and Lanner and Long-legged Buzzard between Boulmane and Tinehir.

ROUTE The airport at Agadir is the gateway to the south of the Atlas, though Marrakech is nearer and has the advantage of a direct route into the Tizi-n-Tichka.

SIDI RAHAL – OUALIDIA

Between El Jadida and Cap Beddouza, the coast runs north-east–south-west. Here huge dune beaches have been built up, broken here and there by rocky outcrops. These dune systems have cut off an almost continuous stretch of marshland between Sidi Rahal and Oualidia, an area that for some reason has escaped receiving a common birders' name. Over the years these marshes have been converted to rough grazing and saltpans, though in the north and the south the sea maintains access and two inter-tidal lagoons have developed. Thus, the landscape varies from virtually dry fields intersected by reed-lined dykes to open shoreline.

This huge area is one of Morocco's outstanding wetlands, offering a vast range of species to thorough explorers: egrets, storks, waders and terns, as well as many warblers and chats. Among the regulars is Slender-billed Curlew, one of the scarcest species, found here only during the late autumn and winter. Even this is not its major Moroccan haunt and numbers are small. Though seabirds often rest on the embankments between the saltpans, most tend to roost either on the beach or on the sandy spits found at the two salt-water inlets. Gulls and terns are often good, with Audouin's Gull and Royal and Lesser Crested Terns present in small numbers. Skuas of several species are often seen in autumn, and there are sometimes good flocks of large shearwaters feeding close inshore. In fact, all the regular shearwaters, terns and skuas may be seen on a good day.

South of the main area lies Cap Beddouza, a rocky headland that has proved a fine seawatching site. Barbary Falcon is regular and, in autumn, the large shearwaters may be present in substantial flocks.

PASSAGE Black-necked Grebe, Cory's, Great, Sooty and Mediterranean Shearwaters, Gannet, Purple Heron, Little Egret, White Stork, Spoonbill, Flamingo, Long-legged Buzzard, Marsh and Montagu's Harriers, Peregrine, Lanner, Barbary Falcon, Slender-billed Curlew, Black-tailed Godwit, Little Stint, Curlew Sandpiper, Ruff, Avocet, Black-winged Stilt, Collared Pratincole, Long-tailed Skua, Audouin's Gull, Royal, Lesser Crested and Black Terns, Hoopoe, Crested Lark, Fan-tailed and Melodious Warblers , Spotless Starling, Serin.

ACCESS The coast road south of El Jadida runs alongside this splendid area and gives views over many of the marshes and saltpans. The first major area is at **Sidi Moussa**, with saltpans to the north and an intertidal inlet to the south. Both can be easily explored on foot. Southwards, there are various marshes and lagoons that should be investigated before reaching the **Oualidia** area. Here the marsh extends for several kilometres north to another large area of saltpans, the whole forming probably the best site along the whole coast. Oualidia itself is a small resort situated on the second intertidal lagoon. At the mouth of this the rocks are an excellent seawatch site. The whole area is worth a thorough exploration, and there are even reports of Andalusian Hemipode here. **Cap Beddouza** lies straight along the coast road southwards. To the north, at **Azemmour**, take a track that leads towards the beach south of the town and river. This excellent scrub-covered area and estuary has Slender-billed Curlew in season and has produced Lesser Crested Tern.

ROUTE Casablanca and its airport are only 130 km or so to the north.

Moussier's Redstart

NORWAY

BÖRGEFJELL

This large national park lies on the border of the provinces of Nordland and Nord-Tröndelag, roughly half-way between Trondheim and Narvik. The main base is Fellingfors, but there are plenty of villages and huts offering accommodation. This is a mountainous landscape with cascading rivers, lakes, marshes, forests and large areas of birch scrub. The birds are typical of northern Scandinavia, with Pied Flycatcher and Bluethroat among the scrub, Phalarope and Temminck's Stint on the marshes, Goldeneye and Goosander on the pine-surrounded lakes and Snow Bunting and Ptarmigan on the open tops. There are Bean and Lesser White-fronted Geese here, though they may take a bit of tracking down, and raptors include Rough-legged Buzzard. To the north is Rössvatn, a huge water with Black-throated Diver and Scoter. This is a remote area, and visitors should be prepared to walk for their birds and treat the mountains with respect.

SUMMER Black-throated Diver, Bean and Lesser White-fronted Geese, Long-tailed Duck, Scoter, Goldeneye, Goosander, Rough-legged Buzzard, Dotterel, Temminck's Stint, Red-necked Phalarope, Long-tailed Skua, Ptarmigan, Willow Grouse, Snowy Owl, Fieldfare, Redwing, Bluethroat, Brambling, Snow Bunting.

ACCESS From Fellingfors a road leads eastward, with Börgefjell to the south and Rössvatn to the north. Smaller roads facilitate exploration, but be prepared to walk to get the best out of this beautiful area.

ROUTE The main north–south road of Norway runs through Fellingfors.

DOVREFJELL

The Fokstua reserve on the Dovrefjell has been a famous bird resort for over a century and attracts hundreds of ornitho-tourists every year. Though relatively small – the reserve is only 7.5 sq. km – the surrounding areas of fjell, marsh, woodland and lakes make this one of the best-known bird areas in Europe. Over the years the Dovrefjell has changed considerably, most dramatically when the Dovre railway was built in 1916–17 through the best area of marsh. Some species abandoned the area only to return later, and others have colonized for the first time. Today, Crane is no longer a regular breeder, though it does breed in most years. Temminck's Stint, Whimbrel and even Lesser White-fronted Goose have bred, along with a fine cross-section of birds usually found much farther north.

On higher ground Snow Bunting, Shore Lark and Purple Sandpiper breed, while Rough-legged Buzzard usually does. This is an excellent, easy-to-explore area, worthy of a short holiday rather than an overnight stop.

SUMMER Red-throated Diver, Crane, Hen Harrier, Peregrine, Rough-legged Buzzard, Dotterel, Whimbrel, Temminck's Stint, Ruff, Purple Sandpiper, Great Snipe, Red-necked Phalarope, Great Grey Shrike, Dipper, Ring Ouzel, Fieldfare, Bluethroat, Shore Lark, Brambling, Siskin, Redpoll, Snow and Lapland Buntings.

ACCESS Permits for the Fokstua reserve may be obtained from the warden near the railway station. Much, however, can be seen from walking the boundary without penetrating the reserve at all. Dombås, to the south offers a range of accommodation and is used as a base by most visitors.

ROUTE By road or rail from Oslo or Trondheim to Fokstua station.

HARDANGERVIDDA

The Hardangervidda is a popular holiday area for the people of Oslo and Bergen in both summer and winter. Though it reaches no great altitude, its hills, marshes, forests and meadows hold a variety of species more typical of land considerably farther north. Indeed, for a number of Arctic birds Hardanger represents their farthest point south. Dotterel, Purple Sandpiper and Temminck's Stint are cases in point. Here too are Tengmalm's and Pygmy Owls, both elusive. Bluethroat, Brambling and Fieldfare are wide-spread and there is often a good population of raptors, though numbers vary according to the lemming population. As elsewhere in Norway, there is an excellent series of huts offering overnight accommodation and meals. They are reached via tracks and well-marked paths and, though they require

White-tailed Eagle

a certain degree of fitness, they are used by all ages. Altogether, the woods, hills and lakes here are among the most accessible sites for northern birds.

SUMMER Golden Eagle, Osprey, Merlin, Scaup, Goldeneye, Velvet Scoter, Dotterel, Greenshank, Whimbrel, Wood and Purple Sandpipers, Temminck's Stint, Pygmy and Tengmalm's Owls, Three-toed and Black Woodpeckers, Fieldfare, Bluethroat, Brambling, Redpoll, Crossbill.
ACCESS Dyranut has a hostel and is a good base for exploring the Bjoreidal valley and then head south to Randhellern on Lake Langesjoen, Sandhang on Lake Normannslagen and Hadlasker to the north-west.
ROUTE Dyranut is on the main Oslo–Bergen road.

LOFOTEN ISLANDS

Despite lying within the Arctic Circle, the Lofoten Islands are green, lush and fertile because the Gulf Stream keeps temperatures above freezing, even in the depths of winter. Only two of the eight major and hundreds of smaller islands extending over 150 km need seriously concern the visiting birder. Röst is the southernmost and also the most important, while the slightly larger Vaeröy is the next island north up the chain. Röst is one of the world's outstanding seabird sites with well over a million birds present at the height of the season. Sadly, the dominant species, the Puffin, has shown a serious decline in recent years, though previous estimates of over 2,000,000 pairs were probably wildly inaccurate. Today there are certainly fewer than the 700,000 pairs estimated in 1964. Other auks are also here in good numbers including over 4000 pairs of Guillemot; 2000–4000 pairs of Razorbill; and 1000–1500 pairs of Black Guillemot. Other cliff-nesters include 17,500 pairs of Kittiwake; 600–1000 pairs of Shag and 300–500 pairs of Fulmar. There are also good numbers of both Storm and

Leach's Petrels. There are also colonies of Eider and Arctic Tern as well as Arctic Skua, Dunlin and Whimbrel. White-tailed Eagle is readily seen and even gathers in spring flocks over Vedöy, a smaller uninhabited island.

SUMMER Storm and Leach's Petrels, Fulmar, Shag, Eider, White-tailed Eagle, Snipe, Dunlin, Whimbrel, Red-necked Phalarope, Kittiwake, Arctic Tern, Arctic Skua, Guillemot, Razorbill, Puffin, Black Guillemot.
WINTER Eider, King Eider, White-tailed Eagle, Gyrfalcon, Purple Sandpiper, Snow Bunting.
ACCESS There are regular steamers to Röst from Bodö on the mainland, as well as from Moskenesöy via Vaeröy. There are also regular daily flights from Bodö with connections to Oslo and other Norwegian cities. Röstlandet, the largest island, offers guesthouse accommodation as well as well-equipped fishermen's huts. Contact Destination Lofoten AS, Postboks 210, 8301 Svolvaer, Loften (Tel. 088 73000). Trips to the smaller islands can be arranged through that organization and locally.
ROUTE To Röstlandet via Bodö and Oslo.

RUNDE

Runde (Rundöy) lies in the south of Norway's fjord coastline not far from Alesund. It is a rugged island with fearsome cliffs that hold huge numbers of seabirds – about 170,000 pairs most years – and the country's largest gannetry. Its human population is centred on Runde and Goksöyr – access is relatively straightforward and accommodation can be obtained. Kittiwake and Puffin are the most numerous species, with largest concentrations at Rundebranden near Goksoyr. Gannets nest at Storebranden: numbers have increased steadily since they first colonized in 1946; by 1974 there were nearly 500 pairs. The seabird cliffs are among the best in Europe. Runde is also home to White-tailed Eagle and Eagle Owl.

SUMMER Fulmar, Gannet, Shag, Eider, Peregrine, White-tailed Eagle, Curlew, Oystercatcher, Kittiwake, Puffin, Guillemot, Razorbill, Eagle Owl.
ACCESS There are regular ferry sailings from Ålesund to Runde, where there are rooms at Christineborg turisthotell (Tel. 070–85950) and at other smaller (and cheaper) hostelries. There is also a camp site. For details write to Heröy og Runde Reiselivslag, v/Knut A. Goksöyr, N–6096, Runde (Tel. 070–85905). Fishermen are usually willing to sail under the seabird cliffs.
ROUTE By air or steamer from Bergen, or by train from Oslo.

VARANGER FJORD

Varanger is the north-easternmost part of the European mainland outside Russia. Opening eastwards into the Arctic Ocean, it gets less benefit from the Gulf Stream and is thus cold and barren, so several species can be found only here, or farther to the east. The White-billed Diver is more common than the Great Northern, and this is the only European site for both Steller's and King Eiders. It is also the only place outside Iceland for Brünnich's Guillemot and even Spectacled Eider is present in winter.

Though these species may be the 'stars' of Varanger from a twitcher's angle, there is much more top-rate birding here. The surrounding fjells and marshes are full of breeding waders, and this is the most accessible spot in 'Siberia'. Red-necked Phalarope, Purple Sandpiper, Turnstone, Bar-tailed Godwit and both stints can be seen, along with skuas, Glaucous Gull, Red-throated Pipit, Snow Bunting and Arctic Redpoll. Exploration is relatively straightforward along the road that clings to the northern shore. Conditions become progressively worse as one proceeds eastward, and several crews have found that more sweaters are required as they progress from Varangerbotn at the head of the fjord to Vardo at the mouth and Hamningberg around the corner on the Arctic Ocean.

SUMMER White-billed, Red-throated and Black-throated Divers, Long-tailed Duck, Velvet Scoter, Eider, King and Steller's Eiders, Gyrfalcon, Dotterel, Bar-tailed Godwit, Temminck's and Little Stints, Purple Sandpiper, Red-necked Phalarope, Arctic Tern, Glaucous Gull, Arctic and Long-tailed Skuas, Snowy Owl, Bluethroat, Arctic Warbler, Shore Lark, Red-throated Pipit, Lapland and Snow Buntings, Arctic and Mealy Redpolls. ACCESS Varangerbotn has a muddy area at the head of the fjord for waders, including summer-plumage Knot and Godwit, and the chance of Arctic Warbler. Nesseby has a quaint church and adjacent wader pool, noted for Red-necked Phalarope. From the promontory there is a good chance of King Eider, which occurs from here eastwards. Vadsö is the main town, with shops and a hotel, and a rubbish dump on an offshore island reached by a motorable bridge. This is a good spot for odd gulls, including late or early Arctic species, as well as both stints and Steller's Eider. Ekkeröy is a prime seawatching spot where Varanger's specialities can be seen. Ekkeröy Island, connected to the mainland by a causeway, has good seabird cliffs in the south, pools in the interior and a sandy shore in the north. This is the spot for masses of stints, Red-throated Pipit, Lapland Bunting and Shore Lark. Steller's Eider is often seen from here. Falkefjell lies inland from Ekkeröy and is worth a walk for scrub-dwelling Arctic Redpoll, Bluethroat and Red-throated Pipit. There are good wader pools, and Dotterel, skuas and even Snowy Owl on the higher slopes. Vardö is a fishing town on two linked islands reached by a 3 km tunnel. The islet of Hornöy has five species of auk and a seawatch from the north-eastern point of the outer island may produce many of Varanger's specials. It is too far to identify Brünnich's Guillemot, but a boat-trip from the town might produce this species without landing on Hornöy. Hamningberg is a splendid climax to the drive along the fjord, with spectacular scenery, snow down to sea level all year and many Arctic birds. Ordofjell lies north of the Varanger Fjord and is reached via Varangerbotn and Tana bru along the minor road that runs north along the eastern bank of the Tana. The spectacular scenery eventually gives way, as the road (the 890) turns east, to open tundra with Long-tailed Duck, Phalarope, Temminck's, two skuas, Red-throated Pipit and Lapland Bunting. Continue on the 891 to Bätsfjord. Pasvik valley is not often visited because it lies on the southern shore in an extension of Norway southwards between Finland and Russia. The only route is via Kirkenes south to Nyrud. The scrub, pools and marshes hold a fine collection of waders, including Bar-tailed Godwit, plus Arctic Redpoll, Bean Goose and other scarce species. ROUTE By air to Vadsö, or by road. The best time is late June and early July, when birding 24 hours a day is available.

POLAND

AUGUSTÓW FOREST AND LAKES

This area lies close to the Russian border in eastern Poland and could be regarded as a northward extension of the Biebrza Marshes to the south. Certainly, any birders getting as far as this should explore both. The present area is, if anything, even more daunting than Biebrza, but there are several lakes around Augustów that can be reached by road, and the Augustów Canal runs conveniently through the area, offering splendid birding from boats. The area is basically wet forest with lakes and marshes, and certainly deserves a thorough exploration.

Among a host of species are Lesser Spotted and Short-toed Eagles, Crane, Black Stork, Eagle Owl, White-backed and Three-toed Woodpeckers, as well as Goldeneye and both Goosander and Merganser.

For those lacking time in this part of the country, a canal trip offers the best chance of making contact with some of these special birds.

SUMMER Little Bittern, White and Black Storks, Goldeneye, Red-breasted Merganser, Goosander, Goshawk, Red Kite, Lesser Spotted and Short-toed Eagles, Hen Harrier, Crane, Eagle Owl, White-backed and Three-toed Woodpeckers, River and Great Reed Warblers, Scarlet Rosefinch.

ACCESS Wigry Lake and Serwy Lake are just two of many waters worthy of exploration in this area. The best method of exploration, however, is to take one of the tourist boats that ply the Augustów Canal. ROUTE Augustów can be reached by train from Warsaw.

BIALOWIESKA FOREST

This famous forest lies in the extreme east of Poland and continues across the border into Russia. It is the home of the only wild herd of European bison and is the largest remnant of the original European forest; it covers 580 sq. km, of which 47.5 sq. km is a national park. Hornbeam, alder, oak, birch, lime, maple and pine are the dominant trees, and there are open glades, wet marshes and park-like areas, offering a home to over 200 species. Though there are eagles, owls, woodpeckers and cranes here, the visitor is unlikely to see many of the more exotic species – including the bison. Lesser Spotted Eagle is common, but Short-toed is scarce. Eagle, Tengmalm's and Pygmy Owls, are here but highly elusive, though the last is said to be fairly common. Hazelhen are definitely here but are difficult to locate. Woodpeckers are, in contrast, easy to locate, but difficult to see. Grey-headed, Black, Middle Spotted, White-backed and Three-toed all breed, though their numbers vary. Thrush Nightingale is common, as are River, Marsh, Icterine, Barred and Wood Warblers, while Greenish breeds in smaller numbers. Both Collared and Red-breasted Flycatchers are common, and Golden Oriole and Scarlet Rosefinch are regularly seen.

Fortunately the Park Palacowy, which lies a short distance from the reserve entrance and also holds the main hotel, is excellent for most of the smaller birds. The reserve can be visited and it is worth watching out for nestboxes with Collared Flycatchers. The best bet for seeing the scarcer birds, however, is to contact one of the local ornithologists and get him to show you birds at known nests. Such a tactic may produce woodpeckers, owls and conceivably Hazelhen.

The Narewka can be walked on both banks, though only for 1 km on the east bank. There are good forest areas south-west of the town, and a good track to the north-west to a wet forest area. On the northern fringe of the Bial/owieska Forest there is a newly created water, the Siemianowka Reservoir, which boasts an excellent collection of breeding and passage waterbirds. These include White-winged Black and Whiskered Terns, Little Gull, Marsh Sandpiper, Osprey, White-tailed Eagle and Tawny Pipit.

SUMMER White and Black Storks, Crane, Honey Buzzard, Osprey, Black Kite, Goshawk, White-tailed, Booted, Lesser Spotted, Spotted and Short-toed Eagles, Hazelhen, Capercaillie, Corncrake, Crane, Green and Marsh Sandpipers, White-winged Black and Whiskered Terns, Little Gull, Tengmalm's and Pygmy Owls, Nightjar, Wryneck, Grey-headed, Three-toed, Black, Middle Spotted and White-backed Woodpeckers, Tawny Pipit, Thrush Nightingale, Bluethroat, River, Marsh, Great Reed, Icterine, Barred, Greenish and Wood Warblers, Red-breasted, Collared and Pied Flycatchers, Golden Oriole, Red-backed Shrike, Serin, Scarlet Rosefinch, Ortolan Bunting.

ACCESS The Hotel Iwa is situated in the grounds of the Palace Park, where many of the small birds can be seen. The reserve entrance is along

the road leading due north, and the scientific staff live in flats in the next street to the east. There is a good track running west just north of the Narewka. Permits can be obtained at the Bialowieska Tourist Office.
ROUTE Train from Warsaw to Bialystok and then through Hajnowka to Bialowieza. The hotel is a short walk from the station. The Siemianowka Reservoir is easily reached by train, bus or car from Hajnowka.

BIEBRZA MARSHES

These great marshes extend along the River Biebrza between Augustów and Lomza to the north-west of Warsaw near Bialystok. Here, the mean-dering river has created a network of channels, backwaters and floods, with islands, lakes and huge marshes. There are areas of woodland and some considerable forests, but the area is thinly inhabited. There is a reserve at Czerwone Bagno, but the whole is worthy of exploration.

The variety of habitats is demonstrated by the wealth of species that can be found here, though even today there is some doubt about what does and what does not breed. Osprey, Red and Black Kites, Goshawk, Spotted and Lesser Spotted Eagles, Golden and White-tailed Eagles, Marsh, Hen and Montagu's Harriers and Hobby make a formidable list of raptors, but all have been seen in a single visit. Wetland birds include Bittern and Little Bittern, Crane, Spotted and Little Crakes, Great Snipe at a significant-sized lek, Jack Snipe, Marsh Sandpiper and Little Gull, and Black, White-winged Black and Whiskered Terns. Aquatic Warbler is common, and Bearded and Penduline Tits both breed.

SUMMER Bittern, Little Bittern, White and Black Storks, Garganey, Ferruginous Duck, Osprey, Red and Black Kites, Goshawk, Spotted, Lesser

Great Snipe

Spotted, Golden, White-tailed and Short-toed Eagles, Hen, Montagu's and Marsh Harriers, Hobby, Black Grouse, Crane, Water Rail, Spotted and Little Crakes, Ruff, Black-tailed Godwit, Marsh Sandpiper, Great and Jack Snipe, Little Gull, Black, White-winged Black and Whiskered Terns, Eagle and Tengmalm's Owls, Barred, Great Reed and Greenish Warblers, Bearded and Penduline Tits, Great Grey Shrike, Nutcracker, Scarlet Rosefinch.

ACCESS The best area extends from Wizna to Goniadz and can be explored via minor roads and tracks on the eastern side. At the centre of this area lies the tiny village of Budy, which has access in most directions and even two observation towers within walking distance. This is a wet area with poor roads, so wellies are essential. The best Great Snipe area is from a causeway 2 km south of Budy, but continue to the observation tower. The terns breed at a small lake just north of Goniadz. There is a hotel in Lomza and a restaurant at Goniadz. Camping at Budy is possible, but take food and mosquito repellent – not necessarily in that order.

ROUTE Take a bus from the PKS Bus Station, Piwnica na Wojtowskiej, Lomza. Change to bus to Trzcianne and get off at Gugny and walk. Alternatively hire a car, but remember that petrol stations are not numerous. Also remember that this is one of the greatest raptor spots in Europe, and may well be worth all the effort of getting there.

CHELM MARSHES

To the north and east of Chelm, between the town and the Russian border, lies an extensive area of peat bogs and wet-meadows some 900 ha of which are protected as a reserve. This wetland holds a wealth of breeding species, including some specialities such as Crane, Bittern, Montagu's Harrier, Bluethroat and Penduline Tit. There are many of the 'eastern' specials that one would expect to see in this part of central Europe. Most attractive of all are breeding Aquatic Warbler, for this is one of the major strongholds of what is a fast declining species.

SUMMER Bittern, White and Black Storks, Lesser Spotted Eagle, Goshawk, Montagu's and Marsh Harriers, Crane, Water Rail, Thrush Nightingale, Barred, Icterine and Aquatic Warblers, Penduline Tit, Scarlet Rosefinch.

ACCESS There are no restrictions on access to the area, which can be explored by road from Chelm. The marshes lie to the north, north-east and east of the town, and part of the area is protected as a nature reserve. Contact Jarowlaw Krogulec, Zaklad Ochrony Przyrody, Instytut Biologii, ul. Akademicka 19, 20-003 Lublin.

ROUTE Chelm can be reached by train from Lublin.

GDAŃSK

Gdańsk lies on the shores of the Baltic near the mouth of the Vistula and forms an admirable base for exploring this exceptionally bird-rich shoreline. Generations of migrant-watchers have counted and ringed the millions of birds that annually pass along this coast, and the variety that puts in an appearance here is quite remarkable. Gdańsk is, however, not just a migration place, for the whole of northern Poland is rich in lakes, and a short distance to the west is an area of water, marshes and woods around Kartuzy. Here breeding birds include White-tailed Eagle, Black Stork, Little Bittern, Thrush Nightingale, Red-breasted Flycatcher and River Warbler. It is in autumn that this region becomes internationally important.

Mierzeja Helska is a narrow sandy peninsula that separates the Bay of Puck from the open sea. It has huge beaches and some quite extensive pine forests, together with areas of meadows and a huge sewage farm. In spring and autumn there is a ringing station near Chalupy, though the area around Jastarnia has a reputation for producing the largest number of rare birds in Poland. Spring brings Citrine Wagtail and Red-throated Pipit as well as good raptor passage, whereas in autumn there are Broad-billed Sandpiper, Richard's and Olive-backed Pipits and the real chance of a new species for the country.

On the south side of the Bay of Puck the River Reda joins the Baltic north of Rewa. The marshes here are excellent for waders, especially in autumn. This area is, however, overshadowed by the area of the mouth of the Vistula east of Gdańsk, which is generally recognized as the best wader–tern–gull site in Poland. Caspian Tern is numerous, and waders include regular Broad-billed and Terek Sandpipers and Red-necked Phalarope. This area is continually being transformed by deposition and storms, and there are lagoons, islands and marshes to explore. In summer, this is the only Polish breeding site of Arctic and Sandwich Terns. Finally, Druzno Lake lies to the south-east beyond Elblag, and is a shallow, reed-fringed water surrounded by marshes. Although less than 1 m deep, there are still areas of open water separating floating islands of reed and sedge. The wealth of breeding species here is impressive by any standards, and includes Ferruginous Duck, Lesser Spotted Eagle, Crane, Little Gull, Black Tern, River Warbler and Scarlet Rosefinch.

SUMMER Red-necked and Black-necked Grebes, White and Black Storks, Little Bittern, Bittern, Ferruginous Duck, Goshawk, Hen and Marsh Harriers, Lesser Spotted and White-tailed Eagles, Crane, Little Crake, Ruff, Little Gull, Sandwich, Arctic and Black Terns, Golden Oriole, Thrush Nightingale, Bluethroat, Icterine, River, Great Reed, Marsh and Barred Warblers, Red-breasted Flycatcher, Scarlet Rosefinch, Ortolan Bunting.

AUTUMN Black-throated Diver, Velvet Scoter, Eider, Smew, White-fronted and Bean Geese, Whooper Swan, White-tailed Eagle, Rough-legged and Honey Buzzards, Broad-billed, Terek, Purple and Curlew Sandpipers, Little Gull, Caspian Tern, Citrine Wagtail, Red-throated Pipit.

ACCESS Kartuzy is 30 km west of Gdańsk, and the best lakes are Reduńskie, Kiodno and Ostrzyckie to the south-west. There is a good network of roads and the area can be reached by train and bus. **Mierzeja Helska** can be reached by train from Gdynia to Jastarnia, the best spot on the peninsula. Rewa, to the south, is reached by road from Gdynia. The Vistula mouth is reached by taking a bus from Gdańsk railway station to Swibno and then proceeding on foot to the river mouth. **Druzno Lake** can be reached via Elblag, which has a good bus service from Gdańsk. Contact the Ornithological Station, ul. Nadwislanska 108, 80–680 Gdańsk 40.

ROUTE Gdańsk can be reached from Warsaw by road or rail in a day; or by air in about an hour.

MILICZ FISH-PONDS

The fish-ponds at Milicz lie in the flat valley of the Barycz, a tributary of the Oder, in southern Poland near Wroclaw. The ponds were created by Cistercian monks in the fourteenth century, and have been largely preserved. The annual crop of carp is huge, but involves draining a number of ponds each autumn. These ponds vary enormously, from over 3000 ha down to tiny 'village' type ponds. They are surrounded by marshes, grazing land and extensive woods that offer a home to a wide variety of species. Though generally shallow with a considerable growth of emergent vegetation, open water is maintained for both fish and birds.

The ponds hold good populations of grebes, harriers, Greylag Goose and Mute Swan, duck and a fine variety of warblers. Outstanding species include White-tailed Eagle and Poland's only breeding Purple Herons. The best areas of water are, from west to east, Radziadz, Ruda Sulowska, Milicz, Krosnice and Potasznia. The surrounding meadows hold Black-tailed Godwit, Garganey and Grasshopper Warbler, while the margins between ponds and meadows have Penduline Tit and Scarlet Rosefinch.

South of Milicz the hills near Skoroszow are covered with mixed deciduous woodland, offering a home to White-tailed Eagle, Black Stork, various woodpeckers plus Red-breasted Flycatcher.

In autumn, the area is a major staging post for geese and duck and the eagles may then be quite numerous.

SUMMER Red-necked and Black-necked Grebes, Purple Heron, Little Bittern, Bittern, Black Stork, Ferruginous Duck, Greylag Goose, Red and Black Kites, White-tailed Eagle, Honey Buzzard, Marsh Harrier, Crane, Little Crake, Black-tailed Godwit, Roller, Grey-headed, White-backed, Middle Spotted and Black Woodpeckers, Golden Oriole, Penduline Tit, Bluethroat, River, Great Reed, Savi's and Barred Warblers, Red-breasted Flycatcher, Great Grey Shrike, Serin.

ACCESS The main pond areas extend east and west along the Barycz valley from Milicz, and can be explored by minor roads. There is a bird station and visitors are well advised to make contact to find the whereabouts of special birds and of local 'hot spots'. Contact Jozef Witkowski, Ornithological Station, Ruda Milicka, 56–300 Milicz, on arrival.

ROUTE Milicz lies no great distance north of Wroclaw and is reached by train or bus. The ornithological station is 4-km to the east at Ruda Milicz, and will issue permits for the ponds included in a nature reserve.

SILESIAN RESERVOIRS

Wroclaw lies in southern–western Poland, and makes an ideal starting point for exploring the border country as well as the famous fish-pond area of Milicz in the Barycz valley. To the south and the south-east two huge reservoirs have been constructed and these, together with the surrounding land, have become the subject of considerable attention from local birders. They are, however, virtually unknown outside Poland.

The Nysa Reservoir lies west of the town of the same name near the Czech border. This lake covers some 20 sq. km and is at its most attractive in late summer and autumn when the water level is at its lowest, exposing huge areas of mud along the margins. It has become the most important inland stop-over place for migrant waders in Poland. Almost all the species one could reasonably expect in this region have occurred, many in substantial numbers. Marsh and Broad-billed Sandpipers are regular, as is Red-necked Phalarope, and rarities are recorded annually. There are also good concentrations of wildfowl. West from Nysa Reservoir lies Otmuchow Reservoir, also worth visiting, having a good variety of water birds.

Turawa Reservoir lies immediately east of Opole and is similarly best in autumn, when the water level is at its lowest. It too attracts large numbers of waders and wildfowl, including the specialities also found at Nysa. Great White Egret is, however, also regular at this site.

Though primarily migration spots, the two areas also hold many of the species one would expect to see in central Europe, even if they are not in full song in autumn. These include Penduline Tit and Scarlet Rosefinch.

AUTUMN Black-necked Grebe, White Stork, Pintail, Black Kite, Osprey, Black-tailed Godwit, Green, Marsh, Broad-billed, Wood and Curlew Sandpipers, Little and Temminck's Stints, Common and Black Terns, Bluethroat, Barred and Icterine Warblers, Tawny Pipit, Great Grey Shrike, Penduline Tit.
ACCESS Nysa Reservoir can be seen from the surrounding public roads, and is best along the southern and western shoreline off the Otmuchów–Paczkow road west of Nysa. Turawa Reservoir is best in the east, and can be viewed via Szczedrzyk.
ROUTE Both reservoirs enjoy easy access from Wroclaw. Nysa and Opole can be reached by both train and bus and thereafter by bus to Siestrzechowice (Nysa) or Szczedrzyk (Turawa).

SLOŃSK RESERVE

This wetland reserve lies at the confluence of the Warta and Odra on the German border south of Szczecin. Over 5000 ha are flooded and, with numerous shallow lakes and splashy pastures, the whole forms the most important wetland in western Poland. The area is particularly significant to migrant waders and wildfowl, and is the wintering ground of thousands of Bean and White-fronted Geese and hundreds of Whooper Swan. All are outnumbered several times over by surface-feeding and diving ducks.

Breeding birds include a wide variety of species: White-tailed Eagle is perhaps the star, though Shelduck are not common in Poland. Gadwall and Shoveler, River Warbler and Penduline Tit can also be found.

SUMMER Red-necked Grebe, Bittern, Cormorant, Greylag Goose, Shelduck, Gadwall, Shoveler, White-tailed Eagle, Marsh Harrier, White-winged Black Tern, Spotted Crake, Corncrake, Water Rail, Barred, Icterine and River Warblers, Penduline Tit.
WINTER Whooper and Mute Swans, Bean and White-fronted Geese.
ACCESS Though much of this wetland can be seen from roads leading eastward from Kostrzyn, the main area and reserve is situated at Słońsk on the Kostrzyn Reservoir. Permits can be obtained from Przemyslaw Majewski, Station of Polish Hunting Association, 64–020 Czempin.
ROUTE By train from Poznań to Kostrzyn, then by bus to Słońsk.

PORTUGAL

ALTO ALENTEJO

The Alentejo is a land of vast rolling plains, broken by rocky outcrops upon which larger towns are strategically sited. There are also areas of cork, holm oak and pine, a network of rivers and large tracts of unploughed grassland. The region is divided into Alto and Baixo Alentejo (roughly Upper-Northern and Lower-Southern Alentejo) by a boundary that extends westwards from the Spanish border to between Évora and Beja.

The Alto Alentejo is generally better known. The best bird sites lie south of Évora, extend east to Elvas and the Spanish border, and consist predominantly of unploughed and fallow grasslands. Little Bustard is widespread, even common, in places and it requires a level of incompetence, or lack of patience, not to see these birds around Évora or Elvas. Great Bustard is also present, but is a little more elusive and less numerous. The secret is to stop on minor roads wherever 'natural' grassland occurs and watch or walk. Actual 'stake-outs' tend to be unreliable because of the changing agricultural activities of increasingly mechanized farmers. Other good grassland birds include Stone-curlew, Calandra Lark, Montagu's Harrier, Common Quail and the highly local Black-bellied Sandgrouse. White Stork is common in villages and riverside vegetation is full of

Cetti's Warbler, Nightingale, Bee-eater and Golden Oriole. There are several good Black-shouldered Kite spots among olive or cork groves.

SUMMER Cattle Egret, White Stork, Black Kite, Short-toed and Booted Eagles, Montagu's Harrier, Lesser Kestrel, Great and Little Bustards, Black-winged Stilt, Collared Pratincole, Black-bellied Sandgrouse, Crested Lark, Golden Oriole, Roller, Bee-eater, Red-necked Nightjar, Common Quail, Red-rumped Swallow, Woodchat and Great Grey Shrikes, Fan-tailed, Great Reed, Cetti's and Orphean Warblers, Penduline Tit, Black-eared Wheatear, Hawfinch.

ACCESS From Évora take the Beja road and explore minor roads to the right for bustards. The Redondo road is good for the first few kilometres and within 18 km of Evora there are several bridges worthy of stops for smaller birds. North of the N4 take the N370 to Mora, turn east to Cabeção. Oak woods here have a high density of breeding raptors including Booted and Short-toed Eagles. They also hold Red-necked Nightjar, Bee-eater and Orphean Warbler. From Elvas head east toward Spain. Southeast of the town take a right to Torre de Bolsa and continue through extensive rice fields to the river. Outside and to the east of the town is a right turn to Padeira. A huge supermarket on the left means that you have gone a few hundred metres too far. This minor road crosses open plains and in a few kilometres a knoll overlooks a fine bustard area. Although Lesser Kestrel no longer breeds in the area, it is abundant in Badajoz across the border and can often be seen around Torre de Bolsa.

ROUTE From Lisbon Airport head northwards to Vila Franca da Xira on the toll motorway. Turn right across the Tagus bridge and continue to the N4 where turn left toward Montomor-o-Novo, Évora and Elvas.

BAIXO ALENTEJO

Until recently this area was largely ignored by birdwatchers intent on the Algarve to the south and the Alto Alentejo to the north. The Portuguese Atlas project and the IBA survey have shown just what had been missed. It is a huge rural area marked by vast plains, much of it unploughed. There are vast cork and olive groves, rocky outcrops and, in the east, gorges cut by great rivers. Here one can find all the typical Portuguese birds, but here too are some of the best concentrations of raptors and other scarce birds usually thought of as Spanish specialities. So, alongside Great and Little Bustards, White Stork, Montagu's Harrier, Bee-eater and Calandra Lark are Griffon, Egyptian and even Black Vultures, Red and Black Kites, Short-toed and Booted Eagles and even Black Stork and Black Wheatear.

SUMMER Cattle and Little Egrets, White and Black Storks, Short-toed and Booted Eagles, Black-shouldered Kite, Griffon and Black Vultures, Great and Little Bustards, Eagle Owl, Bee-eater, Roller, Great Spotted Cuckoo, Calandra and Thekla Larks, Crag Martin, Red-rumped Swallow, Black Wheatear, Blue Rock Thrush, Rufous Bushchat, Woodchat and Great Grey Shrikes, Azure-winged Magpie, Raven, Rock and Spanish Sparrows.

ACCESS The plains between **Moura and Safara** have a few Great Bustards, Little Bustard, Black-shouldered Kite, Stone-curlew, Montagu's Harrier and Thekla Lark, and the road north from Beja toward Vidigueira has

Montagu's Harrier, Little Bustard, Stone-curlew and Calandra Lark. The best areas are either side of this Beja-Moura core area. To the north and east the area between **Mourão and Barrancos** is simply excellent. Barrancos has the vultures, but eagles can be seen along the road to Amareleja and Granja. This is one of the best areas in Portugal for Black-shouldered Kite. The Granja rubbish tip (north of the village) is good and it is worth crossing into Spain east of Mourão at São Leonardo (open daily except at night) and turning left on a track about 500 m after the border. Here a small reservoir is surrounded by stony plains with both bustards, Black-bellied Sandgrouse, Roller and Calandra Lark. West of Mourão the Guadiana bridge on the N256 is a haunt of Rufous Bushchat. The second significant area lies south-west of Beja around **Castro Verde**. The plains here are the major stronghold of Great Bustard in Portugal with upwards of 500 birds. Try the N2 about 7 km to the north and the minor road east towards São Marcos for about the same distance. This area is good for many grassland species including Little Bustard, Stone-curlew, Roller, Calandra Lark, Thekla Lark, Red-necked Nightjar and Black-eared Wheatear.

ROUTE The Lisbon–Faro road, the N2, passes a few kilometres from Beja which, together with Mourão, forms the best base for this region.

CASTRO MARIM

The Guadiana forms the Portuguese-Spanish border. The Portuguese bank is particularly interesting at its mouth near Vila Real and Castro Marim, where a considerable area of saltpans has been created. Together with pines that line the coastal dunes and the adjacent groves, they form a good area with a wide variety of species. The salinas are excellent during passage, with good numbers of the more common species of waders, terns and gulls. There is a chance of Caspian, Gull-billed and Whiskered Terns. Flamingo and Spoonbill put in appearances, while in summer the variety of breeding birds includes good numbers of White Stork together with Little Bustard, Stilt and Avocet, and a variety of larks including Lesser Short-toed, for which this is the only Portuguese breeding area.

A little to the north further areas of saltpans hold similar species, while woods around Azinhal hold Azure-winged Magpie. The breakwater at the mouth of the Guadiana may produce a few seabirds, including Mediterranean and Cory's Shearwaters, as well as terns, gulls and waders.

SUMMER White Stork, Spoonbill, Cattle and Little Egrets, Black Kite, Booted Eagle, Griffon Vulture, Montagu's Harrier, Little Bustard, Kentish Plover, Black-winged Stilt, Avocet, Collared Pratincole, Little Tern, Short-toed, Lesser Short-toed, Calandra, Crested and Thekla Larks, Hoopoe, Red-rumped Swallow, Black-eared Wheatear, Rufous Bushchat, Spectacled Warbler, Short-toed Treecreeper, Azure-winged Magpie, Great Grey and Woodchat Shrikes, Serin.

PASSAGE Cory's and Mediterranean Shearwaters, Gannet, Flamingo, Spoonbill, Avocet, Spotted Redshank, Ruff, Black-tailed Godwit, Caspian, Gull-billed and Whiskered Terns, Black Redstart, Red-throated Pipit.

ACCESS The pines can be explored west of Vila Real where a road runs parallel to the coast. North off this road, the road to Castro Marim crosses a river bridge and a little way on an access track leads left to the salinas.

FARO

Faro is the largest town on the Algarve and offers arguably the best birding in southern Portugal. The city lies behind a complex dune system that extends east as far as Tavira, and which has effectively sealed off a number of lagoons, creating a bird-rich habitat that starts immediately west of the town. Despite its proximity, several teams have found it a difficult area to work properly, though those that have succeeded have been well rewarded.

Passage and winter waders are excellent, with a good variety of the species one would expect along this coastline. Local breeding birds include Cattle Egret, Night Heron, Little Bittern, Red-crested Pochard and Purple Gallinule. The last is a speciality of the best site, the lagoon by the salinas at the western end of the airport, usually seen from 'planes when taking off into a westerly wind – when you are on your way home! The adjacent woods have Azure-winged Magpie, Golden Oriole, Sardinian Warbler, and there are often Waxbills in the area. Caspian Tern and Mediterranean Gull are regular outside the breeding season and in winter there are Spoonbills, Ospreys and Peregrines here along with an important wader population.

SUMMER White Stork, Cattle and Little Egrets, Night and Purple Herons, Little Bittern, Red-crested Pochard, Black Kite, Montagu's Harrier, Purple Gallinule, Little Bustard, Kentish Plover, Black-winged Stilt, Avocet, Collared Pratincole, Little Tern, Hoopoe, Bee-eater, Golden Oriole, Woodchat and Great Grey Shrikes, Azure-winged Magpie, Sardinian Warbler, Waxbill.
PASSAGE Grey Plover, Whimbrel, Black-tailed Godwit, Wood and Curlew Sandpipers, Little Stint, Sanderling, Knot, Avocet, Caspian Tern, Mediterranean Gull.
ACCESS Leave Faro on the main Portimão road and turn left for the airport. Follow signs for 'Praia de Faro' and explore the beach and the connecting causeway. Return to the airport and take the first left. Pass through woods and turn right at a T-junction. At the next junction, turn left through more woods. This track continues to the salinas for waders on the left and a viewpoint over a fresh-water lagoon to the right. The latter is good for Purple Gallinule. However, this is part of the Ludo Farm area and many have been evicted for lacking the appropriate permit. Those who have tried to obtain a permit have usually been frustrated. You have been warned. The Tavira saltpans farther east are also a wader haunt and enjoy a more friendly reputation. They are easily approached and watched via a series of tracks from the coastal road at Tavira which leads to a seaside restaurant. The westernmost marshes at Quinta do Lago are included in the Ria Formosa Natural Park. From Almancil head south to this private estate and pick your way through a maze of luxury developments to the Quinta do Lago Hotel. Park below the hotel and head for the sea exploring to left and right for waders, terns and herons.
ROUTE Faro airport with good birding within walking distance.

MIRANDA DO DOURO

The Douro forms the border with Spain in the north-east where it flows through a steep-sided valley and several spectacular gorges. The surroundings have extensive areas of scrub, some fine holm oak woods and agricultural land. All can be found within a short distance of the town. There is an important colony of Alpine Swift, as well as Rock Sparrow and Serin, and summer nights produce the calls of both Scops Owl and Red-necked Nightjar. A pair of Bonelli's Eagles regularly overfly the town.

It is, however, the gorge that holds most interest. Egyptian Vulture is the commonest raptor and Subalpine the commonest warbler. Griffon Vultures are about, and Hoopoes and Golden Orioles appear from every wood. Even Hawfinch is common and up to twenty may be seen in a day. Raptors include both kites, Golden, and Booted Eagles, while the commoner warblers include Subalpine, Sardinian, Orphean (one of the best areas in Portugal), Dartford, Cetti's, Melodious and Bonelli's. Typical mountain birds are also present with Chough, Crag Martin, Blue Rock Thrush, Black Redstart, Black Stork, Black Wheatear and Rock Bunting.

The area is recommended for those who do not wish to drive or walk too far, though a series of dams downstream is worth investigating. While this is the most important area in Portugal for Griffon Vultures, the number of Peregrines is of truly international significance.

SUMMER Black Stork, Black and Red Kites, Griffon and Egyptian Vultures, Golden, Booted and Bonelli's Eagles, Great Spotted Cuckoo, Scops and Eagle Owls, Red-necked Nightjar, Alpine Swift, Bee-eater, Roller, Hoopoe, Wryneck, Calandra, Crested and Thekla Larks, Woodlark, Crag Martin, Red-rumped Swallow, Black-eared Wheatear, Black Redstart, Blue Rock Thrush, Melodious, Dartford, Subalpine, Orphean and Bonelli's Warblers, Golden Oriole, Great Grey and Woodchat Shrikes, Chough, Raven, Rock Sparrow, Serin, Hawfinch, Rock and Cirl Buntings.

ACCESS Explore along the Douro to north and south on foot and by car along tracks. Drives farther afield should follow roads that lead to the river.

ROUTE Bragança, about 70 km north-west is the nearest airport. Miranda can be reached by road from Lisbon in about eight hours and there is a daily bus service.

SADO ESTUARY AND SETÚBAL PENINSULA

The Sado is quite different from the Tagus, with larger areas of saltings and considerably more exposed mud. It is far less developed and more awkward of access. There are areas of saltpans in the north, to the east of Setúbal, and along the Sado itself as far as Alcácer do Sal. Other parts of the valleys are given over to rice-growing. Waders abound in winter and on passage, with Grey Plover in substantial numbers. Stilt and Kentish Plover breed and most of the villages have White Stork. Large groves of cork oaks hold Azure-winged Magpie, Woodchat, Wryneck and many warblers including Cetti's, Fan-tailed and Great Reed in more marshy areas. Other breeding birds include Red-necked Nightjar, which outnumbers its 'common' relative, Pallid Swift (especially in Setúbal), Hoopoe, Bee-eater and Cirl Bunting, which finds a stronghold here. Waterbirds are not confined to winter or passage periods and, while Little Bittern is scarce there are good numbers of Purple Herons in the reeds and Little Terns among the saltpans.

The Setúbal peninsula is, in contrast, a beautiful rugged landscape, with the Serra da Arrábida falling, in places, almost directly to the sea. Here Peregrine, Bonelli's Eagle, Alpine Swift, Golden Oriole and typical scrub warblers can be found, while in the far west Cabo Espichel is a first-class seawatch spot. Gannet, Cory's and Manx Shearwaters, skuas and terns can all be seen at appropriate seasons, and small migrants should certainly not be ignored. The seasonal listings cover only the Sado Estuary.

SUMMER Little and Cattle Egrets, Little Bittern, Purple Heron, Spoonbill, White Stork, Marsh Harrier, Booted Eagle, Kentish Plover, Black-winged Stilt, Little Tern, Nightjar, Red-necked Nightjar, Pallid Swift, Hoopoe, Bee-eater, Woodlark, Red-rumped Swallow, Cetti's, Fan-tailed, Reed, Great Reed, Melodious and Sardinian Warblers, Great Grey and Woodchat Shrikes, Short-toed Treecreeper, Azure-winged Magpie, Golden Oriole, Spotless Starling, Rock Sparrow, Waxbill, Serin, Hawfinch, Cirl Bunting. **WINTER** Black-necked Grebe, Little and Cattle Egrets, White Stork, Spoonbill, Flamingo, Wigeon, Teal, Gadwall, Pintail, Shoveler, Pochard, Red-breasted Merganser, Hen and Marsh Harriers, Osprey, Avocet, Turnstone, Little Stint, Green Sandpiper, Mediterranean Gull, Hoopoe, Woodlark, Bluethroat, Black Redstart, Cetti's, Fan-tailed, Dartford and Sardinian Warblers, Firecrest, Penduline Tit, Great Grey Shrike, Short-toed Treecreeper, Siskin. **ACCESS** The best area can be reached by leaving Setúbal east on the N10. After about 13 km the railway station of Aguas de Moura can be seen on the right-hand side of the road. A further 200 m after passing some warehouses, there is a large track to the right. Taking this track and passing under the railway line, one enters a splendid area of rice fields, salinas, fish-ponds, salt marsh and reedbeds. This spot is worth a long stop. Southwards, the track crosses the Ribeira da Marateca, a tributary of the Sado which also deserves a look. In winter, the estuary side is good for waders of all sorts. Black-necked Grebe and Red-breasted Merganser. **ROUTE** Leave Lisbon southwards across the Tagus bridge and follow the motorway to Setúbal.

SAGRES AND CAPE ST VINCENT

The south-westernmost point of Portugal sticks out into the Atlantic and has great gathering power. It has a lighthouse and some splendid cliffs, but is devoid of good cover and is too high for effective seawatching. It is also thronged by tourists (just like Lands End), and the best areas lie away from the point of the cape itself. Migrant passerines include Melodious and Bonelli's Warblers, Tawny Pipit, Pied Flycatcher and all the more usual stuff. So far it has had little opportunity to produce the rarities that would undoubtedly appear. Seawatching too has produced no more than Cory's and Mediterranean Shearwaters, Gannet, skuas and terns; yet we know that there are Wilson's Petrel, Sabine's Gull and Great Shearwater offshore. Enthusiasts have joined fishing expeditions or 'hitched' a day out in a local fishing boat to find these species, plus Madeiran Petrel. In fact, all it needs is a good westerly gale to produce these birds off the cape.

Do not ignore local birds. They include Little Bustard, Stone-curlew and quite definite Thekla Lark (there are said to be no Crested), as well as an assortment of typical warblers. Sagres has its own cape, complete with lighthouse, and makes an excellent base. A few seabirds frequent the fishing harbour and there are Chough and Peregrine on the cliffs.

In recent years Portuguese birders have explored the potential of St Vincent, particularly for autumn raptors. With a westerly wind there are virtually none, but with a good easterly or north-easterly blow there are often hundreds of raptors circling, with nowhere to go. Booted Eagle, Black Kite and Sparrowhawk may all be seen in hundreds along with Honey Buzzard, Egyptian Vulture, Short-toed Eagle, Hen Harrier, Buzzard and Black Stork. Other raptors are of more irregular occurrence. Mid-September to mid-October is the best season, with the majority of Black Kites passing earlier. Do not be disappointed by visiting on the wrong wind.

SUMMER Peregrine, Quail, Little Bustard, Stone-curlew, Woodlark, Thekla Lark, Black Redstart, Spectacled, Sardinian, Dartford and Fan-tailed Warblers, Blue Rock Thrush, Woodchat Shrike, Chough.
PASSAGE Mediterranean and Cory's Shearwaters, Wilson's and Storm Petrels, Gannet, Black Stork, Honey Buzzard, Short-toed and Booted Eagles, Hen Harrier, Black Kite, Great and Arctic Skuas, Dotterel, Tawny Pipit, Melodious and Bonelli's Warblers, Pied Flycatcher, Woodchat Shrike.
ACCESS Cape St Vincent and Ponta de Sagres are both easily found. The road between the two has a number of rough tracks leading inland among grassy fields for Stone-curlew and Little Bustard. There are some areas of pines and it is these that hold grounded migrants and raptors.
ROUTE Faro and its international airport are a driveable distance to the east. There are several hotels, including a modern *pousada*.

SANTO ANDRÉ LAGOON

The lagoon at Santo André lies on the west coast of Portugal north of the oil port of Sines. Despite the proximity of such development and the high demand for recreation facilities by the local population, Santo André has managed to survive as a fine bird area. It is essentially brackish in character but has extensive reedbeds. It is surrounded by agriculture with resulting pollutants and disturbance but as a nature reserve has managed to keep both its status and its appeal. Both Santo André and its northerly neighbour, the Lagoon of Melides, are joined to the sea by narrow entrances almost closed by the build-up of dunes along this part of the coast. Though the surrounding land holds a good selection of species, including Black-shouldered Kite, Tawny Pipit, Stone-curlew, Great Spotted Cuckoo and so on, the lagoons themselves are best during passage periods. Seabirds may include Gannet, skuas, terns and oddities such as Scoter. Waders are often interesting on passage and passerines are worthy of attention, though the adjacent woodland does, if anything, offer too much cover.

SUMMER Little Egret, Little Bittern, Purple Heron, Marsh Harrier, Black-shouldered Kite, Black-winged Stilt, Kentish Plover, Stone-curlew, Great Spotted Cuckoo, Great Grey and Woodchat Shrikes, Hoopoe, Bee-eater, Crested and Short-toed Larks, Red-necked Nightjar, Sardinian, Savi's, Cetti's and Fan-tailed Warblers.
PASSAGE Gannet, Spoonbill, Kentish Plover, Little Stint, Sanderling, Sandwich and Gull-billed Terns, Arctic Skua, Bluethroat, Great Reed Warbler.
WINTER Red-crested Pochard.

Great Spotted Cuckoo

ACCESS Leave the N120 near Grândola on the N261–2 to Melides. Both lagoons can be reached by road from this town. The surrounding land and the ground between the two is worth exploring. The smaller Sancha Lagoon to the south is similar in character with breeding Little Bittern, Purple Heron, Marsh Harrier and Black-winged Stilt. It is a noted haunt of wintering Bluethroats.
ROUTE Southwards from Lisbon via Setúbal.

TAGUS ESTUARY

Lisbon, Portugal's capital, lies at the mouth of the most important estuary in the whole of Iberia – the Tagus. Like most such areas, the Tagus estuary is at first sight somewhat daunting but, with the aid of what follows, even the casual visitor should enjoy a really first-rate day of birds.

At low tide the Tagus is a huge maze of mud-banks and shoals surrounded by areas of saltings and, in the north, by stands of reeds. Much of the adjacent land has been reclaimed and is flat and productive. Here and there long-established saltpans have been created and more recently some have been converted to fish farms. These pans and pools are among the richest of bird habitats and many estuarine species resort to them, particularly at high tide. The saltpans at Alcochete and Montijo are easily approached cases in point but their significance has been overshadowed in recent years by the establishment of a nature reserve farther north near the mouth of the Sorraia River. This, together with the Lezirias Land between the Sorraia and the Tagus, forms a quite outstanding birding area.

In summer there are always numbers of egrets together with Purple Heron. There are about ten pairs of Marsh Harriers, plus smaller numbers of Montagu's, Black-winged Stilt, Collared Pratincole and Little Tern all of which breed. Though not part of the estuary proper, the surrounding fields and woodland hold many of the more sought after species including Little Bustard, Short-toed and Booted Eagles together with Black-shouldered Kite, which is quite numerous.

It is during passage periods and in winter that the Tagus comes into its own. Virtually all the regular west European waders turn up, often in staggering numbers. Curlew Sandpiper (1000), Redshank (5000) and

Black-tailed Godwit (12,000) are pretty startling on passage, but in winter Avocet (18,000), Dunlin (30,000), and Grey Plover (9000) are no less impressive. Passage also brings Greater Flamingo, Spoonbill, Kentish Plover, Ruff, Knot, Little Stint, Whimbrel and Spotted Redshank. In winter there are regular ducks and geese, plus Bluethroat and Penduline Tit.

SUMMER Cattle Egret, Purple Heron, White Stork, Black-shouldered and Black Kites, Short-toed and Booted Eagles, Marsh and Montagu's Harriers, Buzzard, Quail, Water Rail, Black-winged Stilt, Stone-curlew, Pratincole, Kentish Plover, Pallid Swift, Bee-eater, Hoopoe, Short-toed and Calandra Larks, Woodlark, Tawny Pipit, Cetti's, Savi's, Great Reed and Melodious Warblers, Short-toed Treecreeper, Great Grey and Woodchat Shrikes, Azure-winged Magpie, Rock Sparrow, Waxbill, Serin, Hawfinch.
PASSAGE Spoonbill, Flamingo, Garganey, Little Ringed and Kentish Plovers, Ruff, Knot, Little Stint, Curlew Sandpiper, Bar-tailed Godwit, Whimbrel, Spotted Redshank, Greenshank, Mediterranean Gull, Black Tern, Alpine Swift, Roller, Bluethroat, Black-eared Wheatear, Subalpine Warbler, Pied Flycatcher.
WINTER Spoonbill, Flamingo, Greylag Goose, Wigeon, Pintail, Hen and Marsh Harriers, Osprey, Merlin, Little Bustard, Avocet, Golden, Grey and Ringed Plovers, Black-tailed Godwit, Spotted Redshank, Greenshank, Green Sandpiper, Short-eared Owl, Water Pipit, Bluethroat, Firecrest, Penduline Tit.
ACCESS There are two distinct areas each worthy of exploration. **Lezirias** is reached by following the autoroute (toll) northwards from Lisbon to Vila Franca de Xira. Cross the Tagus by the bridge on the N10 and watch for a large unsurfaced road on the right to a sailing centre. Drive to the point and walk right along the estuary bank as far as Marinhas da Saragoça with salt-marsh on one side and reeds on the other. The fish-ponds at Saragoça can be excellent. Turn right (inland) and return to the main track and then right again back to Ponta da Erva. Those with less time should attempt to find the track to the fish-ponds direct from the main track – but this is a featureless landscape. The second area is by no means secondary. Follow the N10 eastwards from Vila Franca to Porto Alto and turn right on the N118. Zero the car's trip counter and after exactly 10 km turn right on a small road. Drive about 3 km keeping an oak wood on the left. After a further 1 km a gate bars progress. This is the reserve entrance. Continue on foot for 1.5 km to the superb saltpans for all the Tagus waders. Return and explore the oak wood for both nightjars, Rock Sparrow and Azure-winged Magpie. At the end of the oak wood turn right (south) to Pancas. Beyond here look for Little Bustard as far as another saltpan area.
ROUTE Lisbon Airport.

TAGUS INTERNATIONAL

This stretch of the River Tagus forms the border with Spain, where the frontier runs east to west near Castelo Branco, and is best known for the number of species that are otherwise scarce in Portugal. It is also an area that, combined with adjacent Spain, is highly suited to the know-no-frontiers approach to birding.

The Tagus here has created a steep-sided valley that is lined with scrub and evergreen oaks, though in some parts the cliffs are sheer and vertical. These hold important colonies of both Griffon and Egyptian Vultures, and even Black Vulture is a frequent visitor. It is a stronghold of Black Stork and eagles include Golden, Booted and Bonelli's. There are good colonies of Lesser Kestrel and Montagu's Harrier frequents the surrounding land. There are several pairs of Eagle Owl and Scops Owl is common. Red-necked Nightjar can also be heard, and Thekla Lark and Spanish Sparrow are abundant, the last outnumbering House Sparrow. Other good birds include Black and Black-eared Wheatear, Orphean Warbler and Great Spotted Cuckoo, while both Black and Red Kites are also present along with Black-bellied and the rare Pin-tailed Sandgrouse.

SUMMER Black and White Storks, Black and Red Kites, Egyptian, Griffon and Black Vultures, Montagu's Harrier, Booted, Bonelli's and Golden Eagles, Lesser Kestrel, Little Bustard, Black-bellied Sandgrouse, Great Spotted Cuckoo, Scops and Eagle Owls, Red-necked Nightjar, Thekla Lark, Black-eared and Black Wheatears, Dartford and Orphean Warblers, Golden Oriole, Great Grey Shrike, Spanish and Rock Sparrows, Rock Bunting.
ACCESS Leave Castelo Branco eastwards on the N240. After 28 km pause in Ladoeiro for Spanish Sparrows, which also nest on roadside telegraph poles. After a further 11 km turn right towards Rosmaninhal; a stop at the crossroads might produce Little Bustard, Black-bellied Sandgrouse and Great Spotted Cuckoo. Rosmaninhal, some 15 km farther on holds White Stork. Thereafter continue on motorable tracks toward the confluence of the Rivers Erges and Tagus. This is normally feasible except for the final 2 or 3 km. Open woodland along the way holds Black-eared Wheatear, Azure-winged Magpie, Orphean Warbler and Rock Sparrow. The confluence itself has Black Stork, Black Wheatear, Thekla Lark and, of course, the large raptors. A good map is essential – try the Instituto Geográfico e Cadastral 1:50,000 number 25–C. While in this area an exploration of the pastures around Idanha-a-Nova might produce a few of the small population of Great Bustard, as well as both kites, Calandra Lark and other 'steppe' species. North-east of Rosmaninhal near Segura there is a frontier crossing into Spain (not 24 hours) where the road leads directly to the Embalse de Alcântara on the Tagus. This is the huge dam that extends eastwards to Monfragüe and beyond and there are many areas for Black Stork, Black Vulture and so on. Farther south the area between Brozas and Membrio is a huge grassland, broken here and there by ponds and woods. It forms a major Great Bustard stronghold (800–1000 birds) and also boasts good numbers of both sandgrouse. Even farther south is the Sierra de San Pedro with one of the best populations of birds of prey in Spain. Imperial, Booted and Bonelli's Eagles breed along with a major population of Black Vultures. Largely ignored by birders, this is a sparsely populated area that merits a thorough exploration. At the western end of the Sierra there is another border crossing beyond Valencia de Alcantara that is open 24 hours. Last, but by no means least, the border dam of Embalse de Cedillo has Black Stork, vultures and Eagle Owl.
ROUTE Leave Lisbon northwards and keep on the motorway to Santarém. Continue and exit after 28 km on the new road leading eastwards to Abrantes and Castelo Branco.

ROMANIA

CĂLĂRAŞI-GIURGIU FLOODLANDS

The River Danube floods twice each season, covering a huge area that remains wet and marshy throughout the year. On the Romanian side these floods are particularly extensive and considerable areas of open water remain, forming shallow lakes at almost all times. The area between Călăraşi and Giurgiu is full of such waters, including the large Lake Călăraşi, which is heavily overgrown with reeds and *Salix*, and the similar Lake Greaca above Olteniţa. Just a little way down stream, though on the other bank, is Lake Oltina near Băneasa.

Throughout this huge stretch of countryside the marshes hold the most extraordinary variety of birds, including most of those found in the Danube delta, plus others that are absent from that famous wetland. Though they do not breed here, White Pelicans are regular visitors. Glossy Ibis, most of the herons and egrets, Pygmy Cormorant, Spoonbill, the three marsh terns, and Savi's, Moustached and Great Reed Warblers all breed. Raptors are decidedly more abundant than in the delta, and there is a good chance of Spotted, Lesser Spotted and White-tailed Eagles, Hen and Marsh Harriers, Saker and Red-footed Falcon. Add to this the more widespread smaller birds and the potential for list-building here is outstanding.

Some of the hot spots are the northern end of Lake Oltina, with its Purple and Squacco Herons and Glossy Ibis; the rock outcrops to the east of Băneasa, with Eagle Owl and Pied Wheatear; the southern edges of Lake Călăraşi and its subsidiary lakes Melcu and Rotundu, with Glossy

Ibis, Little Egret and Night and Squacco Herons; nearby Lake Derfu, with a colony of Spoonbills; Lake Greaca, with more heronries; and the adjacent Comana Forest and Lake Mostistea. These wetlands, together with the surrounding forests and agricultural land, are simply outstanding.

SUMMER Black-necked Grebe, Dalmatian and White Pelicans, Bittern, Little Bittern, Purple, Night and Squacco Herons, Glossy Ibis, Spoonbill, Garganey, Corncrake, Spotted and Little Crakes, Honey Buzzard, Lesser Spotted, White-tailed, Short-toed and Booted Eagles, Hen and Marsh Harriers, Saker, Hobby, Goshawk, Black, White-winged Black and Whiskered Terns, Eagle Owl, Alpine Swift, Bee-eater, Roller, Golden Oriole, Hoopoe, Lesser Grey, Great Grey and Red-backed Shrikes, Olivaceous, Icterine, Savi's, Moustached and Great Reed Warblers, Thrush Nightingale, Pied Wheatear, Ortolan Bunting, Spanish Sparrow.
ACCESS Since the first *WWBE* picked out these areas of the Danube as the outstanding bird haunt that they are, comparatively few foreign birders have made the effort to explore them. There are a number of reasons: the difficulties of finding reliable and quick transport, other than a car, in Romania; and more importantly the difficulties of access. One correspondent told me of his three-day wrangle to be allowed to walk through the Băneasa area following a cursory turnback at Călăraşi Perhaps the reduction in east–west tension and the changed regime in Romania will make access easier to what is still a sensitive border area. Nevertheless, old habits die slowly and I still suggest that anyone thinking of working this area should write to the Romanian Embassy asking for a permit to watch birds in the areas concerned. When the letter saying that no permit is required is received, keep it as if it were a permit! If you can get a Romanian translation (try the Tourist Board), so much the better. If this seems too much to go birding, I can only re-quote my correspondent: 'All the hassle', he wrote, 'was completely worthwhile since within one hour I saw Lesser Spotted Eagle, Booted Eagle, Red-footed Falcon and Short-toed Eagle. The woods echoed to the calls of Golden Oriole and Hoopoes, Bee-eaters and Rollers are relatively common.' Access (with the letter!) is along the river banks and minor roads with the aid of the best map you can find.
ROUTE Bucharest is no distance from Oltenita, which is a good starting point. Constant5a, on the Black Sea coast, has charter flights from several parts of Europe serving package holidays at Mamaia, though as I write I can find no UK package holidays offering such arrangements.

DANUBE DELTA

The Danube's is one of the three great European deltas, with the Camargue in France and the Coto Doñana in Spain. While the others have become famous birding resorts, the Danube delta has remained quietly on most people's dream list of places to visit. There are several reasons why this should be, but mostly it is the daunting scale of this great eastern wetland and the lack of any tourist infrastructure to support individual journeys.

The Danube delta is huge. It covers 3000 sq. km of marsh, lake, reed-beds, swamps and forest, all built up by the millions of tons of silt the river dumps at its mouth every year. 100 km from its mouth, the Danube divides into three major channels, the Chilia, Sulina and Sfîntu Gheorghe.

Thereafter there is a maze of waterways known only to local boatmen. Roads and tracks are few or non-existent, and settlements are mostly on islands, and waterborne birding is the norm. This is a leisurely process and a complete contrast to the modern drive-tick-drive school of listing crews. It can, however, provide a unique experience, with great flocks of White Pelicans at close range and Pygmy Cormorant and Glossy Ibis in view at all times. Frankly, I think the Danube to be worth all the effort required.

The other drawback is the general uniformity of the delta. Vast reedbeds broken by open waters and a scattering of willows occupy over 90 per cent of the landscape. To this can be added the riverine forests along the main channels, a little but steadily expanding area of agricultural land, the villages and the shoreline, and that is that. Thus, it is not a huge logistical problem to explore the delta habitats as such.

To the south there are two huge open lakes, Razelm and Sinoie, which are shallow and full of birds. Here Ruddy Shelduck has a European toehold, but there are masses of herons, egrets, waders and duck, substantial breeding colonies of Collared Pratincole, Gull-billed Tern and many small birds in the surrounding dry countryside. A visit to the southern point of Sinoie produced a huge range of species in vast numbers. Migrant waders are often abundant here, and the area is worth more than a single stop.

The delta proper can be explored from Tulcea, from where a system of regular ferry services operates downstream. These slow-moving boats stop frequently to take on and put down passengers, and offer excellent birding opportunities. Birds likely to be seen include White and Dalmatian Pelicans, Glossy Ibis, Pygmy Cormorant, Little and Great White Egrets and Spoonbill. The first recommended stop is Maliuc, where there is a hotel catering for tourists. Try to get a front-facing room to avoid the noisy generator at the rear. From Maliuc, it is possible to hire a boatman for a day's outing to Lake Fortuna and thereabouts, but start before dawn for the best results. Here there are Ferruginous Duck, Whiskered Tern, Roller, Penduline Tit, Thrush Nightingale, Moustached Warbler and Bluethroat.

Farther downstream, Crisan is worth a stop to explore along the embankment that runs to the south. This, at least, is terra firma and using a telescope is a possibility. There are several reserves around here, but permits seem almost impossible to obtain and are not necessary.

Near the mouth lies the port of Sulina and here there is more chance of accommodation and of exploring on dry land. It is not geared up to birders.

The outstanding birds include 2500 pairs of Pygmy Cormorant; 2500 pairs of White Pelican; about 50 pairs of Dalmatian Pelican; 2000 pairs each of Night and Squacco Herons; 700 pairs of Great White Egret; 1250 pairs of Purple Heron; 1500 pairs of Glossy Ibis; 5 pairs of White-tailed Eagle; 300 pairs of Marsh Harrier; 3 pairs of Osprey and a similar number of Saker; 150 pairs of Red-footed Falcon; no fewer than 20,000 pairs of Whiskered Tern and perhaps similar numbers of Black Tern. In winter the delta holds upwards of half a million Whitefronts, though recent counts have produced fewer than 100,000, plus up to 12,000 Red-breasted Goose.

SUMMER Red-necked and Black-necked Grebes, White and Dalmatian Pelicans, Pygmy Cormorant, Purple, Squacco and Night Herons, Great White and Little Egrets, Little Bittern, Bittern, Spoonbill, Glossy Ibis, White Stork, Greylag Goose, Ruddy Shelduck, Garganey, Red-crested Pochard,

Ferruginous Duck, Honey Buzzard, Black Kite, Marsh and Montagu's Harriers, Lesser Spotted, Booted, White-tailed and Short-toed Eagles, Saker, Red-footed Falcon, Hobby, Collared Pratincole, Little and Mediterranean Gulls, Gull-billed, Caspian, White-winged Black, Black and Whiskered Terns, Roller, Bee-eater, Syrian Woodpecker, Calandra Lark, Tawny Pipit, River, Moustached, Great Reed, Icterine and Olivaceous Warblers, Collared and Red-breasted Flycatchers, Bearded and Penduline Tits, Golden Oriole, Rose-coloured Starling.

ACCESS There is a network of reasonable roads around and among Lakes Razelm and Sinoie, both of which are easily reached from Mamaia, the package-holiday resort. In the south of the delta proper the village of Murighiol is welcoming, offering meals and rowboat excursions into the marshes. The starting point for the delta ferry boats is Tulcea, which has a hotel. Maliuc, in the delta, has a hotel which should be booked in advance. Elsewhere, see where the ferries lead and explore on foot or with a local boatman. This is no place for those on tight schedules.

ROUTE Constanţa has an international airport, and Mamaia offers package holidays, though not from the UK. There is even a lagoon here with terns, gulls and waders from rear-facing hotel rooms.

DITRĂU

This is a small village in the central Carpathians that makes a suitable base for those wishing to explore farther than the delta and marshes of the Danube. Here the hills rise to nearly 2000 m, with deep valleys and extensive conifer forests creating an almost 'alpine' landscape. The birds are also typically alpine, with Nutcracker, Black Redstart, Sombre Tit and raptors that may include Golden Eagle. This area is not well explored, but it does have potential and full reports would be welcomed.

Pygmy Cormorant

SUMMER Golden Eagle, Honey Buzzard, Capercaillie, Black Grouse, Hoopoe, Nutcracker, Grey Wagtail, Ring Ouzel, Sombre and Crested Tits, Black Redstart, Firecrest, Crossbill, Raven.
ACCESS The mountains and forests to the north of Ditrău, the Călimani and Rodna, are among the best for a variety of species. They are the only places for Black Grouse in Romania. Even Dotterel may breed in Rodna.
ROUTE Via Bacău, then north-west on Route 15 to Bicaz, thence south-west to Gheorgheni on Route 12C to join Route 12 north to Ditrău.

SATCHINEZ AND THE MUREŞ MARSHES

In the extreme west of Romania, the land drops from the heights of the Carpathians to the steppes of the Hungarian plain. Here the tributaries of the River Tisza meander over the level ground, slowly finding their way to the main river and ultimately to the Danube. Seasonal floods, oxbow lakes, pools and backwaters all created a marsh landscape that was systematically drained during the eighteenth century. Reedbeds which contained Glossy Ibis and Spoonbill until 1914 have given way to vast fields of cereals, and the sedge thickets and primeval oak forests have disappeared. Only in the area around Satchinez, 25 km north-west of Timişoara, has any area of marsh remained. The pools and marshes here were declared a Monument of Nature in 1942, and 101 ha now form the Satchinez Reserve. The area is noted mainly as a breeding haunt of herons – Purple Heron, Night Heron, Little Egret, Squacco Heron and Little Bittern – and these are found principally at Ritul Dutin and Ritul Mărăşeşti though numbers are declining apparently as a result of to the establishment of a colony of Jackdaws in recent years. The reserve also harbours a range of other species that are rare in this part of the country, including Greylag Goose, Ferruginous Duck, Marsh Harrier and White-winged Black Tern. The pond surrounds are the haunt of Penduline Tit, Bluethroat and an interesting collection of warblers, including Reed, Marsh and Savi's. The surrounding drained area is one of the best in Romania for Great Bustard. The marshes are wet meadows and old riparian woodlands that are seasonally flooded along the river near Ceala, Pecica and Bezdin to the west of Arad. There are also extensive modern plantations as well as grasslands and backwaters. Lesser Spotted Eagle is the commonest raptor, but there are also Honey Buzzard, Black Kite and Marsh Harrier. Good numbers of herons and egrets breed and the woods hold Black Woodpecker.

SUMMER Purple, Squacco and Night Herons, Little Egret, Bittern, Little Bittern, White Stork, Greylag Goose, Ferruginous Duck, Spotted and Little Crakes, Marsh Harrier, Black Tern, Great Bustard, Penduline Tit, Bluethroat, Savi's, Reed and Marsh Warblers.
ACCESS Leave Timişoara northwards on Route 69 and fork left to Sinandrei and Satchinez just outside the town. The main marsh and pools lie south of the village and are a reserve, though in fact the reserve covers a very small part of the area and most of the birds can also be seen outside it. The Mureş marshes lie downstream from Arad and can be explored from Pecica.
ROUTE Timişoara and Arad are connected by air and train to other major Romanian cities.

SLOVAKIA

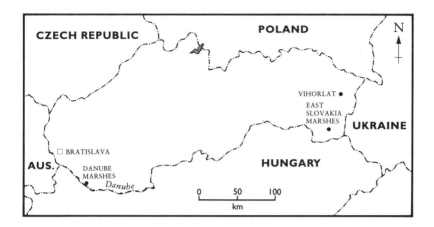

DANUBE MARSHES

The Danube forms Slovakia's common border with Hungary below Bratislava, in the western part of the country. As elsewhere in central Europe, it is prone to seasonal flooding and its banks are lined by marshes and flooded woodland. Many of these areas are quite excellent and have, over the years, been declared reserves. Between Bratislava and Komárno the Danube splits into two major channels, the Danube (Dunaj) proper and the Maly Dunaj, and the area is actually a huge island. This low-lying plain is also the major stronghold of the Great Bustard and there is a special reserve west of Komárno at Zlatná na Ostrove. Between Bratislava and Čičov particularly, the Danube has many islands which offer breeding sites for Night Heron and Cormorant. The marshes of the floodplain have River Warbler, Penduline Tit, Golden Oriole among the many poplar plantations, and more recently Black Woodpecker. The Čičovské Mrtvé rameno is an oxbow in the floodplain with Bittern, Purple Heron, Ferruginous Duck, River and Savi's Warblers, and Penduline Tit. The Istragov Marsh is a regular feeding haunt of Great White Egret. All in all this is a fabulous area in summer and hardly less so in winter and on passage when Bean and White-fronted Geese are present in huge numbers. At this time White-tailed Eagle is also present.

SUMMER Cormorant, Bittern, Little Bittern, Night and Purple Herons, Black and White Storks, Ferruginous Duck, Marsh Harrier, Red and Black Kites, Great Bustard, Corncrake, Black Woodpecker, Icterine, River and Savi's Warblers, Golden Oriole, Penduline Tit.
WINTER AND PASSAGE White-tailed Eagle, Bean and White-fronted Geese.
ACCESS Though the whole of this region is worth exploring, there are several major areas to visit. In the west the Dedinský ostrov, near

Gabčíkovo, is a fine reedbed area, while just to the east is Istragov. Zilizský močiar is near Čilizská Radvaň, the Great Bustard reserve is Zlatná na Ostrove, 13 km west of Komárno, while to the north-east of that town is Parížské močiare near Gbelce. Though technically outside the Danube marshes as such, this small and manageable marsh is a State Nature Reserve with extensive areas of reeds and peat bog. Breeding birds include good numbers of Bittern, Little Bittern, Purple Heron, Ferruginous Duck, Marsh Harrier, Spotted and Little Crakes, Black-tailed Godwit, Whiskered and Black Terns, Bluethroat, Barred Warbler and occasionally 1–3 pairs of Moustached Warbler.
ROUTE Route 63 from Bratislava.

EAST SLOVAKIA MARSHES

Against the Ukraine and Hungarian borders the Rivers Latorica and Bodrog have created a maze of channels, backwaters, oxbows and marshes, with riverine forest and scrub, that is typical of much Central European lowland. Although much of the area has been reclaimed for agriculture, there are several outstanding sites many of which are State Nature Reserves. Breeding birds include most of the wetland species one would expect in this part of Europe, though Black Stork, Spoonbill, Ferruginous Duck, Little Crake and Whiskered and White-winged Black Terns are not found everywhere by any means. Add raptors such as Lesser Spotted Eagle and Red-footed Falcon and one begins to get the impression of a really good spot.

Within the marshes proper the reserves of Zatínske močiare marshes and the Tabja marshes hold most of the best species and there are White Stork, Syrian Woodpecker and Lesser Grey Shrike among the surrounding fields and villages. At no great distance and certainly to be included (along with Vihorlát *q.v.*) in any exploration of this area are the ponds at Senné-rybníky and the eastern end of Zemplínska Šírava Reservoir. Both of the ponds are oxbows of the major rivers and are now State Nature Reserves. Both have good populations of breeding waterbirds including Purple Heron, Little Bittern, Marsh Harrier, Hen Harrier at Zatínske, Spotted and Little Crakes, Black Tern and Roller. Additionally the ponds at Senné-rybníky have Bittern, Spoonbill and Aquatic Warbler, though the last is a somewhat erratic breeder here. The reservoir is best known as a migration stop-over where species include divers, grebes, herons and egrets, Black Stork, Lesser Whitefront, Crane and Great Snipe.

SUMMER Black and White Storks, Bittern, Little Bittern, Night, Squacco and Purple Herons Little Egret, Spoonbill, Ferruginous Duck, Black Kite, Marsh Harrier, Lesser Spotted Eagle, Spotted and Little Crakes, Black-winged Stilt, Black-tailed Godwit, Whiskered, Black and White-winged Black Tern, Short-eared Owl, Roller, Syrian Woodpecker, Bluethroat, Nightingale, Thrush Nightingale, Red-backed and Lesser Grey Shrikes, Aquatic Warbler.
ACCESS Explore via Vel Kapušany and Kral Chlmee and a good map. The marshes proper and the ponds at Senné-rybníky are the best starting points.
ROUTE Bratislava eastwards on the N51 to Zvolen, then eastwards on the N50 to Košice and Michalovce. Turn right (south) along the river to

Ural Owl

Vel. Kapušany. Alternatively enter by crossing from Hungary at Sátoreljaujhely after doing the Hortobágy.

VIHORLAT

This range of hills in the easternmost part of the country is seldom visited by outsiders, despite its obvious attractions. Rising only to 1000 m, the hills are covered with mainly deciduous woods offering a home to a fine range of species, several of which are otherwise undoubtedly scarce in Slovakia. Raptors are particularly important, and species include Lesser Spotted, Short-toed, Booted and probably even Imperial Eagles. Saker and Peregrine both breed, along with both kites. The woods also hold a good range of woodpeckers and even the decidedly difficult Ural Owl.

Though this area is almost the full length of the country away from Bratislava, it would seem well worth the efforts involved in making the journey and certainly worthwhile for anyone visiting the Tatras. The marshes to the south make this an extremely attractive and worthwhile area of Slovakia.

SUMMER Honey Buzzard, Lesser Spotted, Short-toed, Imperial and Booted Eagles, Black and Red Kites, Saker, Peregrine, Goshawk, Hazelhen, Eagle, Pygmy and Ural Owls, Nightjar, Grey-headed, Black, Middle Spotted, White-backed and Syrian Woodpeckers, Wryneck, Roller, Hoopoe, Dipper, Crested Tit, Rock Thrush, Barred Warbler, Collared and Red-breasted Flycatchers, Red-backed Shrike, Rock Bunting.
ACCESS Base at Humenné or Michalovce and explore on minor roads and tracks.
ROUTE Košice is the nearest large town.

SPAIN

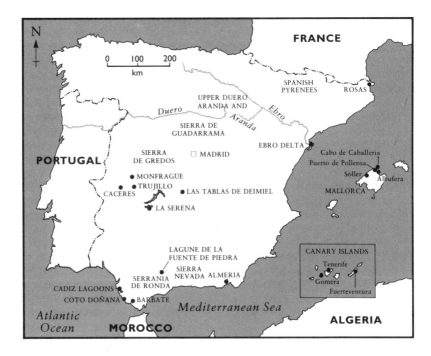

ALMERIA

Sandwiched between the Costa del Sol and the Costa Blanco at the south-eastern corner of the Iberian Peninsula, Almeria has, so far, managed to avoid mass coastal tourism. There are areas of rugged, cliff-girt coastline, as well as sandy shores backed by lagoons and saltpans, where birds still remain relatively undisturbed – unusual for Mediterranean Spain. The saltpans at Cabo de Gata are a regular haunt of up to 2000 Flamingoes and nesting has from time to time been attempted. The same area has good wintering and passage populations of Black-winged Stilt and Avocet, other waders and Audouin's Gull. Across the Gulf of Almeria, a similar area at the Punta del Sabinal includes the saltpans of Cerrillos and San Rafael and several extensive lagoons. Here too Flamingoes are regular and there are good passage waders. Stone-curlew is a relatively common breeder.

It is, however, the semi-desert hinterland that has brought Almeria to ornitho-prominence. To the north of the town lie the rugged slopes of the Sierra Alhamilla with, to the south, the arid wastes of the Campo de Nijar and, to the north, the equally dry slopes of the Sierra de Filabres. The whole area is home to Stone-curlew, Black-bellied Sandgrouse, Thekla Lark, Blue Rock Thrush, Black Wheatear, Spectacled Warbler and, outstandingly, good populations of Dupont's Lark and Trumpeter Finch. The higher areas boast Bonelli's Eagle and Eagle Owl and the area is noted as a major zone for Lesser Short-toed Lark.

SUMMER Flamingo, Bonelli's Eagle, Black-winged Stilt, Kentish Plover, Stone-curlew, Little Bustard, Black-bellied Sandgrouse, Audouin's Gull, Eagle Owl, Alpine Swift, Thekla, Lesser Short-toed and Dupont's Larks, Roller, Blue Rock Thrush, Black Wheatear, Spectacled Warbler, Trumpeter Finch.

PASSAGE/WINTER Black-winged Stilt, Avocet, Kentish Plover.

ACCESS Cabo de Gata is reached by taking a right turning several kilometres beyond the airport. After some 8 km another right turn leads to the village of the same name and then towards the Cape and the lighthouse of Vela Blanca. The saltpans can be explored from this road. For the Punta del Sabinal complex leave Almeria westwards turning left in El Parador to Roquetas de Mar. This road passes the Salinas de San Rafael. Continue to the generally better area of the Salinas de Cerrillos. The 'desert' of Almeria is vast and almost any road around the **Sierra Alhamilla** may produce the 'star' species. However, most crews try first in the **Tabernas** area where a steep-sided canyon has Trumpeter Finch.

ROUTE Airports at Malaga and Valencia are well served by scheduled and charter international flights, but both are long drives.

ARANDA AND UPPER DUERO

The landscape around Aranda, which is traversed virtually non-stop by hordes of birders between Burgos and Madrid, is singularly uninviting. Yet this somewhat barren part of the Meseta holds some excellent birds including really good numbers of birds of prey. There are deep canyons full of Griffon and Egyptian Vultures, with Golden Eagle and Eagle Owl for good measure, as well as fine populations of Chough and Peregrine. Surrounding scrub and wasteland holds Black-bellied Sandgrouse and Little Bustard and the most significant population of Dupont's Lark in Europe. Of course, this species is as elusive as ever, but to be in an area where there are 2000–3000 pairs must improve the chances of contact. The secret is to sit patiently and wait for the birds to appear – desperation has prompted some birders to walk or even run through suitable habitat.

SUMMER Griffon and Egyptian Vultures, Golden Eagle, Peregrine, Little Bustard, Black-bellied Sandgrouse, Chough, Dupont's Lark.

ACCESS There are several widespread areas of interest worth exploring, all of which have raptors and the Lark. Downstream from Sepulveda the gorge of the Duraton has vultures, Peregrine, with Dupont's on the surrounding wasteland. It is signposted west 11 km from the N1 south of Aranda. The Riaza Gorge is reached by taking the minor road east from Fuente Espina a few kilometres south of Aranda. Continue to Maderuelo, exploring *en route*. The Caracena area can be explored by following the N122 from Aranda east as far as San Esteban and turning right (south) to Morcuera. After a few kilometres fork left and later take a left to Hoz de Arriba and Hoz de Abaio and the gorge for raptors. The best place for Dupont's Lark is among the limestone wastes around Barrahona. Take the N122 eastwards from Aranda to El Birgo. About 1 km beyond the town turn right on the C116 and, near Almazan, take the C101 to that town.

ROUTE Madrid Airport is adjacent to the N11 leading north-east to the Barrahona area. Main directions above assume a Madrid–Burgos journey.

BARBATE

Barbate is the centre of the Spanish tuna-fish industry and is an excellent base for exploring a variety of splendid areas along the Atlantic coast of Andalucia. To the west lies Cape Trafalgar, with its old lighthouse, beaches, spring lagoons and enough bushy cover to shelter migrants. Seabird passage may be exciting, with Gannet, shearwaters, skuas and terns all passing in numbers in suitable conditions. This is an excellent area for Audouin's Gull, often seen loafing on the beach, Kentish Plover and Black-winged Stilt. Tawny Pipit is regular. Between Barbate and Trafalgar there is an excellent road through a fine forest of pines, with Woodlark, Dartford, Sardinian and Orphean Warblers, Hoopoe and migrants in season.

To the north is the hilltop town of Vejer de la Frontera, with Jackdaw and Lesser Kestrel. To the south, through a military zone (no binoculars or 'scopes), lies Zahara de los Atunes. Continue south along the coast beyond Zahara to a rocky peninsula, the Sierra de la Plata, the home of Europe's first colony of White-rumped Swifts. These birds breed in disused Red-rumped Swallow's nests in caves alongside the road that zigzags up the headland through a modern villa development. They arrive and breed late – June is probably the best month. The Sierra is important for Griffon Vultures.

Inland, the flat arable and grazing land east of the main N340 south of Tahivilla is home to twelve Great Bustards (very elusive: you may take days to find them) and the more numerous Little Bustard. This area can be explored by taking a small road east off the N340, almost opposite the turning west to Zahara. At first this runs alongside a canal, which is the main drainage channel for what, until the 1950s, was the splendid Laguna de la Janda. It is worth exploring, particularly in winter, when there are extensive floods and it is home to a flock of several hundred Cranes. Farther south lies the Ojen valley, with lush groves, acres of scrub, high ridges and a dam combining to produce one of those special places. A wide variety of birds includes Griffon and Egyptian Vultures, Short-toed, Booted and (with luck) Bonelli's Eagles, Montagu's Harrier, Buzzard, Red Kite and a wealth of small birds including Great Spotted Woodpecker.

Just south of Barbate, along the road to Zahara, is the tiny Barbate estuary, with a modern bridge offering vantage points over the mud-banks and adjacent saltpans. Birds here often include Caspian Tern and Audouin's Gull, as well as several passage waders plus the occasional Spoonbill.

SUMMER Cory's and Manx Shearwaters, Gannet, Cattle and Little Egrets, White Stork, Griffon and Egyptian Vultures, Booted, Bonelli's and Short-toed Eagles, Marsh and Montagu's Harriers, Sparrowhawk, Goshawk, Lesser Kestrel, Peregrine, Black-winged Stilt, Kentish Plover, Sandwich and Caspian Terns, Audouin's Gull, Collared Pratincole, Bee-eater, Roller, Golden Oriole, Red-necked Nightjar, Calandra, Short-toed, Crested and Thekla Larks, Woodlark, Tawny Pipit, Cetti's Warbler, Woodchat Shrike, Stonechat, Corn Bunting, Spotless Starling.

ACCESS The whole area can be explored by road, with walking confined to the bushy area at Cape Trafalgar and the pine woods above Barbate. Drive through the Ojen valley to emerge above Los Barrios near Algeciras, though one of the best areas is by the dam near its western end.

ROUTE Airports at Sevilla, Gibraltar and Malaga.

CACERES AND TRUJILLO

These towns are surrounded by wonderful open grasslands and are themselves important for birds. Both have important colonies of Lesser Kestrel but there the similarity ends – Trujillo is a small and charming historical gem, Caceres a developing urban sprawl. Nonetheless, the grasslands around the larger city are probably more productive of birds than those around Trujillo and both are equidistant from Monfragüe (*see* below).

To my mind the open grasslands around Caceres are the very epitome of the Spanish Steppes. They extend for miles in every direction and, though many areas are now ploughed and irrigated, huge areas of open grassland remain. Here, naturally enough, is one of the strongholds of Great and Little Bustards and with about 12–13 per cent of the total Spanish population of the former, this is clearly the place to see these great birds. There are, however, other steppe birds including sandgrouse, Stone-curlew, Calandra Lark, Montagu's Harrier as well as Lesser Kestrel and Roller, both of which have been persuaded to breed in nest boxes.

Both towns are built on rocky mounds and are surrounded by a peculiar landscape of huge boulder-strewn slopes. Beyond, the grasslands are cut through by steeply banked streams lined by areas of scrub and open woodland. Here Bee-eaters and Rollers are often very common and a wide variety of smaller birds finds a suitable niche. At Caceres the low, but significant, Sierra de Fuentes, extends south-eastwards offering breeding opportunities to raptors and Black Storks.

SUMMER White and Black Storks, Cattle and Little Egrets, Grey Heron, Booted and Short-toed Eagles, Black-shouldered and Black Kites, Montagu's Harrier, Lesser Kestrel, Great and Little Bustards, Stone-curlew, Pin-tailed and Black-bellied Sandgrouse, Hoopoe, Bee-eater, Roller, Calandra Lark, Azure-winged Magpie, Great Spotted Cuckoo, Great Grey Shrike, Hawfinch.
ACCESS The plains are criss-crossed by roads leading from both Caceres and Trujillo. It is possible, however, to drive round all day without seeing a Great Bustard. Improve your chances by concentrating on the smaller roads and, even better, by exploring the roads and (mainly) tracks that connect the outgoing town roads to each other. Sadly, many tracks are suitable only for those with a total disregard for their suspension. If that is you, the tracks that join the C520 and the N630 north of the Embalsa del Salor are highly productive as are tracks joining the N630 to the N523. For the more cautious the road from Valdesalor on the N630 west to Velduernas Station is a good bet, particularly looking west over the railway line at the end. A little farther south on the N630, a track westwards starts just north of the Arroyo de Salor, crosses an appalling old bridge, but is then driveable deep into bustard country. Similarly the road just east of Caceres to Sierra de Fuentes has always been a favoured bustard route. Around **Trujillo** take the old main road to Madrid and after 3 km turn right to Belén. Pass through the village and scan for bustards. A further 11 km towards Madrid the road on the right to Torrecillas de la Tiesa gives access to plains and a broken landscape for bustards as well as raptors, sandgrouse and important colonies of storks and egrets. Here again resorting to tracks southward is required to get the best from the area. Although these details are biased toward the bustards, most of the other

birds of this superb area will be seen by exploring the areas recommended. I do, however, take no responsibility for damage to cars caused in pursuit of bustards, or any other birds come to that.
ROUTE The area is reached on the NV southwards from Madrid.

CADIZ LAGOONS

This is the name for several groups of small, low-lying lagoons in western Andalucia, the most famous of which is Laguna Medina. In fact these waters are all very similar with emergent vegetation that may be confined to the margins, or may cover virtually the entire lagoon. Such vegetation varies not only on a seasonal basis, but also according to rainfall and the depth of water. The variability of these factors can drastically affect both number and species present at any particular time and virtually all birds move between lagoons in search of better feeding and nesting opportunities.

The lagoons are generally divided into five main groupings. Though a search of the literature may produce more than five groups, this is largely a result of using different names: the Lagunas de Espera are also referred to as the Lagunas de la Zorilla. The Lagunas de Santa Maria are similarly called the Lagunas de Terry and include a Laguna Salada as does the Espera group! Laguna Medina is always Laguna Medina but there is a tiny lagoon nearby called the Laguna Istata that should not be ignored. The Lagunas of Punto Real and Lagunas de Chiclana are fortunately not confused in this way, though each lagoon has its own individual name.

Though the Cadiz Lagoons are important all year it, is their breeding populations that most attract birders. Here is one of the strongholds of the rare White-headed Duck, virtually the only Crested Coots in Europe and, somewhat erratically, one of the few places for Marbled Duck. Purple Gallinule is actually quite common as is Red-crested Pochard and Little Bittern. The elusive Baillon's Crake breeds but is seldom seen.

Passage, particularly in spring when water levels are high, produces a variety of terns and waders. Some, like Black-winged Stilt, Kentish Plover and Collared Pratincole, stay to breed. In winter duck are often numerous. Though Marsh Harrier is the only breeding raptor, several other species use the lagoons as hunting grounds: Black Kite, Egyptian Vulture, Short-toed and Booted Eagles and Montagu's Harrier are regularly present.

SUMMER Great Crested and Black-necked Grebes, Little and Cattle Egrets, Shoveler, Gadwall, Garganey, Teal, Marbled and White-headed Duck, Pochard, Red-crested Pochard, Marsh and, Montagu's Harriers, Black Kite, Short-toed and Booted Eagles, Egyptian Vulture, Purple Gallinule, Coot, Crested Coot, Baillon's Crake, Black-winged Stilt, Kentish Plover, Collared Pratincole, Sardinian, Melodious, Cetti's, Fan-tailed and Great Reed Warblers, Woodchat Shrike.
PASSAGE Ruff, Greenshank, Wood Sandpiper, Little Stint, Whiskered, Gull-billed and Black Terns, Mediterranean Gull.
ACCESS Permits to visit all of the lagoons must be obtained in advance and written applications should show evidence of serious ornithological interest and some qualifications. Address applications to: Agencia de Medio Ambiente, Junta de Andalucia, Ana de Viya 3–3, 11004 Cadiz, Andalucia, Spain. An International Reply Coupon to cover return postage

could do no harm. **Laguna Medina** Lies alongside the C440 east of its junction with the A4 toward Medina Sidenia near Jerez. Its small neighbour Laguna Isteta lies on the western side of the same road about 1 km farther north beyond a cement factory – excellent for Purple Gallinule. The **Lagunas de Espera (Zorilla)** are reached by taking the Arcos turning from the NIV. There is a large and quite excellent roadside cafe here that has all the characteristics of what we used to call 'Transport Caffs'. After 10 km the lagoons lie to the left. Walking is required. The **Lagunas de El Puerto de Santa Maria** lie some 6 km north of that town and are reached via the minor road towards Sanlucar or the intersection with the Jerez road. Walking is required. The **Lagunas de Puerto Real** are marked on maps as Laguna de Tarage, east of Puerto Real on minor roads toward the C440. Walking is required. The **Lagunas de Chiclana** lie east of that town off the C346 road to Medina Sidonia. Walking is required. *Please* do not visit or attempt to visit any of these lagoons without prior permission. Uncontrolled visits are having a detrimental effect on the bird populations of what are an internationally important group of wetlands. ROUTE Jerez de la Frontera has an airport with international and domestic flights and unlimited quantities of Sherry.

CANARY ISLANDS

These volcanic Atlantic islands have over the past twenty years developed into a favourite winter-sun haunt of north Europeans and have all the tourist infrastructure necessary for birders. In winter, when they bask in the sun that one expects just outside the tropics, there are six (previously seven) endemic species, and a few other high-value residents to find. The winter sun is also a bonus in December or January. However, package holidays are generally more expensive in winter, especially at Christmas, than the rest of the year so a summer break that produces the same birds is more cost-effective on a price per tick basis. Summer also has the seabirds. Little and Cory's Shearwaters breed as does Madeiran Petrel, which otherwise only breeds in Europe on the Berlengas Islands of Portugal, and Bulwer's Petrel. Cory's apart, these are three much sought after species that almost all determined visitors to the Canaries should get from May to July.

So the choice lies between winter sun and the seabirds: if you want all the birds May or June would be best, but avoid Whitsun which is expensive.

Of the seven major islands in the Canaries, the birder need visit only three, or get away with only two if pressed for time or money. Tenerife is the largest, 80 km across at its widest. It has an international airport, lots of package hotels and apartments, and regular ferry services to the two other islands of interest. It rises to 3718 m at the active volcano of Teide. The best birds are found along the upland ridge and in the drier southern half of the island. On Tenerife there are the endemic Canary, Berthelot's Pipit, Plain Swift (no longer an endemic with its discovery along the coast of Morocco), Boll's and White-tailed Pigeons and, of course, the Blue Chaffinch.

Gomera is nearest to Tenerife and a smaller version of it. It has the best laurel forest remaining in the Canaries and the ferry from Tenerife provides the best seawatching in the islands. It is not strictly necessary to visit as all the endemics can be found by visiting only Tenerife and Fuerteventura. The latter is different in character, being both low-lying and arid, with rolling dunes and lava fields. This is the only island with Canary Islands Chat and also has Houbara Bustard and Cream-coloured Courser. The Canary is widespread in northern Tenerife. Try La Esperanza near km stone 9 and in the Botanic Gardens at Puerto de la Cruz. Plain Swift is often seen from hotels in the evening and is common at Santa Cruz and at the bridge on Calle Galceran. The laurel pigeons are at Ergos south-west of Icod in the western part of the island. For Blue Chaffinch try either La Esperanza up to the Mirador Pico de los Flores and to beyond the 15 km stone, or Las Lajas picnic area 9 km north of Vilaflors on the Teide road. Fill a basin of one of the drinking fountains and wait for it to come to drink. Berthelot's Pipit can be found at many sites, particularly in the south. Try the Punta de la Rasca, or La Esperanza and Los Rodeos Airport.

On Fuerteventura the main species is the Canary Islands Chat and the hot spot is Willis' Baranco near the Airport (named for the birder who discovered the site). The birds can be found among vegetation on the dam, but not at weekends when the local shooters are out in force. Berthelot's Pipit is also common here and in other drier parts of the island. Houbara is in the Correlajo–La Oliva area and the Cotillo–Taca area, both in the north of the island. There are also Courser, Black-bellied Sandgrouse, Lesser Short-toed Lark, Trumpeter Finch and Berthelot's Pipit.

Waders have a hard time in the Canaries and virtually any area of fresh water is worth a look. Near Tenerife airport the El Medano pool has turned up American waders and should be checked. It is not far from Santa Cruz.

The ideal way to work the Canaries is to fly to one of the two necessary islands – Tenerife or Fuerteventura – and fly back from the other with a few days on each between. Sadly, holiday operators do not offer such arrangements. So, second best would be to fly to Tenerife on a B and B package, explore for the endemics, take an internal flight to Fuerteventura (booked with Iberian Airlines in advance) stay a couple of days and return to Tenerife (also pre-booked). Additionally, take the Tenerife–Gomera ferry, from Christianos to San Sebastian, and back for a full day seabird trip.

SUMMER Cory's and Little Shearwaters, Madeiran and Bulwer's Petrels, Little Egret, Egyptian Vulture, Sparrowhawk, Buzzard, Eleonora's and Barbary Falcons, Barbary Partridge, Quail, Houbara Bustard, Stone-curlew, Kentish Plover, Woodcock, Cream-coloured Courser, Turtle Dove, Boll's and White-tailed Pigeons, Plain Swift, Hoopoe, Great Spotted Woodpecker, Lesser Short-toed Lark, Berthelot's Pipit, Great Grey Shrike, Sardinian Warbler, Canary Islands Chat, Trumpeter Finch, Canary, Blue Chaffinch. ACCESS 'Pigeon Point' is reached from Icod on the north coast by taking the C820 to Ergos. On leaving Ergos watch for a track on the right opposite the Casa Forestal. Follow this to the laurel forest and, at the end of the descent zero the kilometre counter and climb for 5.6 km. There, on a left-hand bend, is a rocky outcrop on the left marked by a weathervane-type structure that few have failed to find. A pinnacle to the left confirms the spot. Climb the roadside rocks, walk farther up the road, or stand to the right of the rock base and keep eyes peeled for pigeons. Mid-morning and late afternoon are recommended, though this may be due to the timing of previous visits. La Esperanza is reached from La Laguna 9 km stone for Canary. From there follow the main ridge road towards El Portillo and past the Mirador Pico de los Flores to the 15 km stone. Continue upwards on foot for Blue Chaffinch. Alternatively take the Tiede road from near Granadilla de Abona in the south to Vilaflor. After a further 9 km stop at the Lajas picnic site. The **El Medano pool** lies east of the motorway and the international airport Reina Sofia. The road to the town lies north of the airport. Just outside the town turn right behind the beach. After a short distance the pool lies behind the beach before an obvious rocky area. **Punta de la Rasca** is a good seawatch site at the extreme south-west of Tenerife, though good and more comfortable seawatching can be enjoyed from hotel balconies at Playa American, for example. Rasca is difficult to access, but is reached from the motorway via an equally difficult to find track next to a prominently walled field. The rough fields behind the Punta have Lesser Short-toed, Trumpeter, Barbary Partridge and Berthelot's. On Fuerteventura **Willis' Baranco** is reached by leaving Puerto del Rosario south on the coast road towards the airport. After 3 km and just before a small cutting, the road crosses a gully. Walk 2 km to the dam. The Chat is either before the dam or either side of it. Also here are Trumpeter Finch and Barbary Partridge. For Houbara head inland from Puerto del Rosario to La Matilla, La Oliva, Lajares and Cotillo. Take the road south towards Taca through semi-desert and back to La Oliva. Either side of Taca is Houbara country. North, the La Oliva–Correlajo road has lava plains on the right for Houbara, Berthelot's, the Partridge and Lesser Short-toed. ROUTE Package holidays to Tenerife, with internal flights to and from Fuerteventura (pre-booked) and ferry crossings to and from Gomera.

Coto Doñana

The Doñana area of south-western Spain is a place of pilgrimage for thousands of birders each year and is an outstanding bird haunt at all seasons. Along this coast, the Atlantic has built up a huge dune beach that has diverted and restricted the outlet of the Guadalquivir, creating behind it a vast area of seasonal floods known as *marismas*. From late autumn until the following summer, this area is covered by water which gradually dries out to leave islands (*vetas*) and later huge expanses of mud.

Taking a cross-section from west to east across the Coto, the sea attracts a variety of seabirds including terns, skuas, Gannet and large flocks of Scoter. The beach may be full of Sanderling and Oystercatcher, with seasonal influxes of Whimbrel and other waders and a variable population of gulls that often includes Audouin's. Kentish Plover breed. Then there are the dunes, varying in width from 100 m to 1 km or more. They have a variable growth of stone pines and scrub, but are highly mobile. Defensive towers along the beach often hold Peregrine, and there are Short-toed Eagle, Stone-curlew, and Dartford and Sardinian Warblers. The next area, between the dunes and the marismas, is wooded, with open glades often creating a parkland effect. Huge numbers of birds breed, including Europe's greatest concentration of raptors, and it is here that Imperial and Booted Eagles must be sought among the hordes of Black and Red Kites. Alongside the wet marismas large colonies of herons and egrets can be found, including Little and Cattle Egrets, Night and Purple Herons, Spoonbill and White Stork. The marismas are the great feeding ground on which all of these birds ultimately depend. In winter they are full of geese and duck, but as spring comes they are alive with migrant and breeding waders,

Whiskered and Gull-billed Terns and the recently established Flamingo. Collared Pratincole is often numerous and Marsh Harrier abundant.

Across the marismas lie further areas of wood and grassland where raptors are again abundant and where visiting vultures are more often seen. Much of this land is being converted to agriculture, but some excellent areas of dwarf pines and scrub remain where Azure-winged Magpie and Great Spotted Cuckoo abound.

SUMMER Purple, Squacco and Night Herons, Little and Cattle Egrets, Little Bittern, White Stork, Spoonbill, Flamingo, Marbled Teal, Red-crested Pochard, Egyptian and, Griffon Vultures, Imperial, Booted and Short-toed Eagles, Red and Black Kites, Peregrine, Purple Gallinule, Avocet, Black-winged Stilt, Collared Pratincole, Slender-billed and Audouin's Gulls, Whiskered and Gull-billed Terns, Great Spotted Cuckoo, Scops Owl, Red-necked Nightjar, Bee-eater, Roller, Hoopoe, Calandra, Crested and Short-toed Larks, Golden Oriole, Azure-winged Magpie, Green Woodpecker, Cetti's, Savi's, Great Reed, Melodious, Orphean, Sardinian, Subalpine, Spectacled, Dartford and Fan-tailed Warblers, Crested Tit, Tawny Pipit, Great Grey and Woodchat Shrikes, Spotless Starling, Hawfinch, Serin.
SPRING Black-tailed Godwit, Ruff, Greenshank, Spotted Redshank, Wood Sandpiper, Little and Temminck's Stints, Marsh Sandpiper, Black Tern.
WINTER Geese, duck.
ACCESS Large parts of the area are within the Parc Nacional de Doñana, with its HQ at the Acebuche Centre, while the main egret colonies and the heart of the Coto are a scientific reserve with restricted access. The Co-operativa of El Rocio runs half-day excursions by four-wheel-drive vehicles through the Parc, but these are often full of tourists with no interest in wildlife and are expensive and pointless for birding. Fortunately much can be seen without leaving rights of way, and I suggest the following as offering

Purple Gallinule

the best birding opportunities. The bridge at **El Rocio** is outstanding when there is water in the *marismas*. Excellent views of huge variety of birds from the roadside. Late evening produces flights of Night Heron. Walk north to the town and examine every corner of the marsh as far as you can go. **La Rocina Centre** is a sub-centre of the Parc, with an excellent hide overlooking the marsh west of El Rocio. Good for Purple Gallinule, Little Bittern, Savi's and Great Reed Warblers. Walk westwards to several hides. **Acebuche Centre** is the Parc HQ where the Co-operativa is based. Excellent shop, refreshment area, educational displays and free hides for watching for Purple Gallinule. Red-necked Nightjars sit out on the track after dark and there are many scrub birds here. **Palacio del Rey** In El Rocio (do not miss fabulous church except in the last week of May, when 2,000,000 'pilgrims' hold a festival here), find the main 'square', and with your back to the bar-restaurant 'La Rocina' head east along the left-hand side. After leaving the square, take the second left past the school to a modern concrete bridge. Continue out over a wooden bridge (excellent wader spot) to a rough track along the northern edge of the marismas towards Palacio del Rey. Beware getting bogged down in sandy area between the bridges. Explore woods, watch for raptors. Before the Palacio, fork right on to an ever-roughening track into the *marismas*. With four-wheel-drive vehicles it is possible to reach a reservoir area, but this is a long, tough ride and not necessary. **Beach** Drive as far south in Matalascanas as possible and park. Walk south along the beach for waders, gulls and terns. In a long day (a long walk), you may reach the mouth of the Guadalquivir opposite Sanlucar de Barameda: watch for Slender-billed Gull. **Western Park** Take the Matalascanas–Huelva road, and after a few kilometres watch for a building on the right. Take the next right for typical scrub birds, plus Bee-eater (nesting under the track) and raptors. Also explore tracks on the left among the beach pines for Azure-winged Magpie etc. **Agricultural Area** Just south of El Rocio look for a turning on the right with a large green notice. This road leads out among fields for Calandra and other larks, and more besides.

ROUTE Airports at Sevilla and Faro (Portugal). Leave the Sevilla–Huelva autoroute signposted to Ballullos (not the Ballullos a few kilometres from Sevilla) and Almonte. Drive straight to El Rocio and on to Matalascanas.

EBRO DELTA

Despite its obvious attractions, the Ebro delta on Spain's Mediterranean coast remains somewhat neglected by northern birders. Over 1200 ha are a game reserve protecting some of the country's most important seabird colonies, yet still visitors pass by on their way to what are seen as better birding areas. Perhaps this is because the Ebro delta lacks any 'special' birds, species that cannot be found elsewhere in Spain. Yet careful searching has produced breeding Lesser Crested Tern, some of the first in Europe.

The delta has large lagoons, reedbeds, channels, ricefields and seasonally flooded areas of scrub. Each should be thoroughly searched, but the area nearest the sea is of greatest importance. Here the lagoons shelter breeding terns, including good numbers of Sandwich and Little, centred on Punta de Fangal. Gull-billed breed at Punta de la Baña, while Whiskered are widespread over the ricefields. Buda Island has Purple Heron in its vast reedbeds and, though numbers vary, is an important site for the species. Marsh and

Montagu's Harriers are usually seen. Spoonbill and Flamingo are regular, sometimes in large numbers. Passage waders and terns deserve attention.

SUMMER Purple Heron, Spoonbill, Little Bittern, Red-crested Pochard, Marsh and Montagu's Harriers, Black-winged Stilt, Avocet, Kentish Plover, Gull-billed, Whiskered, Sandwich, Little and Lesser Crested Terns, Cetti's, Savi's, Great Reed and Fan-tailed Warblers.
ACCESS Minor roads lead into the delta from the N340 near Amposta. To the areas mentioned above should be added an exploration of La Encanizada, La Tancada and Canal Vell.
ROUTE Valencia, to the south, has an airport.

LA SERENA

La Serena is an extensive upland plain west of Merida, though it is here taken to include the huge reservoirs created by damming the two major arms of the River Zújar, as well as the extensive plains to north and south. The landscape, which is all but treeless, consists of somewhat bleak rolling plains, broken here and there by rocky outcrops. The area is only sparsely inhabited and mostly consists of the grasslands beloved by steppe species. The two large reservoirs of Orellana and Zújar form a roost for the important concentrations of birds that winter in La Serena, as well as offering a distinctly different habitat to many other species.

Strangely, La Serena has been largely overlooked by visiting birders and only recently received the attention it deserves. It is described in *IBA* as 'probably the most important (for steppe species) in Spain' and lives up to that reputation. Some 20,000 Little Bustards and over 500 Great Bustards find a home here, along with thousands of Stone-curlews and Pin-tailed Sandgrouse, and hundreds of Black-bellied Sandgrouse and Collared Pratincoles. In winter it is home to tens of thousands of Lapwings and Golden Plovers and, quite outstandingly, the single largest concentration of Cranes in western Europe. Official figures talk of 2000 here and 3000 there, but experienced visitors calculate a total population in the order of 25,000 birds. Only Gallocanta in northern Spain can rival such numbers.

The Embalse de Orellana is bordered to the north by low sierras: the Sierra de Pela, Sierra de los Pastillos and Sierra de Orellana, all well vegetated in comparison with La Serena. Cattle and Little Egrets, Black Storks and birds of prey including Griffon and Egyptian Vultures, Golden Eagle and Eagle Owl all breed. Farther north the rolling landscape with rocky outcrops between Zorita and Madrigalejo holds large populations of Short-toed and Booted Eagles along with smaller numbers of Lesser Kestrel, Montagu's Harrier and Black-shouldered Kite. Both bustards, Stone-curlew and Pin-tailed Sandgrouse are present in good numbers.

SUMMER White and Black Storks, Griffon and Egyptian Vultures, Golden, Short-toed and Booted Eagles, Red, Black and Black-shouldered Kites, Lesser Kestrel, Great and Little Bustards, Stone-curlew, Pin-tailed and Black-bellied Sandgrouse, Calandra Lark, Red-rumped Swallow, Great Spotted Cuckoo, Great Grey Shrike.
WINTER Griffon Vulture, Crane, Golden Plover, Lapwing, Great and Little Bustards, Stone-curlew.

ACCESS This is a huge area, but not one that should daunt even a casual visitor. In winter it is difficult to miss the Cranes, and in spring and summer the bustards should not be too difficult to locate. Nevertheless, some places are better than others and the route that follows traverses most of them. Leave Trujillo south-eastwards on the C524 to Zorita. Follow this road to Madrigalejo watching for raptors, especially Montagu's Harrier and Short-toed Eagle, and scanning the open grasslands for Great and Little Bustards. Continue to the N430 and turn left (east) and after 4 or 5 km turn right to Navalvillar de Pena. Turn right to Orellana de la Sierra and Orellana la Vieja. Explore the reservoir along this northern shore for breeding egrets and wintering Cranes with good chances of raptors. Follow the route across the dam into La Serena. The triangle bounded by the roads between the dam, Castuera and Cabeza del Buey should be explored – it is the bustard and Crane stronghold. The range of hills between Puerto de Mejoral and Cabeza del Buey is good for Black Stork and several raptors. ROUTE Madrid to Trujillo thence as above. The area is also easily approached via Merida.

Lagune de la Fuente de Piedra

When I first visited the second breeding site of Flamingoes in Europe, way back in the 1960s, I was able to drive right across its dried-out wastes in my second-hand Austin A60 Estate and saw nothing whatsoever. Today, this formerly secret site is a fully protected nature reserve and access, even to serious birders with or without A60s, is prohibited. It is, however, an easy site to work from the surrounding roads and fields.

Even today, however, the propensity of this saline lagoon to dry out makes it highly susceptible to predators and the Flamingoes often fail in their breeding attempts. Flamingoes (and there may be several thousands present) apart, this is also a good spot for Slender-billed Gull, Gull-billed Tern, Avocet and Black-winged Stilt. The surrounding fields and olive groves hold the species one would expect in this part of Spain, including good populations of Stone-curlew and Montagu's Harrier.

A somewhat awkward drive to the north, near Aquilar, brings one to the Laguna de Zonar, which holds water all summer when all around is bone-dry. There are some areas of reed with the usual species, and Purple Heron, Purple Gallinule, Red-crested Pochard, grebes and other waterbirds can be found. Zonar is, however, one of the famous places for pure, wild White-headed Duck – the most important breeding area in Spain. Farther north, the area west of the N331 around San Sebastian de los Ballesteros holds Little Bustard. These areas are not included in the checklist below.

SUMMER Flamingo, Red-crested Pochard, Marsh and Hen Harriers, Stone-curlew, Avocet, Black-winged Stilt, Gull-billed Tern, Slender-billed Gull, Hoopoe, Woodchat Shrike.
ACCESS From Antequera, take the N334 Sevilla road to Fuente de Piedra. Drive through this small town, cross the railway, and take a track on the left to the rubbish dump and a small hill beyond, with excellent views over the north of the lagoon. Early morning is best before heat haze makes viewing impossible. Return to the road and continue around the northern shore to the other roadside viewpoints at the north-western corner.

ROUTE Malaga Airport, then directly northward to Antequera. This area is a must for anyone using Malaga as an entry port for a Doñana trip.

LAS TABLAS DE DAIMIEL

In the Mancha region of Spain, the word *tablas* is used for an area of flooding where rivers regularly overflow their banks to create uncontrolled marshland. As part of its conservation programme, the Spanish government has declared Las Tablas de Daimiel a national park – the smallest in the country. Here the waters of two rivers, the Ciguela and the Guadiana, create a huge network of waterways, lagoons and floating reedbeds. There is an excellent, modern park information centre, and it may be possible to arrange exploration by boat. In any case, the birds of the marshes and surrounding land are relatively easy to work via paths and roads.

There are extraordinary numbers of Red-crested Pochard, which is the most abundant duck species; others include Shoveler and Gadwall. Marsh and Montagu's Harriers are relatively common, and Hobby more or less regular. Other waterbirds include Little and Great Crested Grebes, Little Egret and Purple Heron, and White Storks are regular foragers here. Water Rail, Black-winged Stilt, Pratincole, plus a variety of passage waders can be seen, and Gull-billed and Whiskered Terns are regular.

SUMMER Little and Great Crested Grebes, Little Egret, Purple Heron, White Stork, Gadwall, Shoveler, Red-crested Pochard, Pochard, Marsh and Montagu's Harriers, Hobby, Quail, Black-winged Stilt, Stone-curlew. Collared Pratincole, Little Ringed Plover, Gull-billed and Whiskered Terns, Bee-eater, Hoopoe, Calandra Lark, Woodlark, Woodchat and Great Grey Shrikes, Cetti's, Savi's, Moustached, Great Reed, Olivaceous and Bonelli's Warblers, Black-eared Wheatear, Bearded Tit, Reed Bunting.

ACCESS Leave the main Madrid–Sevilla road westwards (signposted to Cuidad Real) at Manzanares or Puerto Lapice for Daimiel. From here the national park lies to the north-west over rough roads, but it is signposted. If in doubt ask for 'La Parque Nacional por favor' and be prepared for a volley of Manchegan directions and much pointing; the latter is the best to follow. The park centre has maps and guidebooks, and the staff will be able to help secure the best from this remarkably rich wetland.

ROUTE Madrid airport is linked via the N1V, the main road south from the capital, which now has a fast motorway through its centre.

MALLORCA

From July to September Mallorca is crowded with mainly British and German visitors, though at other times it can be pleasantly empty. The island has also always been a popular birding site and worth a week or two of exploration. Most birding visitors come in spring, from March to May, and stay in the north in the Puerto Pollensa area. This is undoubtedly the best bird area, as well as one of the most pleasant parts of the island, even if it is, at times, a bit like a warm 'Minsmere'. There are, however, excellent bird spots scattered through the island.

Mallorca offers three major attractions. Black Vulture (twenty birds and two breeding pairs) finds one of its strongholds here and is regularly seen in the mountains in the north-west. Eleonora's Falcon breeds at several places, and Marmora's Warbler can be found locally here and there. Additionally, there are several exciting migration spots that regularly produce superb birds, and the range of breeding species includes Osprey, Peregrine, Booted Eagle, Scops Owl, Audouin's Gull, Cory's Shearwater, etc.

A visitor based at Puerto Pollensa is within easy reach of the Boquer Valley for excellent migrants, Blue Rock Thrush and Rock Sparrow. To the north lies Cape Formentor, with Eleonora's Falcon, Marmora's Warbler and excellent seabird passage. To the east is the Albufereta and the Albufera Marsh, the latter is a nature reserve and Mallorca's most famous bird spot. Here are Purple Heron, Little Egret, Osprey, Marsh Harrier and abundant Little Bittern and Moustached Warbler. The Albufera is also a noted feeding ground of Eleonora's Falcon. Even the best spots for Black Vulture are only a short distance away. The lovely wooded Ternelles Valley produces these birds, as does the road immediately west of Tomir, a substantial peak on the road between Pollensa and Soller. Vultures also appear at the two reservoirs beyond Tomir, where there are Rock Thrushes too. In the south of Mallorca there are several habitats, including the excellent Salinas de Levante. Here, Flamingo, Avocet and Kentish Plover can be found alongside many migrant waders. Porto Colom is another fine area, with Marmora's Warbler and Thekla Lark among others. This is also one of the better places for Audouin's Gull. Passage brings an exciting variety of species, especially in spring.

SUMMER Mediterranean and Cory's Shearwaters, Purple Heron, Little Egret, Little Bittern, Flamingo, Black Vulture, Marsh Harrier, Eleonora's Falcon, Osprey, Peregrine, Red Kite, Booted Eagle, Stone-curlew, Kentish Plover, Avocet, Black-winged Stilt, Audouin's Gull, Scops Owl, Hoopoe, Woodchat Shrike, Pallid Swift, Crag Martin, Short-toed and Thekla Larks, Blue Rock and Rock Thrushes, Tawny Pipit, Fan-tailed, Great Reed, Cetti's, Moustached, Marmora's and Sardinian Warblers, Serin, Cirl Bunting, Raven.

ACCESS Cape Formentor is reached by road out of Puerto Pollensa. At the far end a path leads from the lighthouse to an excellent seawatching spot near the cliffs, but Eleonora's can be seen from the road just before the lighthouse. It is worth stopping at several points between Puerto Pollensa and Cape Formentor, especially where the road approaches the western cliffs, for Marmora's Warbler. Pleasure boats from Puerto Pollensa to Cala San Vicente pass around the cape and can give excellent views. **Boquer Valley** is a short walk from Puerto Pollensa along the road to Formentor, turning left along a track between two rows of pines. Simply follow the track through the farm to the valley and eventually to the sea. **Sierras:** to look for Black Vulture drive along the road between Pollensa and Soller to Tomir peak and beyond. Alternatively, walk the Ternelles valley, which is signposted from the main road north of Pollensa town. Permits must be obtained on Mondays from the Banca Marco in Pollensa; they are valid day of issue only. There is very limited car parking at a set of private gates. For **Albufera** drive east from Puerto Pollensa to Alcudia and continue along the coast road towards Arta. The marsh is just past the Esperanza Hotel. Park and walk or drive inland along the southern bank of a wide drainage channel to the farm; ask the staff for news. Continue back towards the sea along one of two tracks. Finish by walking back to the Esperanza along the main road. For the **Salinas de Levante**, find your way to Petra in the south-east and then check carefully that you take the road signposted to Vila Franca and Felantix. In Campos, follow signs for Colonia San Jordi and continue to the salinas. The main entrance is on the right 1 km after a sharp S-bend. Access is highly restricted and liable to change. Birdwatchers have been denied access. To the south the Lagunas de Salobrar de Campos hold breeding Stilt and passage waders. **Porto Colom** lies in the south-east of Mallorca, and the main area of interest is easily found by turning left on reaching the harbour and proceeding along the peninsula to the lighthouse. The scrub is good for Marmora's as are the fields for Thekla Lark. The harbour produces Audouin's Gull. ROUTE Abundant flights to Palma and easy car hire.

MONFRAGÜE

Monfragüe (the ü is pronounced as a w) is a natural park centred on a precipitous ridge running roughly west to east north of Trujillo alongside the now dammed River Tajo. It is one of Spain's outstanding raptor haunts.

Above all else, Monfrague is known as one of the strongholds of the Black Vulture. This species may be seen at almost any point in the park, but the best watchpoint is from the Embalse de Torrejon southwards along the ridge of the Sierra de las Corchuelas. This spot is also good for Imperial, Golden and Short-toed Eagles, Black Kite and Griffon and Egyptian Vultures. The most spectacular birding, however, can be had at the rocky pinnacle of Peñafalcón. Here Griffon and Egyptian Vultures breed, and soar endlessly overhead viewed from the road on the eastern side of the Tajo. The pinnacle also holds Black Stork – look into low cracks on the right-hand side – and White-rumped Swift, which has colonized in recent years. Here too there are Chough, Crag Martin, Red-rumped Swallow, Alpine Swift and Black-eared Wheatear. The road running eastwards along the southern side of the River Tietar descends into a wooded valley with cork oaks that has Cetti's Warbler, Hawfinch, Azure-winged Magpie, Woodchat Shrike, Booted Eagle and Black-shouldered Kite.

SUMMER White and Black Storks, Egyptian, Griffon and Black Vultures, Golden, Imperial and Booted and Short-toed Eagles, Red, Black and Black-shouldered Kites, Little Bustard, Stone-curlew, Woodlark, Alpine and White-rumped Swifts, Hoopoe, Crag Martin, Golden Oriole, Azure-winged Magpie, Great Grey Shrike, Hawfinch, Chough.

ACCESS Some areas of the park are closed to traffic, but all of the birds can be seen from a good network of public highways. To the south roads penetrate the plains, though walking is advised. **Monfragüe** has a tiny park HQ with a resident naturalist at Villareal de San Carlos; also a couple of cheap bar-restaurants. The park itself is reached along the Plasencia road from Trujillo where it crosses the River Tajo. **Peñafalcón** is across the dammed river on a vicious hairpin bend in the main road. Park before or beyond and watch vultures and raptors; search the low caves on the right for Black Stork. **Saltos de Torrejon** is the dam where a road crosses the empoundment. Continue on the north side, climbing steeply until a parking area is seen on the right. Look south over the Sierra de las

Corchuelas for Imperial and Golden Eagles and Black Vulture. Black Stork may overfly the reservoir to the north. Further viewpoints are northward along this road, which runs south and east of the River Tietar. Farther north still, the road descends towards Bazagona through good forest for Black-shouldered Kite. **Castillo** This castle atop the Sierra de las Corchuelas is reached via a motorable track on the right-hand side about 1 km south of Peñafalcón. It is excellent for vultures, including Black, and also has White-rumped Swift in summer. Most visitors approach the area via Trujillo to the south from the fast Madrid–Badajoz road. The C524 leads directly northwards to Peñafalcón, through a delightful area of cork groves full of Azure-winged Magpies, Great Spotted Cuckoos, Woodlarks, Orioles and Hawfinches. Black Vultures are often to be seen overhead. Before Monfragüe, the road crosses two deep river systems. The bridge on the first has Kingfisher and Little Ringed Plover, the second a small colony of Spanish Sparrows.
ROUTE From Madrid via Trujillo. Or from the capital via the Sierra de Gredos and Plasencia.

ROSAS

The Costa Brava has become an international playground for northern Europeans and the tourist infrastructure has changed the Mediterranean coastline in just 35 years. Estartit and La Escala, which once gave so many birders, including me, their first taste of Spanish birding, are now almost uninhabitable by birds. Fortunately, the marshes just along the coast, to the north of the Roman town of Ampurias, remained 'difficult' to develop and have been accorded reserve status by the Catalan government. Since October 1983 the marshes around the mouths of the Rivers Fluvia and Muga have been known as the Aiguamolls de l'Emporada.

Inland lie areas of lagoons and floods, while there are extensive salt-marshes nearer the sea. Even the beach here is relatively unfrequented.

Almost 300 bird species have been recorded and, with improved management, it is hoped that an increasing number will breed. Penduline Tit, Purple Heron, Cetti's, Savi's and Fan-tailed Warblers, as well as many less specialized wetland birds such as Lesser Grey Shrike, already fall into this category and Purple Gallinule has been successfully introduced. Waders are plentiful on passage, and Cattle and Little Egrets are often abundant. Flamingoes are regular visitors, and raptors include Marsh Harrier and Short-toed Eagle. The sea is a regular winter haunt of divers and sea-duck, so there is something for everyone throughout the year.

The surrounding countryside, though much despoiled, is still interesting enough a little way inland. In particular, the hills between La Escala and Estartit are still full of warblers in the scrub and backing pine forests. Here is a likely spot for Marmora's Warbler (do be careful for there are still good ornithologists who doubt their existence along this coastline), Black Wheatear and occasional Eleonora's Falcon.

SUMMER Little and Cattle Egrets, Purple Heron, Little Bittern, Flamingo, Marsh Harrier, Short-toed Eagle, Purple Gallinule, Kentish Plover, Stone-curlew, Black-winged Stilt, Little Tern, Scops Owl, Bee-eater, Hoopoe, Short-toed Lark, Blue Rock Thrush, Alpine and Pallid Swifts, Red-rumped

Swallow, Tawny Pipit, Lesser Grey and Woodchat Shrikes, Penduline Tit, Black and Black-eared Wheatears, Savi's, Cetti's, Fan-tailed, Great Reed, Moustached, Orphean, Spectacled, Sardinian, Subalpine, Dartford, Marmora's and Olivaceous Warblers, Serin.

ACCESS From La Escala, drive north to Ampurias and walk into the reserve. There are signs, but access may change – so enquire locally. Alternatively, the reserve may be approached from the north through Rosas. For scrub and forest, leave La Escala southward along the shore road and continue towards Estartit. The best areas are near the coast and, in the southern part, inland of Estartit where roads lead into forest areas.

ROUTE Gerona airport is a short drive. There is plenty of accommodation.

SERRANIA DE RONDA

Ronda was for many years regarded as the best area for mountain birds in Andalucia, and even today the town remains a splendid centre for exploring this area's sierras. The town, divided in two by its deep gorge, is unique and has attracted tourists for generations. Today there are more hotels and hostels, and the scope for exploration is considerably greater. Many of the birds remain and, though the vultures of Ronda have disappeared, they can still be seen in many areas. The town still has Chough, Lesser Kestrel and Crag Martin, and the surrounding mountains holds Golden, Short-toed, Bonelli's and Booted Eagles, Peregrine, Goshawk, Egyptian Vulture, Black Wheatear, Blue Rock Thrush and Rock Bunting. Eagle Owls can also be found here but as ever they are elusive.

Probably as good as any of the mountains of Andalucia are those that surround the charming *pueblo blanco* of Grazalema. Two roads lead northwards through superb valleys that easily produce Griffon and Egyptian Vulture, plus Short-toed and Booted Eagles. The road westwards is excellent for Golden Eagle and Chough, with Dartford Warbler at the adjacent pass. Beyond here is the Sierra de Grazalema Nature Park, a pine forest thronged by Spanish school children. Nevertheless, the area is excellent for Bonelli's Eagle and even holds White-rumped Swift in summer. Around the town itself boulder-strewn slopes hold Rock and Cirl Buntings, Black Wheatear, Blue Rock Thrush and Little Owl.

To the north, beyond Zahara, lies the tiny massif of the Sierra de Lijar with high limestone cliffs and a strong breeding colony of Griffon Vultures, plus Egyptian Vulture, Bonelli's Eagle and Eagle Owl.

SUMMER Griffon and Egyptian Vultures, Golden, Short-toed, Booted and Bonelli's Eagles, Buzzard, Goshawk, Sparrowhawk, Peregrine, Lesser Kestrel, Little and Eagle Owls, Alpine Swift, Woodlark, Blue Rock Thrush, Black Wheatear, Crag Martin, Red-rumped Swallow, Grey Wagtail, Chough, Raven, Rock Sparrow, Cirl and Rock Buntings.

ACCESS Almost any of the minor mountain roads radiating from Ronda will produce birds, and exploration of the high passes is strongly advised. A favoured area lies south of the C339 to the west of Ronda, in the area of the Sierra Margarita south to the Sierra Ubrique and bounded in the west by El Bosque. The Puerto del Boyor above Grazalema to Zahara is likewise first-class, with vultures, eagles, Choughs and many other typical birds. Farther south the C341 leads south-west from Ronda, with

minor turnings to the right such as the MA549 and MA511 being particularly worthwhile. Ronda offers a variety of accommodation, but do buy
a drink at the Reina Christina for magnificent views from the clifftop gardens. Ice-cold beer and Lesser Kestrel at a few metres – delicious!
ROUTE Airports at Malaga and Gibraltar are roughly equidistant, and
the route then follows the Costa de Sol to San Pedro. Although it then
winds through the village, it is fast beyond there.

SIERRA DE GREDOS

Gredos is usually regarded as one of the very best ornitho-mountain
ranges in central Spain and, while there is no doubt that its reputation is
justified, it does not always part with its secrets easily. These are high and
rugged mountains with alpine-type grasslands, areas of scrub, extensive
pine forests and, of course, some quite fearsome cliffs. There are good
populations of raptors with Golden, Imperial and Booted Eagles sharing a
major stronghold. Both kites are abundant and Griffon and Black Vultures
are present in about equal numbers, making this one of the major areas
in Europe for the last species. Crested Tit, Firecrest and Bonelli's Warbler
are common in the pines and there are also Crossbill and Ortolan Bunting.
Higher slopes should produce Water Pipit, Black Redstart and Rock
Thrush, and this area boasts the largest population of Bluethroat in Spain.

To the south the Rio Tietar has been dammed at Rositario and Navalcan
near Candeleda. A loop on the surrounding roads, off the N501, passes
through scrub and cork oak 'parkland' for Imperial, Booted and Short-
toed Eagles and Black-shouldered Kite. Cranes are present in winter.

SUMMER White and Black Storks, Griffon and Black Vultures, Golden,
Imperial, Booted and Short-toed Eagles, Black-shouldered, Red and Black

Black-shouldered Kite

Kites, Goshawk, Hobby, Azure-winged Magpie, Great Spotted Cuckoo, Golden Oriole, Hoopoe, Bee-eater, Woodchat Shrike, Calandra Lark, Crag Martin, Black Redstart, Rock and Blue Rock Thrushes, Firecrest, Melodious and Bonelli's Warblers, Crested Tit, Crossbill, Rock Bunting.

ACCESS The best part of Gredos is reached via series of minor roads leading in most directions out of Arenas. From the north the Parador de Gredos offers exceptional views and to the west a road penetrates deep into the Sierra. From Arenas the N501 leads westwards to Candeleda. About 5 or 6 km farther a minor road on the left takes one to the Pantano de Rosarito. Along the way explore along the reservoir banks.

ROUTE From Madrid, leave the NV at Talavera on the C502 to Arenas. Allow plenty of time for Gredos – it's worth it.

SIERRA DE GUADARRAMA

Guadarrama is the easternmost of the mountain ranges that extend roughly east to west across the Spanish plateau, the Meseta. It is also the nearest to Madrid and, therefore, a favoured playground of the capital's citizens. As a result there is considerable pressure from tourism, leisure developments and their associated rubbish tips, power lines and other mess. Despite such pressures, Guadarrama continues to maintain its status as one of the best areas for birds in central Spain. It is particularly noted as a stronghold for birds of prey and Imperial Eagle is as common here as anywhere else in the country with at least twenty pairs in the area – some 20 per cent of the world population of what is now regarded as an endemic species. The hills are also an important centre for Black and Griffon Vultures, Golden and Bonelli's Eagles, Peregrine, Eagle Owl and a few pairs of Black Stork. Small birds are equally attractive and Great Grey Shrike, Rock Thrush, Dartford and Subalpine Warblers, Rock Sparrow and Golden Oriole can all be found. Open ground will produce Calandra and Short-toed Larks and the higher bare areas have Citril Finch.

SUMMER White and Black Storks, Griffon and Black Vultures, Golden, Imperial, Bonelli's and Booted Eagles, Black and Red Kites, Buzzard, Honey Buzzard, Goshawk, Hobby, Peregrine, Crag Martin, Great Grey and Woodchat Shrikes, Rock Thrush, Calandra and Short-toed Larks, Hoopoe, Roller, Bee-eater, Golden Oriole, Firecrest, Dartford, Subalpine, Melodious and Bonelli's Warblers, Crested Tit, Citril Finch, Cirl, Ortolan and Rock Buntings, Rock Sparrow.

ACCESS The best parts of Guadarrama lie either side of the major A6 and NVI roads north-west of Madrid and both should be explored. To the west the ranges between El Escorial and San Martin de Valdeiglesias are still relatively rural and a major area for Imperial Eagle. There is a good network of roads. To the north and east the Puerto de Navacerrada is a more concentrated watchpoint on the Madrid–Segovia route. The northern slopes have fine pine forests and there are small roads and tracks to higher altitudes. From Navacerrada a minor road runs parallel to the A6 to Colmenar Viejo. From this small town a minor road runs along the eastern side of the Embalsa de El Pardo. The surrounding estates, one of which belongs to the royal family, are important for breeding Black Vulture, Imperial Eagle and other woodland birds. Do not trespass; the great raptors can be seen from the roads. The reservoir holds Black Stork at the end of the breeding season. Though not strictly part of Guadarrama there is a good area for Great and Little Bustards a few kilometres east of the N1 north of Madrid. The easiest way to locate the area is by taking the N11 to Guadalajara and then taking the C102 to Casar de Talamanca. Continue for 7 km and the bustards are often on the right. ROUTE Madrid.

SIERRA NEVADA

Reaching over 3350 m, within 40 km of the Mediterranean, and now well developed as a ski resort, the Sierra Nevada is one of the easiest high-altitude regions of Spain to explore for birds. It is also well situated for those for whom a trip to Andalucia would not be complete without a visit to Granada to see the Alhambra and the Generalife. *Warning*: these sites are so overrun with tourists that early-morning visits are essential for self-preservation. Nevertheless, they are fabulous.

Granada is the gateway to the Sierra Nevada, and a narrow mountain road twists and turns its way upward from the south-eastern suburbs of the city. At first it passes through an agricultural valley, but later there are pine woods, grazing meadows and ultimately the bare mountain itself. Each habitat is worth exploring, with different species at different levels until at the top there is not much more than Alpine Accentor – though this is a common bird outside the Parador Hotel.

SUMMER Golden and Bonelli's Eagles, Peregrine, Eagle Owl, Chough, Short-toed Lark, Alpine Swift, Crag Martin, Alpine Accentor, Black Wheatear, Woodchat Shrike, Hoopoe, Rock Thrush, Sardinian Warbler, Serin, Rock and Ortolan Buntings.
ACCESS The Parador in the Sierra Nevada is signposted from Granada. There are several large skiing hotels, but book in advance for the Parador.
ROUTE From Malaga airport, drive eastward through the city and take the coastal road to Nerja and Motril. Turn left to Granada.

SPANISH PYRENEES

The Pyrenees are one of the best birding spots in Europe, with birds of prey in both number and variety together with a wealth of other mountain, as well as lowland, birds. Several species declining in other parts of Iberia find their last stronghold among the mountain massifs.

Outstanding is the Lammergeier in one of its three last European strongholds. They are the only Lammergeiers left in Iberia since the demise of the Cazorla birds in the 1980s. There are other vultures, plus a variety of raptors which includes Golden, Bonelli's, Booted and Short-toed Eagles, Peregrine, Hobby, Red and Black Kites and Montagu's Harrier. Other species of particular interest include Black Woodpecker but there are plenty of other, more widespread birds as well.

As with all mountain areas, the essential is to explore fully at various altitudes, from the lush meadows and streams via the forests to the high passes. By and large, there is no need to trek into remote areas or climb high peaks though it is necessary to cover considerable distances to get the best out of what is, after all, a huge region. Most birders concentrate on the area between Pamplona and Jaca.

SUMMER Lammergeier, Griffon and Egyptian Vultures, Golden, Short-toed, Bonelli's and Booted Eagles, Buzzard, Red and Black Kites, Montagu's Harrier, Peregrine, Sparrowhawk, Eagle Owl, Black and White-backed Woodpeckers, Alpine Swift, Crag Martin, Golden Oriole, Alpine Accentor, Dipper, Wallcreeper, Woodchat Shrike, Blue Rock and Rock Thrushes, Black Wheatear, Bonelli's and Melodious Warblers, Crested Tit, Citril Finch, Rock Sparrow, Alpine Chough, Cirl and Rock Buntings. **ACCESS** A good base is the town of **Jaca**, though the villages of Berdun, Anso and Hecho are nicer and right among the birds. **Ordesa** has long been the most famous area in the Pyrenees and was, at one time, regarded as the most reliable Lammergeier site in Europe. It still produces this bird, as well as Griffon, Booted Eagle and, among the lower pine forests, Black Woodpecker and Crested Tit. From Torla, which lies east of Jaca, simply follow the road northwards then east to the head of the valley. There are plentiful walks and a good guidebook detailing tracks, paths and a variety of overnight accommodation for those who wish to walk through the park. For **San Juan and Riglos,** head westward from Jaca on the C134 to the turning on the left (south) towards San Juan de la Pena. This magnificent road has breeding Griffon and Lammergeier before San Juan Monastery. At Bernues turn right to Santa Maria. Here turn left toward Ayerbe and watch for pinnacled red rocks on the left. Take the next turning to Riglos. Drive to the village and walk right along the foot of the pillars. Here are Lammergeier, Griffon Vulture and one of the best spots for Wallcreeper; also Blue Rock Thrush, Black Wheatear, and Rock Sparrow in the church tower. **Fos de Binies** is a dramatic gorge with close-up views of Griffon, plus Chough, Alpine Swift and Dipper. Leave Jaca westward on the C134 to Berdun, turn right (north) to Binies and continue to the gorge. Follow this road to just before Anso and turn right to Hecho for possible Lammergeier and Golden Eagle, plus Griffon, Red Kite and Booted Eagle. At Hecho, turn left and explore as high as possible for Wallcreeper near Selva de Oza camp site. For **Fos de Arbayun,** head west from Jaca, passing Berdun and the huge Yesa Reservoir, and watch for the turning to the right (north) to Lumbier. In this village fork right to the Fos de Arbayun, which holds vultures, both kites, Booted Eagle, Golden Oriole and both rock thrushes. The Fos de Lumbier, lower down, is an afternoon site for Lammergeier and has Rock Sparrows. A torch is useful for walking the tunnels, but beware of cars in the dark. The Sierra de Abodi lies north of Lumbier and is reached by following the C127 to Aoiz and thereafter forking right along the Rio Irati. Take a right before Gerralda and a left to Arive. Continue to the Pantano de Irabla. The woods here are an important site for Black and White-backed Woodpeckers and other woodland birds. If some of the valleys that extend northwards from the N240 between Lumbier and Jaca have been omitted from this account, do not be deterred from exploration. All of the minor roads have produced all of the Pyrennean specialities in their time. **ROUTE** Nearest airports are Bilbao and San Sebastian, but do not ignore the possibilities of a French connection via Toulouse.

SWEDEN

ABISKO

Twenty years ago, Abisko was one of the most remote birding spots in Europe and could be reached only by rail. Today there is a road through to Narvik in Norway and Abisko can be explored by car.

Abisko lies 170 km north of the Arctic Circle near the Norwegian border. The iron-ore deposits of Kiruna are carried westwards to the port of Narvik during winter, when the Gulf of Bothnia is closed by ice.

The area is simply beautiful, with mountains rising steeply from the shores of Lake Torneträsk. In the distance is the 'Lapp Gate', a prominently raised U-shaped valley. A full exploration of the area is essential. The high tops are basically tundra, with Snow Bunting, Long-tailed Skua, Ptarmigan and Dotterel. Descending to the edge of the tree line, there are Lapland Bunting and sometimes Arctic Warbler. The latter is now only irregular here as elsewhere in Sweden, though there were nine singing males in 1993. The woods are full of Willow Warbler and Arctic Redpoll, while the marshes hold Bluethroat, Whimbrel and Greenshank. Red-necked Phalarope and Temminck's Stint are common breeding birds.

As a visit to Abisko requires considerable planning and equipment, it would also be a good idea to check on the likelihood of the season turning out to be a 'lemming year'. Visitors during such seasons will enjoy far greater numbers of the major raptors and breeding skuas.

SUMMER Red-throated and Black-throated Divers, Slavonian Grebe, Long-tailed Duck, Velvet Scoter, Rough-legged Buzzard, Merlin, Ptarmigan, Willow Grouse, Golden Plover, Dotterel, Whimbrel, Greenshank, Temminck's Stint, Broad-billed Sandpiper, Red-necked Phalarope, Long-tailed Skua, Hawk Owl, Redwing, Fieldfare, Ring Ouzel, Bluethroat, Wheatear, Willow Warbler, Pied Flycatcher, Great Grey Shrike, Arctic Redpoll, Pine Grosbeak, Brambling, Lapland and Snow Buntings.

ACCESS To get the best from Abisko, one must be fit, prepared to walk and carry a hefty rucksack all day. Hiking is the main summer sport of the Abisko National Park, and the Swedish Touring Club has established a network of huts at walkable distances to enable tourists to explore the area. These huts vary from the very simple to comfortable, wardened places, but they all require visitors to bring their own sleeping bags, food, cutlery and crockery (plastic?) and to look after themselves. Though they cannot be booked in advance, they have the reputation of never turning anyone away, a reassuring policy that can lead to overcrowding. Do not venture into this area without: walking boots, proper waterproofs, survival rations, compass, map (BD6), and insect repellent. The mosquito is the most abundant species in Abisko. The Abisko Turiststation, 980 24 Abisko, is actually a hotel that can be booked via Svenska Turistforenin, Stureplan 2, Fack, 108 80, Stockholm (Tel. 8 22 72 00). It opens from mid-June until near the end of September and is decidedly expensive. Next door is a two-dormitory 'hut'. The best time to visit is June, preferably the second two weeks. There is a skilift that makes access to the high tops quite simple.

ROUTE By road through Kiruna, which has an airport, or by train from Sweden or Norway five times daily. The railway has many small stops and it is a good idea to get a return ticket to Narvik so that one can explore stations westwards on the same ticket as that used for Abisko. Note: Abisko Turiststation, not Abisko Östra, is the correct station.

ÅNNSJÖN

This is a large shallow lake in central Sweden lying near the Norwegian frontier west of Östersund. It has some surrounding hills and quite extensive forests, but the main ornitho-interest is centred on the surrounding peat marshes and deltas, where a quite excellent collection of breeding birds can be found. These include Whimbrel, Red-necked Phalarope, Ruff, Temminck's Stint and, sometimes, Broad-billed Sandpiper. Cranes regularly breed here, as do both divers and both scoters. Most of these birds breed on the northern and eastern sides of the lake, but Red-necked Phalarope can be found along the shore south of Ånn and at the delta at Handöl. The woodland holds a good variety of species, including the elusive Hazelhen.

There are excellent areas within striking distance of Ånnsjon including the best known Great Snipe lek in Sweden. To the south the Bunner plateau rises to 900 m and offers open country birds not found around the lake. Here are Long-tailed Duck, Ptarmigan, Dotterel, Purple Sandpiper and Lapland and Snow Buntings. The Vålådaten valley south-east of Ånnsjön has extensive areas of virgin conifer forest and holds Golden Eagle, Rough-legged Buzzard, Hawk Owl, Three-toed Woodpecker and Siberian Jay. To the west, at Storlien is the famous Great Snipe lek.

SUMMER Black-throated and Red-throated Divers, Scaup, Goldeneye, Velvet Scoter, Scoter, Osprey, Rough-legged Buzzard, Hen Harrier, Merlin, Willow and Black Grouse, Capercaillie, Hazelhen, Crane, Golden Plover, Whimbrel, Greenshank, Wood and Broad-billed Sandpipers, Temminck's Stint, Great Snipe, Ruff, Red-necked Phalarope, Arctic Tern, Pygmy, Tengmalm's and Hawk Owls, Great Grey Shrike, Three-toed and Black Woodpeckers, Siberian Jay, Bluethroat, Icterine Warbler, Crossbill, Brambling, Scarlet Rosefinch.

ACCESS Explore via the roads that meet at Ånn. Handöl, with its delta, is about 8 km away. This is a popular tourist and winter sports area, and there is accommodation in Våladen, Ånn, Enafors, Handöl, Storulvan, Storvallen and Storlien. There are also camp sites at Ånn, Handöl and Storlien as well as several restaurants. The lake is relatively straightforward. In contrast, the **Bunner Plateau** requires at least a two-day hike to get the high-altitude species. Walk in from Tjallingen or south from Ånnsjön and take camping gear and mountain walking equipment. The Våladen valley is reached by road via Underåker to the east of Ånnsjön. The Storlien area, lies west of Ånnsjön on the road to Norway. Start at the Storliens Högfjällshotel and follow the blue-marked trail. Follow the marked trail west from Bånggårdsliften to a hide. During the lekking season it is forbidden to leave the trail or stand outside the hide. Great Snipe display from late May to late June with peak activity from 11 p.m. to 2 a.m. The lack of real night this far north makes for good viewing in reasonable light.

ROUTE Ånn can be reached by road on the E75 from Östersund. All trains stop at Ånn and Enafors. Join the railway at Östersund. Both means of transport can also be started from Trondheim in Norway.

ARJEPLOG AND AMMARNÄS

These two areas of southern Swedish Lapland lie just below the Arctic Circle. They are over 100 km apart, and nearly 200 km by road. Nevertheless, they do offer similar birds in similar habitats. There are vast areas of woodland, birch-lined lakes, swamps and bogs and high, semi-tundra-topped hills and plateaux. Both areas lie off the main routes northward to Lapland and there has been a tendency for foreign birders to work Arjeplog, while Swedish birders have Ammarnäs to themselves particularly in early June, when many species wait in the valley for the snows to

Hawk Owl

clear from the hills. The roads to both areas are now surfaced and equally accessible. Gyrfalcons do, incidentally, exist at Ammarnäs, but are extremely rare in their appearances. Arjeplog has many lakes and several important quaking bogs where Whimbrel, Wood Sandpiper and Jack Snipe can be found. There are a few breeding Smew here, and the woods hold Siberian Jay and Siberian Tit, as well as a few Waxwings in the damper places.

Ammarnäs offers the occasional White-tailed Eagle, and Great Snipe, Spotted Redshank, Purple and Broad-billed Sandpipers, Hawk Owl, and the decidedly scarce Shore Lark. The main bird haunt is the delta in late May or early June, but a thorough exploration of the woods, mountains and lakes is needed to find all the specialities. A total of 216 species has been seen, including some 130 breeding birds.

SUMMER (Arjeplog): Black-throated Diver, Smew, Scaup, Goldeneye, Rough-legged Buzzard, Whimbrel, Jack Snipe, Spotted Redshank, Wood Sandpiper, Greenshank, Siberian Jay, Waxwing, Siberian Tit, Great Grey Shrike. (Ammarnäs): Scaup, Long-tailed Duck, Scoter, Golden and White-tailed Eagles, Rough-legged Buzzard, Hen Harrier, Merlin, Willow Grouse, Ptarmigan, Hazelhen, Capercaillie, Dotterel, Great Snipe, Spotted Redshank, Greenshank, Purple and Broad-billed Sandpipers, Temminck's Stint, Red-necked Phalarope, Long-tailed Skua, Hawk and Tengmalm's Owls, Three-toed Woodpecker, Siberian Jay, Shore Lark, Siberian Tit, Bluethroat, Great Grey Shrike, Lapland Bunting, Pine Grosbeak, Parrot Crossbill, Arctic Redpoll, Snow and Rustic Buntings.

ACCESS Arjeplog is a particularly good centre, with roads leading in several directions to facilitate exploration. To the east, the woods and lakes at Stensund are good, and the village of Laisvall to the west is also recommended. There are several hotels, as well as a youth hostel. **Ammarnäs** has two hotels, one of which also has cabins. Exploration is mainly on foot, with Marsivagge good for waders and Högbacken for high-altitude species. The village can be reached by mailbus from Sorsele (90 km), which connects with the train: one of each per day. During the summer Lund University operates a small research station near Tjulträsk. **ROUTE** By rail or road from Norway or Sweden.

FÄRNEBOFJÄRDEN

This is a unique area where the Daläven spreads out in a series of shallow lakes with an abundance of islands, surrounded by large areas of marsh and moist forest, much of which is flooded in spring. Large areas have been remarkably little affected by man. It is unique because all seven Swedish woodpeckers breed (White-backed is now very rare). This is also the place in Sweden to see (or at least hear) Ural Owl, some 20–25 pairs of which breed. It is expected that the area will be declared a National Park in the near future. Access is restricted in some areas in spring to protect the White-backed Woodpecker. Färnebofjärden is in the border zone between the southern and northern taiga and houses a remarkable mixture of forms, about 100 species breed, which is a very high figure for a predominantly taiga area. There are no fewer than 30 breeding pairs of Osprey, several pairs of White-tailed Eagle, as well as Goshawk, Hazelhen and both Pygmy and Tengmalm's Owls. The best period to visit this area is late March–early April when woodpeckers are drumming, grouse lekking and owls calling, but most of the interesting species are resident and can be found in any season, though it is of course more difficult than in the spring.

SUMMER Black-throated Diver, Goldeneye, Osprey, White-tailed Eagle, Goshawk, Hobby, Crane, Capercaillie, Hazelhen, Wood and Green Sandpipers, Ural, Pygmy and Tengmalm's Owls, Grey-headed, Green, Black, Three-toed, Great Spotted , Lesser Spotted and White-backed Woodpeckers, Redwing, Brambling.
ACCESS Take Route 72 from Uppsala to Heby. Turn right on Route 254 for 10 km, then left through Runhällen and Enåker. After 10 km cross the river Költorsån and take the first turning right until the road is blocked by a boom. This is the best area for owls and woodpeckers. Elsewhere take any road leading to the lake for White-tailed Eagle and others. Of free access except to areas where White-backed Woodpecker breeds.
ROUTE Taking the fast motorway from Stockholm's airport to Uppsala you can be watching or hearing woodpeckers and owls here within an hour of collecting your baggage and renting a car – tempting for owl-starved British Euro-twitchers. Gysinge in the north of the area has a hotel.

GETTERÖN

Getterön is a peninsula north-west of Varberg on the west coast. Formerly an island, it has been joined to the mainland by the dumping of dredged mud and this forms an important marsh for both breeding and passage birds. Avocet, Ruff and Black-tailed Godwit breed and there is a significant Great Snipe lek. Gadwall, Garganey, and Bearded and Penduline Tits breed. Outside the reserve is a large colony of Little Tern. Osprey and Caspian Tern are seen daily in summer. Migration brings most of the waders one would expect in southern Sweden with Spotted Redshank and both stints 'common'. Great Snipe and Red-throated Pipit are regular in autumn. In March and April Getterön is an excellent spot to watch migration at the point of Gubbanäsan. Here large flocks of divers and eiders pass offshore, often with the odd King Eider, even occasionally Steller's, and regularly with a few White-billed Diver in company. Grebes, Little Gull, Arctic Tern and skuas are also numerous. In autumn it is one of the best seawatch sites in Sweden following north-westerly winds, with large numbers of gulls and auks, both storm petrels, skuas, shearwaters and, in November, Little Auk.

Other good locations nearby include bird towers at Galtabäck to the south and at Båtafjorden (between Bua and the nuclear power station at Ringhals) to the north. Inland, some 20 km east of Varberg, are good woods and lakes at Åkullabokskogar, with Black-throated Diver, Osprey, Black Woodpecker and Nutcracker. In March–April five owl species may be heard – hearing them requires good fortune, seeing them amazing luck.

SUMMER Garganey, Gadwall, Osprey, Marsh Harrier, Spotted Crake, Great Snipe, Black-tailed Godwit, Ruff, Avocet, Little and Caspian Terns, Marsh Warbler, Bearded and Penduline Tits, Blue-headed Wagtail, Red-backed Shrike.
PASSAGE Divers, wildfowl, raptors, seabirds, waders, Red-throated Pipit.
ACCESS The road west from the E6 north of Varberg passes south of the nature reserve (follow signs to Grenå). On the eastern side of the reserve a Visitor Centre provides up-to-date information. There is also a hide, a bird tower and an observation platform. Follow sign Fågellokal. Facilities for watching birds are always accessible. Varberg has several hotels and youth hostels as well as camp sites. Varbergs Turistbyrå will always help to find suitable accommodation (Tel. 0340 887 70). This account is based on one kindly supplied by the warden, Magnus Forsberg.
ROUTE Varberg is an ideal base on the E6 80 km south of Göteborg.

GOTLAND

Gotland is the largest Baltic island, 130 km long and 50 km wide with the mildest climate in Scandinavia. The influence of the sea can also be seen in the ruggedness of the limestone cliffs, caves and stacks that dominate the shoreline. Off the west coast are the islands of Stora and Lilla Karlsö, where the limestone has been eroded into ledges favoured by breeding seabirds. North of Gotland, Farö is a military security zone and foreigners are not allowed. Nevertheless, there are many other attractions and several species are on the northern fringe of their range. The Collared Flycatcher, for instance, is found nowhere farther north and is really quite common. There are five pairs of breeding Golden Eagle. Over 1400 pairs of Barnacle Geese breed along the east coast. These are descended from migrants not feral birds and are largely based at Laus holmar. Though foreign birders are unlikely to visit Gotland during the winter, perhaps regular flocks of Steller's Eider from December to March might tempt them.

SUMMER Greylag and Barnacle Geese, Crane, Golden Eagle, Osprey, Goshawk, Black-tailed Godwit, Ruff, Avocet, Green Sandpiper, Little Gull, Caspian Tern, Guillemot, Black Guillemot, Razorbill, Black Wood-pecker, Thrush Nightingale, Redwing, Icterine and Marsh Warblers, Collared Flycatcher, Bearded Tit.
ACCESS Allekvia äng A small deciduous wood with large areas of open grassland. It is an interesting place because of the mixture of southern and northern species, including Collared Flycatcher and Redwing. Take Route 147 from Visby and turn right (signposted Dalhem) after 3 km. In

6 km there is a small green sign on the right that shows the way to Allekvia äng. **Lina Myr** Marshland area with a growth of reeds surrounded by large wet-meadows and an excellent collection of regular breeding birds that includes Ruff and Black-tailed Godwit. In some years River and Marsh Warblers occur. Take Route 147 east from Visby and turn right after 35 km on to Route 146. After 10 km turn right for 1.5 km and fork right. Pass the bridge over the Gothemsån and after 1.5 km turn left on to a road going down to the marsh. **Gothems storsund** An attractive lake set in a coniferous wood, has a bird tower on the south shore giving views over the lake, which has emergent vegetation and attracts a wide variety of marsh birds. The most outstanding are Crane and Greylag Goose but non-breeding visitors include White-tailed Eagle, Osprey, Caspian Tern, Little Gull and Great Reed Warbler. The woodland holds Black Woodpecker, Goshawk and Green Sandpiper, which can often be seen near the bird tower.Back on Route 146 go a further 2 km, pass Gothem church and in 1.5 km is the road to Botvaldevik. Soon after there is a small track going off to the left to a car park from which the bird tower can be seen. **Stockviken** A shallow marshy water with fringe vegetation and wet-meadows with a bird tower to the east of the lake which gives excellent views. Though breeding marsh birds are the main attraction and include Greylag Goose, Avocet and Bearded Tit, the area is noted for the rarities that turn up, probably a result of its strategic position in the south of the island. Vagrants have included Blue-cheeked Bee-eater, Little Bittern, Greater Flamingo and Black Stork. From Burgsvik in the south of Gotland, take the last road east south of the village and fork right after 2 km. Continue 3 km southwards to the Stockville signpost and in 2 km the bird tower is on the right. **Stora Karlsö and Lilla Karlsö** are Sweden's only accessible seabird colonies. The latter is a nature reserve of the Svenska Naturskyddsföreningen covering 152 ha of sheep pasture. Both lie a few kilometres off the west coast south of Klintehamn, and hold breeding auks. A regular passage of passerines often includes Greenish Warbler (a scarce but regular breeder on Gotland) and Scarlet Rosefinch. Red-breasted Flycatcher is a summer visitor. They can be visited by daily excursion boats during summer.
ROUTE There are daily ferries (a four-to-five hour crossing) from the mainland towns of Södertälje, Nynäshamn, Västervik and Oskarshamn to Visby and in some cases to Kappelshamn and Klintehamn. Gotland is only an hour by air from Stockholm. Because of the mild climate, interesting buildings and beautiful scenery, the island is a favourite holiday resort and there is plenty of accommodation.

HAMMARSJÖN AND ARASLOVSSJÖN

These two shallow lakes lie south and north of Kristianstad respectively, in the east of Skåne in southern Sweden. They are easily reached from Malmö and by visitors to Falsterbo. Both lakes have extensive reedbeds and the surrounding meadows are excellent for breeding birds. The Håslövs ängar to the east of Hammarsjön are carefully protected for breeding Black-tailed Godwit and Ruff, both numbering about 50 pairs. A smaller number of Black Terns also breed, along with Marsh Harrier, Spotted Crake and Bittern. Ospreys are regular summer visitors, and there are Bean Geese and Whooper Swans in autumn.

SUMMER Bittern, Garganey, Marsh Harrier, Hobby, Osprey, Spotted Crake, Corncrake, Black-tailed Godwit, Ruff, Black Tern, Bearded Tit. AUTUMN White-tailed Eagle, Goosander, Bean Goose, Whooper Swan. ACCESS Hammarsjön lies immediately south of Kristianstad, and the northern shore is the most accessible. There are bird-observation towers just south of the town and on the western shore near Norra Assum. There is a footpath around Håslövs ängar and a bird tower at the southern tip. The nearby Herculesdammarna, to the north-east of Håslövs ängar, is an area of ponds left by an abandoned brick works. It has acquired a reputation for producing rarities and should not be ignored. It can be reached north of Rinkaby before turning west to Håslövs ängar. Araslovssjön is best watched from the observation tower on the southeastern shore near the car park. This is open at weekends, but not always on weekdays owing to military activities. No photography. ROUTE Kristianstad is easily reached by Route 15 from Malmö.

HJÄLSTAVIKEN

This shallow lake was once part of the huge Ekolsund bay of Lake Mälaren, but is now a separate water. It lies just north of the E18 some 70 km west of Stockholm and is a noted haunt of breeding birds, with some excellent passage wildfowl and waders. Bittern, Marsh Harrier, Osprey, Spotted Crake and Ortolan Bunting all breed, and both Great and Jack Snipe regularly display in May before moving on to their breeding grounds elsewhere. Passage waders include Temminck's Stint, and both Bluethroat and Red-throated Pipit are local migrant specialities.

SUMMER Slavonian Grebe, Bittern, Garganey, Marsh Harrier, Osprey, Spotted Crake, Long-eared Owl, Ortolan Bunting.
PASSAGE Bean Goose, Rough-legged Buzzard, Sparrowhawk, Hen Harrier, Hobby, Great and Jack Snipe, Bluethroat, Red-throated Pipit, Lapland and Snow Buntings.
ACCESS The extensive growth of reeds around the lake makes observation awkward, although there is a path right around the lake starting from a car park off the E18 in the south-eastern corner. The adjacent hill of Kvarnberget gives excellent views from the south-east, and another hill in the north, Enbärsbacken, serves a similar purpose.
ROUTE 70 km on the E18 from Stockholm. Watch for the lake on the right on emerging from an extensive pine forest.

HORNBORGASJÖN

This famous lake lies south of route 49 between Skarna and Skovde about 130 km from Gotebörg. Attempts to drain the lake over the last hundred years have resulted in total failure, and instead the creation of a reed and willow marsh of international importance. Restoration, involving management of the water level, has helped to restore its former glory. Although 100 species breed in the area, Hornborgasjön is famous for the migration of Cranes in spring. From 10–25 April, up to 2500 of these splendid birds may be seen feeding (and displaying) on the potato fields south-west of the lake and flighting to roost between Bjurum church and

Collared Flycatcher

Dagsnäs *en route* to the lake. At other seasons the eastern shoreline is best, and there is a visitor centre and a bird tower at Fågeludden. This is an excellent spot for Slavonian Grebe, some 40 pairs of which breed here. There are also a few Black-necked Grebe (now the only reliable site in Sweden) plus Red-necked Grebe, Marsh Harrier, Hen Harrier (the only breeding site in southern Sweden), Montagu's Harrier, Crane, Bittern, Osprey, Wood Sandpiper, Ruff, Black Tern, Great Reed and Icterine Warblers, Bearded Tit and Scarlet Rosefinch.

SUMMER Red-necked, Black-necked and Slavonian Grebes, Greylag Goose, Garganey, Goldeneye, Bittern, Marsh, Hen and Montagu's Harriers, Hobby, Osprey, Crane, Water Rail, Spotted Crake, Wood Sandpiper, Black Tern, Ruff, Long-eared Owl, Blue-headed Wagtail, Redwing, Icterine and Great Reed Warblers, Bearded Tit, Scarlet Rosefinch.
SPRING Crane.
AUTUMN Hen Harrier, Crane, Spotted Redshank.
ACCESS View the Cranes early in the morning or late in the evening as they flight across the road between Dagsnäs and Bjurum church. They can also be seen feeding, by taking the road from Bjurum church to the south-west. Fågeludden is reached by leaving the road along the eastern side of Hornborgasjön 1 km north of Brodedetorp church on a track leading westward. There are hotels in Skara and Falköping.
ROUTE Take the E3 from either Gotebörg or Stockholm to Skara, then follow signs toward Falköping past the lake at the Crane corner. It is illegal to enter the Crane feeding fields.

ÖLAND

Öland is an island in the Baltic just off the eastern coast of Sweden and joined to it by a road bridge and a ferry system. It is 137 km long but only 16 km wide, and runs north–south parallel with the mainland. The west has a range of limestone cliffs and the land gradually falls away to the low-lying east coast. There are some huge areas of woodland, areas of grazing with dry-stone walls, and a characteristic limestone heathland called alvar.

Öland is traditionally Sweden's prime birding area with Ottenby by far the best spot for rarities. Among summer birds are Slavonian Grebe, Marsh and Montagu's Harriers, Hobby, Corncrake, Ruff, Avocet, Black-tailed Godwit, Black Tern, Red-backed Shrike and exciting eastern species such as Thrush Nightingale, Icterine and Barred Warblers and Red-breasted Flycatcher. Caspian Tern breeds on a few islets and Barnacle Geese do so off the east coast – these are genuine wild birds. During passage periods there are good numbers of geese, Crane, plus a variety of raptors that regularly includes Golden and White-tailed Eagles in November. Waders are excellent, especially at Ottenby, and the numbers of migrating Eider are simply staggering. Daily spring totals of the latter of over 50,000 (late March–early April) have been counted, along with 30,000 returning birds per day (early October). Rarities usually occur in May and the first half of June, but migration here is both dramatic and productive of species.

Öland has many distinct sites, each of which is outlined below. It is worth a holiday at almost any time of the year.

SUMMER Slavonian Grebe, Greylag Goose, Garganey, Pintail, Marsh and Montagu's Harriers, Corncrake, Avocet, Ruff, Black-tailed Godwit, Golden Plover, Black and Caspian Terns, Wryneck, Hoopoe, Red-backed Shrike, Icterine and Barred Warblers, Thrush Nightingale, Red-breasted and Collared Flycatchers, Bearded and Penduline Tits.

PASSAGE Black-throated and Red-throated Divers, Long-tailed Duck, Velvet Scoter, Scoter, Eider, Steller's and King Eiders, Bean, Brent and Barnacle Geese, Whooper and Bewick's Swans, Golden and White-tailed Eagles, Rough-legged Buzzard, Crane, Whimbrel, Bar-tailed Godwit, Spotted Redshank, Greenshank, Knot, Ruff, Broad-billed Sandpiper, Wryneck, Ring Ouzel.

ACCESS Ottenby The southernmost area of Öland and the bird observatory is situated near the lighthouse. Visible migration is watched from the southern tip and grounded migrants in the whole area. Ottenby Fagelstation, P1, 1500, 38065 Degerhaven, Sweden (Tel. 0485 610 93), has limited accommodation. There are passage geese on Vastrevet to the west, and the meadowland to the east, known as Schaferiangarna, is a breeding ground of Avocet and Ruff. The woods of Ottenby Lund are a stronghold of Icterine Warbler and a few pairs of Red-breasted and Collared Flycatchers. To the west is an area called Tokmarken, where Barred Warblers breed. There are two observation towers: one at the southern end of Ottenby Lund near the car park, the other in the north at the end of the east–west Allvägen. Both are open to the public. The woods to the north of this road are also open via a gate near the youth hostel in the north and a tall stile farther south. Bee-eater and Roller no longer breed but do appear from time to time. Accommodation is limited, and there are few shops. **Beijershamn** An area around an old causeway on the western shore with interesting marshland and some splendid wildfowl and wader passage. This is one of the best spots for breeding Marsh Harrier, Ruff and visiting Caspian. Passage of geese and duck, viewed from the end of the breakwater, can be dramatic, and passage waders may include Broad-billed Sandpiper. The adjacent woods and scrub are a stronghold of Thrush Nightingale and Icterine Warbler and, with care and patience, a Barred Warbler may be located. **Stora Rör** The ferry terminal opposite Revsudden north of Kalmar. Either spot makes an excellent base for watching the spectacular movements of wildfowl, divers and waders in spring and autumn. **Möckelmossen** A shallow lake 5 km east of Resmo church. It holds breeding Slavonian Grebe, Black Tern and Black-tailed Godwit, and is an autumn stop-over for Crane. Please view from the road along the southern shore to minimize disturbance. **Södviken** A shallow, sandy shore backed by meadows situated on the east coast in the north of Öland. Breeding birds include Avocet, and the area is excellent for migrant waders. **Mellby Ör** A small island connected to the east coast of southern Öland. It has breeding Black Tern, Avocet and Ruff and an excellent passage of waders, particularly at the southern tip. It is easily reached from the village of Mellby. **Petgärde Träsk** A reedy marsh some 15 km north of Borgholm. Breeding species include Little Gull, Black Tern, Godwit, Marsh and Montagu's Harriers, and Bearded and Penduline Tits. There is a bird tower on the right-hand side of the road north of Löt. The road to Stacktorp is a little farther on. Paths are marked. **Kapelludden** Lies on the east coast opposite Borgholm, the only town on Öland. The meadows along the shore hold Avocet and are excellent for migratory waders. There is a lighthouse and easy access. **ROUTE** The bridge to Öland is at Kalmar, which also has a provincial airport. Accommodation is available at several places on Öland, including Borgholm, and there are summer cottages to rent. Contact Ölands Turistforening, Box 115, 380 70 Borgholm (Tel. 0485 302 60).

SOUTHERN SKÅNE

Skåne is the southernmost province of Sweden and is one of the country's best areas for birds. Though best known for its migrants, especially waders and birds of prey at Falsterbo, there are several lakeland areas that attract breeding birds that are otherwise decidedly scarce as far north as this. Best of these are Red Kite and Golden Oriole.

Falsterbo lies at the end of a peninsula south of Malmö and faces west towards Denmark. Here the two coastlines of Scandinavia come together, and migrating birds of prey have no choice but to set out over the sea. In autumn they gain height by circling over the heath of Ljungen, and numbers are often very impressive, though many experienced birders now prefer to raptor-watch along the Falsterbo Canal where birds are more concentrated. Though lacking the variety of Gibraltar or the Bosporus, numbers are certainly greater, with over 14,000 birds counted on an exceptional day and over 1000 a day occurring several times a season. Late August and early September is best for Honey Buzzard and October for Buzzard and Rough-legged Buzzard. Other species include Sparrowhawk, Osprey, Marsh Harrier, Red Kite, plus the occasional Spotted or White-tailed Eagle. Best weather is clear and sunny with light westerly winds. When winds are from the south or south-east, birds cross the straits on a broad front.

Falsterbo Bird Observatory is just south of the village and has an active ringing programme. To the south the small hill of Kolabacken is a good raptor-watching spot, while just to the west is the lighthouse with its garden, good for small passerines. Migration of small birds in October can be very dramatic, with 1,000,000 on a good day. Waders concentrate mainly at the northern end of the peninsula at Slusan, Bakdjupet and

Revlarna. The last is particularly good, but easily disturbed. Birds include Temminck's and Little Stints, Spotted Redshank and even Broad-billed Sandpiper. The inlet of Foteviken in the north at the base of the peninsula is also good for these species, and both Avocet and Kentish Plover breed.

Inland are the lakes of Börringesjön, Häckerbergasjön, Krankesjön and Vombsjön. Though mostly worked over by summer visitors, these waters should not be ignored during migration. The woods at Börringesjön have Red Kite, Golden Oriole and Thrush Nightingale, while the marsh at the northern end has breeding Black Tern. Bean Geese and sometimes Crane appear on passage, as do many birds of prey. Krankesjön has extensive reedbeds, with breeding Bittern, Marsh Harrier, Black Tern and, occasionally, Great Reed Warbler. Vombsjön has passage Bean and White-fronted Geese. Eagles regularly winter, and Crane use the area as a September stop-over. The beautiful, wooded Fyledalen valley south-east of Vombsjon and north of Ystad has plentiful Red Kite and two pairs of Golden Eagle – the most accessible eagles in Sweden. Clearly there is much to be enjoyed in southernmost Sweden throughout the year.

SUMMER Red-necked Grebe, Greylag Goose, Red Kite, Marsh Harrier, Osprey, Sparrowhawk, Bittern, Kentish Plover, Avocet, Ruff, Black-tailed Godwit, Black Tern, Golden Oriole, Thrush Nightingale, Great Reed and Marsh Warblers, Bearded and Penduline Tits.
AUTUMN White-tailed Eagle, Buzzard, Honey and Rough-legged Buzzards, Osprey, Hen and Marsh Harriers, Sparrowhawk, Peregrine, Hobby, Crane, Spotted Redshank, Temminck's and Little Stints, Broad-billed Sandpiper, Red-throated Pipit.
WINTER Bean and White-fronted Geese, Golden Eagle, White-tailed Eagle, Rough-legged Buzzard.
ACCESS The Falsterbo area is well built-up and of open access. There are two hotels, and the bird observatory caters for the serious birder. All tend to be fully booked during September. There are also camping sites, but they close in mid-September. The best place for raptor-watching is along the north-to-south road that extends along the western side of Ljungen or along the Falsterbo canal to the east. Waders are concentrated in the northern part of the peninsula, north and west of Skanor. The southern point, Nabben, is always popular. Foteviken, the wader bay, is easily reached between Hölviksnäs and Vellinge. For the lakes, follow country roads with the aid of a map. Börringesjön is near Börringekloster. From there, turn north to Håckeberga at Dalby. From here, take minor roads to Silvakra for Kranesjön; Vombsjön lies 4 km east of Krankesjön.
ROUTE Falsterbo and the lakes are easily found from Malmö, which is itself reached by ferry from Copenhagen, or by road from Gothenburg. Ferries across the North Sea will determine which is the best route. Malmö does, however, have an airport for those in a hurry.

Store Mosse

This huge peat bog, now a national park, lies in southern Sweden, yet is more typical of the landscape of the far north. Huge marshy areas with ill-defined lakes, often well out of sight, make this a difficult place to work, but as the landscape is typically northern so are the birds. Store

Mosse is thus a very convenient place to see breeding birds such as Crane, Whooper Swan, Wood Sandpiper and Ruff. It also has Tengmalm's Owl, Hazelhen and Three-toed Woodpecker in the surrounding woodland. But note! These are very difficult birds to locate.

In the middle of the Mosse lies Kävsjön, a splendid lake with remarkably useful bird towers – take a telescope. Some other areas of open water can be seen from roads and there are plenty of trails.

SUMMER Red-throated Diver, Goldeneye, Whooper Swan, Goshawk, Marsh Harrier, Osprey, Hobby, Capercaillie, Black Grouse, Hazelhen, Crane, Golden Plover, Wood Sandpiper, Ruff, Tengmalm's and Pygmy Owls, Black and Three-toed Woodpeckers.

ACCESS The road between Hillerstorp and Värnamo passes the centre of the area near Kävsjön, where there are two bird towers east of the road. There is a car park near the first and marked trails facilitate exploration.

ROUTE The E4 between Helsingborg and Jönköping passes through Värnamo.

TÅKERN

This shallow lake is one of the best-known resorts in central Sweden and lies immediately east of the huge Lake Vättern. It is the combination of emergent vegetation and surrounding marshes that has produced such an enviable list of both breeding birds and migrant species. Among the former are Red-necked and Slavonian Grebes, Bittern, Osprey, Black Tern and Great Reed Warbler. Bearded Tit is abundant and even Penduline Tit may breed. Migrants include up to 47,000 (normally 30,000) Bean Geese from early to mid-October. The birds roost on the lake and fly out at dawn to graze the fields to the north-east. The sights and sounds of these great flocks are quite staggering – 'The most spectacular big bird event in inland Sweden' says Tommy Tyrberg, who did so much to ensure that the Swedish chapter of this book adequately represented the superb birding his country has to offer. The numbers of breeding birds have been increasing in recent years, and the numbers of duck in spring and autumn are quite outstanding. The Bean Geese are often accompanied by a few Whitefronts and even Lesser Whitefronts, and there is invariably a good selection of raptors present. Reedbeds restrict visibility in many areas and comparatively little can be seen from the surrounding roads. Fortunately there are bird towers in the north and the south as well as trails in the same areas. Waders are generally rather few.

SUMMER Red-necked and Slavonian Grebes, Bittern, Greylag Goose, Garganey, Marsh Harrier, Osprey, White-tailed Eagle, Crane, Water Rail, Spotted Crake, Black Tern, Icterine, Marsh and Great Reed Warblers, Red-backed Shrike, Bearded and Penduline Tits, Parrot Crossbill.

PASSAGE Bean and White-fronted Geese, Whooper Swan, Hen Harrier, Peregrine, Merlin, Short-eared Owl.

ACCESS From the south, take the E4 and then fork left on Route 50 at Ödeshog. Minor roads to the right lead around the lake, with other minor roads leading to the lake and to the three bird towers. Although Tåkern is a huge and somewhat unmanageable place and access is restricted in some areas during the breeding season, it is still possible to sample the various habitats quite well. Svalinge, in the north, is often the best place in spring, when the reeds and willows are good for Bearded and Penduline Tits. In summer both Black Tern and Bittern are often seen here. There is a car park and a trail leading to the hide. In the autumn the Hov area in the east is good for wildfowl, waders and the Bean Goose spectacular. In the south Glänås offers the best chance of White-tailed Eagle and Caspian Tern. A path leads westward from this tower to another at Svanshals (Swan's neck) udde where the church is crowned with a flying swan weathervane. The path is good for Bearded Tit, the hide for Black Tern. Väversundamaden, in the south-west, is good for spring waders including lekking Ruff and, in the last few years, the odd Great Snipe in mid-May. There are always Greylags here in summer and usually a few calling Spotted Crake on June evenings. Nearby, a little to the east, is Tåkern Field Station at Kvarnstugan. This offers limited, but reasonable, accommodation from April to August and in October and is the place to get the latest gen. Write to Tåkerns Fältstation, Box 204, S-595 22 Mjölby (Tel. 144-32119).

ROUTE Gothenburg is 250 km and Stockholm 350 km. Jönköping has a provincial airport and the main road from Stockholm to south Sweden passes quite close to the lake.

TYRESTA

Situated literally on the south-eastern outskirts of Stockholm, Tyresta is Sweden's most recently established national park. It consists of coniferous forest (largely virgin) and forms the largest block of such forest in the southern half of the country. The birds are mostly what one would expect of southern Sweden with Osprey, Black Grouse, Hazelhen, Pygmy Owl, etc, but to find such a collection so close to the capital is bound to attract future visitors to Sweden in some numbers. For the tight-scheduled businessman it may be possible to get Ural Owl at Färnebofjärden before breakfast, do a multi-million kroner deal before lunch, take in the Eagle Owl at the abandoned gas works at Frihamen actually in Stockholm itself and still manage Pygmy Owl at Tyresta before flying home in the evening. Please let me know if you attempt, let alone achieve, this remarkable coup, with or without the deal.

SUMMER Black-throated Diver, Osprey, Goshawk, Capercaillie, Black Grouse, Hazelhen, Tengmalm's and Pygmy Owls, Black Woodpecker, Parrot Crossbill.
ACCESS Leave Stockholm on Motorway 73 and exit at Handen. Take Route 227 and turn left after a few kilometres to Tyresta village in the south-west corner of the national park. Several footpaths facilitate exploration.
ROUTE Stockholm has excellent international air connections.

SWITZERLAND

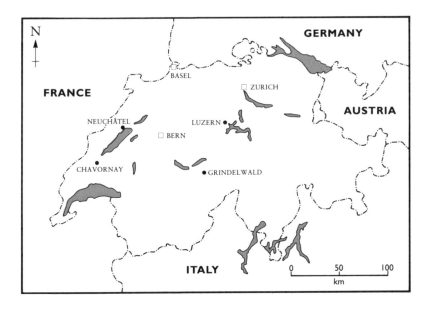

CHAVORNAY

For the lower part of its course, before joining Lac de Neuchâtel, the River Orbe runs over a flat plain that is particularly liable to flooding in spring. Here too are the old clay pits around Chavornay with their reedbeds, willow thickets and permanent open water. During the early part of spring the area is a favourite haunt of duck, but as the water level drops it offers fine opportunities for migrating waders. Birds such as Temminck's Stint and Marsh Sandpiper are regular and in most years there is a scattering of herons, including Little Egret and Night Heron. In fact, species as varied as Hobby, Baillon's Crake and Red-necked Phalarope use this lowland 'channel' to pass between the Jura and the Alps on their way northward.

Of course, most visitors will bird this area during the summer on their way to the mountains. At this time there are plentiful Black Kite, Hobby and Great Reed Warbler to be seen to add to the more spectacular high-altitude birds of this superb mountainous country.

PASSAGE Little Egret, Night Heron, Honey Buzzard, Marsh Harrier, Wood and Marsh Sandpipers, Temminck's Stint, Red-necked Phalarope, Bluethroat.
SUMMER Black Kite, Hobby, Little Bittern, Great Reed Warbler.
ACCESS Leave the Chavornay–Orbe road northwards 2 km west of Chavornay on a narrow road to the pits. The whole of the area along the Orbe between Bavois and Yverdon is worth exploring at any season.
ROUTE Northwards from Lausanne.

GRINDELWALD

This ski resort in the Bernese Oberland is the place where summer tourists touting binoculars should not be confused with fellow birders. They gather here to watch the intrepid perform on the North Face of the Eiger. Though decidedly touristy, Grindelwald makes an ideal base for alpine birding, with skilifts for easy access to the high slopes and a railway that actually runs inside the Eiger itself to Jungfraujoch at high altitude. Most of the facilities do not operate between the end of the ski season in mid-April and the start of the summer season in June.

The town itself has Alpine Chough and Black Redstart, while the odd Golden Eagle glides overhead. The first chair-lift north of the town has Peregrine, Nutcracker, Crested Tit, Firecrest, Crossbill and Citril Finch. Higher up there are Alpine Accentor and Snow Finch, while in the woods around the town there are Grey-headed Woodpecker and Fieldfare.

Down the valley near Interlaken, the rack-and-pinion railway at Wilderswil rises to Schnige Platte, with Honey Buzzard, Alpine Chough and Citril Finch. The Brienzer See, east of Interlaken, has Goosander as well as the ubiquitous Red and Black Kites. Farther east, beyond Brienz, is Meiringen and the nearby Reichenbach Falls. The woods here have both kites and Honey Buzzard, with Wallcreeper on the waterfall itself.

SUMMER Goosander, Buzzard, Honey Buzzard, Black and Red Kites, Grey-headed Woodpecker, Alpine Swift, Alpine Accentor, Ring Ouzel, Fieldfare, Water Pipit, Red-backed Shrike, Wallcreeper, Crested Tit, Redstart, Black Redstart, Firecrest, Citril and Snow Finches, Nutcracker, Alpine Chough.
ACCESS As detailed above, with plentiful and easy access to the tops.
ROUTE South-east on Route 6 from Berne.

Snow Finch

LUZERN

Luzern is a good centre from which to explore in every direction... including upwards. It also connects easily with the Grindelwald area, offering further opportunities of finding alpine birds. In that direction, south-west, is the Sarner See, where woodlands hold both buzzards and both kites. In Luzern itself the tower of the old bridge has Alpine Swift, while the parks and woodland along the northern shore of the lake have Black and Green Woodpeckers, together with Golden Oriole and Wood Warbler.

To the south, beyond Stans, is the ski resort of Engelberg, with Alpine Chough, Water Pipit and Rock Bunting together with a selection of raptors that includes Golden Eagle and Goshawk. To the east the lake turns sharply southwards through a wooded gorge, with Peregrine, both 'green' woodpeckers and breeding Red Kite. The best spot in this area is Seelisberg on the southern (western!) shore. Farther south Goldeneye summer around Flüelen, while at nearby Altdorf a road leads eastward to the Klausen Pass, with Nutcracker, Rock Thrush, Snow Finch and Alpine Chough.

SUMMER Goldeneye, Golden Eagle, Black and Red Kites, Buzzard, Honey Buzzard, Goshawk, Peregrine, Black, Green and Grey-headed Woodpecker, Alpine Swift, Water and Tree Pipits, Golden Oriole, Wood Warbler, Black Redstart, Rock Thrush, Nutcracker, Alpine Chough, Snow Finch, Rock Bunting.
ACCESS Sites detailed above.
ROUTE Luzern lies a short drive south of Zurich with its international communications.

NEUCHÂTEL

The northern end of Lac de Neuchâtel has extensive marshy margins extending for many kilometres along the shore between Neuchâtel town and Portalban. These are arguably the most important wetlands in Switzerland, both for breeding and for migrant birds. Waders flock the shoreline, and the damp marshes and the larger reedbeds hold Swiss rarities such as Little Bittern and Purple Heron. There are always Black Kites here and Marsh Harrier is a regular passage visitor.

The nearby hills are not high by local standards but their woods hold many species including Bonelli's Warbler, Crested Tit and Pied Flycatcher. At Le Fanel, a reserve covers both marsh and woodland and is as good a place as any to start working the area.

SUMMER Black-necked Grebe, Purple Heron, Little Bittern, Shoveler, Pochard, Black Kite, Bonelli's Warbler, Pied Flycatcher, Crested Tit.
PASSAGE Marsh Harrier, Little and Temminck's Stints.
ACCESS Start by walking the embankments along the canalized Broye River. These turn westwards off the road between Campelin and Cudrefin 16.5 km south-east of Neuchâtel. Le Fanel is administered by the Societe Romande pour l'Étude et la Protection des Oiseaux, Case Postale 548, 1401 Yverdon, CCP20–117 Neuchâtel, which issues permits.

TUNISIA

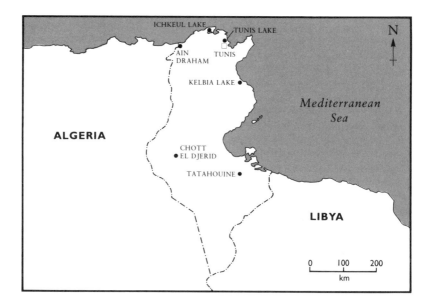

AIN DRAHAM

The road GP17 between Tabarka on the north coast and Jendouba to the south passes through an excellent area of rugged hills reaching the highest point at the Col des Ruines, near Ain Draham. The forests here are extensive and worth exploring for birds common in northern Europe but highly localized in Tunisia. Both the Col and the village have produced things such as three species of woodpecker, including Levaillant's, Bulbul, Blue Rock Thrush, Crossbill and Hawfinch. Doubtless there are more to be found.

SUMMER Woodpigeon, Tawny Owl, Levaillant's, Great Spotted and Lesser Spotted Woodpeckers, Jay, Bulbul, Blackcap, Sardinian Warbler, Blue Rock and Song Thrushes, Blackbird, Short-toed Treecreeper, Chaffinch, Crossbill, Hawfinch, Cirl Bunting.
ACCESS Drive to Ain Draham and continue northwards towards Col des Ruines. After 1.5 km stop and explore the woods. The woods south of Ain Draham are also worth exploring wherever there are large oaks.
ROUTE Jendouba is reached from Tunis on the GP6. Some groups link this area with Lake Ichkeul via Beja.

CHOTT EL DJERID

Djerid lies in central western Tunisia near the Algerian border, and is a vast salt lake variably flooded in winter. On occasion Flamingo and Ruddy Shelduck breed and there may be wader passage, but mostly this shallow lake is dry and virtually devoid of birds. Its inclusion here depends more on its surroundings, for the Sahara is nearby and the area is one of the best in North Africa for desert and semi-desert species. The two main areas of interest lie to the north-west, around Tozeur, and to the south-east, around Douz. Both should be included in any Tunisian itinerary.

The oasis at Tozeur supports Laughing Dove and Olivaceous Warbler, with House Bunting in the town. The surrounding area should produce Red-rumped Wheatear (common), with Desert, Mourning and White-crowned Black Wheatears. Desert and Bar-tailed Desert Larks with Bifasciated, and sandgrouse, Courser and Trumpeter Finch complete the normal desert species. Peregrine, Lanner and Long-legged Buzzard are all possible, and the edge of Djerid beyond Driz has produced Houbara Bustard.

In most seasons it is possible to drive the GP16 across the northern edge of Djerid to Kebili, with more larks, wheatears, falcons and some Little Swifts. South of Kebili, the road to Douz passes through oases with Fulvous Babbler, while at Douz itself there are Brown-necked Ravens on the rubbish tip. From Douz, a road leads to Hessai Oasis and then out into the desert. This route will probably be blocked by sand but it is worth exploring on foot for Tristram's, Desert and Scrub Warblers and Desert Sparrow. The last breeds at the end of the road at Ksar Rhilane but this spot requires an expedition or a specially chartered vehicle, driver and guide.

This area offers a splendid alternative to sub-Saharan Morocco for desert species. It deserves more attention than it has so far received.

SUMMER Flamingo, Ruddy Shelduck, Long-legged Buzzard, Lanner, Peregrine, Barbary Falcon, Houbara Bustard, Stone-curlew, Spotted Sand-grouse, Laughing Dove, Little Swift, Desert, Bar-tailed Desert, Bifasciated, Crested and Thekla Larks, Spotless Starling, Raven, Brown-necked Raven, Bulbul, Sardinian, Spectacled, Tristram's, Desert, Scrub, Marmora's and Fan-tailed Warblers, Mourning, Desert, Red-rumped, Black and White-crowned Black Wheatears, Blue Rock Thrush, Moussier's Redstart, Fulvous Babbler, Rock and Desert Sparrows, Trumpeter Finch, House Bunting.

Little Swift

ACCESS From Tozeur, explore along the various roads, seeking out different terrains. It is worth driving nearly to the Algerian border, and out towards Kriz. To the north, reach the Gorges de Seldja from the Gafsa road; watch for a sign to Thildja. This gorge has Marmora's Warbler, Little Swift and Rock Sparrow. The Tozeur area is worth a couple of days. The road across Djerid produces wheatears and larks, Little Swift and Trumpeter Finch. At Kebili turn south toward Douz, inspecting oases for Fulvous Babbler. Drive through Douz watching for a National Guard camp on the right. Turn left and continue to Hessai Oasis. Carry on into the desert for a few kilometres, then turn left (south) at the National Guard camp to the rubbish tip. Continue on the road toward Zafrane and turn right to Naxil. Chott Naxil is on the left after 5 km – for duck, herons, etc.
ROUTE Gabes is the nearest substantial town. Approach on the GP16.

ICHKEUL LAKE

This large lake near the north coast lies a few kilometres inland from Bizerte and is connected to the sea via the lake of that name. Five rivers run into Ichkeul, flushing through the lake each autumn and considerably increasing its size. Thereafter the water level drops until the following autumn, though some sea water flows into the lake when it is at its lowest. Ichkeul is a major wetland and a primary staging post for migrants crossing the Mediterranean and Sahara. In spring there is an enormous passage of waders, especially Ruff, and in winter huge numbers of geese stay here.

In fact, there are birds at all seasons at Ichkeul, with breeders including Marbled Teal and White-headed Duck, egrets and herons, Marsh Harrier and many warblers. During spring and autumn the wader flocks regularly include large numbers of Little Stint and Curlew Sandpiper and a few Marsh Sandpipers. There are Avocet and quite substantial flocks of Flamingo and, in late summer, Eleonora's Falcon regularly appears here.

The Jebel Ichkeul to the south rises to over 450 m and holds a few species, such as Crag Martin, that help build up a substantial list. Long-legged Buzzards use the mountain as a winter roost.

PASSAGE Flamingo, Osprey, Avocet, Kentish Plover, Temminck's and Little Stints, Curlew and Marsh Sandpipers, Ruff, Spotted Redshank, Greenshank, Sandwich Tern, Yellow Wagtail.
SUMMER Cattle and Little Egrets, Marbled Teal, White-headed Duck, Marsh Harrier, Lanner, Eleonora's Falcon, Water Rail, Purple Gallinule, Kentish Plover, Little Owl, Kingfisher, Crag Martin, Lesser Short-toed and Thekla Larks, Bulbul, Cetti's and Fan-tailed Warblers, Moussier's Redstart, Spanish Sparrow.
WINTER Little Egret, Flamingo, Wigeon, Teal, Pintail, Shoveler, Pochard, Marsh Harrier, Long-legged Buzzard, Barbary Falcon, Peregrine, Avocet, Golden Plover, Red-throated Pipit.
ACCESS The village of Tindja lies on the eastern shore and is an ideal starting point. To the north, the MC57 road offers many viewpoints and it is easy to explore. The various river mouths are often productive. In the south, the Jebel Ichkeul involves leaving the Tindja–Mateur road and exploring westward along the southern shore. This is an easily worked area that is as good as most other wetlands in the Mediterranean.

ROUTE Though Bizerte is an ideal base, most visitors arrive from Tunis on the GP7. Turn right on the MC54 12 km before Mateur to Tindja.

KELBIA LAKE

Ranked within the top category of wetlands of international importance, Kelbia is a substantial lake that is close to the main tourist areas of the Tunisian coast. Sousse is about 35 km distant and Monastir airport about 20 km farther, so it is frequently visited by birders with families and by those using a package holiday as the base for a birding trip. Its size varies according to season and rainfall and it does sometimes dry up completely. In normal circumstances, its emergent vegetation holds a good collection of breeding birds, including Squacco Heron, White-headed Duck, Purple Gallinule and Black-winged Stilt. It can, depending on water levels, also be a wintering ground for a variety of species, including Flamingo and Crane. On passage, wader numbers are often very impressive. The usual species include both stints, Ruff, Greenshank and Spotted Redshank, but there is often a concentration of Kentish Plovers and a regular flock of Dotterel. Birds of prey are often noted, and interesting terns are to be seen. Collared Pratincole may be present in large flocks and there are resident Crested and Thekla Larks. The arid hills to the west are worth a look. Black-bellied Sandgrouse and Coursers have been noted here.

SUMMER Squacco Heron, Little Egret, Shelduck, White-headed Duck, Purple Gallinule, Black-winged Stilt, Crested and Thekla Larks, Fantailed Warbler.
PASSAGE AND WINTER Flamingo, Little Egret, Squacco Heron, Glossy Ibis, White-headed Duck, Osprey, Bonelli's Eagle, Hen Harrier, Lanner, Peregrine, Crane, Purple Gallinule, Kentish Plover, Dotterel, Little and Temminck's Stints, Ruff, Greenshank, Caspian and Gull-billed Terns, Collared Pratincole, Black-bellied Sandgrouse, Cream-coloured Courser, Calandra, Short-toed, Crested and Thekla Larks, Marmora's, Spectacled and Fan-tailed Warblers.

White-headed Duck

J.D

ACCESS The best access point is at the north-western corner on the GP2 near the junction with the MC48. From here, a walk south along the shore will produce most of the birds. Because of the variable water level, there are no particular 'hot spots' and a general exploration is required.
ROUTE Leave Sousse northwards and turn left beyond Hamman-Sousse towards Kebira on the MC48. Monastir is the nearest airport.

TATAHOUINE

This is an alternative to Chott el Djerid for sub-desert species and is convenient to anyone staying on Djerba, or working the shorebirds, terns and gulls of Bahiret El Biban. Oases and semi-desert areas are north and south of the town, as well as along the minor roads and tracks that extend in all directions. Tatahouine is more a base for exploration than a bird spot itself. To the north of the town is an area of dry fields with Trumpeter Finch, Desert Lark and Temminck's Horned Lark. To the south is a dry river valley with Tristram's, Desert and Scrub Warblers and more besides.

SUMMER Lanner, Long-legged Buzzard, Stone-curlew, Desert, Bifasciated and Temminck's Horned Larks, Brown-necked Raven, Tristram's, Desert and Scrub Warblers, Trumpeter Finch.
ACCESS Do not suppose that the areas mentioned are outstanding or even particularly worth visiting. They are simply spots where others have seen birds that are almost certainly more widespread. A full report on this area would be most welcome. North of Tatahouine, watch the kilometre stones and stop halfway between 23 and 24. A sandy track leads eastward. Park and walk north for 200 m to an area of fields for Temminck's Horned and Desert Larks. The Oued Dekouk crosses the GP19 road 25 km south of Tatahouine. This is excellent for all the warblers.
ROUTE Medenine is the nearest large town 49 km north on the GP19. Ben Guerdane could be good near the coast to the east – via the MC111.

TUNIS LAKE

The visitor to Tunis with only a little time available has one of the best wetlands in the country just beyond the hotel doorstep. A quick taxi ride to the esplanade, north of the port area, leads to the lake and the birds. Two roads lead out towards the coast; both provide excellent birding.

Lake Tunis is a salt-water lagoon connected to the Mediterranean and, therefore, a home to many seabirds. It often has several thousand wintering Flamingoes, is Tunisia's major haunt of Cormorant (about 5000), has several hundred Black-necked Grebes and a good population of wintering duck. Egrets and waders are present during passage, and gulls regularly include Slender-billed. At the end of the road lie the ruins of Carthage.

PASSAGE AND WINTER Black-necked Grebe, Cormorant, Little Egret, Flamingo, Teal, Avocet, Kentish Plover, Little Stint, Slender-billed Gull, Sandwich Tern.
ACCESS Take either the road along the northern shore or that through the lagoon towards Carthage and La Marsa, both eastward out of the city.
ROUTE Tunis environment.

TURKEY

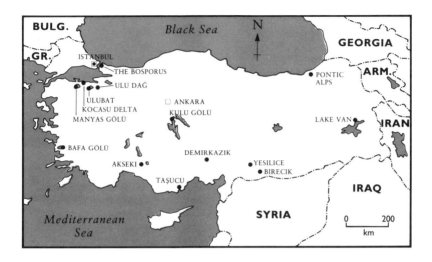

AKSEKI

Akseki has an unfriendly hotel, its prison and its graveyard. The last of these is full of interesting birds and especially Olive-tree Warbler. This is one of the specialities of the area, with White-backed Woodpecker and Krüper's Nuthatch. There are other birds here too, including Rüppell's Warbler, Masked Shrike, Great Spotted Cuckoo and Cretzschmar's Bunting.

SUMMER Long-legged Buzzard, Booted and Short-toed Eagles, Syrian and White-backed Woodpeckers, Krüper's Nuthatch, Great Spotted Cuckoo, Masked Shrike, Roller, Blue Rock Thrush, Orphean, Rüppell's, Subalpine and Olive-tree Warblers, Cretzschmar's Bunting.
ACCESS The graveyard opposite the prison in the south-east of town has Olive-tree Warbler and Masked Shrike. Take the Konya road for 7.9 km to a lay-by on the right. A clearing in the woods across the road has White-backed Woodpecker. 50 m farther on a path leads left to a radar station. After 600 m there is another clearing for the 'pecker. Krüper's Nuthatch is numerous. South of Akseki there are Rüppell's, and after 8 km a small conifer wood on the left is followed by a turning on the right. Olive-tree Warbler can be seen among scattered trees behind the plantation, as can Masked Shrike and Great Spotted Cuckoo. For raptors, a track east from the south of the plantation leads to a rocky area beyond a small village.
ROUTE Konya has an airport.

BAFA GÖLÜ

This splendid area lies on the coast of south-western Turkey, and consists of the large Bafa Gölü, plus the nearby coastal Karine Gölü and the mouth of the River Büyük Menderes. The whole was formerly the delta-estuary of the Menderes but has been extensively reclaimed for cotton growing. It is particularly attractive to those taking a package holiday along this coast (many mass-holiday companies feature Izmir and its surroundings).

The bird list is extensive, regularly producing Pygmy Cormorant, Dalmatian Pelican, a variety of herons and egrets, Ruddy Shelduck, Spur-winged Plover, Penduline Tit, and both sought-after kingfishers. Migrants include Hobby, White-winged Black Tern and waders, and the only drawback to the area is the apparently ferocious dog near the main access point which is now an integral part of the Turkish birding scene having been a pest for more years than any reasonable dog could expect to live.

Between Bafa Gölü and Karine Gölü lies an area of fields, bounded in the north by interesting but relatively unexplored mountains (Peregrine and eagles) and in the south by scrub-covered hills with Cretzschmar's Bunting. This area regularly produces Fan-tailed Warbler, Bee-eater and Eleonora's Falcon. The latter is also found at Karine Gölü, along with Flamingo and more pelicans, and this is probably the roost for the herons that fly westwards from Bafa at dusk. Clearly the collection of breeding and passage birds makes this an excellent and accessible area, but in winter the numbers of duck rise to a staggering 300,000, with additional numbers of geese. Outstanding are over 100,000 Wigeon, 60,000 Pintail, 3000 Red-crested Pochard, plus 3500 Great Crested Grebe. The whole area is quite beautiful.

SUMMER Pygmy Cormorant, Dalmatian Pelican, Little Egret, Squacco, Night and Purple Herons, Little Bittern, Flamingo, Ruddy Shelduck, Short-toed and White-tailed Eagles, Long-legged Buzzard, Peregrine, Hobby, Eleonora's Falcon, Mediterranean Gull, Kentish and Spur-winged Plovers, Black-winged Stilt, Alpine Swift, Great Spotted Cuckoo, Bee-eater, Rufous Bushchat, Cetti's, Fan-tailed and Icterine Warblers, Penduline Tit, Lesser Pied and Smyrna Kingfishers, Cretzschmar's Bunting.
WINTER Great Crested Grebe, Cormorant, Pygmy Cormorant, Dalmatian Pelican, Great White Egret, Teal, Mallard, Wigeon, Pintail, Shoveler, Red-crested Pochard, Pochard, Ruddy Shelduck, White-fronted Goose, Curlew.
ACCESS Take the road south from Soke to the bridge over the Menderes. Turn left, past the tea house, on a track for 2 km to a dilapidated farmhouse (dog). Walk to the shores of Bafa Gölü with reedbeds for Penduline Tit, etc. A scrubby hill south of the track leads to Cretzschmar's Bunting etc. North of the Menderes bridge drive east along the embankment to the lakeshores. Only the south-west of Bafa Gölü has reeds and cover.

Return to the bridge and tea house and take the turning to Akkoy. Turn right in the village and cross the Menderes again. Walking the river may produce the kingfishers. The track continues along the landward side of Karine Gölü and at the end joins an east–west track between Doganbey on the beach and the main Soke road.
ROUTE There is an airport north at Izmir where the main package holiday companies land.

BIRECIK

Birecik is a small village in eastern Turkey just a few kilometres north of the Syrian border. A colony of Bald Ibis formerly bred on the crags above the village, but repeated visits by Ibis-twitchers have produced a good range of Anatolian species in the area. Local specialities include Bruce's Scops Owl in the tiny park in the south of the town, and two species of sandgrouse that regularly fly in from the east at dawn to drink from the Euphrates on the islands north of the town. Lesser Pied and Smyrna Kingfishers haunt the river, and Menetries' and Graceful Warblers are common along the adjacent scrub. The extensive wadi just north of town, east of the river is worth exploring for both species of rock sparrow, and there is often an Eagle Owl present. Blue-cheeked Bee-eater can be found on the west bank north of an enclosed wood, as well as in sand pits some 5 km to the south on the eastern bank. The sand pits also hold Dead Sea Sparrow, which is, however, common among the orchards and scrub to the north of the wadi. Other species of note include Desert Finch, Chukar and See-see Partridges, Desert Lark, at its only known Turkish site, and Bimaculated Lark and even regular Long-eared Owl.

SUMMER Egyptian Vulture, Short-toed Eagle, Long-legged Buzzard, Lesser Kestrel, Chukar, See-see Partridge, Little Ringed and Spur-winged Plovers, Black-bellied and Pin-tailed Sandgrouse, Laughing Dove, Nightjar, Bruce's Scops and Long-eared Owls, Little Swift, Lesser Pied and Smyrna Kingfishers, Blue-cheeked Bee-eater, Syrian Woodpecker, Desert, Short-toed, Lesser Short-toed and Bimaculated Larks, Rufous Bushchat, Black-eared and Red-tailed Wheatears, Graceful, Great Reed, Olivaceous, Upcher's and Menetries' Warblers, Spanish, Dead Sea, Pale Rock, Yellow-throated and Rock Sparrows, Black-headed Bunting.
ACCESS There is a hotel in Birecik, as well as a bank and an 'excellent' restaurant. The main areas are the small park in the southern part of the town and the sand pits some 5 km south on the east bank. To the north, there is a track leading northwards just beyond a café on the west bank. The east bank, north of the town, is the best, with the main wadi about 3 km away. Continuing north, a small stream joins the Euphrates and beyond here is an area of scrub and orchards. Allow two or three days here.
ROUTE Gaziantep, some 60 km to the west, is the nearest town. As everywhere in Turkey, there is a bus service.

DEMIRKAZIK

This high mountain area is noted as the best place in Turkey for Caspian Snowcock but it also offers a good range of high-altitude species to those intrepid enough to face the efforts of searching for them. Snowcock are far from obliging. Firstly, one must leave for a 90–150-minute hike in darkness to arrive at the high snowfields before dawn. Then, as the light emerges, listen for the 'Curlew-like' call and locate the birds before they climb up among the screes and crags. Once they have done that, there is little chance of finding them again. Calling stops by about 8 a.m. in mid-May, while by mid-June the snow is disappearing and with it any reasonable chance. There is, however, much more to Demirkazik than this species. Radde's Accentor is regularly seen, along with Finsch's Wheatear, Shore Lark, Rock Bunting and Red-fronted Serin. The gorges are one of the most reliable places for Wallcreeper, and there are usually a few Lammergeier and Griffons to be seen. Other good birds include Crimson-winged and Snow Finches, with Bimaculated Lark and Isabelline Wheatear lower down.

SUMMER White Stork, Griffon Vulture, Lammergeier, Golden Eagle, Caspian Snowcock, Chukar, Scops Owl, Alpine Swift, Bimaculated, Short-toed and Shore Larks, Crag Martin, Water Pipit, Grey Wagtail, Alpine and Radde's Accentors, Black Redstart, Wheatear, Isabelline and Finsch's Wheatears, Rock Thrush, Cetti's Warbler, Rock Nuthatch, Wallcreeper, Alpine Chough, Chough, Snow Finch, Red-fronted Serin, Serin, Crimson-winged Finch, Rock Bunting.

ACCESS Off the E98 between Nigde and Kayseri. North of Nigde turn right just beyond Ovacik to Baldaras. Continue towards Camardi and watch for the hill village of Demirkazik to the left. Continue and turn left across the river (some 8 km before Camardi), then proceed over a motorable track to the village. Beyond Demirkazik is a path to a mountain lodge which offers accommodation, but no food. Two gorges open out above the lodge. Take the right hand one up to the snow line, allowing 90–150 minutes prior to dawn for Snowcock. Cross to the left and descend down the second gorge back to the lodge. A cup-shaped hollow at the top of the second gorge holds Radde's Accentor, Finsch's Wheatear, etc.

ROUTE Kayseri has an airport with flights from Ankara.

ISTANBUL AND THE BOSPORUS

The spectacular migration of storks and birds of prey attracts hordes of birders every autumn. The main period is from late August, when Honey Buzzard reaches peak numbers, until early October. Birds vary according to season, but generally mid-September has the largest variety, with up to 18 different species of raptor seen in a day. At this time, Lesser Spotted Eagle, Buzzard, Short-toed Eagle, Booted Eagle, Goshawk, Levant Sparrow-hawk and Black Kite are regularly seen. White Storks pass over in their thousands, but much earlier in the season. Return passage is lighter, but still produces the species variety from mid-March to early April.

Though these birds are the main attraction, there are many other migrants in the area including Levantine Shearwater. Among small birds in the bushes are Red-breasted Flycatcher and occasional Green Warbler. Istanbul is noted for Laughing Dove and abundant Alpine Swift.

White Stork

AUTUMN Levantine Shearwater, White and Black Storks, Lesser Spotted, Short-toed and Booted Eagles, Buzzard, Honey Buzzard, Griffon and Egyptian Vultures, Goshawk, Levant Sparrowhawk, Black and Red Kites, Hobby, Lesser Kestrel, Red-footed Falcon, Wryneck, Alpine Swift, Laughing Dove, Redstart, Red-breasted Flycatcher.

ACCESS Istanbul has many hotels and restaurants, and is connected to the Asian shore by two modern bridges and by frequent ferry services. The main watchpoint is a café on Buçuk Çamliça, the larger of the Çamliça Hills. This can be reached by taking the northern motorway bridge and exiting on the D100 signed 'Çamliça'. Keep following signs – often obscure. There is also a bus from Uskudar, reached by ferry across the Bosporus. In peak season the café tables will be protected by the owner for bona fide customers, but there is no problem in standing by the balustrade overlooking the Bosporus and and Istanbul. A zealous gardener will ask you to move if you settle on the lawn in front of the balustrade. The valley to the right beyond the radar towers often gets huge concentrations of raptors rising on thermals depending on wind direction. Though there are other good raptor-watching sites around the Bosporus, Çamliça remains the classic and most dependable site. Arrival at 10 a.m. is fine.

ROUTE Istanbul has international flights.

KULU GÖLÜ

This small (by Turkish standards) lake lies south of Ankara and is generally regarded as an essential ingredient in any tour of Turkey. It is easily found, relatively easy to work, and regularly produces a variety of breeding and passage birds. The shallow margins hold passage waders and the reedbeds produce the odd heron and occasional Thick-billed Reed Bunting. The flock of White-headed Duck is significant and may on occasion exceed 500 birds in late summer. Flamingo is also regular and other interesting species include Gull-billed (200 pairs) and White-winged Black Terns, Mediterranean (390 pairs) and Slender-billed Gulls (100 pairs), Ruddy Shelduck (50 pairs), Glossy Ibis, plus a variety of waders that includes Marsh Sandpiper, Red-necked Phalarope and, outstandingly, Greater Sand Plover, five pairs of which breed. The most abundant pipit is usually Red-throated, and Citrine Wagtail is sometimes seen. The surrounding land has Great Bustard.

SUMMER Black-necked Grebe, Purple and Squacco Herons, Glossy Ibis, Flamingo, Ruddy Shelduck, Gadwall, Garganey, Pintail, Red-crested Pochard, White-headed Duck, Red-footed Falcon, Hobby, Great Bustard, Avocet, Black-winged Stilt, Kentish and Greater Sand Plovers, Little and Temminck's Stints, Red-necked Phalarope, Ruff, Marsh Sandpiper, Collared Pratincole, Little, Mediterranean and Slender-billed Gulls, Gull-billed and White-winged Black Terns, Black-bellied Sandgrouse, Roller, Short-toed, Lesser Short-toed, Calandra and Bimaculated Larks, Red-throated and Tawny Pipits, Citrine Wagtail, Great Reed Warbler, Isabelline Wheatear.

ACCESS Leave the E5 south of Ankara on Route 35 towards Konya. Stop in Kulu and turn left past the Turkish I.S. Bank. Continue over a stream on a gravel track to the south-west corner of the lake. Walk from here along the western shore, the Sand Plovers often being found at the end along the northern shore, and explore the reedbeds and fields. Return and explore the southern shore; a sandy spit often holds waders. There is a hotel in the town (poor reports).

ROUTE Reached on the E5 from Ankara with its international airport.

LAKE VAN

Van is a huge inland sea in the far east of Turkey near the Russian border. It is a magnificent blue and virtually devoid of birds. It does, however, have a number of small rivers running into it, plus a number of adjacent marshes with a splendid variety of interesting birds. There are several islands, such as Aknamara, that hold breeding Armenian Gull, Night Heron, Ruddy Shelduck plus Lesser Kestrel and Olivaceous Warbler.

Van town is a bustling place with several hotels that have apparently improved over the years. It is about 5 km from Van Citadel, which is a good spot for exploring the marshes south of the railway which are among the best birding spots in Turkey. Crane, Marsh Harrier, Caspian and White-winged Black Terns, Little Bittern, Roller, Moustached Warbler and White Stork may all be seen. The marshes to the north across the railway have waders and duck, including White-headed Duck.

East of Van, the railway runs through a gorge where Eagle Owl may be seen and where Grey-necked Bunting and Pied Wheatear are relatively common. Alternatively, the road to Ercek has these species, as well as Lanner, Long-legged Buzzard, Crimson-winged Finch and Bimaculated Lark, with Red-necked and Black-necked Grebes, White-winged Black Tern, Ruddy Shelduck, Crane and Stilt on the various waters viewable from the road.

In the north-east of Van, just beyond where the road to Muradiye turns off, is the Bendimahi marsh. Here, there are often good concentrations of White Pelican, Gull-billed and Caspian Terns, Black-winged Pratincole, White-headed Duck, Crane and Ruddy Shelduck. Citrine Wagtail may be found among the areas of short grass and Broad-billed Sandpiper is pretty regular. Rock Thrush may be quite common along the road to Ercis.

Several of the roads leaving Van lead through high-level passes. Some are known to hold Radde's Accentor and Red-fronted Serin among others, and there is no reason to suppose that others do not. Several other excursions from Van may be rewarding. To the north, Dogubayazit and adjacent Ishakpasa have Rock Nuthatch, Snow Finch, Rock Sparrow and Finsch's Wheatear, while farther north still the marshes alongside Mount Ararat have Marsh and Montagu's Harriers, Crane and Ruddy Shelduck.

One of the most outstanding birds of the Van area – Demoiselle Crane – is worth the effort involved. This species may be found along the River Murat north of Bulanik but it is a 6-km walk plus a possible 4-km exploration to find them – even if they are there. Other birds include Crane, Pygmy Cormorant and Quail, plus possible Great Bustard. Bulanik marsh lies some 10 km to the west and is good for Glossy Ibis and Pygmy Cormorant. There is still much to explore in the Van area.

SUMMER Red-necked and Black-necked Grebes, Pygmy Cormorant, White Pelican, Little Bittern, Night, Squacco and Purple Herons, Little Egret, White Stork, Glossy Ibis, Flamingo, Ruddy Shelduck, Ferruginous and White-headed Duck, Egyptian and Griffon Vultures, Marsh and Montagu's Harriers, Goshawk, Golden Eagle, Lesser Kestrel, Hobby, Quail, Crane, Demoiselle Crane, Great Bustard, Black-winged Stilt, Avocet, Greater Sand Plover, Armenian Gull, Gull-billed, Caspian, Whiskered and White-winged Black Terns, Black-bellied Sandgrouse, Calandra and Bimaculated Larks, Citrine Wagtail, Isabelline and Finsch's Wheatears, Bluethroat, Rock Thrush, Savi's, Marsh, Moustached, Great Reed and Olivaceous Warblers, Rock Nuthatch, Penduline Tit, Rock Sparrow, Red-fronted Serin, Crimson-winged Finch, Ortolan and Grey-necked Buntings.

ACCESS The area of eastern Van is easily worked at the Citadel, at Erçek Gölü and the other waters along the Van–Erçek road, and at Bendimahi marsh. Baskale is a plateau above the army camp just north of the town, beyond which a track leads up to a hillside village with a narrow valley beyond for Radde's Accentor and Bluethroat. Grey-necked Bunting is below the village; lower still are Crimson-winged Finch and Red-fronted Serin. There are Cranes in many areas but Demoiselle are found at Bulanik. There is a dilapidated bridge across a river immediately north of the town, which is on Route 60 north-west of Lake Van. Watch for an 'orange' building. A track leads to the River Murat. At the river explore westwards. For Bulanik marsh, head west to the fork for Muş and Varto. At this point a path leads south to the marsh, which cannot be seen from the road. A short distance along the Varto road, more or less in Balatos, a path/track leads to the River Muret. Take care to find the bridge across a narrow stream and in 4 km walking you will find the Murat. Walk westwards for Demoiselle Crane on one of the islands. Great Bustard, Lesser Short-toed Lark and Black-bellied Sandgrouse have all been seen here.

ROUTE There is an airport at Van and a train service from Ankara, and a train service also from Istanbul (on the Asian shore) to Tatvan. Regular ferries connect Tatvan and Van. There are hotels in most towns: the standard of accommodation varies from satisfactory to downright disgusting. Take a padlock and key and/or large wooden wedges to ensure privacy.

Black-headed Bunting

MANYAS GÖLÜ

Kuş Çenneti on the north-eastern shore was Turkey's first bird reserve, mainly for breeding herons and egrets, with up to 2500 pairs among the lakeside willows. These include Grey, Night and Purple together with Little Egret, Little Bittern and Spoonbill. Dalmatian Pelican also breeds and large numbers of White Pelican regularly pass through. The reedy woodland holds Pygmy Cormorant, Scops Owl, Penduline Tit and, in the more open areas, Great Reed and Savi's Warblers. There are Spur-winged Plover, Marsh Harrier, Roller, Bee-eater, Great Spotted Cuckoo and Rufous Bushchat among over 90 breeding species. Some 200 species have been seen here.

Passage often brings huge numbers of White Storks, and Red-footed Falcons may be present in significant flocks.

SUMMER White Stork, Pygmy Cormorant, Dalmatian Pelican, Night and Purple Herons, Little Egret, Little Bittern, Spoonbill, Lesser Kestrel, Spur-winged and Kentish Plovers, Scops and Long-eared Owls, Roller, Bee-eater, Great Spotted Cuckoo, Penduline Tit, Great Reed, Savi's and Olivaceous Warblers, Rufous Bushchat, Black-headed Bunting.
PASSAGE White Stork, White Pelican, Glossy Ibis, Ferruginous Duck, Red-footed Falcon, Caspian and White-winged Black Terns.
ACCESS Kuş Çenneti is signposted at the north-east of the lake near Sigirciatik. It is well fenced and you may have to raise the warden by making local enquiries. Most species can be seen from outside anyway.
ROUTE Leave Route 2 south of Bandirma, on the Sea of Marmara.

PONTIC ALPS

This area of the Pontic Alps lies north of the road from Gümüşhane to Erzurum and is one of the least explored areas in Turkey. Though parts are known and attract birders every year, there is much to explore and un-doubtedly many more places that would produce the region's special birds.

In 1972, I rode from near Gümüşhane up into the hills to a summer village, where Scarlet Rosefinch was common and where Water Pipit, Shore Lark, Sombre Tit and a variety of eagles were easily seen. No doubt there are other, more accessible villages, where these and other species occur.

Sivri Kaya lies between Ispir and Ikizdere, high on the shoulder of Kirkla Dağ, and is a prime spot for Caucasian Blackcock and Caspian Snowcock. Both can be found among the crags and rhododendron scrub high above the road north of the village. Access is difficult and you must get there before dawn. Mountain Chiffchaff is another attraction here.

Ikizdere has Green Warblers in good woodland, but they are as easily found at Sumela Monastery near Macka inland from Trabzon, where there is also Red-breasted Flycatcher. In the other direction, Ispir has Semi-collared Flycatcher among valley orchards north and south of the town. From here, a track leads through woodland for Syrian Woodpecker, Golden Oriole and Hobby. Borçka is in north-eastern Turkey near the Ukraine border and the Black Sea. It lies in the Çoruh Valley at the head of a route that funnels migrating raptors through the Pontic Alps before they spread out on their southward journey through the eastern Mediterranean. This funnelling effect was discovered in 1976 but has so far attracted relatively few foreign birders. Nearly 400,000 birds of prey use this corridor around the eastern side of the Black Sea, more than the Bosporus concentration. Buzzard, Black Kite and Honey Buzzard are dominant, and there are numbers of other birds scarce or absent from the westerly route, including Pallid Harrier, Saker, Spotted Eagle, Steppe Eagle, Golden Eagle, White-tailed Eagle and Imperial Eagle. There is a disgusting Sparrowhawk trapping industry here, and appalling hunting of raptors, but do not interfere.

SUMMER Egyptian Vulture, Black Kite, Goshawk, Golden and Booted Eagles, Hobby, Caucasian Blackcock, Caspian Snowcock, Hoopoe, Green, Great Spotted and Syrian Woodpeckers, Shore Lark, Water Pipit, Grey Wagtail, Dipper, Alpine Accentor, Dunnock, Black-eared Wheatear, Black Redstart, Rock Thrush, Marsh and Green Warblers, Mountain Chiffchaff, Semi-collared Flycatcher, Chough, Scarlet Rosefinch, Crimson-winged Finch, Rock Bunting.
AUTUMN White-tailed, Short-toed, Spotted, Lesser Spotted, Steppe, Imperial, Golden and Booted Eagles, Egyptian and Griffon Vultures, Black Kite, Marsh, Hen, Montagu's and Pallid Harriers, Goshawk, Levant Sparrowhawk, Sparrowhawk, Buzzard, Honey and Long-legged Buzzards, Lesser Kestrel, Kestrel, Red-footed Falcon, Hobby, Saker, Peregrine.
ACCESS Sumela Monastery is easily reached from Trabzon via Macka. There is a zigzag path through lovely woodland, with Green Warbler and Rosefinch, to the monastery, which is set into a sheer rock face. Continue upwards, join a track to the left and descend back to the river (Dipper and Red-breasted Flycatcher) via another track. Sivri Kaya lies on the Rize–Erzurum road between Ispir and Ikizdere. About 800 m on the Ispir side, an inconspicuous path leads up the hill, passes a few houses and continues into an area where small rhododendrons can be seen above and below. This spot, where the path disappears, is best for Snowcock and Blackcock; but you must be here before dawn. Mustapha Savri lives opposite the tea room in the village; arrange for him to act as guide – pay him! There is a hotel. Across the river, opposite the village, the conifer woods hold Mountain Chiffchaff. Ikizdere About 1.5 km south of the village of Ikizdere, a bridge crosses the river. Take this, and turn back for 400 m alongside the stream where a steep path zigzags through the woods for Green Warbler. Ispir lies just off the Erzurum–Rize road. Take the village road and search the orchards on the right near the river for Semi-collared Flycatcher. It may be elusive and may also be in an orchard near the bus station north of the village. Continue up the river valley for other species. Hotel here. Borçka lies inland from the Black Sea coast and is reached by taking the road north from Erzurum. This largely follows the Çoruh Valley which is the main funnel for raptors across the Pontic Alps. Late September would seem to be the best time, but birds pass from late August to mid-October. ROUTE Airports at Trabzon and Erzurum with car-hire possibilities at the former.

TAŞUCU

Taşucu nestles in a small bay on the south coast and is one of the ferry ports for Turkish Cyprus. It is handy for exploring the largely reclaimed, but still internationally important, Göksu delta. All who have worked this area have found it a slog, including determined walkers and motorists prepared to drive along the beaches. The collection of species is what one could reasonably expect in this part of the Mediterranean, with Spur-winged Plover, Ruddy Shelduck, White Pelican and Marbled Teal heading the bill. There is also Purple Gallinule at its only Turkish site, White-tailed Plover and Graceful Warbler, and good passage of waders that may include Greater Sand Plover. Crakes can be regularly seen crossing gaps in the reeds. A fine collection of breeding waterbirds includes White Pelican (probably), Little Bittern, Night Heron, Great White Egret, Glossy Ibis, Spoonbill and Ferruginous Duck. There are also Lesser Kestrel, Black Francolin, Pratincole, and Smyrna and Pied Kingfishers. Audouin's Gull breeds along the coast and is regularly seen from the pier in the evening. The hillsides above the village have Yellow-vented Bulbul.

Inland, the Göksu River has good, if undramatic, cliffs where vultures, eagles, Bulbul and other rocky-based birds can be found. This is an outstanding area and worth much more than a few days' exploration. In winter there are great numbers of wildfowl plus Flamingo and Spotted Eagle.

SUMMER Great Crested Grebe, Shag, Pygmy Cormorant, White Pelican, Squacco Heron, Little Bittern, Little and Great White Egrets, Purple Heron, White Stork, Glossy Ibis, Ruddy Shelduck, Marbled Teal, Egyptian and Griffon Vultures, Lesser Spotted and Short-toed Eagles, Hobby, Eleonora's Falcon, Chukar, Black Francolin, Water Rail, Purple Gallinule, Little, Baillon's and Spotted Crakes, Black-winged Stilt, Greater Sand, Spur-winged and White-tailed Plovers, Audouin's Gull, Syrian Woodpecker, Rock Nuthatch, Red-rumped Swallow, Crag Martin, Blue Rock Thrush, Yellow-vented Bulbul, Black-eared Wheatear, Graceful Warbler, Spanish Sparrow, Cretzschmar's Bunting.

ACCESS The pier at Taşucu and the road north from Silifke to Mut are easily found. The Göksu delta is more awkward. Leave Taşucu on the Silifke road and after a fenced-off factory area of about 2 km, a track on the right leads to the beach. Motor or walk left, hopping over the dunes from time to time in the search for an extensive reed-fringed lagoon. A hired motorbike might prove the perfect way of exploring the whole of the estuary. The development of a holiday village among the dune scrub (excellent for small migrants) that separates the Akgöl lagoon from the sea will doubtless damage the area, but will facilitate access for birders.

ROUTE The E24 runs westwards from Adana, which has an airport. To the south of Adana lies the multiple delta known as Çukurova. Though it still has some excellent birds, it is best known as the cotton growing centre of the country. Dead Sea Sparrow is said to be common here.

ULUBAT, ULU DAĞ AND THE KOCASU DELTA

Ulubat, or Apolyont as it was formerly known, is the central of the three famous lakes that lie on the southern shore of the Sea of Marmara, west of Istanbul. Manyas to the west is treated separately, while Iznik to the east is generally disturbed by tourists, though still having some good breeding and passage birds.

Ulubat is shallow, with extensive areas of reeds along the western end and the north-western shores. As spring turns to summer large areas of mud-bank dry out, especially at the mouth of the Mustafakemalpassa, and this then becomes the breeding ground of Spur-winged Plover and Stilt. Later, the number of passage waders here may be most impressive.

The western reedbeds and tamarisks are the most obvious and easy to work area and a walk along the motorable track produces a variety of species, including Night Heron, Bittern, Little Bittern, Purple Heron and Ferruginous Duck. Whiskered and Black Terns breed among the lily pads, and there are many interesting smaller birds in the surrounding fields. An equally productive site is the village of Gölyazi, which is sign-posted from the main road that skirts the northern shore. Before reaching this charming, unspoilt village there are views over the reedbeds to the right for Marsh Harrier, egrets and Pygmy Cormorant. In the village itself there is a fish factory on the right and a request for access gives views over a superb area of reeds and mud for Whiskered and Black Terns, Pratincole and harriers. Continuing to the end of the village, park outside the church and examine the shoreline on either side of the bridge for waders. Be nice to the kids, who are curious and do not beg.

Between Gölyazi and the western end of the lake a signed track leads to Kuş Çenneti (not to be confused with signs at Manyas bearing the same inscription). This is another area of rough marsh with views over the lake.

Ulu Dağ is a significant mountain rising to almost 2130 m above Bursa. It is a national park and has good road access and even a cable-car. Its fame rests on its convenient situation adjacent to the well-known lakes and within easy distance of Istanbul. Here is one of the best areas to see Alpine Accentor, Krüper's Nuthatch, Red-fronted Serin and Lammergeier.

The Kocasu delta lies at the mouth of the Kocacay River that drains Ulubat. Three large lakes, Arapciftligi, Poyraz and Dalyan Gölü, lie adjacent to the river and shoreline, and the whole area offers some of the best birding to be found in the western part of the country. As with so many other good bird areas, it is the variety of habitat that accounts for its richness. Shoreline, lakes, reeds, mud, flooded woodland and fields and scrub-covered hillsides are all found within a small area. The result is a remarkable variety of species for such a generally underworked area. Stilt, Ruddy Shelduck, White-tailed Eagle, Whiskered Tern, Stone-curlew and Kentish Plover breed, as does a decent-sized colony of Pratincole along with a few Tawny Pipits and Short-toed Larks.

West of Dalyan Gölü is a superb area of flooded forest over which Lesser Spotted Eagle and Honey Buzzard display, and where a thorough investigation may produce Olive-tree Warbler, White-backed Woodpecker, Masked Shrike and River Warbler. There are really outstanding numbers of birds here, with Nightingale and Red-backed Shrike dominating.

SUMMER (Ulubat) Great Crested and Black-necked Grebes, Pygmy Cormorant, Purple, Night and Squacco Herons, Bittern, Little Bittern, Little Egret, Glossy Ibis, Greylag Goose, Ferruginous Duck, Marsh and Montagu's Harriers, Lesser Kestrel, Whiskered, Black and Common Terns, Black-winged Stilt, Kentish and Spur-winged Plovers, Collared Pratincole, Rüppell's and Olivaceous Warblers. (Ulu Dağ) Golden Eagle, Lammergeier, Goshawk, Buzzard, Alpine Accentor, Rock Thrush, Isabelline Wheatear, Water Pipit, Shore Lark, Krüper's Nuthatch, Ortolan Bunting, Crossbill, Siskin, Red-fronted Serin. (Kocasu Delta) Pygmy Cormorant,

Ruddy Shelduck, Short-toed, White-tailed and Lesser Spotted Eagles, Honey Buzzard, Marsh Harrier, Kentish Plover, Stone-curlew, Pratincole, Short-toed Lark, Tawny Pipit, Golden Oriole, Roller, Red-backed and Masked Shrikes, White-backed Woodpecker, Nightingale, Rufous Bushchat, Olivaceous, Olive-tree and River Warblers.

ACCESS Ulubat Leave Route 2 at Ulubat, which is the birthplace of Hassam, the first to scale the walls of Istanbul in 1453. His statue marks the track that leads to the embankment along the lake shore. **Ulu Dağ** Leave Bursa westwards and turn left past the airport to Huseymalani. Turn left to Ulu Dağ. Stop for Krüper's where the first major group of conifers line both sides of the road. It can, of course, be found throughout these woodlands. In Ulu Dağ centre turn left past the Grand Hotel Yazici (open in summer) and fork right downhill then up to a huge quarry for the other three main species. **Kocasu Delta** The road from Karacabey to the coast follows the river to the shoreline where a modern holiday resort has been built. Turn right behind the beach and motor over sandy tracks eastwards with good woodland on the right.

ROUTE Bursa is the best centre for all sites and is easily reached from Istanbul. Hotels at Ulu Dağ save the tedious daily trek up and back.

YESILICE

Yesilice (or Büyük Arapter as it is sometimes called) lies 23 km northwest of Gaziantep and is, therefore, often worked by visitors to Birecik. It is an area of rocky outcrops and hillsides with fields and orchards, and is a strangely fruitful place for several otherwise decidedly elusive species. It may, however, be a little awkward to find, as some observers are unsure as to whether they visited the correct place or not! The interesting birds include Red-tailed Wheatear and Eastern Rock Nuthatch, as well as the more regular Upcher's Warbler (fairly common), Cinereous Bunting, Desert Finch and Pale Rock Sparrow.

SUMMER Chukar, Bimaculated Lark, Rock and Eastern Rock Nuthatches, White-throated Robin, Red-tailed and Black-eared Wheatears, Upcher's Warbler, Cinereous and Cretzschmar's Buntings, Desert Finch, Pale Rock Sparrow.

ACCESS From the Gaziantep direction, continue through Yesilice and watch for a lime kiln on the right after 1.5 km. A track on the left opposite this leads past a village and on up a valley with rocky outcrops and sides. Continue to the far end for Red-tailed Wheatear, with Eastern Rock Nuthatch on outcrops and Upcher's in orchards to the north. Pale Rock Sparrows are on the right-hand slopes of the valley. If this fails, return towards Yesilice and take a track right 200 m before the town. Continue for 4 km to the village of Isikli and then, on foot, up a valley for Wheatear and Eastern Rock Nuthatch on crags. If this also fails, head towards Gaziantep to about 1.5 km before the Maras fork, where a restaurant on the right is followed by a stream leading from a gorge. Here at least you should get Upcher's, Cinereous and Pale Rock Sparrow. There are no hotels in Yesilice, but several in Gaziantep.

ROUTE Gaziantep is on the E24. The nearest airport is Malatya to the north-east.

HAMLYN

NATURAL HISTORY BOOKS

A complete range of Hamlyn Natural History titles is available from all good bookshops or by mail order direct from the publisher. Payment can be made by credit card or cheque/postal order in the following ways:

BY PHONE
Phone through your order on our special *Credit Card Hotline* on **0933 410 511**. Speak to our customer service team during office hours (9 a.m. to 5 p.m.) or leave a message on the answer machine, quoting your full credit card number plus expiry date and your full name and address. Please also quote the reference number NATHIS 2.

BY POST
Simply fill out the order form below (photocopies are acceptable) and send it with your payment to:
Cash Sales Department,
Reed Book Services Ltd.,
P.O. Box 5,
Rushden,
Northants, NN10 6YX

NATHIS 2

I wish to order the following titles:

	ISBN	Price	Quantity	Total
Hamlyn Guide to the Birds of Britain and Europe	0 600 57492 X	£8.99	....	£ ....
Photographic Guide to Birds of Britain and Europe	0 600 57861 5	£9.99	....	£ ....
Where to Watch Birds in Eastern Europe	0 600 58076 X	£16.99	....	£ ....
Behaviour Guide: Birds of Prey	0 540 01277 7	£14.99	....	£ ....
Behaviour Guide: Waders	0 600 57974 3	£14.99	....	£ ....

Add £2.00 for postage and packing if your order is worth £10.00 or less £ ....

Grand Total £ ....

Name _____ (block capitals)

Address _____

_____ Postcode _____

I enclose a cheque/postal order for £ _____ made payable to Reed Book Services Ltd
or
Please debit my ☐ Access ☐ Visa ☐ American Express ☐ Diners

account number ☐☐☐☐ ☐☐☐☐ ☐☐☐☐ ☐☐☐☐

by £ _____ Expiry date _____ Signature _____

SPECIAL OFFER: FREE POSTAGE AND PACKAGING FOR ALL ORDERS OVER £10.00, add £2.00 for p+p if your order is £1u.00 or less.

Whilst every effort is made to keep our prices low, the publisher reserves the right to increase the prices at short notice.

Your order will be dispatched within 5 days, but please allow up to 28 days for delivery, subject to availability.

Registered office: Michelin House, 81 Fulham Road, London SW3 6RB.

Registered in England no 1974080.

If you do not wish your name to be used by other carefully selected organizations for promotional purposes, please tick this box ☐